THE SOCIAL FABRIC OF HEALTH

An Introduction to Medical Anthropology

THE SOCIAL FABRIC OF HEALTH

An Introduction to Medical Anthropology

John M. Janzen
University of Kansas

Boston   Burr Ridge, IL   Dubuque, IA   Madison, WI   New York   San Francisco   St. Louis
Bangkok   Bogotá   Caracas   Kuala Lumpur   Lisbon   London   Madrid   Mexico City
Milan   Montreal   New Delhi   Santiago   Seoul   Singapore   Sydney   Taipei   Toronto

McGraw-Hill

*A Division of The **McGraw·Hill** Companies*

THE SOCIAL FABRIC OF HEALTH: AN INTRODUCTION TO
MEDICAL ANTHROPOLOGY

Published by McGraw-Hill, an imprint of The McGraw-Hill Companies, Inc.
1221 Avenue of the Americas, New York, NY, 10020. COPYRIGHT © 2002,
by The McGraw-Hill Companies, Inc. All rights reserved. No part of this publication may
be reproduced or distributed in any form or by any means, or stored in a data base or retrieval
system, without the prior written consent of The McGraw-Hill Companies, Inc., including, but
not limited to, in any network or other electronic storage or transmission, or broadcast for
distance learning.

Some ancillaries, including electronic and print components, may not be available to customers
outside the United States.

This book is printed on acid-free paper.

2 3 4 5 6 7 8 9 0 DOC/DOC 0 9 8 7 6 5 4 3 2

ISBN 0-07-032831-5

Publisher: *Phillip A. Butcher*
Senior sponsoring editor: *Carolyn Henderson*
Editorial Assistant: *Julie Abodeely*
Senior marketing manager: *Daniel M. Loch*
Project manager: *Ruth Smith*
Production supervisor: *Gina Hangos*
Media producer: *Shannon Rider*
Supplement producer: *Vicki Laird*
Photo researcher: *Jeremy Cheshareck*
Coordinator of freelance design: *Mary Kazak*
Cover and interior design: *Kay Fulton*
Typeface: *10.5/12 Palatino*
Compositor: *Shepherd Incorporated*
Printer: *R. R. Donnelley & Sons Company*

Library of Congress Control Number: 2001092036

www.mhhe.com

PREFACE

OVERVIEW

Medical anthropology is the study of health, illness, and healing across the range of human societies and over the course of human experience. It includes the study of the patterns of disease within particular environments and the ways in which diseases relate dynamically to other organisms—especially humans. Medical anthropology also includes the ways that the human community understands and responds to these challenges to its existence, with an emphasis on how members of the community direct their behaviors, articulate their ideas, and organize their resources. It may also include attention to the community's access to the resources to maintain or restore health, or the way power is wielded to privilege some and deprive others of those resources. Finally, medical anthropology studies the meaning of the signs of illness and suffering as part of the overall study of cultural traditions, and strives to interpret them in the light of wider traditions of technology, ritual, and religion.

ORGANIZATION AND APPROACH

The Social Fabric of Health: An Introduction to Medical Anthropology covers the familiar and important themes in medical anthropology. Yet it features a particular perspective to guide the reader through that subject matter. Like an anthropological monograph or a novel, it has a storyline that goes as follows: Chapter 1 sets the stage by defining the field and briefly illustrating it. Chapter 2 describes how medical anthropology as a special field of study emerged, and some of the ways in which it has been theorized. Chapters 3 to 9 tell the main story, how the "fabric of health" (the title of the first of these chapters)—health, illness, and healing—is seen and studied by medical anthropologists. Chapter 10 examines how these an-thropological insights may be applied to "shaping the fabric of health" (the title of the chapter).

Within this main story, the **fabric of health** may be looked at as a set of cultural ideas and practices in a number of healing traditions and health campaigns, ancient and modern, large and small scale, and the social pat-terns and institutions by which they are carried (Chapter 3). The fabric of health may also be seen in the way diseases and population dynamics af-fect the human community, historically and today (Chapter 4). But anthro-pologists do not look only at the collective level of cultural ideas, tech-niques, societies, and aggregate statistics. They also focus on individual lives, particularly in the way that individuals move through life within culturally defined societies, within the "life cycle" or "lifecourse" (Chap-ters 5 and 6). One of the reasons for giving health an emphasis equal to ill-ness or disease in medical anthropology is that not all of life should be medicalized. Birth and birthing, even if they occur in hospitals, are not dis-eases. Death, an inevitable stage of life, is more tricky, but it too is not re-ally a disease. So the broader subject matter of medical anthropology is health and life, which include disease, suffering, and death. Chapter 6 fea-tures personhood as a way to examine how individual identity is affected by society's and medicine's standards of life and death, and how it is shaped by sickness and chronic illness.

The human experience of sickness and the human effort to find healing is at the heart of medical anthropology. Chapter 7 looks at this subject both within and beyond the boundaries of medicine. A broader concept of cul-tural definition is required to understand how we, or people in other soci-eties and other times, identified those conditions which were held to be "disease," how the process of being sick was handled, and how healing of that condition was attempted. The application of sign theory is particu-larly appropriate here, so some of the concepts introduced earlier are fur-ther developed. Tracing the signification of sickness and healing is particu-larly important in light of such phenomena as "voodoo death," placebo healing, and the symbolic power of ritual and social relationships.

"Medicine," as distinct from sickness and healing, is the subject of the next two chapters on "medical knowledge" (Chapter 8) and "power and or-ganization in medicine" (Chapter 9). Of course "knowledge is power," but how is knowledge constructed so as to create distinctive traditions of heal-ing? And how is this knowledge taught and transmitted from one generation to the next within a living tradition? Chapter 9 is an application of organiza-tional ideas to medicine, in order to understand how the institutionalization of medicine within professional, scientific, and state bodies gives enormous authority and legitimacy to the concepts held and practices used by those within these institutions. Power and organization account for the allocation of society's resources in a particular way to health, illness, and healing.

Finally, Chapter 10 covers a number of areas in which anthropologists have drawn upon their understanding of health, illness, and healing to help "shape" the social fabric of health. This is a subject that is often discussed under the rubrics of "applied medical anthropology," "clinical anthropology," or "action anthropology." The single most important narrative thread running through the book is the story of the social fabric of health, how it is defined and represented, and how it may be restored when compromised.

A second thread, or theme, has to do with the experience of suffering and healing and how these experiences are represented. This textbook puts forward the perspective of signs—commonly known as **semiotics**—as a way to formulate the nuances of both the subjective realm of individual experience and of the more objective, public world of symbols, codes, and laws. In medical anthropology, semiotics offers one of the best ways to think about the signification of the relationship between biology and culture. The closing sections of Chapters 2 and 7 provide fuller discussion of these issues, although other passages throughout the book reflect the semiotic perspective to medical anthropology.

This textbook is designed to be helpful to a wide range of users and classroom settings. It grew out of the needs of an Introduction to Medical Anthropology course I have taught for several decades at the University of Kansas, a large public university typical of public higher educational institutions across North America. The course has drawn undergraduates and a few graduate students in classes up to 25 students, among them anthropology majors, as well as prenursing, premedicine, music therapy, biology, and a range of other students of varied capability.

The course and this textbook reflect the way medical anthropology has evolved at the University of Kansas since the 1960s. After a brief attempt to run a graduate program jointly with the Community Health Department at the KU Medical School in Kansas City, we returned to couching medical anthropology within the "four fields" of our department, meaning that medical anthropology exists and is taught at the cross-section of sociocultural and biological anthropology. It is enhanced by faculty members who focus on such cognate areas as growth and nutrition, reproductive ecology, demography, genetics, paleontology, political anthropology, postmodern studies, and applied anthropology, among other anthropological specialties. This textbook has thus been developed within a course in medical anthropology whose distinctive feature is the emphasis on the role of culture in the human experience of health, illness, and healing. The textbook bears traces of this uniquely Kansas profile in the special case studies of PhD research by some of these students.

Still, despite this local specificity, I have tried to couch medical anthropology in a distinctly global perspective. A stint during the 1980s as editor of the series "Comparative Studies in Health Systems and Medical Care" published by the University of California Press deepened my familiarity with top research work in most of the major healing traditions of the world. My own central and southern African research will be evident in the text. Since beginning the project in 1994, I was privileged to participate in relief and fieldwork in the postwar, postgenocide zone of central Africa; this has added the dimension on war violence and the anthropology of trauma that appears in the book. I have traveled widely for professional and personal reasons during this time, which has further enhanced the book's global perspective.

During the years of preparing this textbook, other more personal types of socialization into humanity—beyond being a scholar, traveler, and teacher—have left their mark on this work. The particular point at which I find myself in my lifecourse has meant that I have experienced the advanced aging and death of parents, and my wife and I have become grandparents. It is hoped that such experiences will add broader human wisdom to this work.

LEARNING AIDS

CHAPTER OUTLINES, VIGNETTES, END-OF-CHAPTER SUMMARIES

Most chapters are punctuated with several vignettes about research projects in the topic of that section. Each vignette sketches the general issue that was researched, the methodology used, and the findings of the project. An attempt has been made to represent a number of continents, cultural traditions, and global regions in the vignettes and other illustrations, although central Africa, my primary area of research, has been highlighted and is more fully represented than other world regions. At the end of each chapter, the material of the chapter is summarized and a few **key works** may be listed to aid further exploration of the subject of the chapter.

REVIEW QUESTIONS

Review questions at the close of each chapter will assist the instructor in organizing topics for discussion and for emphasis in assignments. Instructors, students, and other readers are encouraged to think of other questions and exercises that illuminate the chapter's material and the issues that surround it.

KEY TERMS AND GLOSSARY

Key terms are highlighted and defined in the text the first time they are mentioned. The reader will find these terms listed in a glossary at the close of the book where they are given additional brief discussion. The index allows the reader to explore all uses of the term throughout the book.

ILLUSTRATIONS AND PHOTOGRAPHS

Each chapter features several photographs and figures that illustrate the text material. The lead photograph or illustration that appears at the beginning of a chapter visually represents the subject of the chapter. The lengthy caption should serve to offer a parallel learning experience to the verbal text introduction.

BIBLIOGRAPHY

The bibliography includes all references cited in the text and additional standard readings in medical anthropology.

IN SUM

The Social Fabric of Health is designed to provide a well-rounded medical anthropology for the opening of the 21st century. It takes advantage of the interpretive semiotic approach in medical anthropology without turning its back on some of the basic health information offered by the ecological and biocultural perspectives. This work is intended for upper-level undergraduate and beginning graduate students in medical anthropology, but it should be of interest as well to students in sociology and in health care fields such as nursing, medicine, and international health who are interested in a cultural and comparative understanding of health, illness, and healing.

INSTRUCTOR SUPPLEMENTS PACKAGE

As a full-service publisher of quality educational products, McGraw-Hill does much more than just sell textbooks. The company creates and publishes an extensive array of print, video, and digital supplements for students and instructors. This edition of *The Social Fabric of Health* is accompanied by the following:

- Instructor's Manual/Testbank—chapter outlines, overviews, objectives, lecture notes, essay questions, and more.

This Instructor's Manual is provided free of charge to students and instructors. Orders of new (versus used) textbooks help us defray the cost of developing such supplements, which is substantial. Please contact your local McGraw-Hill representative for information on the above supplement.

ACKNOWLEDGEMENTS

I wish to thank the many and varied readers who have contributed to the development of this work. First and foremost, I am grateful to several generations of students—the classes of '95, '97, '99, and graduate students during those years—who read earlier drafts of this text and offered their suggestions for improvement. Among all my students I single out Meagan Zimbeck who took the time to thoroughly critique Chapters 3 and 4 after she had taken the course. I acknowledge the critical reading of the 1997 manuscript by Marike Janzen and Terry Chappell MD, who were gracious enough to offer their thoughts for improvement. Among the specialized medical anthropology readers I sought out, and who gave me collegial critiques and encouragement, I single out Kathryn Staiano-Ross. She diligently read all versions of the manuscript and was my ultimate adviser on Peircian semiotics, as well as the general American health care scene. Marcia Good Maust, an anthropologist of reproductive health and birthing, and Stanley Yoder, Africanist and international health consultant, read earlier drafts of the text and gave expert advice on revisions.

The Wellcome Medical Institute's Library in London has been an inspiration for the overall conceptualization of this project. I was able to make several research visits to the Institute while writing this book and have been able to incorporate images from the Wellcome Institute's print and illustration collection into the book so as to enhance the topics covered.

I acknowledge the several series of readers engaged by McGraw-Hill who gave me many good suggestions for improvement of the text:

John Ross—Eastern Washington University
Wenda Trevathan—New Mexico State University
Ellen Gruenbaum—California State University—Fresno
Barbara Miller—George Washinton University
Lynette Leidy—University of Massachusetts, Amherst
R.A. Halberstein—University of Miami
Kathy Nadeau—California State University—San Bernardino
Andrea Wiley—James Madison University

Some of these reviewers imagined using the text in their classes, and all reported back with extremely helpful revisions. I am also grateful to the editorial staff at McGraw-Hill who worked with me in a most efficient and professional manner to bring this material into shape for the rest of the world.

My family, especially Reinhild, were encouraging and long-suffering during the years this project was in gestation. Although I acknowledge the wide circle of others who supported and helped inform this book, I take full responsibility for the views and perspectives voiced between these covers.

John M. Janzen

CONTENTS

c h a p t e r   6

Personhood, Liminality, and Identity   137

c h a p t e r   7

The Transforming Signs of Sickness and Healing   149

c h a p t e r   8

Medical Knowledge   187

THE SOCIAL FABRIC OF HEALTH

An Introduction to Medical Anthropology

INTRODUCING MEDICAL ANTHROPOLOGY

Photo 1.1 *Collecting and identifying medicinal plants in western equatorial Africa. Bill Arkinstall, MD, and Kusikila kwa Kilombo, mayor of Kivunda commune, collect plants indicated by healer-herbalist Kitembo of Muyeni region in Balari commune. Leaf press is visible in grass beside Kitembo.*
SOURCE: J. M. Janzen.

1

THE SOCIAL FABRIC OF HEALTH AND THE CORE
OF MEDICAL ANTHROPOLOGY

Fabric is a common metaphor for that which enables life. Derived from the Latin verb *faber* which means "to make" or "to create," fabric has come in English to refer especially to woven textiles. By extension, we speak of fabric as human-created patterns that serve a range of useful ends, including the enhancement of health. Recent uses of "fabric" in relation to health include social fabric, social and economic fabric, solid social fabric and health care, cultural fabric, and moral fabric. Reference is also widely made to "support networks" and "safety nets." The "social fabric of health," like these other fabrics, may be imagined to envelop the individual body with life-enabling means such as basic fresh water, shelter, significant others of family, friends, and community, as well as concepts, medicinal substances, therapeutic techniques, and institutions with which to come to terms with health problems and to seek healing. To extend the metaphor, once we have identified the basic features of this social fabric of health, we can explore how it is maintained or how it changes, or where it is "tattered," "torn," or "cut," (where individuals or segments of society have, as we say, "fallen through the safety net") or where the fabric has been withheld from parts of the community. In these areas it may be repaired or restored in new ways. In this book fabric will become a useful image to show how medical anthropologists speak about health, illness, and healing, as represented in social and cultural images, society and institutions, and ideas.

Medical anthropology[1] is the study of health, illness, and healing across the range of human societies and over the course of human experience, with an emphasis on how members of the community direct their behaviors, articulate their ideas, and organize their resources in these realms. It includes the study of the patterns of disease within an environment and the ways in which diseases relate dynamically to living organisms—especially human organisms. It includes the ways in which the human community understands and responds to these challenges to its existence. Medical anthropology may also include the community's access to the resources that maintain or restore health, or the exclusion from such resources by the community's power structure. Medical anthropology studies the meaning of the signs of illness and suffering as part of the overall study of cultural traditions, and strives to interpret them in the light of wider traditions of ritual and religion.

The social fabric of health as introduced here carries many aspects of what anthropologists, social scientists, and the general public call **culture,** a usage that is often seen as the distinctive hallmark of medical anthropology's approach to its subject matter. In its anthropological application, culture (with a small *c*), covers further dimensions to include creatively fashioned techniques, lifeways, and deeply held convictions and assumptions in a community. Additionally, the complex body of culture, much of which is stored and articulated in language, is learned rather than transmitted genetically, although anthropologists see the capacity for cultural learning as part of the human genetic makeup. Since it is learned rather than inherited genetically, culture needs to be taught to, or learned anew by, each generation in order to persist. Culture is constantly adjusted to overcome the limits of material conditions—climate, food sources, shelter, distance—and make the most of available technology. The unique way that a community of individuals organizes itself and marshals its skills, knowledge, and energies to combat disease is thus a very central part of culture. Likewise, the anthropology of health seeking and health restoring is an excellent inquiry through which to understand the central values and character of a culture.

As a discipline, anthropology often includes social or cultural anthropology, archaeology, biological or physical anthropology, and linguistics, making it the only academic discipline to span all of the university divisions: the humanities, the social sciences, and the natural sciences, as well as the applied sciences pertaining to health. The four (or more) types of anthropological inquiry within such a single setting combine to create an appreciation of living and historical communities that contribute to understanding all of humankind. For this, the anthropological perspective has often been called **holistic.**

The distinctive claim to understanding and insight in anthropology is gained by research into particular communities and social settings. Close extended participation and observation in such a setting yields text called **ethnography** through which the vivid particulars of a single case study show the way to more general insights. Although anthropologists may not always and immediately try to relate the particulars of individual and community health and healing behavior to the universal human level, they try to find a common basis for diverse local practices. Thus, the anthropological perspective is also **comparative.** The comparative method of anthropology enables us to find the universal within the particulars of individual human experience. For example, birth and death are universal human experiences, but they are thought of and handled in somewhat distinctive ways because of unique language, beliefs, and degrees and types of available techniques. The anthropologist's use of controlled comparison is in some sense a substitute for, or an alternative to, the experimental method of the scientist's laboratory. The anthropologist selects a question to consider and then marshals evidence from the approaches of two or more societies to those issues. Conclusions may be drawn about the diversity and effectiveness of approaches taken to the health challenges.

The "medical" in medical anthropology deserves further explanation because it no doubt includes more, and different, dimensions of health and healing than most medical practitioners may anticipate. **Medicine**—the medical—in medical anthropology is used somewhat generically to refer not only to official medicine, but to any and all practices that are intended to address or alleviate what a given group of people or practitioners consider to be an affliction in need of attention. So, as the examples of medical anthropology projects that follow will show, "medicine" may include the study of malaria or health intervention efforts to reduce its occurrence, as well as a shaman's song about his mystical journey beneath the sea to bring back the soul of a sick person. Medical anthropologists thus might speak of "medicines" or "medical traditions" to designate the diverse curing and health-upholding practices found across human history and society.[2] The medicine of hospitals and mainstream doctors of the industrialized world are usually spoken of today by medical anthropologists as **biomedicine.**[3] This name identifies the specific character of this medical tradition, its basis in science, and its emphasis on the physical body. Although this medicine is globally distributed (leading one author [Leslie 1976] to speak of it as "cosmopolitan" medicine), it is seen as a specific medical tradition, distinct from other medical traditions such as Chinese medicine, or Indian Ayurvedic medicine, the medical traditions of Africa, or any number of distinctive schools of healing and bodies of knowledge.

The "medical" in medical anthropology is in a way a misleading specification for this anthropological focus, because the subject matter of this focus includes health, illness, and healing. Health covers a broader range of subject matter than the illness and healing that is medicine. **Health,** whether it is defined as the absence of disease, a dynamic condition combining individuals, society, and an adaptation to the environment, or a part of a grand scheme of thought and life, needs to be included in the set of key concepts at the beginning of this introduction to the field. In the planning sessions of the executive committee of the Society for Medical Anthropology that accompanied the founding of the *Medical Anthropology Quarterly* journal, a debate occurred over the merits of using "medical" or "health" in the title. The consensus was that although much of the attention of medical anthropologists was on health promotion, health development, and health concepts—that is, the social fabric of health—we would continue to use the term *medical* because anthropologists and others had become used to the name.

Sickness, suffering, illness, disease, and *healing* are additional terms central to the anthropological perspective, and the way culture and comparison are used in the exploration of issues of health and medicine. Although these words are taken from the common vocabulary, they have come to have somewhat distinctive uses in anthropology or, rather, they express types of issues and inquiries that interest anthropologists. Thus, **sickness** is the individual or group experience of **suffering,** from the onset of a condition to the outcome, whether that be a return to health, the experience becoming chronic, or resulting in death. Sickness and suffering are subjective. For the anthropologists this subjectivity is of interest whether or not a medical expert finds a physical source for the experience.

The **illness/disease** dichotomy has been a way to distinguish the sufferer's perception of the experience from whatever objectively discovered entity or process may be established. An individual may be ill or have an illness without there being a corresponding disease that can be established by another person or expert. Likewise, an individual may have a disease— for example, cancer, HIV positive infection—without knowing this or feeling ill. The illness/disease distinction made by medical anthropologists is a matter of the vantage point of the speaker. A sufferer experiences "illness." Those who professionally study, examine, or test the object of this suffering will usually speak of "disease," in particular if it can be identified with a medical label or diagnostically established name. The term **healing** is used generically in medical anthropology to describe both the sufferer-defined resolution of the sickness experience, as well as the medically defined overcoming of disease and disorder. In some cultural traditions, the term for healing is derived from wholeness, and refers to the restoration of wholeness.

A further refinement of the study of the cultural dimension of medical anthropology is to explore the ways in which the experiences of health, sickness, illness, disease, and healing (or medicine) are represented or couched in the expressions of different kinds of signs. This study of signs that has flourished in linguistics and the humanities, as well as in the biological sciences, is called **semiotics.** For medical anthropologists, it provides the basis for a unifying perspective of the subject matter, as can be seen through the brief elaboration of three basic notions that can establish the beginning working vocabulary of semiotics in medical anthropology: *Sign, symptom*, and *symbol.*

A **sign** in its broadest working sense is a sensory object with a signification—that is, a message or a meaning.[4] The sign is any presence that can be felt, heard, smelled, seen, or tasted, which conveys some direct or indirect additional association. The sign points to something else as soon as it emerges. In medical texts and dictionaries the sign is the objective measure of illness or disease, while the symptom is an expression of the felt condition of the patient. Signs in health and healing are the basis for significant information whether they are in consciousness or out of consciousness, whether they are put into words or not, and whether they are felt with the doctor's fingertips or seen through a CAT scan.

The **symptom,** with the same prefix and connotation as sign, is a happening or attribute that indicates the personally felt, that is, subjective, evidence of disease or physical disturbance.[5] A temperature of 104 degrees Fahrenheit is a sign in the medical sense, while the feeling of fever experienced and expressed by the person who is sick is a symptom. Thus, sign and symptom are dimensions of the same event; the difference between them is the object or referent. The first is the disease or other affliction, the second is the sense of a feeling of or conviction about the physical attribute. The terms convey a strong sense of the temporal or logical co-occurrence of the two. The relationship between sign and symptom can be illustrated by the case of measles. The red blotches on the skin are signs that everyone can see. They are objective (though they may be variously interpreted). The feeling of illness which accompanies the red blotches—perhaps itching or burning—is of a subjective nature and is therefore a symptom.

Associated with the same stem as sign and symptom is the notion of **symbol.**[6] It refers to a token or sign of identity verified by a point of reference outside the sign, such as an independent set of ideas or source of meaning. This means that the symbol's relationship to its referent is arbitrary. Thus, the splotches on a measles sufferer may or may not be interpreted as the presence of spirits. This property of the symbol establishes an important distinction between it and the symptom on the one hand, and the basic sign on the other. Whereas the sign may be seen as a natural mark of a condition, the symptom and the symbol establish greater reality in the felt and thought perception of the subject, the sufferer, and those around the sufferer. Symptom and symbol thus open the way for the medical anthropologist to "see" culture in sickness and healing without losing touch with the immediacy of the signs of the physical world.

The disposition of culture in health, illness, and healing is thus at the center of the medical anthropological perspective. The metaphor of social fabric of health provides a broader context for the study of health, while semiotics offers a more nuanced close-up tool for the analysis of suffering, healing, and identity of persons and communities.

THREE CLASSICAL (AND CONTINUING) PROJECTS IN MEDICAL ANTHROPOLOGY

Another way of introducing medical anthropology is by looking at what medical anthropologists have done, the way they have worked, and the projects they have undertaken. In the several decades since its beginnings as a field of emphasis within anthropology, medical anthropology has become quite diverse. We can hardly identify a single scholarly volume or practitioner's work that depicts the entire field. Yet it is possible to identify some of the common concepts of the foregoing pages at work in particular projects that have attracted numerous scholars over decades, and have resulted in clusters of research teams, conferences, articles, books, and activities that have driven and created medical anthropology. I speak of these projects as "classics" because they show the reader not only a cross-section of the field, but projects that have helped create and shape the field. Of course, this is my list, drawn from my teaching, from the colleagues and those who have influenced me, and the heroes I have accumulated.

"The Case of the Cannibals' Curse"

This is the first project to be presented. At first flush the story has the character of a murder mystery, but by the end of this account the reader will understand that this project is really about the use of the anthropological perspective in collaboration with epidemiology, virology, and public health to unlock the puzzles of a new and deadly disease. This disease was **kuru,** and it plagued the Fore (pronounced for-ā) people of highland New Guinea and some of their neighbors during the 1950s when the first outsiders (representatives of the Australian administration) made contact with them. Manifestations of kuru would begin with tremors and loss of coordination. Within months, the affected individual would be unable to walk, focus eyes, or maintain emotional equilibrium; death invariably followed within a year of onset. The Fore commonly blamed the disease on a type of sorcery, also kuru, and would try to identify the sorcerer through divination. Grieving the many kuru victims (up to half of Fore deaths at one time) included a gathering of close kin to partake of the flesh of the deceased, a ceremonial act considered to be a sign of love and respect to the deceased. Women and children especially took part in this; the men believed it weakened them, especially when it entailed eating women's flesh which they mostly avoided doing.

An Australian colonial health officer, perplexed by this fatal disease so regionally restricted, asked Carleton Gajdusek of the U.S. National Institutes of Health to help him understand it. Gajdusek then led an interdisciplinary team, including anthropologists, to study kuru among the Fore. From 1957 to 1959 Gajdusek and his team created special hospitals for kuru sufferers and traced the pattern of infection. They soon discovered that infected women and children far outnumbered men. Several hypotheses were advanced about the source of the infection and its transmission. These included that kuru was caused by an environmental toxic substance, that it was due to a nutritional deficiency, and that it was a genetically inherited disease. However, the genetic hypothesis did not quite fit. Although the disease tended to follow families, it predominantly affected women and children of both sexes, but not men. Also, it did not seem likely that a genetically transmitted disease could carry itself in the population if so many children died from it.

In the early 1960s anthropologists Shirley Lindenbaum and Robert Glasse came to the Fore to study the cultural aspects of kuru—the peoples' perception, memory, and feelings about this scourge in their midst. The anthropologists interviewed elderly Fore about kuru and learned that both the disease and this method of cannibalistic grieving had entered Fore society within the lifetime of these individuals: first the grieving practice, then at a later time, kuru. This information led the anthropologists to be the first researchers to make the association between cannibalism and kuru (Lindenbaum 1979). As if to confirm this hypothesis, kuru had been in decline among the Fore since their abandonment of the cannibalistic form of grieving. Not a single child who had not tasted human flesh had ever suffered kuru. Even with this suggestive correlation of kuru and cannibalism, the mode of transmission of the disease remained a puzzle. Gajdusek and his colleagues then conducted laboratory experiments, taking the tissue from the brains of kuru victims and injecting the substance into chimpanzees. These animals soon contracted kuru, confirming the scientists' hunch that a virus was the cause of kuru, and that eating the flesh of its victims had been the mode of transmission. In 1976 Gajdusek received the Nobel Prize in medicine for his work on kuru and other neurological diseases. He and his colleagues at the National Institutes of Health were central figures in research on viral-transmitted diseases that included not only kuru, but neurological diseases such as Creutzfeldt-Jacob, Parkinson's, and other afflictions of the central nervous system (Gibbs and Gajdusek 1979a, b; Gajdusek 1985). This work has become a foundation for later work in AIDS research and in looking at "new" viral diseases such as ebola whose method of transmission is not yet understood. Anthropologists became the primary researchers to look at HIV-positive and AIDS-related behaviors associated with the spread of the disease and patterns of transmission, and ideas of the disease and stigmas associated with those who have it (Schoepf 1995, 1998; Farmer 1992). Anthropologists also became involved in the research and promotion of culturally sensitive public health education campaigns (Schoepf 1995; Green 1994; MacDougall and Yoder 1998).

Medical anthropologists in the work on kuru collaborated with a team of other scientists to unscramble the pattern of an unknown and deadly disease. We can learn from this project that medical anthropology is often a collaborative effort across disciplines, indicative of the holistic vision of anthropology. Medical anthropology is sometimes an adventure in discovery. Medical anthropologists, like other scientists, are driven by their desire to figure things out. They also have a compassionate streak in their work, wishing to genuinely help those confronted with terrible diseases such as kuru, ebola, and AIDS.

"BIRTHING IN ONE, TWO, FOUR, TEN, ALL SOCIETIES"

The second classical project in medical anthropology to be introduced here covers birthing. So central a human activity as birth, at the source of individual life, brings together many of the themes around which medical anthropology has crystallized. Birth is a "natural" process but everywhere it is framed by cultural values and forms. Following from this fact, the comparative agenda has been common in the anthropological analysis of birthing. Comparative study may be able to establish those practices that are universal, essential, or necessary, and those that are idiosyncratic and aberrant, and how they are tied to belief systems and authority structures. Birthing is also of great interest because, although a physical process, it is not a disease. Thus, how it is handled, and by whom, demonstrates the extent to which a society has "medicalized" a realm of life or condition, that is, redefined it as a medical problem.

Brigitte Jordan's landmark *Birth in Four Cultures* (1984) studied birthing in Mexico (Yucatán), the Netherlands, Sweden, and the United States. This selection of national society settings demonstrates well the strategy of comparison to sketch the underlying commonness against the specific and different, in a human realm. In her work, Jordan was interested in contrasting the preindustrial (Yucatán) to the industrial. This selection of case settings also compared those societies in which midwives are the main attendants at birth (Yucatán, Sweden, the Netherlands) and a society (the United States) in which midwives were replaced by doctors, thereby "medicalizing" birth. She also was able to demonstrate the implications of home-birth (Yucatán, the Netherlands) versus hospital birth (Sweden, the United States).

The comparative study of birthing has been used to examine different approaches within a single society and to examine the policy consequences in advocating one or the other approaches. Carol Laderman (1983) carefully examined the health consequences of a complex set of practices in Malay birthing that included dietary restrictions and keeping the mother warm near a fire after delivery—a practice called "roasting" which conjured up an image of severe burns—both practices criticized by health officials. In her study Laderman used nutritional analysis of the food of women who were following the restrictive regimen. She found that their diets were adequate because of the total combination of foods to make up for those they could not eat because of dietary rules. In this case the anthropologist corrected some misperceptions about practices that were not well understood.

In her comparative study of birthing, *Birth as an American Rite of Passage* (1992), Robbie Davis-Floyd gathered and analyzed narratives by a hundred American women during the course of their pregnancies and following their deliveries. The majority of women gave birth in mainstream wards in hospitals. They demonstrated in their attitudes and convictions an acceptance of what Davis-Floyd called the "technocratic" model of birth in which the full array of monitors and surgical procedures—shaving of pubic hair, the episiotomy cut, sometimes the cesarean section birth—were used. A small minority were uncomfortable with giving up the control that these procedures entailed, preferring a more "holistic" model of birth embodied in LaMaze birth preparatory courses. A few of the women preferred and identified with the "natural" model of birth. Davis-Floyd's tone, along with that of some other studies of birthing, is critical of the technocratic mode of birthing, suggesting that it is a form of ritual full of symbolic messages about the control of women and the medicalization of birth.

The anthropology of birthing has become a major area of interest. It includes attention to reproductive issues ranging from concerns over infertility to fertility enhancement, the new technologies of prenatal testing and their social and moral consequences, the health of women and infants, and family planning and population trends. The recent volume *Knowledge of Birthing* (1998) demonstrated that this "project" is at the pivot of many other anthropological issues.

UNDERSTANDING ASIAN MEDICINES

Our third project in medical anthropology represents a significant concern, and may be taken to reflect the interest in all non-Western, nonbiomedical medicines, but not necessarily to the exclusion of Western, or biomedicine. As the first two projects—understanding kuru and the study of birthing—suggested, every issue medical anthropologists take on has dimensions of beliefs, concepts, practices, and social organization. However, a large concern within medical anthropology is the understanding of the world's medical traditions for their own sake. I will here sketch the most visible of those efforts, the study of Asia's medical traditions. One name, and two books, provide the most influential scholar and visible work in this area: Charles Leslie and the now classic *Asian Medical Systems* (1976) and its sequel, *Paths to Asian Medical Knowledge* (1992), coedited with Allan Young.

The medical traditions of Asia follow the great civilizations of Asia: China, India, and Arabia (or Islam), although the many local or regional medicines have their own distinctive flavors. The great traditions of Asia are all based on literacy and their knowledge is grounded in texts, the earliest of which were penned several thousand years ago. Chinese medicine has some affinity with Taoism, the ancestral religion of China, as well as ancient demonism, the theory of the "meridians," along with other layers of knowledge based on particular cures and treatments. These come together in the well-known technique of acupuncture which has an ancient history in Chinese medicine.

Indian and South Asian medicine, called *Ayurveda* after the Sanskrit term for doctor or medicine, is similarly constructed around ancient ideas of Indian philosophy and religion. A key concept in Ayurveda is the *dosha*, variously translated as element or humor, in a system that relates wind to fire and water, thus hot and cold, the bodily organs and fluids, and the universe. Meditation and well-known yoga disciplines are combined in Indian medicine with many herbal treatments and dietary practices.

Arabic medicine was spread into Asia by Islamic expansion eastward following the Prophet Muhammad's appearance in the seventh century. The medicine of Islam includes the central ideas of ancient Greek medicine, known in Arabic as *Unani*, from Ionia, a Greek city and early art style. The four humors of earth, wind, air, and fire, as well as the bodily fluids are main aspects in this classical medicine of Europe. This learning and practice simply spread with Arab doctors and scholars to places conquered by Islamic armies and settled by Islamic merchants, clerics, and travelers. The other dimension of Islamic medicine was appropriately called "Medicine of the Prophet" because it was based on Muhammad's moral teachings from the Koran and varied cures from Arabia.

The anthropology of Asian medicine is thus a very broad and diverse object of study that no single individual can master. Rather, medical anthropologists and their practitioner and scholar colleagues from related disciplines such as history or pharmacy usually work in one region or nation, or with the texts of one of the great traditions. One main finding that has come out of the study of Asian medicine is that multiple medicines may coexist in the same society, representing differing specializations, social classes or ideological interests (Leslie 1976). All of the nations of Asia incorporate a diversity of religious and ethnic communities which tend to privilege and maintain their own ancestral medicines. Thus, the Chinese merchant colonies of Malaysia maintain Chinese medicines. Typically, learned scholars, practitioners with vast medical lore, and religious healers including shamans may coexist in the same city or region, alongside advanced biomedicine with its medical schools and specialists.

Another finding that has resulted from several decades of the study of Asian medicine is a better appreciation for the continued appeal of spiritual healing by shamans—that is, healers who work with or through spirits to rescue victims from a range of psychological and metaphysical afflictions and anxieties. "Soul loss" is commonly treated by the shaman journeying in the spirit to find the lost soul and to return it to the sick individual. In a time of rapid social change resulting from labor migration, urbanization, and industrialization, the shaman's work seems to be more important than ever. Medical anthropologists have studied this phenomenon and explained why and how these healers are persuasive healers for their clients.

The common interest among scholars and practitioners of Asian medicine has become great enough that participants in these conferences and publications have organized their own professional society which meets periodically to compare notes and pursue common interests. The wider consequence of the study of Asian medicine within anthropology has been the emergence of a more sophisticated understanding of the coexistence of multiple medical traditions, or as bodies of practice and thought, within cultures and civilizations, a circumstance that anthropologists have come to call **medical pluralism.** It has also led to a greater understanding of the role of culture in biomedicine, a theme that will be taken up in later chapters.

This section has shown the subject matter of medical anthropology defined by several of its major projects: figuring out the nature of a disease; interpreting and comparing a natural process, birth, that is always framed culturally; and studying and organizing a major medical tradition that is part of a civilization outside of the Western world. The range of interests revealed in these projects will help the reader gain an appreciation of the scope and unique perspective of medical anthropology.

THE RESEARCH BASIS OF MEDICAL ANTHROPOLOGY

The energy that drives the desire for new understanding in a discipline like medical anthropology is both very practical and very scholarly. It includes all of the following urgencies of the just recounted classical projects: the desperate need of kuru victims and their families in highland New Guinea; the curiosity of scientists to figure out the mechanisms of disease transmission; the anthropologist's participant observation with the elderly Fore to learn their language and to talk with them about what they remembered of their own history; the anthropologists interested in figuring out the implications and consequences of very different practices of birthing; the women who were genuinely concerned about the restrictions on their freedoms to give birth as they wished; the students of medicine of an entire continent, organizing and meeting to share their approaches to reading and translating texts in order to comprehend strange metaphors of the body, of truth, of life, and of the natural universe. Pursuing these interests in the projects we have seen, designing a focused inquiry, following through on the inquiry with tact and rigor, and then presenting the findings in some form of lecture, publication, or action program—all these tasks are part of **research.** The anthropological perspective of medical anthropology is clearly reflected in and generated through research.

Research in medical anthropology thus follows the procedures and strategies of anthropology in general. But the spread of anthropology across the humanities, social sciences, and natural sciences may make research in medical anthropology extremely different from one instance to the next, even though the different inquiries may be related to the same issue. For example, heart disease may be studied from the physiological or biochemical angle using exercise tests and other laboratory examinations. The medical anthropologist may also, however, look at the self-perception of the sufferer of heart disease, using a humanistic inquiry that entails narratives by the afflicted about his or her own life situation. Or, the medical anthropologist may look at the organization of sufferers of heart disease who get together in a support community to maintain their hope and to work toward a new adaptation following a heart attack. Medical anthropology, as anthropology itself, utilizes a variety of research approaches determined by the nature of the issue studied. But it is the fieldwork component that provides the most unifying and compelling source of information.

In the following pages the first of a series of vignettes[7]—or case studies—appears that profile particular medical anthropology research projects and researchers to illustrate how a given research problem was defined, how the study was conducted, a sketch of the society in which it was done, and the findings of the research. The first of these vignettes is from my own early work in medical anthropology.

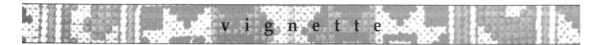

vignette

A Week in the Life of a Fieldwork Project: The Quest for Therapy in Lower Congo

From January to August 1969 I undertook a research project on African medicine in Kongo society of Lower Congo.[8] This project was formulated in part because of encouragement by local Kongo leaders interested in the validity of their healing traditions, and in part because of the puzzle by hospital and dispensary directors over the continued use by the Kongo people of African healing alongside Western medical treatment. From a scholarly perspective, it seemed an interesting way to study Kongo culture and health issues. Finally, while conducting earlier research in north Kongo on social and religious issues, I had met a Canadian medical doctor, William (Bill) Arkinstall, who was interested in collaborating in this study.

Photo 1.2 *Healer Madeko treats patient Bakulako for aggressive and disoriented behavior. Her aunt and therapy manager carefully watches the progression of the healer's massage.*
SOURCE: J. M. Janzen.

continued

continued from previous page

I obtained a postdoctoral grant from the Social Science Research Council's Africa Program. My wife and young son went to live with her parents in Germany for the term of this project. Arkinstall's wife and young son went to live at Kimpese, a big mission hospital complex in Lower Congo where he had worked previously. Bill and I set out for the Manianga, north of the Congo River, where I had worked previously, to study the Kongo approach to healing.

Our base was at Kumba, an independent school and center that had been set up by Fukiau kia Bunseki, a Kongo teacher interested in the study and revalorization of Kongo culture and history. From 1964 to 1966, I had lived and worked in the village of Kisiasia nearby, so it was relatively easy to incorporate research on health seeking in my overall program. Bill arranged to be on call at the local Protestant mission dispensary and the Catholic hospital of Mangembo, neither of which had access to a physician at this time.

I kept a daily log of our work and my impressions and feelings. This log often served as a reminder of what we had done during those

Photo 1.3 *A very exhausting week! We (the author and his research associate Dr. William Arkinstall) returned to base at Kumba where we were with friend and host Fukiau, his family and students. We spent time in much-needed relaxation, writing in our journals and indexing our notes, both essential dimensions of successful anthropological fieldwork.*
SOURCE: J. M. Janzen.

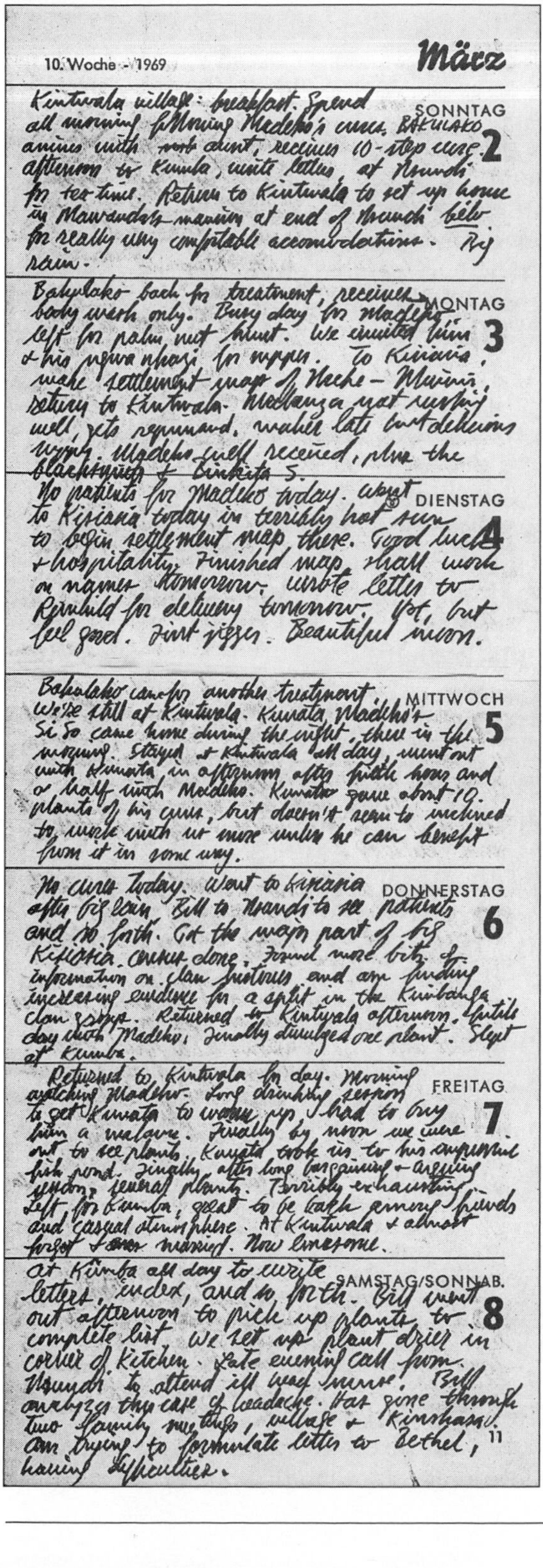

periods when work became too hectic and the write-up could only follow several days later. Photo 1.4 at left shows one week from this fieldwork log. It should provide you, the reader, with an impression of this fieldwork.

Our research proposed to understand the classification of illnesses and medicines, as well as the Kongo people's basis for judging whether to consult an African healer or to go to a nearby Western medicine dispensary or hospital. After some false starts, we devoted much time to tracking cases that seemed representative and interesting—like the two mentioned in this week's notes—and in interviewing and observing practitioners, like the uncle/nephew pair Madeko and Kunata.

During this week of March 2–8, we tried to witness and understand the case of Bakulako, brought by her aunt, her "therapy manager," to the care of healer Madeko. The week's treatments were but one segment of her more complex "quest for therapy" that became a chapter, "A History of Madness," in our book.

After leaving Congo, I took up a position at McGill University in Montreal while Arkinstall worked at the Royal Victoria Hospital there. We held several seminars on our work and published *The Quest for Therapy in Lower Zaire* in 1978. This work was awarded the Wellcome Prize of the Anthropological Institute of Great Britain and Ireland for its contribution to medical anthropology. ■

Photo 1.4 *Diary text recording highlights of each day during fieldwork. Side comments 30 years later suggest that changing memory and continuing reflection may alter our understanding of the original experience.*

Source: J. M. Janzen.

As we saw in the "classical projects" above and in the first vignette, most research in medical anthropology begins with a research issue or problem for which there may be no ready answer, or there may be several plausible answers but little evidence to support one or another of them. Some researches in medical anthropology are descriptive ethnographies that seek to be as inclusive as possible or thorough in the account of a focused issue. In others, a hypothesis is generated through discussion and reading around the issue. An appropriate method and sample will reflect the theory and the problem. The "findings" will reflect the theories and the methods.

Thus, the inquiry on Kongo medicine described in the vignette required several levels of research. First, what was—or had been—Kongo medicine? Second, why did people use it? And third, why and how did they use it alongside the Western or biomedical institutions. Because of extensive change in colonial Kongo society since the early 20th century, many features of Kongo medicine had been discarded or had gone underground by the time we conducted our study. Kongo people were able to talk about this in general, but were less willing, or able, to explain what they would actually do. This is why we settled on the case-study approach, because we knew we could identify current practices from current cases. Optimal sample size became a few good extended cases with individuals who would explain their actions and thoughts.

The first question above—what was Kongo medicine?—was best answered with a great deal of observation of both healers and their clients, the people who came to them. The second question—why did people use it?—required more discussion with the principal decision makers in the cases. Our work eventually highlighted this decision-making process and the negotiation among "therapy managers" who were often responsible kinsmen of the sufferer. From these conversations emerged a picture of a dualistic worldview of the causes of misfortune. There were "illnesses of God," what we might call "natural" illnesses, that could be treated with symptomatic treatment or taken to dispensaries and hospitals. There were also "illnesses of man," human-caused or agent-caused illnesses that would not respond permanently to symptomatic treatment, and thus required divination by experts to figure out which agent, human or spirit, or social circumstance might be wishing the victim's affliction. Almost universally the Kongo thought that an illness bearing such a cause could not be cured in a Western-created medical institution. This was the basic insight of our research, although we needed a year and much analysis to dig out this simple understanding.

Our approach to fieldwork emphasized what has come to be known as "key informants" related to the cases, and from the ranks of the healers. In such an approach to gathering information, reliability can be gained only by comparing stories and various experiences. Other studies may take a cross-section of the community and conduct periodic interviews from standardized protocols. We were interested as much in "how the system works, and what is its logic," as in understanding the range of opinions or of personal experiences, or even in discerning the distribution of types of illnesses and therapies. The nature of the research question thus often dictates the required method and sample.

CONCLUSION

This introductory chapter has sought to provide an accurate impression of the nature of medical anthropology for the uninitiated student and reader. As part of anthropology in general, the perspective of medical anthropology is comparative—that is, it seeks to situate single examples of health, illness, and healing within a wider framework, potentially to all human history and all kinds of human societies. It is contextual, that is, it stresses the uniqueness of each community and culture within which the social fabric of health, the suffering of illness, and the search for healing occur. It is holistic in that it looks at the physical, social, and mental aspects of health, illness, and healing.

The point has been made that medical anthropology develops this distinctive perspective and builds its knowledge through research. Often, as in the vignette in this chapter, that research takes the form of fieldwork. Such fieldwork may also be clinical, in a setting of healing, or it may be an applied program that seeks to change the conditions of health. But the distinctive approach of anthropology to research is to go out and see what is actually occurring, and to talk to the people themselves. Only secondarily, or to complement fieldwork, would an anthropologist go to archives or a library for information on the research problem.

A useful source for further work on the basic nature of medical anthropology is the journals published by the leading societies of medical anthropology. In the United States the *Medical Anthropology Quarterly* is published by the Society for Medical Anthropology, a branch of the American Anthropological Association. *Medical Anthropology* is an independent U.S. journal. For an introduction to British medical anthropology, consult the journal *Anthropology and Medicine;* in France, *Sciences Sociales et Santé;* in Germany, *Curare.* International journals of note include the medical anthropology section of *Social Science and Medicine.* This journal is published in the United Kingdom, but it has a global editorial body. These journals, among others, offer a contemporary overview of the thriving field of medical anthropology both in academia and beyond. The next chapter turns to how the field of medical anthropology began, and the ideas that have inspired it.

REVIEW QUESTIONS

1. In light of the key terms and classical projects, formulate in your own words and thoughts a response to the question, "What is medical anthropology?"

2. What are the distinctive features of the anthropological perspective? Explain how this perspective is met in one or more of the studies or projects described in this chapter or elsewhere.

3. How has research in medical anthropology served to solve human problems and to create a distinctive perspective to understanding health, illness, and healing within anthropology?

NOTES

1. Anthropology, (*anthro*[p] = human, *ology* = the study of) humankind.

2. This use of "tradition" is quite different from speaking of "traditional" practices. As used here, tradition is based on the Latin root *Traditium* to refer to that which is handed down, either orally or in written text or other codified manner (Janzen 1989; Marty 1982: 3–4; Sullivan 1988). This use of the term is similar to the approach of archaeologists and cultural historians to account for sets of cultural features that remain recognizable, although not static, over time and space. A health and healing (or medical) tradition would reveal characteristic ways of identifying and classifying disease, organizing treatments, and expounding its teachings. The elements of the tradition are not disembodied and free-varying. They are embedded in the logical and ideological contexts of living communities; they are shaped by economic, social, and political forces (Janzen 1992: 163).

3. This term evokes very different connotations to Terry Chappell, M.D., who suggests that most physicians, especially of alternative medicine, see "biologic medicine" as stimulating and nurturing normal biologic mechanisms, whereas mainstream medicine, defined as drugs and surgery, is invasive.

4. *Sign* derives from the ancient Greek *syn* or *sym* (by way of Latin and Middle English and Old French). The difference between the two variants of sign is one of alternative phonetic contexts; for example, *syn* is used by itself or with consonants such as a *d* following it, as in syndrome, or in a cluster of signs of a condition; *sym* is used when a *b* or *p* follow the stem, as in symbol or symptom. The common term means "with, together, together with, or along with"; that is, as the signum, mark, token, image, seal, or sign together with the object to which it refers. In the context of sickness, sign stands for a condition of affliction (Liddell and Scott 1968).

5. *Symptom* is more specifically derived from the Greek *symptomat* and the late Latin *symptoma* (Liddell and Scott 1968).

6. *Symbol* is derived from the Latin *symbolon* or the Greek *sym-ballein,* meaning "to throw together." There is a historic link between symbol and cymbal, the instrument, whose two metallic discs are struck together to create a powerful sound resonance (Liddell and Scott 1968). Just as the cymbals create a sound from their impact upon each other, so the symbol creates a meaning that resonates from the outside to the sign that it interprets.

7. *Vignette* has come to refer to the running ornament on a book's title page, or at the beginning or end of a chapter; to the picture on a postage stamp; and, as it is used here, to a short literary sketch that illustrates a larger topic.

8. The name Congo refers to the vast river that drains the Congo Basin of Central Africa, to the country that extends over most of this territory (the Democratic Republic of Congo whose capital is Kinshasa), and to the region (e.g., Lower Congo, near the mouth of the river). Colonial conquerors claimed this region as the Congo Free State (1885–1908), and the Belgian Congo (1908–1960), after which time it became the Democratic Republic of Congo. From about 1966 to 1997 the river and the country were renamed "Zaire," a Portuguese term derived from *nzadi,* the KiKongo word for the great river. Liberators of Congo in 1997 renamed the country the Democratic Republic of Congo. In scholarly convention the people of the Lower Congo and their culture are referred to as Kongo (with a *K*) and, following the structure of Bantu language, their language is KiKongo, they are the BaKongo people, and an individual would be a MuKongo.

THE ORIGINS AND THEORIES OF MEDICAL ANTHROPOLOGY

Photo 2.1 *A medical anthropology seminar at the University of Helsinki in May 1999 reflects current themes and perspectives of the discipline. Participants and their research topics (left to right) included Juha Soivio (off camera), hypertension and ischaemic heart disease in Finnish society; Meri Larivaara, disease ecology and the HIV epidemic in Tanzania; Reea Hinkkanen, divination and knowledge in the Sukuma-Nyamwezi area, Tanzania; John M. Janzen, anthropological perspectives on war trauma in the African Great Lakes region; Tapio Nisula (organizer and moderator), pluralistic modes of health care organization in Zanzibar; Eva-Marita Rinne, perceptions of water in a Nigerian community; Marja-Liisa Honkasalo, the ambiguity of chronic pain; Marja Tiilikainen, everyday knowledge of health and illness among Somali refugee women in Finland.*
SOURCE: J. M. Janzen.

How did the interest in health, illness, and healing among anthropologists become a full-fledged specialization among a group conscious of its own identity and with its own professional journal? What were the ideas that inspired its work and how did they reflect anthropology at large? This chapter responds to these questions about the origins and theories of medical anthropology. The first part of the chapter describes the beginnings of medical anthropology in the context of the wider academic and health care world. The second part situates medical anthropology within the theories and writings of anthropology and related disciplines. The third part situates some of the unique approaches of this text within those ideas.

THE RISE OF MEDICAL ANTHROPOLOGY

The Society for Medical Anthropology, a branch of the American Anthropological Association, was organized in 1968, with its own newsletter. Its journal, *Medical Anthropology Quarterly,* was begun in the early 1980s. So medical anthropology is a "kid on the block" in terms of some other disciplines. Why did this field emerge within anthropology at this time? It was not that there were no anthropological projects before the 1960s concerned with health, illness, and healing. Early 20th-century British anthropologists C. G. Seligman and W. H. R. Rivers, who had been medical researchers before they entered anthropology, conducted research on the disease concepts and therapies of Melanesian islanders (Rivers 1924). Anthropologist Forrest Clements (1932) studied the ideas about sources of misfortune and causes of disease. The study of shamanic healers was prominent in the work of scholars Waldermar Bogoras (1904–1909) and Mircea Eliade (1964) well before the dawn of medical anthropology. The study of the distribution of cultural patterns by the World Ethnographic Survey and the Human Relations Area Files (Murdock 1967, 1980) identified the types and distribution of ideas of disease causation, healing methods, and practitioner roles. Attention to health, illness, and healing was subsumed within anthropology without being a special focus.

The emergence of medical anthropology as a visible specialty in the 1960s may be traced to several distinct developments that have been noted by reviewers of the scene. The first of these was the desire to better understand health care practices in cultures in which anthropologists and health workers found themselves in the 1950s and 1960s. With the broadened understanding of non-Western health settings, the awareness also grew that the members of societies within which Western health workers were engaged had their own distinctive ideas about the nature of the human being, including anatomy, relationships between individuals and between humans and the spirit world, and the basis of disease. Anthropologists began to study non-Western medical traditions and to write about them. In regions such as China, India, the

Middle East, where historians and scholars of language had studied the medicine and cultural traditions with their own famous doctors and scholars, medical anthropologists began to collaborate with, and to incorporate the methods of, linguists and other types of specialists.

A second development in the rise of medical anthropology was the desire to improve health care programs by making them more culturally appropriate and effective (MAQ 1981). In the 1960s, as Third World countries were achieving self-determination, anthropology was marshaled to teach methods of improved health. These projects included, for example, the study of culture to improve the introduction of new techniques such as boiling water, building latrines, and finding ways to raise public awareness of health-promoting techniques such as oral rehydration for diarrheal diseases and other disease conditions with well-known causes. The collection *Health, Culture, and Community: Case Studies of Public Reaction to Health Programs* (1955), edited by Benjamin Paul, was the first scholarly work to use the term *medical anthropology* in an analysis of the cultural context of health improvement measures, and why they were not always successful or easy to institute.

A third reason for the emergence of medical anthropology as we know it today lies within the Western world, and has to do with what some authors call a "crisis in medicine" (MAQ 1981: 7–8). This crisis was defined as the inadequacy of the formerly prevailing single-cause explanation of disease to account for many of the illnesses for which people in advanced industrial societies increasingly sought care. Gone, or greatly diminished in seriousness, were many of the contagious diseases such as smallpox, measles, and diphtheria attributed to single causal agents—microorganisms, bacteria, germs. They had been steadily replaced in peoples' concerns by a myriad of degenerative, environmental and lifestyle related conditions such as Alzheimer's disease, cancer, or toxic shock syndrome. This gradual change in the type of illness suffered by many people has given rise to the growing desire by practitioners, health agencies, and the general public to understand the nature of complex sets of influences upon health, and to gain a better understanding of the place of cultural agents such as beliefs, lay knowledge, diet, and communication in clinical processes and diagnostic settings.

This shift in the nature of disease and health, and the related expansion of the focus of medical anthropology, has become worldwide, although it may occur along class lines in many countries. That is, upper classes reflect the decline of contagious diseases, and the rise of degenerative and other diseases related to a longer life span, while lower classes continue to suffer contagious diseases and diseases related to inadequate housing, poor diet, polluted water, and lack of access to health care. This epidemiological pattern continues to spread throughout the globe, accompanied by demographic changes from high birthrates to lower birthrates.

However, with the decline of the old contagious diseases, some of which have been eliminated globally (such as smallpox), new diseases have taught us about the dangers of putting our faith in "magic bullet" cures. Antibiotic-resistant bacteria or parasites (e.g., tuberculosis, malaria) have evolved from the misuse of earlier pesticides and medicines. This widespread pattern of medicine-resistant microorganisms (smart germs) has amplified the crisis of medicine mentioned above and raised awareness of the need to see the source of health in lifestyle, diet, preventive medicine, and social and economic institutions. It has also prompted drug companies to redouble their search for new medicines (e.g., antibiotics) in the non-Western herbal traditions. This has in turn stimulated anthropological research on plant uses and understanding. It has also raised ethical questions about the rights of native and national peoples to the uses of knowledge and to the economic proceeds from these substances.

On a somewhat different plane, technological advances in health and reproductive functions have created a new horizon of "designer medicine," featuring patients' choices on weighty life outcomes in such areas as the gender and predisposition of disease in infants. Techniques for the examination of the amniotic fluid around the fetus are routinely applied in India and China to assure the gender of offspring; in the United States and western Europe widespread screening is done of both gender and genetically inherited conditions. This vision of the way the person is constructed biologically and how this knowledge is used by communities and nations has brought into new focus the signification of the body in health and disease. A global marketplace of health and healing concepts, techniques, opportunities, and materials has emerged which includes an interest in alternative (to biomedicine) therapies, many of which derive from ancient therapeutic traditions. Both dealing with the new knowledge and opportunities in medicine, and knowing how to use them in relation to ancient therapies, makes a discipline like medical anthropology more necessary than ever.

All these changes have come to the health scene at a time when the long-held premise that health was steadily improving through the intervention of the state has been questioned. No longer is the notion of "health as a right for all" held to be possible. The collapse of state socialism in the Soviet world and the retreat from fully socialized economies in the West have eroded the possibility of even being able to pay for complete health care. In some places free market institutions are taking the place of state-promised and -provided health care. In the United States, health has become a huge and aggressive capitalist business at the same time that millions no longer have access to much medical care. In other places, as a result of the gradual collapse of some states, neither free-market nor state-socialized care is available. This is especially alarming in light of the reappearance of old diseases such as tuberculosis and malaria, and the rising burden of the AIDS epidemic. Increasingly, all countries of the world are divided into healthy upper classes and continuing unhealthy underclasses (WHO 1999).

These trends may seem unprecedented, but they merely represent the continuing "history" of health conditions and of medical thought and practice in our modern world. Insofar as medical anthropology responds to them with its distinctive perspective—that is, comparative, contextual, historical, holistic—a fourth reason for the rise and continuing importance of medical anthropology may be noted. The perspectives that emerged in the anthropology of non-Western settings have gradually been brought back to the biomedical settings of the Western world, to the dominant paradigm of medicine in North America, Europe, and in the nation-state and academic-controlled circles: The cultural analysis of concepts, institutions, and practices of biomedicine have become the domain of the medical anthropologist. Culturally sensitive health surveys and improved language and nonverbal manners in clinical care have become the realm of medical anthropologists working with health care personnel. Medicine as science, and the very notion of "nature," have come to be seen by some medical anthropologists as culturally constructed realities.

Medical anthropology has responded to these changes and issues with a certain "stretching" to cover the following complementary perspectives: On the one hand there continues to be an applied perspective that emphasizes the insinuation of cultural sensitivities into health development programs and clinical practice; on the other hand, there is an emphasis on the interpretation of beliefs, disease constructs, and therapies, including the somewhat newer demonstration of the cultural or symbolic character of biomedicine. Proponents of the first perspective stress action, such as Thomas Johnson, the 1994 president of the Society for Medical Anthropology, who suggested that the field is moving out of academe into the arena of practice, and that medical anthropology should create its own professional certification (1994). Proponents of the interpretive approach suggest that medical anthropology is called to "deconstruct" the culture of medicine so as to humanize its practice.

The two approaches are different, but they are complementary. They are also a reflection of the steady change in medical anthropology's concept of itself and of where it is headed. Medical anthropology, within anthropology and other disciplines, has gone through phases that reveal a dominant set of ideas and other subordinate or opposing perspectives. For advanced students and scholars in medical anthropology, this continual shifting of orienting ideas is of great importance in defining the field, its research issues and projects, and in charting new directions. This is why this chapter continues with a brief history of the theories that have come and gone, or persisted, in the few short decades of our discipline.

MEDICAL ANTHROPOLOGY: A BRIEF HISTORY OF THEORY

Theory is a conversation between practitioners of a discipline about the ideas that give the subject matter its coherence. There is even something of aesthetics in theory; a good writer may bring a beautiful theoretical coherence to bear on an issue, just like a well-honed speech or performance is convincing in its eloquence. But sometimes this conversation over the coherence of a field becomes more like a debate between those who agree on perhaps only a small part of the subject matter, and differ on much of the rest. Because of the many-sided nature of the anthropology of health, illness, and healing, it is common for there to be both collaboration between members of the subdisciplines and between anthropology and other fields, as well as debates over which approaches are most appropriate for a given project. Often new theoretical perspectives begin as innovative commentary and research on old research problems. Just as there is often a left wing and a right wing in politics, so are alternative approaches and trends common in the disciplines. Medical anthropology thus has reflected the larger issues and debates within anthropology. Many of the discussions over theory in medical anthropology have revolved around the question of how culture is to be defined and handled in the study of health and healing. For some it is the lens through which all of illness and healing are seen. For others, culture is a reality balanced against biology.

These stances toward culture in health, illness, and healing correspond roughly to the four-field distribution within anthropology. On one side, sociocultural anthropology stresses the cultural reality of experience; biological anthropology, on the other hand, while acknowledging culture, either puts it aside methodologically or simply focuses on the biological dimensions of human experience. Medical anthropology as presented in this work, and generally in the modern field known by that title, is seen to be distinctive from biological anthropology because of its active consideration of culture. The two major long-standing approaches to culture in medical anthropology may be identified by the labels "sociocultural" and "biocultural." These in turn reflect the leanings and distinctions that have reigned within anthropology itself during much of the 20th century. Our consideration of a brief history of medical anthropology within anthropology begins with a discussion of each of these two orientations.

THE SOCIOCULTURAL PERSPECTIVE, 1950S–1970S

This perspective in medical anthropology must be aligned with "social anthropology" and its British origins, as well as certain threads coming from the French sociology of Emile Durkheim in which society, its structure and consciousness about it, is seen as the prime focus of the study of the human condition. In the sociocultural perspective, the biological or material realm is considered, known, and understood through the prism of cultural knowledge, whether that be a folk theory of illness and healing, or the cultural knowledge of biomedical science. The "hard facts" of biology and physiology are not denied, but the interest lies in the cultural consciousness about them, and the ways society organizes that knowledge and related behavior.

A leading paradigm or theoretical pattern within much of anthropology in the immediate post–World War II period in North America and Europe came to be called **structural-functionalism.** The two terms arose from different emphases, but they were often put together into a hyphenated set of concepts. One definition of functionalism saw human behavior as meeting a variety of biological, material, community, emotional, and spiritual needs. In the work of Bronislaw Malinowski (1948, 1965), all human institutions had a "function" in meeting a particular range of human needs. It was relatively easy to direct this functionalist perspective toward issues of health, illness, and healing. A medical treatment served the function of meeting the need raised by the disease or affliction which it addressed. The very circularity of this theoretical perspective, however, often made its practitioners blind to the forces of change and to the possibility that behavior might have multiple, haphazard, or even contradictory reasons for being.

With the influence of French social thought as expressed in the work of Durkheim, anthropological thinking in some European and North American centers turned toward the forms of society for an understanding of institutions. Rather than emphasizing material and psychological needs as the basis of society's institutions, social thinkers thought of society through the natural metaphor of the "organism" made up of multiple organs each with its own structures. Just as a biological body had its organs with distinctive functions, so society had its distinctive and complementary institutions or individuals in a community, individual roles in a web of social roles, or institutions in a social whole. This perspective was brought into anthropology by the work of A. R. Radcliffe-Brown, who founded numerous departments of "social anthropology" in the United States, Australia, and Africa.

This perspective found its way into several influential medical anthropological projects in the 1970s. The first of these, fittingly named *Social Anthropology and Medicine* (1976), edited by physician-anthropologist J. B. Loudon, covered the cultural study of non-Western healing practices, the culturally sensitive introduction of health care innovations, and alluded briefly to the cultural study of Western medicine. The organizers of this work saw themselves in the older tradition of C. G. Seligman and W. H. R. Rivers (1924), British physician-anthropologists mentioned previously, who studied Melanesian perceptions of disease and healing practices. These works and others led the "social anthropologists of medicine" to a keen interest in comparative theories of disease causation and the study of their relative rationality vis-à-vis each other. The debate over rationality, or comparative rationality, became very important because it essentially asked the question: Does a practice that seems strange, and whose workings we don't understand, make sense from some other viewpoint? Often it meant the judgment of others' theories as irrational or "magical" in relation to Western rationality. E. E. Evans-Pritchard's (1937) study of the interpretation of misfortune among the Azande of Central

Africa, however, highlighted the alternative rationality of witchcraft as a theory, as a special circumstance alongside natural laws. For the Azande, illness or accident could in certain circumstances be seen as resulting from human relationships, if divination or diagnosis produced the evidence.

One interesting consequence of the early studies in non-Western perceptions of illness and healing was the reinterpretation of the experience of some conditions in the West that had not previously been understood or even recognized. Anthropologists, using the methods developed in their non-Western studies, identified shell shock, that is, war trauma, as a major psychiatric condition among the many veterans of World War I who were unable to readily overcome their combat experiences.

Another major British social anthropologist, Meyer Fortes, thought that too much of this early medical anthropology, and the concern over the rationality of collective customs in illness and healing, had been misguided because it was insufficiently focused upon the person in health and disease for comparative study (Loudon 1976: xvi–xviii). Rather than to look at beliefs and practices and theories of disease as cultural systems, Fortes stressed the empirical focus upon lived experience of individuals, families, and communities. However, in this collection and in others, the stress upon experience, in all its contradictoriness, would often be subsumed under the rubrics of beliefs, concepts and customs, and ritual practices of entire societies. The emphasis upon the social and cultural context of health-related behaviors would prove to be extremely valuable and enduring as a feature of medical anthropological work.

A further perspective that emerged in the sociocultural stream of medical anthropology reflected the growing interest in **symbols** in human life. Debates about the role of consciousness compared to social roles and structures in human behavior, especially in kinship, had the effect of highlighting ritual and myth. Claude Lévi-Strauss's research on myth had a widespread impact on anthropology and, in a selective way, upon medical anthropology. His article on the efficacy of symbols has been published in most anthropology and medical anthropology readers since it was first published in 1949 (Lévi-Strauss 1963). It describes the healing work of a Panamanian Cuna Indian shaman in a song-recitation to relieve a woman's anxiety during a long and difficult birth. By suggesting that the symbolic component in much healing ritual might actually help to achieve its intended goal, Lévi-Strauss suggested that the earlier dichotomy between rationality and magic might not be so clear-cut. He argued that the symbolic potential of human communication and therapeutic performance contained incredible power that truly affected both mind and body.

The symbolic view of society found some remarkable converts in the 1960s, with far-reaching implications for medical anthropology. David Schneider's influential work on society and kinship took a turn toward the symbolic in his *American Kinship, A Cultural Account* (1968). Society's categories were in the minds of society's members after all, rather than "out there" in rules or behavior. Most important for later thinking on the image of the body in medical anthropology, Schneider suggested that blood ties in kinship were really symbols of "diffuse, enduring solidarity." In other words, the "glue" of society was not innate biological blood or genes, but the symbol of blood in peoples' minds and feelings. This symbolic approach to society was accompanied by Schneider's critique of the static, presumed purpose in structural-functionalist views of kinship, and the emergence of feminist and gender correctives in kinship studies. This had the cumulative effect of recasting in symbolist perspective, especially a gender-specific perspective, many topics that had previously been couched in a social determinist framework. At the same time Clifford Geertz's approach to the symbolist perspective, which he put forward in the form of "interpretive" anthropology (1973), brought about a veritable paradigm shift in sociocultural anthropology that had a profound impact on medical anthropology.

Another often-cited author on the role of symbols in sickness and healing is Victor Turner, whose detailed analyses of the symbols of ritual healing among the Ndembu of northern Zambia on the southern savanna of Africa showed the power of cultural expression as it engulfed both material and ideational dimensions of human experience. Turner's (1967, 1968) analysis and writing on the ritual symbol led to the development of one of the most sophisticated formulations of this area of anthropology, and for medical anthropology. For Turner the symbol began with a simple sign, such as a twig of a tree, milk, or blood. It was, however, in the way that meaning was given this sign that created the power of the symbol. The symbol had two "poles of meaning," one rooted in the physical, the body; the other was an idea, such as society, lineage, the moral force of ancestors, or God. Use of the sign in a ritual brought into full play the emotional force of the physical pole of meaning, as well as the lofty abstraction of the ideational pole. Ritual symbols had a power even greater than words because they condensed such many-sided feelings and ideas into a shorthand language of objects and movements. Turner's work on ritual symbols grew into a flourishing scheme of important ideas for medical anthropology, including the following: the "liminal," the betwixt and between status of individuals in the transitional part of a life cycle ritual; "communitas," the same idea applied to an entire community during celebration; "social drama," the explanation of crisis and conflict as a kind of ritual; and "metaphor," the use of stories or symbols of identity by individuals and societies.

A tangible outcome of this impact of the symbolic perspective in sociocultural anthropology upon medical anthropology was the publication in 1984 of an anthropological textbook by Cecil Helman, a professor of medicine at University College London, for his own medical interns. He sought to bring into the perception of the interns the culture of the individuals with whom they would deal as doctors. Helman explained the importance of such topics as the patient's folk views of anatomy and disease causation, the meaning of diet, the importance of symbolic power in healing—in general, the cultural meaning of medicine for the patient.

In keeping with his sociocultural perspective, however, Helman studiously avoided explication of the biological-material dimensions of medicine. He offered a section on folk ideas of anatomy, but did not discuss the cultural character of academic biomedical anatomy. His segment on culture and diet offered many folk recipes, but no valid analysis of dietary science. His work seems to be an anthropological supplement for physicians, rather than a well-rounded presentation of the culture of biomedicine. That would come later, from other medical anthropologists.

Parallel to the foregoing developments in anthropology and medical anthropology, two further, and related, perspectives entered sociocultural anthropology in the late 1950s and 1960s when many of Europe's colonies were gaining independence and social scientists, politicians, and development agencies anticipated the courses these newly independent nations would seek and experience. These perspectives can be identified by the key terms of **modernization** and **Marxism,** two terms that informed the rhetoric of the Cold War which pitted the West, as the champion of a free market, liberal democratic vision of modernization, against the East, as champion of a centrally planned economy under state-dominated Marxian socialism. The academic versions of these perspectives contained a healthy dose of prescriptive rhetoric within their theoretical formulations which, in practical application to health, meant the advocacy of particular lines of action. In the modernization scenario, it was considered necessary to help modernity along with education, health care, and the condemnation of "traditional" conditions that were a drag on modernity. In the Marxist perspective, the excesses of capitalism would be overcome by the unfolding of the contradictions of class conflict. This would lead to a communist or socialist revolution and the ushering in of state-fostered egalitarian society, complete with a state-provided health infrastructure. The state would become the caretaker and vehicle of such a revolution. Both modernization and Marxism are now seen as utopian notions spawned in the 18th or 19th centuries, and which have run their course. But their social visions and their academic theories were very important in the development of aspects of medical anthropology, and need to be reviewed here.

Modernity, as modernism was called in the social sciences, was held to be the embodiment of the modern person and society in the 20th century. Individualism, rational action in the context of the nation-state, and a goal-oriented, rational bureaucratic society characterized modernity, in contrast to the collectivism, intuitive action, and impulsive present-oriented character of traditional society, the polar opposite of the modern. This perspective within the social sciences had inherited some elements from earlier scholars such as Max Weber who had studied the rise of industrial society in Europe. It also reflected the belief in "progress" in the Western world, and the not-so-subtle conviction that the West was superior to all other societies, especially those of the Third World. In this view the Third World was engaged in a "catching up" act that would follow what had occurred in the West. This view provided the premise for much postcolonial development assistance in the Third World, including efforts to improve health.

Not surprisingly, medical anthropology offered its corollary of modernization thinking and analysis. George Foster and Barbara Anderson (1978) divided the Western from the non-Western world and described their distinctive health and medicine conditions in terms of the "modern" and the "traditional," predicting that the former would replace the latter. The shamans, witch doctors, and other curers would give way to the physicians, nurses, and specialists as Third World societies "modernized." Foster and Anderson saw modernization as inevitable and desirable; medical anthropologists should lend their hand to the forces of progress.

Other medical anthropologists who use modernization theory have not embraced it as a positive experience. Some, such as Ann McElroy and Patricia Townsend (1979), saw the process as disastrous for the health of those experiencing it. With a combination of adaptive ecology, nutrition, and "culture contact" analysis—a perspective developed in North America with special reference to Native American societies—they see modernization (i.e., industrialization, cash economies, individualized labor) as a disastrous and deeply traumatic experience that medical anthropology may help clarify and cushion for those societies that have been engulfed or overrun by Western industrialism. More will be said of adaptive ecology under the rubric of the biocultural perspective below.

Marxism or **political economy,** although a major influence during the 1970s and 1980s in social anthropology, was represented in medical anthropology by a number of scholars and writers with varying approaches to the issues. Social critics of biomedicine such as Vicente Navarro (1986, 1992, 1993) and Ray Elling (1986) saw medicine as an instrument of colonial domination of Third World societies that could only be thrown off by establishing collective, worker- or people-controlled health care practices. Marxist demographers Dennis Cordell, Joel Gregory, and Victor Piche (1987) studied mortality, fertility, and migration in terms of the diseases caused by the forces of capitalism upon the health environment, and the political-economic forces of class access to resources and state policies. British anthropologist Ronald Frankenburg raised the political economic voice in a variety of issues in Central Africa and in Great Britain (1992). Hans Baer (1982, 1989) brought this same perspective as a focus on health issues in the United States. These issues would continue to be raised in the 1980s and 1990s by those who called their perspective "critical medical anthropology," which will be taken up later.

The Biocultural Perspective, 1950s–Present

As was suggested earlier, the designation **biocultural** emerges as a generalized label to bring the holism of the four-field anthropological perspective to bear on medical anthropology. In much of Europe by the 20th century, anthropology had come to mean physical anthropology, since descriptive ethnography and ethnology (the theoretically inspired analysis of ethnographic accounts) designated the more specialized social and cultural inquiries. Eighteenth-century philosophers had used the term "anthropology" to describe everything from geography to theories of knowledge and to religion. An anthropology or theory of humanity was part of every religion and philosopher's scheme. Franz Boas brought this inclusive perspective to the United States early in the 20th century. Boas (1940) practiced all fields in his research, including projects such as linguistic surveys, the perception of color, the physiology and culture of race, art, ritual, and religion. Boas emphasized descriptive empiricism (the view that knowledge is based only on what we can see) as the basis for an enlightened science of humanity. His broad and inclusive type of anthropology laid the groundwork for the American style of biocultural medical anthropology. René Dubos's popular *Man Adapting* (1965) also did much to promote the perspective.

The principal hallmark of the biocultural perspective in medical anthropology is that it seeks, as its title "bio-cultural" suggests, to bridge the cultural and biological, or material, realities of life in one perspective. Key words that began to be used in the 1960s and 1970s to show how the cultural and biological could be bridged included "adaptation" and "ecological." The contents of all these writings featured themes in evolutionary biology, genetics, ecology, and cultural adaptation, at once an inclusion of the changing subject matter of physical anthropology, and a renewed attempt to bring the holism of general anthropology to bear on issues of health, disease, and medicine, the newly emerging field of medical anthropology.

One of the central themes in the ecological understanding of the world is that of a **community of organisms.** Organisms, from microscopically small to the largest mammals, must find food in their niche or they die out. They must also not destroy their source of food, or means of reproduction. A degree of specialization occurs among species as one organism comes to depend on another for its livelihood. The exchanges of energy in this process come to resemble a food chain, a hierarchy of energy dependence. Where does this energy originate? Ultimately, all energy is held to have originated from the sun, even though it is stored in carbonized biomass such as coal or gas, or in soil nutrients on which growing plants thrive.

Organisms adapt to these conditions of opportunity and threat. **Adaptation** may be short term within the single organism, or it may be longer term through random reproduction of offspring that are able to come to terms with changing circumstances. Insofar as this ability to adapt to a changing circumstance is transmitted hereditarily, **genetic change,** the basis of evolution, is an important ingredient of the ecological or biocultural view of anthropology.

Nutrition clearly becomes a logical focus for this view of medical anthropology since the central feature of the ecological perspective is the intake and outflow of energy, the nature and requirements for a given organism or species survival. In keeping with this central feature in ecological thinking, human nutrition becomes a central piece of the curriculum in medical anthropology.

The ecological view of energy flow between organisms brings into being a distinctive view of **disease** as well. As an independent concept, disease is problematic in any absolute sense, since the source of nutrition for one species may be the cause of death for another; or, the niche for one species is the invaded life space of another. Indeed, it is not clear exactly how a view of an energy chain could even have a species-neutral concept of disease. A medical anthropological application of the ecological perspective necessarily introduces a human perspective from which vantage point human survival and quality of life is privileged, and "disease" as a relative concept becomes that which places the human community at an adaptive disadvantage. Cultural consciousness, however, frames what the human community will define as disease. This may or may not correspond to what is adaptive.

From the human perspective, adaptation to a given constellation of organisms within a food chain in which humans participate is never just biologistic, or a meaningless flow of energy. The fate of the human organism in the ecological view has led to the inclusion in some texts and analyses of **population profiles** and patterned changes—that is, birthrates, death rates, fertility rates, life expectancies, epidemiologies of various diseases and conditions, and overall population numbers—within given environments.

The human privilege factor in an ecological medical anthropology is usually spelled out in terms of the role of **culture** in human adaptation. Culture is, of course, the most remarkable human resource of all for adaptation. As any student of introductory anthropology can identify, culture includes not merely tools but techniques needed in food foraging and cultivation, as well as language, abstract thought, the arts, and areas of focused human endeavor. In this view **medicine** becomes a part of adaptive culture, possibly the part that consciously reflects thought about interventions with explicit ideas about responding to those conditions perceived to be troubling, and about which one can do something.

Health, in the ecological perspective of biocultural anthropology, is no longer the "absence of disease," since "disease" depends on the organisms involved and the cultural definitions of pathology and suffering. Rather, health becomes in some way related to or defined by adaptation. Often health is not defined explicitly, but is implicitly understood to be synonymous with adaptive equilibrium, echoing structural-functionalism. In such a view the organism exists within an energy circuit or a community of organisms, each of which is at home and at peace with its niche. The real world is of course rarely, if ever, like this. Terry Chappell (1998) has suggested that the concept of **eustasis**—a dynamic balance of forces—is a more appropriate view of the human condition.

With the ecological perspective of disease came the interest in patterns of adaptation over the long term, and of the individual lifetime in a community setting. This may have reflected the rise of **human development** studies, **gerontology,** and then the entire **life span** as a focus for study and health care attention. In medical anthropology and in anthropology at large, this focus has come to be called the **life course perspective,** with interest in birth, transitions, traumas, growth, adulthood, and death. These points and passages of life are seen not as disease, but as the anticipated, integral phases of life. These "normal" life events are too frequently presented as diseases, when in fact the life course perspective may show them as times of appropriate ritualization during periods of transition and trauma. All of Chapter 5 is devoted to this subject.

The broad, integrative biocultural perspective in medical anthropology has continued to find adherence in the work of scholars such as George Armelagos (1994), Peter Brown and Marcia Inhorn (1990), Robert Hahn (1995), and others.

APPLIED "DEVELOPMENT" AND "CLINICAL" ANTHROPOLOGY

Applied anthropology is a school of thought that seeks to find immediate practical results of anthropological insight into the range of human problems and needs. Although most anthropological knowledge is in a sense applied to whoever internalizes it, "applied anthropology" is usually thought of as an intentionally focused application of anthropology to specific ends. Here we are interested in specific and intentional uses of anthropology for health purposes. Both the sociocultural and the biocultural perspectives of medical anthropology have put their insights and experience to use in resolving a range of health problems throughout the world. Although initially much of this application was in non-Western settings (as mentioned in presenting the origins of medical anthropology), the uses of medical anthropology have increasingly been applied to industrialized settings and even within medicine itself.

Medical anthropology applied to "development" refers to the uses of cultural research and involvement to enhance the health infrastructure. This has taken the form of anthropologists becoming involved in the creation of community health programs or primary health care systems. The anthropologist seeks to understand local social and political organization and to assure that the program being created is compatible with existing institutions and power structures. Many applied anthropology projects have sought to facilitate the innovation of health improvement techniques. One of the earliest of these was a study in a Latin American country to determine why drinking water was not being boiled when most people there knew that boiling water eliminated intestinal tract diseases (Polgar 1968). Rather than condemning the communities that did not take the obvious action to protect their own health, the anthropologist determined through careful inquiry that women had no time left in their day to collect the firewood needed to boil water. Once this was understood, time and energy adjustments could be made to facilitate the women's overall ability to adjust their already busy schedules and make room for the labor required to boil drinking water. Many anthropologists have been involved in the cultural research to gain background knowledge on diseases targeted for attention, or education about them. In regions of the world where infant mortality remains high because of diarrheal diseases, anthropologists have studied mothers' perceptions of these conditions and have collaborated with public health teams to publicize home-prepared oral rehydration therapies in culturally appropriate terms (Yoder 1995). Public health education campaigns about public scourges such as sexually transmitted diseases, in particular AIDS, have often employed anthropologists to develop culturally appropriate television or radio messages that explain the dangers of behaviors in the light of the particular disease. Anthropologists are able to study cultural categories of disease, the socially appropriate roles involved, the emotional associations and reasons of risky behaviors, and then to relate these findings to the new information being introduced to offset that risk (Green 1994; Farmer 1992).

"Clinical" applied medical anthropology takes either the form of already-practicing nurses, doctors, or other therapist acquiring anthropological skills to enhance their clinical work, or the form of a research anthropologist relating to a clinical setting as a member of a team. Anthropological learning can equip the nurse or therapist to see the subjective experience and perception of the patient or community more clearly, rather than to impose an objective medical fact upon the client individual or community. This is where the illness/disease dichotomy becomes helpful to the clinician as a tool. Essentially, the insinuation of the concept of culture into the clinical process permits the healer to see and hear the patient-other, and to shape the knowledge base of the clinical encounter between the doctor and the patient (Chrisman and Johnson 1990).

The Comparative Study of Health Systems and Medical Care, 1970s–1980s

For many anthropologists interested in issues of health and healing in the 1970s, among whom this author was one, the driving force was a straightforward interest in non-Western traditions and what they could reveal about the human experience. Theory was not highly developed; primary interest lay in how to understand and compare one tradition of medicine with another in the hope of understanding in general the nature of human response to disease. In the introductory chapter the study of Asian medicines was highlighted as a long-standing project in medical anthropology. Here the development of theory in that project will be stressed, as well as other projects and their insights.

Charles Leslie's contributions to medical anthropology lay not only in his research on South Asian medicine. Perhaps of equal or greater importance was his role in organizing conferences, editing their results, and thereby initiating and stimulating much of the writing and debating of the "medical systems" approach in anthropology. As was suggested, the study of Asian medical traditions provided the basis for this work in the 1970s, and that is where the theories were formulated. In *Asian Medical Systems* (1976), Leslie wrote that the classical healing traditions of the Old World could be studied in concert—in terms of their own integrity and in terms of what they had in common (1976: 2). Their great founders or reformers wrote key texts, founded institutions and laid out divisions of labor and (often) articulated or formulated anew concepts of cosmology, physiology, and the basic active notions of disease and healing. In the Mediterannean, Persian, South Asian, and Chinese traditions, this active notion of the energies or humors was sufficiently similar that a true comparative approach could be undertaken (1976: 4–5). Leslie's own research interests were in the comparative study of science and how its teaching and practice were organized. For Leslie, however, a genuine comparative approach of medical traditions needed to include a **biological approach** to interpret the patterns of health and illness that are part of a medical system; a **cultural approach** that looks at the knowledge in a society regarding ecology, nutrition, pathology, and the utility of health practices; and a **social approach** that looks at the health dimension of behaviors, as well as the role of relations and authority patterns in all health and medical matters (1976: 10–11). Leslie's inclusive approach to medical anthropology incorporated much of the sociocultural as well as the biocultural perspective sketched earlier. Indeed, he encouraged open dialogue and comparison of analytical approaches between not only anthropologists, but also historians, sociologists, behavioral epidemiologists, and medical scholars and practitioners. He would foster this same broad debate encouraging inclusiveness as senior anthropology editor of *Social Science and Medicine,* and in launching the first major monograph series devoted to medical anthropology with the University of California Press, which was titled: "Comparative Studies in Health Systems and Medical Care." The roots and branches of a great deal of medical anthropology during the 1970s and 1980s can be found in conferences and publications sponsored by Leslie.

Thus, we can find in the papers to a 1977 conference on "Theoretical Foundations for the Comparative Study of Medical Systems" (Leslie 1978) the distinctive streams represented. By invitation and design, these included the sociology of science and medicine (David McQueen, sociologist); disease in history (William McNeill, historian); medical systems as cultural systems (Arthur Kleinman, psychiatrist M.D. and anthropologist, scholar of Chinese medicine); narrative analysis of classic Ayurvedic medical texts (Francis Zimmerman, anthropologist, South Asian scholar); political economy of medical institutions (Ray Elling, medical sociologist, professor of community medicine); interrelated and changing social character of small-scale clinical processes and the larger-scale political and economic changes affecting health and medicine (John Janzen, anthropologist, Africanist). In Leslie's vision for this sprawling field, theory served the purpose of stimulating research, writing, and application in a multidisciplinary arena of usually complementary—although sometimes contradictory—perspectives.

Some of these insights were carried forward and joined with others in a decade-long project devoted to health and healing in Africa, called the "Medicine and Society Project" and directed by Steven Feierman and this author for the Joint Committee for African Studies of the Social Science Research Council and the American Council of Learned Societies from 1979 to 1989. As in the work on Asia, the conferences, workshops, and publications of this Africa project stressed the importance of the social, economic, and cultural context of health, disease, and healing (Janzen and Feierman 1979; Janzen and Prins 1981). Diseases do not just happen in a vacuum, it was argued; social conditions and behaviors create the conditions for the increase in malnutrition, malaria outbreaks, and AIDS pandemics. Similarly, health is not just there, it is maintained by a social basis of adequate nutrition, housing, healthful behaviors, and medicine. In the introduction to the final project volume *The Social Basis of Health and Healing in Africa,* the editors (Feierman and Janzen 1992) highlighted this social basis of health and healing with the case of widespread tuberculosis (TB) in southern Africa. Originally introduced by miners from Great Britain in the 1890s, tuberculosis spread quickly to the African population, and has been endemic to this day. TB is a well-known disease indicator for many kinds of health stresses; where diet, housing, and overall well-being are adequate, TB vanishes (Packard 1989). Poverty, labor policies that uproot individuals from their homes, and inadequate preventive and curative medicine allow this perfectly well-understood disease to remain endemic over a wide area. So disease and health do not just happen. Disease is socially triggered, and health is socially upheld (Feierman and Janzen 1992: xvi–xvii). The ideas about the social bases of health have been summarized as the **"social reproduction of health"** (Janzen 1992), and are at the foundation of the popular phrase of the **"social fabric of health"** in the present volume.

In the perspective that emphasizes the social basis of health, medicine needs to be seen as a process of maintaining health. In Africa, where medical traditions are not as monolithic as those in Asia, understanding their impact on health needs to be seen in terms of practices and ideas rather than centralized institutions (see the vignette "Discovering *obusinge*" in Chapter 3). A healing cult, a well-organized lineage, or a biomedical public health campaign may all enhance health because they maintain contact between people, provide a sharing of resources, and offer social support for the sick. In the African setting, where biomedicine may not be available in an effective form, it is important to understand all the aspects of society, economy, and medicine that contribute to health, or detract from it.

The comparative perspective in medical anthropology has not been limited to Asia and Africa. Commonly, health issues in the Western world are discussed and initiatives evaluated in comparative terms. Titles such as *The Health Planning Predicament: France, Quebec, England and the United States* (Rodwin 1984) and *Medicine and Culture: Varieties of Treatment in the United States, England, West Germany, and France* (Payer 1988) suggest the extent and type of uses of comparison in medicine, even outside anthropology.

CULTURAL MEDIATION IN THE BIOCULTURAL PERSPECTIVE, 1970s–1980s

Among scholars who subscribed to either the Leslian multidisciplinary or comparativist perspective, or to the basic coherence of the biocultural program in medical anthropology, there were a number who sought to intensify the focus on the cultural dimension in living, sickness, and healing. For some this had to do with their training in social or cultural anthropology rather than in medicine and biology. For others, it had to do with their interest in the manner in which the cultural dimension figured in the experience of sickness or in the dynamics of healing.

An influential group of scholars at the Department of Social Medicine of Harvard Medical School spearheaded, or at least reflected, many of the ideas around the role of culture in sickness and healing, and in medicine. Arthur Kleinman, the head of the department and founding editor of the journal *Culture, Medicine and Psychiatry*, had spelled out his vision of medical anthropology in his contribution to the previously mentioned 1977 forum on the theoretical basis of the comparative study of medical systems. The language of his paper was that of biocultural anthropology and medicine, but the emphasis was on the role of culture. Although health care was seen as a part of the adaptation to a given population or society's environment, a central argument was over the cultural construction of illness and strategies of health seeking. The paper's subtitle was "The Biocultural Context of Health Care Systems, and Its Relation to Socio-psycho-somatic Interrelationships in Sickness and Healing" (1978:90). Of the cultural dimension in the biocultural context, he wrote:

> [T]he cultural construction of illness as a psychosocial experience entails complex psycho- and socio-somatic processes that both feed back to affect disease and play a role in the process of healing disease and illness.

This "biosocial bridge," as he called it, offered many opportunities for original research. Culture on the one hand, and a strong biological dimension on the other, needed to be appreciated in order to grasp the mechanisms that bridged them in sickness and healing, or "adaptation," in the language of biocultural anthropology. Only a few of the sequence of research topics can be mentioned here to show the direction taken by Kleinman and his colleagues.

Early writing with colleagues established the importance of the distinction between **disease** and **illness** and provided an entry to the world of the bio-psycho-social bridge, or the place of culture in mediating the biocultural. Disease was held to be the objective reality of a pathology, mainly known to medical professionals, whereas illness was the subjective experience of the suffering, clearly shaped by cultural precepts. It was possible therefore to experience "disease" without "illness," and to have "illness" without "disease." This formulation was later to come under criticism that it expressed excessive medical arrogance, and the absence of culture in the medical perspective. In short, the lay sufferers had culture, the professionals had objective knowledge.

Nevertheless, medical practitioners needed to take seriously the perceptions and ideas of their clients. In order for medical communication between practitioner and client to be effective, each needed to understand the other's **Explanatory Model,** or each other's definition of etiology, onset of symptoms, pathophysiology, course of sickness, and treatment. This notion endorsed the clinical reality of experience in doctor/patient encounter, and provided a comparative framework to allow the scholar or practitioner to look at a variety of healing traditions and practices side by side.

For Kleinman and his colleagues, earlier writing on the **symbolic effect of healing** by Claude Lévi-Strauss and Victor Turner was prime evidence of strong but little understood forces in the bio-psycho-social bridge of illness and healing that they sought to understand. In his writing on Taiwan, Kleinman had documented the work of Tang-Ki shamans and noted their extremely effective clinical manner. Most of their patients had strong faith in their powers to heal. In trying to understand the active dimension in this largely ritual healing, Kleinman together with Robert Hahn developed a scheme derived from research on the **placebo,** meaning "to please," the inert treatment that is nevertheless efficacious, with its obverse, the **nocebo,** meaning "to destroy," in which an equally inert substance is nevertheless harmful (Hahn and Kleinman 1983). The most well-known cases of the nocebo effects were the documented "voodoo deaths" in which persons died of no known organic cause, but were convinced they had been cursed. Later, in Chapter 7, we will cover some of this ground as we look at sickness and healing in medical anthropology.

Other topics in the bio-psycho-social bridge have been thoroughly reviewed by the Harvard social medicine group. The mental illness of depression has been studied in Asia and in the West in order to establish the relationship of cultural context to underlying common bio-psycho-social factors. Studies arising from the research of Kleinman and his associates in China and the United States suggest that Asian manifestations of depression are **somatized,** that is, expressed in a variety of physical symptoms, to a greater extent than their counterparts in the West, where mental illnesses are legitimate conditions with well-known treatments.

These studies on depression have provided more refined evidence in debates over the phenomenon of the **culture-bound syndrome,** the notion that affliction syndromes and treatments may be so specific to a given cultural setting that they cannot be generalized or compared. Those who adhere to a radical cultural relativism in medical anthropology tend to embrace the culture-bound syndrome, whereas those who maintain the comparativist perspective of at least some objective parameters in the study of health and illness seek to locate culturally specific entities within or alongside the common human and physical dimensions of health and disease.

The study of **pain** represents another area in which the Harvard group has sought the psycho-socio-cultural bridge between biology and culture. Taking off from Mark Zborowski's pioneering study in the differential cultural perception of pain in several American immigrant groups, **narratives of suffering** have been analyzed to provide greater nuance to a subject that defies objective analysis, yet is at the center of healing and care.

These projects that have been enumerated all adhered to the conviction of the reality of the biocultural program in which it was axiomatic that society and culture were somehow related to the biological realm of human life. Even for those who were mainly concerned with the social dimension or the study of the ideas behind "exotic" healing traditions, there was no doubt about the continuum of culture and biology. For some, modern medicine remained the arbiter of physical reality and the nature of health and disease. Physicians and medical researchers had the key to reality. The social and cultural researchers could contribute to a better understanding of patients' beliefs or to the ideas of other cultures about health and healing.

THE CULTURAL CONSTRUCTION OF BIOMEDICINE AND NATURE, 1980s–1990s

Other scholars took this emphasis on culture in health and healing to a much more radical conclusion. The scrutiny of the cultural elements within medicine would shift the focus directly upon biomedicine, the culture of biomedicine, its practice, its practitioners as human beings, the teaching of medical knowledge—in short, a perspective they called the "cultural construction of biomedicine." The justification for cultural studies in relation to medicine now shifted subtly from making medicine more effective, to humanizing it by "deconstructing" it.

It is useful to identify several of the major trends in anthropology, the humanities, and social sciences that lie behind this development. First, the previously mentioned writing in the late 1960s and early 1970s by University of Chicago anthropologists David Schneider and Clifford Geertz on the symbolic nature of kinship, which had formerly been seen as naturalistically and socially determined, now was reinterpreted as symbolic in character. Schneider's own reformulation of American kinship as a cultural system, and Geertz's interpretive approach to cultural anthropology, exerted a strong ripple effect into other areas of anthropology, especially medical anthropology.

The impact of modern literary criticism upon anthropology may be identified as a second influence of **cultural constructivism** upon medical anthropology. Methods that had been developed and refined in the analysis of text could easily be extended into cultural studies and, often, where language held the key to culture, culture was language. Thus, one could "read culture as text," and analyze or interpret a cultural process just as one analyzed or interpreted a work of literature. Agency, actor, scene, metaphor, plot, narrative, and similar technical terms from literary criticism began to appear in cultural anthropology and medical anthropology.

A third factor in the emergence of the cultural constructivist approach in medical anthropology may be in the very social context of its practitioners. Intriguingly, the movement was most strongly represented by some of the medical anthropologists within elite medical schools—McGill University in Canada, Harvard and Stanford Universities in the United States. A nonbiological critique of medicine appeared to offer these anthropologists a certain visible place, especially if the basic axiom of this critique was that "biomedicine" gained its power and stature from the assertion that disease, medicine, nature, and science were synonymous with reality, with things as they really are. Therefore, to treat this premise of "invariant reality" as a "construct," to be "deconstructed" by the cultural scholars, would give them immense influence within the establishment to which they wished, as outsiders, to belong.

Allan Young wrote in this way about the "discourse on stress," and traced the history and emergence of post-traumatic stress disorder (PTSD) among Vietnam veterans (1995). In his study in Veterans Administration hospitals, Young showed the ways in which PTSD was manipulated—"constructed"—by some veterans and medical administrators to make their complaints legitimate and certifiable for third-party insurance payments. Other scholars began to deconstruct various syndromes and therapies. Margaret Lock wrote about *nevra* among Greek immigrants in Montreal (1991) and about the trapped housewife syndrome among Japanese women, both of whose conditions manifested widespread physical symptoms. Donna Haraway argued in her work that the medical concept of the immune system was based on Cold War imagery and ideology transferred to the human body (1993), bristling with "defenses," "attack cells" against "intrusion." The whole idea of the immune system, she suggested, was in large part a cultural construct. A more reasoned cultural history of the American view of the immune system was Emily Martin's *Flexible Bodies: The Role of Immunity in American Culture from the Days of Polio to the Age of AIDS* (1994).

Two important colloquiums appeared in the early 1990s (Pfleiderer and Bibeau 1991; Lindenbaum and Lock 1993) that followed "postmodern" understandings that would include Western biomedicine especially in the domains of health and healing that could be analyzed culturally. These works stressed that class power and knowledge strongly shape particular thought, expressions, formulations, and behaviors, and that is how they must be studied.

CRITICAL MEDICAL ANTHROPOLOGY, EMBODIMENT AND PHENOMENOLOGY, 1980S–PRESENT

At an earlier time, the prefix "critical" in anthropology or the social sciences would have referred to a political-economic or Marxist analysis of an institution or a social condition. With the disenchantment of such an exclusively materialist perspective, however, and the entry of the tools and perspectives of literary criticism into anthropology, the term *critical* has come to mean both the **political-economic** as well as the **cultural-literary** perspective. Within medical anthropology such a new, unified critical perspective has argued that biomedical and scientific enterprises often reflect privilege of class and power built upon knowledge constructed around an ideology of unchanging "nature." This perspective is inspired by and resonates with a critique of all that is colonial, imperialistic, patriarchal, elitist, and medical with a capital *M*.

Such varied perspectives have in common several basic features that are of interest and importance in medical anthropology. In contrast to objective constructions, claims, and viewpoints, all emphasize the subjective dimension of individual human experience. They pose the problem of place and the role of the bodily senses in relation to ideas and experience. Finally, for most writers discussed here, there is a central interest in the way that resistance to these types of oppression occurs, and the "sites" or situations where this happens. For medical anthropology in the critical perspective, the body becomes the vehicle, the site, the metaphor of expression, where all these issues come together and may be studied. The results of such studies demonstrate the socially negotiated and socially embedded character of reality and of knowledge, including science.

The implications for medical anthropology are that constructions of knowledge and portrayals of experience must be trimmed to their bare bones to reveal what is most essential to the phenomenon under study, or to the subjective element of human experience, in pain, in suffering, in healing, and in life. This perspective used by medical anthropology has drawn on the philosophical movements of phenomenology and existentialism, which in their original European manifestations in the 1940s and 1950s were reactions (by Martin Heidegger and Edmund Husserl) to the misused rationalism in fascism, particularly National Socialism in Germany, and (by Jean-Paul Sartre and Maurice Merleau-Ponty) to colonialism, especially in France.

The emphasis on the subjective dimension of human experience in this perspective brings to the foreground the place of emotions and everyday life, and puts into the background abstract explanations by officials and formal creeds. Renewed interest by medical anthropologists in the meaning of suffering and pain (Kleinman and Kleinman 1991; Kleinman 1995, 1997) provides anthropological theorist Michael Jackson (1996: 1–3) with examples of research which go beyond language to the subjective experience that may not be transmissible in words, or may be felt and only put into words inaccurately as meaning is gained through experience. "Being-in-the-World," coined by German philosopher Heidegger, is one of the hallmark phrases used extensively by phenomenologically inclined philosophers and anthropologists to describe the "raw experience" prior to language and intellectual discourse (Jackson 1996: 1; Merleau-Ponty 1964: xi). Among medical anthropologists, Arthur Kleinman has taken this phrase and adapted it to speak of the "local moral world" within which suffering usually finds legitimate meaning for most people, and which anthropologists should be concerned to understand. Thus the program for medical anthropology that is being prescribed here is one of vivid description possible only in the ethnography of feeling, emotions, and of sensory expression, rather than of causal analysis and esoteric theory.

Although reference to the body is obviously not new in medical anthropology, no word is more used by scholars in the critical medical anthropological perspective than "the body," where often it would seem that a commonsensical use might be "the person," "the self," or "the human being." What these authors definitely do not mean by the body is the circumscribed biological body of 19th- and 20th-century Western medicine, the material organism or system of organisms seen in the pathology lab. They draw rather on the early 20th-century work of French anthropologist Marcel Mauss who saw the body as a "total social fact" (1960) that cannot be explained by any other idea or ground. Societal and cultural *techniques du corps* were for Mauss the ways that unspoken but powerful images and urges of the emotions are expressed in body imagery. Note that the French term for body, *corps,* is derived from the Latin verb *corpore,* from which we derive a variety of social usages, all with Latin origins, such as corpus (as in a body of texts), incorporate (in either a physical or social sense), and corporation (a politically organized social group). We gain a better idea of what is meant by the way Thomas Csordas titled the introduction to his edited volume *Embodiment and Experience* as "the body as representation and being-in-the-world" (1994: 1–26). Referred to here is not the bounded enduring physical body of 19th- and 20th-century biology and medicine, but the historically shaped body of consumer culture that may be enhanced by products made to be fit through techniques of exercise, diet, or tonics. This body has become a performing self that is constantly involved in impression management (1996: 2). Csordas hoped that the new body in anthropology will allow us to add "sentience and sensibility to self and person" (1996:2).

Nancy Scheper-Hughes and Margaret Lock, in their seminal article "The Mindful Body: A Prolegomenon to Future Work in Medical

Anthropology" (1987), sketched the outline of an embodiment approach for medical anthropology based on the "individual body," the "social body," and the "body politic," each of which was commonly used as a metaphor for the others. This plain outline, drawn from everyday language, suggested that in our language use we assume a continuum of meaning across the spectrum of individual to society, and individual to authority and power, realms that can "inscribe" themselves back upon the individual as body. The renewed interest in the study of the uses of the body as metaphor for society and state (as in the body social and the body politic) in medical anthropology have also echoed the feminist movement. The many ways in which media, institutions, medicine, and men shape the definitions and meanings of women's bodies have become a central topic in medical anthropology. Scheper-Hughes's own award-winning *Death without Weeping: The Violence of Everyday Life in Brazil* (1992) masterfully incorporated the analysis of economic injustices related to the sugar industry and the state on Brazilian women and children and the impact upon their bodily health and life. It is particularly poignant in its depiction of the excesses of "medicalization" of hunger in the way mothers are taught to see the reasons for their children's misery in diseases rather than in the political economy of northeast Brazil.

Hans Baer, Merrill Singer, and Ida Susser, in their book *Medical Anthropology and the World System: A Critical Perspective* (1997), described critical medical anthropology as "a perspective which views health issues within the context of encompassing political and economic forces that pattern human relationships, shape social behaviors, condition collective experiences, re-order local ecologies, and situate cultural meanings, including forces of institutional, national, and global scale" (1997: 3–4). The inquiry into the resistance against manipulation, oppression, and exploitation—or lack thereof—is a recurring theme in the work and writing of critical medical anthropologists. Concurrent resistance and embrace of systems of power among Sudanese women (Greenbaum 1998), "science as resistance" among Egyptians seeking health care (Morsy 1998), mothering among lesbian women in the United States (Lewin 1998), and resisting some medicalized approaches to breast cancer treatment in the United States (Kaufert 1998), are several of the themes that appear in *Pragmatic Women and Body Politics* edited by Margaret Lock and Patricia Kaufert (1998), a volume that illustrates the continuing life of this perspective.

In critical medical anthropology, all topics and issues come together in the body, a site of experience, control, resistance, articulation, and identity.

DISCERNING SIGNS: STEPS TOWARD A UNIFIED EPISTEMOLOGY FOR MEDICAL ANTHROPOLOGY

Medical anthropologists have tried to bridge some of the dichotomies that seem to always crop up in discussing disease, medicine, and human nature, dichotomies such as body and mind, material with nonmaterial, or even the realms of biology and culture within anthropology. Unfortunately, many formulations that attempt to overcome these dichotomies—for example, "psychosomatic"—are themselves couched in terms of a dichotomy, so they tend to reinforce yet again the very dichotomy they are seeking to transcend.

Sign theory as presented here carries a number of features that helps medical anthropology span some of the (false) dichotomies mentioned above that have plagued Western sciences and worldviews. One of these properties of the sign is that it may vary in the extent of "compulsion" that relates the sensory part of the sign to its object and its meaning, its significance. This variance or "continuum" may range from full compulsion or necessity to a totally arbitrary association. A second property of the sign is that signification is an ongoing process, called **semiosis.** The relationship of the sign to its object and its meaning may change continually, as in the process of an illness/disease. It may for example move from a close association of necessity to one that is arbitrary, or both conditions, or degrees of the two, may co-occur. One anthropologist who uses semiotics has spoken of "fluid signs" in describing this characteristic of signification (Daniel 1985). An illustration of semiosis that is very direct will show how, and why, this concept is important in medical anthropology.

Imagine what occurs to an individual who, while hammering a nail into a board, accidentally hits the fingers holding the nail. The first "signification" of the cluster of signs involved will be the nerves in the damaged finger tissue signaling to the brain a message of overwhelming, focused pain. This reflexive response is barely in consciousness. The association of the sign to its object is compulsive and necessary. The pain may continue, but then another series of associations emerges in which further signals will produce responses.

Most likely there will be a reflexive response in which the hand is withdrawn instantly and perhaps grabbed by the other hand. Then follows the usual outcry. But already at this stage of the "semiosis" the pain has been processed from an immediate reflexive response into a cultural symbol in language, where the relationship of sign to signification is arbitrary. The outcry may be "ouch" (English), *auwa* (German), *mpasi* (Kikongo), or *quelle douleur* (French), depending on the language of the injured person. Then, in a further semiosic step, the injured person may pinpoint this particular type or moment of experience by fixing it within memory and culture. If the person is a building carpenter who regularly shingles roofs, he may be able to ignore the incident. A smashed finger may become an index for a certain kind of sharp pain, although other injuries also give sharp pain. Merely reading about a smashed finger may touch off painful memories in the minds of some readers.

The double property of the sign that features a range of necessity or arbitrariness in the way signification occurs, and the continual "fluidity" of signification process, makes sign theory very useful for medical anthropologists in establishing a unified perspective around and through the various dichotomies mentioned above. Not only individual experience, but also describing the world around us, is enhanced with such a perspective. We must be careful not to conclude that all signs of culture that occur in language, art, and music are assumed to have an arbitrary relationship to their object, whereas those within physical, organic communication do not. Music may affect our feelings and our very physical nature, as well as allow us to imagine abstractions. There is growing evidence to suggest that signs in our neurons, the signs in DNA sequences, and messages within our bodies are quite capable of alternative or arbitrary expressions. Equally, the realm of signs goes beyond human experience. Immunologists now speak of "smart germs" which anticipate attempts to eradicate them by mutating to better resist the medicine designed for them.

In any event, a focus on the sign that has been suggested here permits us to "read" the diverse kinds of communication in human experience from language to microorganismic processes, from conscious to unconscious human experience, and from human to animal communications. A growing number of anthropologists have taken up this perspective to describe and evaluate the issues within medical anthropology in order to create a unitary medical anthropology (Staiano 1992, 1999; Ots 1991; Good 1994; Bibeau and Corin 1994; Daniel 1984).

"Body and mind must be treated as one," noted Staiano (1992) in her work on the black Caribs of Belize in Central America. She cited a Carib man describing a condition that affects his nerves. It begins with signs or sounds that make him ill. A relationship may get him to start feeling nervous and cause him to have loose bowels and palpitations. Staiano argued that there is no fully "natural" sign system in human life, totally resistant to "what we have perhaps carelessly labeled 'cultural' influences" (1992: 413).

"The inside and the outside of the body are one," she continued. She used the experience of possession in the *dugu* ceremony to illustrate this process in which the self transcends the body's boundaries, a state in which the "previously inexpressible may be expressed." As the individual is possessed by an ancestor, the boundary between life and death becomes an illusion, the boundary between two selves becomes blurred. She

Communicating Vessels or the Oneness of Inside and Outside the Body

The theme of the oneness of inside and outside is strongly visualized in this 1938 print by Mexican artist Diego Rivera titled *The Communicating Vessels.* Its subject matter and iconography were derived from a 1932 essay of the same title by surrealist writer and poet André

Breton who visited Mexico at the time. Breton explored the interpenetration of waking life and dreams, and the principal image of the dream as the "capillary tissue" between the exterior world of facts and the interior world of emotions, between "what is intellectually understood and

Photo 2.2 The Communicating Vessels, *1938 red and black linoleum print (23 × 33 inches) by Mexican artist Diego Rivera; also called* Hommage to Andre Breton *and* Surrealist Head.

Source: RIVERA, Diego. *The Communicating Vessels.* (1938). Linoleum cut, printed in color, compositon: 23 3/4 x 33 5/16" (60.3 x 84.7 cm) The Museum of Modern Art, New York. Gift of Nelson Blitz, Jr. Photograph © 2002 the Museum of Modern Art, New York.

continued

continued from previous page

what is grasped by the senses," between the structures of society and revolution. In Rivera's print, this imagery appears as the veins and arteries flowing into and out of the subject's brain. Breton's title "communicating vessels" was taken from a scientific experiment in which vessels joined by a tube through which a gas or liquid passes from one to the other and rises to the same level in each, whatever the form of the vessel. In the print, vessels as glasses, and vessels as veins and arteries, merge. The glasses are held up to the subject's eyes and connected by a tube that passes through two large veins above the nose. For Breton the passage back and forth between two modes is the basis of surrealist thought. Personifying these modes are the two imagined figures of sleep, the closed eye on the left, and wakefulness, the open eye on the right (Figura ca. 1999: 18–21). We may take the image to offer a metaphorical illustration of the ways that body and mind, biology and culture, and other artificial dualisms faced in medical anthropology, are two aspects of one and the same thing. ■

---

compares possession in the *dugu,* and the fluidity between self bodies, to the issues at stake in fetal rights, the responsibility of criminals who violate others, donor and recipient in organ transplants, and the issues of sperm and egg in conception (1992: 414).

"If 'inside' and 'outside' are one, then signs which are external to the self must have the same capacity to affect the bounded body/self as those generated from within the organism enclosed by skin" (1992b:416). Staiano offered many examples of how "inside" and "outside" are linked in health, illness, and healing. To name a few, she recalled the work on trance states and voodoo death and the place of the central nervous system in these dramatic instances of personal transformation by dance, meditation, and curse. She noted the rapid shifts between sympathetic and parasympathetic systems; the manufacture of endogenous opiates to kill pain by suggestion; the effect of social stressors such as bereavement, marital disruption, loneliness, and other life changes; and the powerful physiological effects of autosuggestion, meditation, hypnosis, relaxation, and biofeedback. Staiano saw all of these as transformative "semiosic" processes that require a unitary sign theory in order to provide medical anthropologists with a truly unitary perspective on health, illness, and healing in the societies of the world.

The key terms and the unitary perspective offered by semiotics will be taken up from time to time where appropriate in the chapters of this introduction to medical anthropology. The perspective is a helpful tool for medical anthropologists in identifying and analyzing the very immediate levels of existence, as well as the continuum of significations of the cultural realm. Medical anthropologists have striven from the beginning of their work to gain a holistic perspective in issues of health, illness, and healing.

CONCLUSION

Medical anthropology, like the signs of health, illness, and healing, is an unfolding set of significations that, once created, continue to unfold as its practitioners create projects and think out perspectives. Theory in medical anthropology is the equivalent in health, illness, and healing to the symbols and words that give a reflected character to the signs. Although theory in medical anthropology—as in all academic disciplines—sometimes has the appearance of a faddish preoccupation as spokespersons for one perspective and another vie for a hearing of their favorite ideas, the continual refocusing that this provides is important in establishing where we are, and where we are headed. There is no such thing as atheoretical med-

ical anthropology, that is, medical anthropology without underlying assumptions. Therefore, it is important for medical anthropologists—students, practitioners, teachers—to know which perspective they are using, and what the implications are of its use.

This chapter has sought to present the origins of medical anthropology as a focus within anthropology, and the dominant and changing perspectives that have given this field articulation. The chapter closed with a review of semiotics as a growing theoretical direction in medical anthropology, and one that promises to provide a vehicle for the unified analysis and epistemology of all aspects of health, illness, and healing.

REVIEW QUESTIONS

1. Explain the rise of medical anthropology. What are several sources of the "crisis in medicine" suggested as an important source for the emergence of medical anthropology?

2. What is the difference between the "sociocultural" and the "biocultural" perspectives in medical anthropology? Develop your own working understanding of the culture concept for application in health and illness.

3. What are the research questions in studies illustrated in this chapter or in

readings assigned in this section? Can you identify the author's theoretical orientations? Can you offer an example of how a study's basic research question affects the choice of theory and method?

4. Identify and briefly describe some of the approaches that medical anthropologists have used to achieve an integrated perspective that relates biology to culture, and shows the many ways that body and mind are part of the same whole?

THE FABRIC OF HEALTH

Photo 3.1 *Greek god of medicine Aesculapius points the staff of life with the coiled serpent at the figure Death to overcome him, while Ceres, the Roman goddess of agriculture, offers milk to the starving. Both medicine and nutrition are seen as fundamental to life and health. Pen and ink drawing and gray wash, by Jacques-Charles Bordier du Bignon (1774–1826).*
Source: Wellcome Library, London.

"Catching Cold" and "Being Cool"

In the legacy of ancient Greek thought, we "catch a cold" and thereby become sick. Grandmother's hot chicken soup is the appropriate cure for this affliction. Good health is therefore shaped by "keeping warm" sensitive parts of the body when it's cold. The set of assumptions behind this simple formula for keeping healthy has come down to the present from the ancient Mediterranean region and today may be found in large areas of Europe, North and South America, and in Southwest and South Asia.

In the legacy of African thought, graceful and balanced actions are "cool," just as health is defined as "keeping or being cool." Disease is a reflection of excessive "heat" such as conflict, envy, or greed in interpersonal affairs. Restoring coolness and keeping in balance the excessive heat of passion shapes good health. These ideas came with the Africans who were, for the most part, brought to the Americas as slaves. Nevertheless, they were able to retain some parts of their worldview. In due course, parts of this worldview, including musical and body movement aesthetics, were adopted by mass culture in North America.

Those who share these features of the Mediterranean and the African (enriched by Native American) worldviews should, one would think, be confused by these contradictory orientations of "hot" and "cold" in life and health. And yet, it appears that most people know how to keep catching cold and being cool in context. The two sets of ideas are totally separate codes from which we draw our formulas for living. As students of culture, we can see how they contribute to a more inclusive picture of health.

These two familiar examples of health perspectives are introduced at the outset of this chapter to make an important point about the **"fabric of health"**—the practices, the social arrangements, the words and related concepts. "Health" is everywhere culturally particular and varied. There are many different codes for health; some are popular, others deeply embedded in local, national, or civilizational traditions[1]; others are taught in medical schools and uphold biomedical research or public health; and still others reflect the constraints and opportunities of particular natural environments.

Medical anthropologists are interested in learning how these varied codes define the world of health and illness, how they shape techniques that are practiced to bring about such worlds. Knowledge of such codes and practices enables medical anthropologists to advise health agencies, for example, in the promotion of public health measures or health education campaigns. It is important for medical anthropologists to study not only official medicine or the official policy of an agency, but also the perspectives that inform ordinary peoples' assumptions and practices about health. With such culturally visualized health understanding, anthropologists may, in the words of Steven Polgar (1968), facilitate appropriate "health action" in initiatives for more culturally sensitive clinical care, health development projects, primary health care, and popular health education campaigns.

The health cultures found in many Western cities and communities today reflect a cross-section of the global health traditions that came into being and developed over centuries. They have been brought along on migrations, or have been discovered by health enthusiasts. A cursory study of any telephone directory in an American city[2] will reveal specialized therapies such as acupuncture, Qi Gong, Tai Chi Chuan, various versions of energy therapy, and herbal medications derived from Chinese medicine; yoga, meditation, and karma therapies derived from Indian medicine; astrology from ancient Persian medicine; chiropractic, Swedish massage, body work dating from Western 19th-century innovators; Gestalt, psychotherapy, and psychiatry; Christian psychology and other forms of faith healing in churches. These will be listed under "Alternative Medicine" or alongside mainstream biomedical listings which are usually identified by the staff of Aesculapius (see photos 3.1 and 3.2). Official medicine includes a range of medical doctors in internal medicine, family medicine, cardiovascular, cosmetic, gynecological, surgery, obstetric, oncology, orthopedic, pediatric, sports, and many other medical specialties.

Increasingly, healthful living is defined in the Western industrial world not only as the absence of disease but as a specific diet, avoiding or dealing appropriately with "stress," or maintaining defined-as-healthy mental perspectives and relationships, and having a reliable doctor or clinic. The nature of diet and the type of exercise keep changing as new "medical" information comes out, along with marketing products and techniques for health.

Thus, my colleague Kathryn Staiano reminded me in a letter (1997) one could trace the ideas behind the recent history of exercise techniques and technology in the United States, beginning with the observation that once upon a time people exercised without equipment. But then we acquired rowing machines (who still has them?). Then we got Nordic Track and Soloflex. The traditional Nordic Track is still around, but all sorts of new exercise equipment for the home have been developed by the company that manufactures it. Each item, whether a stairmaster, treadmill, or exercise bicycle is marketed as offering the best exercise you can get.

The cultural basis of health can be studied in classical or popular traditions such as those having their origin in the Mediterranean, Asian, American, and African regions, as well as in modern biomedicine. This chapter continues with sketches of the basic ideas of health within a number of recognizable medical traditions and health campaigns: (1) the classical medical traditions of Eurasia (Greece, India, and China), the Americas, and sub-Saharan Africa; (2) the primary ideas of modern biomedicine; (3) the Primary Health Care Campaign and the Reproductive Health Campaign of the World Health Organization; and finally, (4) a sketch of the model of ecological health and the social reproduction of

Photo 3.2 *Aesculapius (left), the father of medicine, son of divine Apollo and the nymph mother Coronis, was thought to have great healing powers, and the ability to raise the dead. This power is symbolized by the "rod of Aesclepius" with a serpent coiled around the staff of life that associates medicine with the snake's power of renewal by the shedding of its old skin and emerging anew. Hygeia (right) also holds the staff of life with a serpent coiled around it. Hercules (center) is depicted struggling with the hydra. The caption reads "The Herculean powers of medicine overcoming disease, for the health and preservation of mankind." Watercolor painting, unknown painter and date.* SOURCE: Wellcome Library, London.

health. Several vignettes of local studies by anthropologists show these dominant ideas often embedded in or often blended with other concepts and realities in the articulation of local, culturally particular, health.

THE CLASSICAL MEDICAL TRADITIONS

EUROPE AND ASIA

One of the most widespread health paradigms is that of **balance** between contrasting forces. This is a perspective which extends across the ancient

Photo 3.3 *Panacea, another daughter of Aesculapius, holds up a flask of urine for examination. Her workshop is chock-full of containers, potions, and assorted medicines. Patients or buyers of medicine appear in the background seeking help. "Panacea" is the word used widely to describe a usually implausible or unrealistic hope for a cure to all ills. 16th-17th century engraving by T. Galle.* SOURCE: Wellcome Library, London.

world of Europe and Asia (sometimes Africa and the Americas are included as well). **Humors** are bodily fluids or states that are thought to be fundamental aspects of human and all life. They are often made up of combinations of natural elements or forces such as fire and water, earth and air, which are considered to exist within the body and the basic attributes of the person. These systems of correspondences between outside nature and inside body-person define affliction as an imbalance between the two opposing sets of "humors" or elements. Health is therefore defined as balance between opposing forces, humors, and elements. The "Golden Rule" of moderate living is an example of this thinking. Scholars who study the traditions of ancient Greece, Persia, Arabia, India, and China thought that these ideas arose in connection with an active exchange of ideas along the east-west corridors of trade in the ancient world. Ideas of the masters of each tradition were circulated to the centers of learning of the other traditions to constitute what has been called an Old World Civilization (an *Oikumene,* from the Greek term for "the known world") (Leslie 1976:1–6).

In classical India (i.e., about 2,000 years ago), whose medical tradition is called Ayurveda, the basis of medical ideas was the five elements of ether, wind, water, earth, and fire, and the three humors, or *dosas* of wind, phlegm, and bile (Obeyeskere 1976:201–2; 206). Elaborate correspondences between the elements and the humors created a scheme for the diagnosis of, and therapeutic intervention into, conditions affecting human health. Ayurveda developed into an extensive set of practices for surgery, curative and preventative medicine, as well as elaborate dietary rules that sometimes articulated the caste system. The Hindu and later Buddhist doctrines of karma, the cycles of life and the eternal fate of the soul, influenced Ayurveda and some of the parallel healing traditions. Yoga is the best known of these other traditions that pertain to meditation, diet, exercise, and the general place of the individual in the universe (Mazar 1978).

In classical Greece (over 2,000 years ago), the consolidation of the features of a health system occurred around deities that bore such names as Aesculapius, the father of medicine, Hygeia, the goddess of health, and Panacea, the goddess of all materia medica (see photos 3.1 to 3.3). This roster of divine heroes of medicine and health was eventually accompanied by a less personal system of elements and humors that were used to define health. As in other Old World medical traditions, in Greek medicine the four elements of fire, earth, water, and air were aligned into a system of correspondences with the four humors of blood, phlegm, yellow bile, and black bile. The early Greek philosophers wrote about this medicine, but it was not until the great physician Hippocrates (ca. 460–377 B.C.) systematized it and wrote about diagnosis and prognosis, the treatment of various diseases, and the ethics of the physician (as formulated in the Hippocratic oath) that Greek medicine became an influential and coherent set of ideas about health. Later Galen (A.D. 129–199) would write additional works on this medicine. Many of the treatments hinged on offsetting excesses of the humors or other forces with their opposite, to restore an equilibrium (Ackerknecht 1982: 47–54). Greek medicine, as described here, spread wherever Greek colonies and conquests occurred around the Mediterranean Sea, places such as Alexandria in Egypt, as well as into northern Europe under the Roman Empire. With the appearance of Islam in the seventh century and the creation of Arabic centers of learning, a combined Greco-Arabic-Islamic medicine spread westward and eastward, combined in places with another set of ideas which has been called Medicine of the Prophet. This synthesis, emphasizing one part or another, spread westward to West Africa, and across the Atlantic to the Americas with the Spanish conquistadores, southward to East Africa, and eastward to India, Indonesia, and Malaysia (Good and Good 1992). A vignette from Malaysia demonstrates a local instance of the blending of all these traditions—Ayurvedic medicine from India brought by merchants and Hindu priests two thousand years ago, Greek

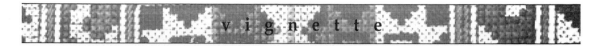

Are "Postpartum Roasting" and "Avoiding Bisa Fish" in Malaysian Medical Practice Healthful for the Birthing Mother?

Carol Laderman, anthropologist, has studied aspects of health ideas and practices on the Malay Peninsula. An early interest, explored in her 1982 work *Wives and Midwives*, seeks to determine whether the practices associated with birthing are deleterious, of no consequence, or beneficial to the mother and child. Laderman traced the dietary dimension of Malay women because it appears to involve rather extensive food prohibitions. The public health officials of Malaysia believe that these dietary restrictions, which permit few foods except rice, lead to malnourishment and should be ended.

Laderman therefore explored the meaning of both the *bisa* concept of food toxicity which is applied to seafood, and the nature of humoral properties associated with most other foods. She determined that the belief that foods bearing *bisa* are dangerous to women and therefore prohibited to those going through pregnancy and childbirth was nutritionally valid following an investigation of their chemical properties.

Malay thinking emphasizes the need of a woman to maintain equilibrium by taking in "hot" foods or stimuli when experiencing an excessively "cold" condition, and vice versa. Although some studies have shown a certain bodily sensation equating with feelings of hot and cold, these humors are not regarded as measurable "temperatures." Thus, the following foods are "hot": fats, both animal and vegetable; alcohol; most spices; animal proteins such as eggs and milk; salty foods; and bitter foods. "Cold" foods include juicy fruits and vegetables; viscous fruits and vegetables such as okra, associated with phlegm, the cold body humor; sour fruits and vegetables, craved by pregnant women, who are "hot"; plants that taste *kelat*—for example,

tea, vines and creepers (Laderman 1982: 44–46). The main neutral dishes are rice and fresh fish, considered essential for daily diet.

Laderman studied the diets of a number of women from pregnancy to birth and into the postpartum period. The increasingly hot period of pregnancy till childbirth was marked by avoiding hot foods but eating cold foods. The immediate postpartum mother is considered to become very "cold." At this point she is "roasted" over a low fire on a special bed. The roasting and the dietary deprivation of certain foods considered nutritious by Malay health authorities prompted Laderman to study the actual food intake. She discovered that most women had an adequate diet by nutritional standards if they followed the Malay humoral prescriptions. She learned that the women often eat fruits and vegetables which they do not consider to be part of their meals of rice alone (they consider rice to be a staple). Their diet is thus more varied than the humoral food ideology would suggest. As far as the roasting is concerned, the English term is far more fearsome than the actual practice which consists of a box of live coals kept beneath the bed to give the woman on the bed the sensation of being cozy for a few postpartum days.

The humoral program as depicted here for pregnant and birthing women is greatly simplified from the elaborate full traditions that come together in the Malay region. In her 1991 work on Malay shamanism, *Taming the Winds of Desire,* and in a 1992 essay, Laderman outlined the layers of medical thought and practice that were brought, through trade, travel, and conquest, into juxtaposition with aboriginal Malay ideas. The full contingent of civilizational layers that are evident in Malay ideas about health include shamanism and singing and "hot"

continued

continued from previous page

and "cold" as the oldest local tradition; ideas of the Ayurvedic-Indian humoral schemes and Hinduism associated with conquests two millennia ago; humoralism of Greek medicine and certain ideas about spirits brought with Islam in the 15th century; notions of curative biomedicine introduced through British colonialism; and finally, postcolonial community health of the late 20th century.

Among the aboriginal Orang Asli of the Malay Peninsula, Laderman reported, the coolness of the forest and the cool breath, bodies, and colorless blood of "original" inhabitants are associated with good health; heat, and anything associated with the heat of the sun, are unhealthy. Coolness and moisture are associated with everything positive in Orang Asli society: self-control, harmony, fertility, health, and life. Heat epitomizes disease, death, destruction, and disorder (1992:274–75).

With the introduction of Ayurvedic ideas on the coast of the South China Sea, the direction of the heat/cool humors are reversed. Coolness comes to be considered associated with ill health and infection; warmth with health. This is reinforced by the introduction of Mediterranean-Greek ideas described above, introduced through the spread of Islam. ■

---

humoralism brought by Arab merchants and Muslim clerics a thousand years ago—with surviving local health culture of the interior of the Malaysian Pennisula.

The reader may wish to compare the humoral ideas of this vignette with the ideas and practices put forward in the vignette from Hispanic New Mexico near the close of this chapter. These two cases about the health culture surrounding childbirth represent the extreme Eastern and Western expansions of the Greek, or Mediterannean, humoral system.

We turn next to the Chinese medical tradition in which the basic elements—five rather than four—were aligned with several other sets of principles of classification. In ancient Chinese medical thought, the five elements of wood, fire, metal, water, and earth were correlated with the dualism inherent in the cosmic dichotomy of the yin and the yang, "universal designations for the polar aspects of effects" (Porkert 1974:13). Yin is everything that is "structive, contractive, absorbing into or within, centripetal, responsive, conservative, and positive," whereas yang is everything that is "active, expansive, bringing to the surface, centrifugal, aggressive, demanding, and negative" (Porkert 1974: 23). The dichotomy of yin and yang also divided a number of concrete positions, elements, and states, respectively: earth/heaven, moon/sun, autumn and winter/spring and summer, female/male, cold and cool/heat and warmth, moisture/dryness, the inside/the outside, darkness/brightness, water and rain/fire, night/day, right/left.

The dynamic spark of chi, or energy, is manifested in all these contrasting states or the dynamic balance between them. Chi must be allowed to flow, to indwell and energize the organs of the body. Invariably, disease is imbalance between a set of features and the blockage of chi, whereas

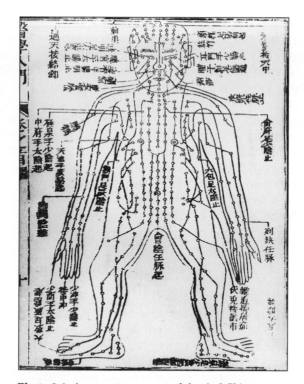

Photo 3.4 *Acupuncture, a part of classical Chinese medicine that has been integrated into modern medicine as pain treatment and for a range of purposes, is practiced by the insertion of long needles into the body at particular points. These points, in the corresponding theory, are located along the principal "meridians" or "canals" in the human body. Here, the meridians and acupuncture points are shown from a medical manuscript dating from the Ming Dynasty (1406–1420). Writing in the left upper side refers to the eight principal meridians as "eight different valves or doors of the body."* SOURCE: Snark/Art Resource, NY.

health is balance between the elements and dichotomous principles such that chi is present and allowed to circulate.

Although the roots of the yin/yang opposition may be traced well into the ancient Chinese belief of Taoism, it has provided the mainstay for further elaborations of thinking on health over several thousand years of Chinese medicine, including acupuncture (see Photo 3.4). Texts and histories of Chinese medicine usually present transformations between dualities and their correspondences, using them to interpret seasons, bodily functions, and organs, as well as appropriate diets and treatments for disease.

As Chinese medicine experienced growth and development, other organizing principles emerged. Under the centralization of progressive dynasties of imperial China, a new system called the meridians appeared, which aligned organs and attributes within the body along specified axes and canals which have been compared to the neurological system or the veins in Western anatomy and physiology. The meridians came to be used along with the yin and yang, as well as other correspondences and alignments in theorizing health and ill health. Today, Chinese medicine continues under the rules of these ancient ideas, as well as those it has incorporated from other medicines. The therapy of acupuncture, for example, has been explained in terms of each of these ancient doctrines, as well as by Western medical sciences and current ideas such as neurological currents (Unschuld 1985; 1992). The constant exchange of the ideas of health and healing in Asia suggests that proven practices may be effective throughout the coming and going of transient theories.

THE AMERICAS

The medicinal traditions of North and South America are as diverse as those of other continents. One student of South American native healing has suggested that in a continent with 1,500 distinct language groups, there are "hundreds of separate medical traditions" to be considered (Sullivan 1989: 397). In addition, across these two vast continents before European contact in the 15th century and in native societies since then, some societies continued as hunters and gatherers while others had developed into centralized empires and cities. Medicine and healing reflected this diversity and complexity.

This brief account will concentrate on the general characteristics of shamanism, the rich plant heritage of American medicine, and a few examples of healing rituals. The process of mixing different medical traditions, with which this chapter opened, has certainly also characterized the relationship of native American healing arts with those of the Western humoral and biomedical traditions. The resulting combination of practices and ideas are sometimes spoken of as "syncretic" medicine.

Shamanism, considered by many scholars to be the earliest type of healing arts, is considered to have been brought to the Americas from Asia in a succession of migrations across the Bering Straight millennia ago. The word *shaman,* as used by scholars, is derived from the Siberian Tungus term *samán,* their name for the specialist of the sacred (Furst 1997d: 244). In this local history, and far more widely in Asia and the Americas, shamanism is characterized by several features: the sickness of the individual who is called to be a shaman, and whose acceptance of the calling is his or her only cure; trance, travel in the spirit to a distant location; association with spirit or animal familiars who are thought to host the human when outside of the body; the common illness diagnosis of **"soul loss"** and the corresponding therapies of "soul retrieval," singing, and a variety of other techniques used in connection with sickness, life transitions, and social crisis (Eliade 1964; Hultkrantz 1989; Furst 1997d).[3]

American shamanism has many variants. In the American Northwest coast the canoe journey taken by the shaman to recover lost souls with a magical canoe pole is an important annual ceremony. On the North American plains and in the Southwest the journey takes the form of a "vision quest." In the Amazonian rain forest it takes the form of trance through hallucinogenic drugs followed by divining and curing.

The focus upon the spirit and spirits in the shaman's worldview reflects the prominence of spirits in the native American vision of the world in general. A scholar of Central American medicine and healing (Ortiz de Montellano 1989: 368–69) described the world of souls located in the human body (head, heart, liver) as well as the world beyond among the historic Aztecs and their contemporary descendants of Mexico. Each of these souls is characterized as having complex functions which must occur satisfactorily and in harmony for the individual to be healthy. Arising from the harmonization of these souls was a life force that bestowed on individuals a certain temperament. The relationship of these world souls with the particular souls of the individual was seen as affecting illness and well-being. These qualities of soul vitality come close to resonating with the humors of the Old World, in a picture of the world of souls, bodily functions, and vital forces that extends to the realm of plants as well, a complex schema of correspondences across multiple cultural domains.

The use of plants in native American medicine is extensive and impressive. Not only have scholars documented the hundreds of applications of medicinal plants by herbalists, healers, and lay people alike, but the native American pharmacopoeia has given to global medicine such important drugs as quinine, aspirin, digitalis, as well as medicinally applied stimulants such as cocoa, coca, and tobacco. That plants such as these should be integrated in a world of souls might mystify the rational Western observer. Yet comparative scholars of medicine understand that culturally complex bodies of knowledge can easily contain different points of reference so apparently distinct as knowledge of souls and of plants. Some societies have separate specialists to deal with the two realms. Others integrate them within general roles of healer. Researchers in botany, anthropology, and medicine have established impressive records of native American uses of plants (*Ancient Healing* 1997: 177): for the Iroquois of the Northeast and the Great Lakes region, 2,237 medicinal uses of plants; for the Cherokee of the East and southern plains, 2,722 uses; for the Navajo-Ramah of the Southwest, 1,037 uses.

Ritual therapies that occur in groups or communities are also an important kind of medicine in native America. Many of the performances of shamanic healers already described occur within the community and for the society, and are often spoken of as "spirit dancing." In the

Southwest many Pueblo societies have annual winter festivals that include generally therapeutic or renewal dimensions. The widespread Sun Dance of the Great Plains region of North America brings together the entire community to renew life. Åke Hultkrantz has identified the underlying concept of health in these ceremonial events of the Pueblo of the Southwest and the communities of the Great Plains, as incorporating the ideology of traditional hunting societies with the ideology of "cosmic balance" that ultimately derived from the advanced horticultural societies of Mexico (Hultkrantz 1989: 329). In the hunting societies, human life and health was considered a gift from the high god or guardian spirits. In the horticultural societies, human beings, the supernatural, and the world constituted one integrated whole to which humankind contributed by conducting rituals intended to reflect or stabilize this harmony. Thus, bodily and mental health are an integrating part of cosmic harmony (Hultkrantz 1989: 330).

The resilience of native American medicine in the face of centuries of sometimes ferocious attempts to discredit it is evident in its survival in communities and in the practices and teachings of its specialists. Further glimpses of these traditions are offered in vignettes later in the book.

SUB-SAHARAN AFRICA

Sub-Saharan African understandings of health, sickness, and healing, as in other classical healing traditions, are couched in a basic set of ideas about the nature of the world and life within it, and which readily offer powerful metaphors with which to make sense of suffering and uncertainty. These ideas are sometimes discernible in verbal concepts that have a deep history and broad geographical and cultural distribution, and a continuing use in diagnosis, the formulation of the sickness experience, and in therapeutic traditions.

A first example of an idea that organizes the events of health, sickness, and healing to give them meaning and to fit them into a paradigm consistent with other organizing principles of the society, is simply the idea of an ordered structure of the body as a whole. Any disruption, negation, or distortion of this ideal suggests sickness, defined in terms of the appearance of redness on the otherwise whole skin surface (a verbal root which extends at least from the Yoruba of West Africa (*eela* or *ele*) (Buckley 1985) to the Kongo of the equatorial central African coast (*beela*) (Janzen 1978). In many regions of sub-Saharan Africa this notion of the departure from health is expressed by a common color code in which the use of white chalk or clay stands for purity and wholeness; the red of camwood and certain dyes, or simply a red cloth, as transition and danger sometimes associated with shed blood; and charcoal black as the danger of human chaos as found in situations of anger and witchcraft. Healing rituals from sub-Saharan Africa usually incorporate this color code in some way, along with plants, material substances, physical manipulations, songs, and prayers.

A second idea expresses purity, a ritual state in which the dimensions of the human world are in order and right. The opposite is a state in which human affairs are out of order, confused, causing ritual pollution or sickness; see Douglas (1966) for this idea among the Lele of the Kasai in Zaire, Ngubane (1977) among the Zulu, Janzen (1978, 1982) among the Kongo, and Green (1996) in Mozambique. Edward Green, in connection with the incorporation of healers in health education programs, believes that purity and pollution concepts represent a traditional set of natural contrasts that are not bound by spirit or human forces and which may have served in the past as a foundation for ideas of health and the prevention of disease. He argued in a recent book that purity and pollution have offered a source of ideas of contagious disease whose idioms should be adopted by public health workers (Green 1999).

In a third idea, "balance" or "harmony" is necessary to a state of health in the relationship between an individual and surrounding persons, as well as between the human community and the natural and spiritual environment (*lunga,* in Zulu of South Africa, and Kongo of western Congo, where this is also an attribute of God). In regions and societies in western, northern, and eastern Africa influenced by Galenic humoral theory by way of Islamic medicine, balance may have the connotation of an equilibrium between the humors, and between heat and cold, balance between opposing humors or fluids leading to health, imbalance to disease. But the African perspective on thermal metaphors of health is rather different than this set of ideas of Mediterranean origin.

Fourth, the "coolness" of grace, style, and health that has entered the North American, and perhaps even the global community—as the opening of this chapter illustrates—is part of a more complex African perspective that operates similarly to thermal contrasts elsewhere, but with some distinctive features. In the African context, "cool" stands in contrast to "heat" (*tiya* in Kikongo, *yuhya* in KiHemba). This heat expresses conflict and ill health. Therefore "cooling down" is a widespread notion that is used to speak of being cured. Among the Kongo and neighboring groups, it has been associated with the use of the cupping horn which when sucked extracts the heat or the impure substance from the sufferer's body (Janzen 1992). In Thomas and Pamela Blakeleys' study of the performance of funerary memorials among the Hemba of eastern Congo, both heat and cold have good and bad connotations. Imbuing "heat" in a good performance—that is, to put much energy into it—may have salutary effects on social relations, thereby cooling them off, and making them harmonious. Out-of-control interpersonal hostility, illness, and death are associated with negative heat, whereas competence, vigor, and energy are associated with positive applications of heat. Negative "cold" pervades undesirable states as fatigue, incompetence, and despair. Positive coolness is associated with self-control, social harmony, and health (Blakeley and Blakeley 1994: 429). The sub-Saharan African concept of the cool thus extends an aesthetic notion widely seen in the arts and in human relations into a definition of health.

Fifth, the concept of flow and blockage is very widespread, often seen as a homology between the physical realm of the body and exchanges in society. Just as the flow of milk, semen, and blood are necessary for the well-being of physical beings, so the community can endure and thrive only if these fluids and other exchanges lubricate the society (Taylor 1992; Janzen 1978). Flow and blockage is a dominant metaphor by which these substances flow within the body social and physical, contributing to health, whereas blockage through envy and ill-will may lead to constipation, infertility, witchcraft, disease, and death.

A widespread concept whose radical is abstracted as *gidu* refers to the role of social prohibitions, taboos, and the consequences of violating them. Sometimes this is mentioned with reference to the restriction on eating or killing one's clan or individual emblem-animals or totems. Rwandan medical scholar Pierre-Claver Rwangabo (1993) observed that these prohibitions help individuals to adhere to social codes in general, including health-promoting restrictions on such things as overconsumption of alcohol, overeating, or health-destroying excesses of any kind. Thus, the adherence to social rules, by implication, maintains health and life by maintaining the fabric of society.

Another widespread notion concerning the human cause of sickness or misfortune, and therefore also health, stresses the power of words and motives in human community for good and ill. This notion is so ancient in Africa that its root term (*dog* or *dok*) is considered to be a part of the basic vocabulary of Bantu languages of at least 3,000 years ago. Its distribution, because of its centrality to the African worldview, extends from Cameroon and the Kongo coast in the west, to the Swahili coast in the east, to the Nguni speakers in South Africa such as the Zulu. Derivations of this concept are often negative, as in the destructive power of wishing ill or gossiping, or even of poisoning or some kind of destructive manipulation. But the power of words suggested by this concept is what a good orator needs to weave a skillful speech to bind the community together, and what a ruler needs to wield power constructively so as to maintain social harmony and justice.

The foregoing images of health from naturalistic (the ordered body, purity and pollution, balance, flow and blockage) and human sources (prohibitions, power of words, will) presuppose the interconnectedness of all life. In the following vignette from the center of the African continent, we will see how one of these notions is drawn out to provide a focus for community health. The concept of *obusinge* featured here was discovered to be helpful in launching a Primary Health Care campaign in one society of the Democratic Republic of the Congo (then known as Zaire). The term has to do with the connectedness that is required to maintain the social fabric in health.

Discovering Obusinge in the Health Zone of Boga, Northeast Congo

Pat Nickson, PhD, an English health development worker, and Nyangoma Karabole, a Zairian public health nurse, have written a remarkable story of how the primary health care team of Boga, in Hema society of northeastern Zaire, decided to explore the underlying concept of health in order to improve the effectiveness of their already good program (Nickson and Karabole 1992). They noticed that some infants who had received their inoculations and whose mothers were aware of health program expectations for the care of their children, nevertheless suffered from or even died of malnutrition in a food-producing setting in which there was adequate food. Suspicious that something was not quite right about the model primary health care program, they set out to learn what the people, the affected mothers in particular, thought about their infants' health and ill health. One mother, whose infant had died of malnutrition after the birth of a younger sibling, although the child had been inoculated and otherwise cared for, was asked why she had not brought it to the clinic. She replied that her child had been miserable and cried all the time, adding that the foreign hospital had no treatment for "misery." She had taken the child to a healer, but that had not helped either.

Nickson and Karabole decided to explore more widely these concepts and beliefs regarding health, so they could guide primary health efforts more effectively. They organized focus groups and went to the local health teams, as well as to the regional chief who had jurisdiction over the health zone of Boga, a political-administrative area of 10,000 persons. What, they asked, is the notion of health that needs to be held up to make certain that such victims are not repeated? Out of this process emerged a "health study team" made up of two senior nurses, the chief, one of the village leaders, a community health worker,

and a secretary. As part of the committee's methodology, they asked health care workers to write stories of typical women with children and the health care problems they faced. From these stories they prepared a fictional but typical story which they circulated to elder men's drinking groups, church women's groups, and other leaders of the area. They asked them to identify the problems and what needed to be done to solve them in this typical case. They learned that *ugonjwa,* illness, is only one of the reasons a person may not be healthy. They found that the community was familiar with health care facilities, but there were other conditions considered to be inappropriate for the health center, and more appropriate for herbal therapy, spiritual healing, and other work of healers. In listening to responses to the story of the sick child, the word *obusinge* was frequently repeated; it referred to what was broken or missing from the child's household and life situation. At first the people of Boga were unable or reluctant to translate *obusinge.* They were able, however, to identify problems associated with "broken *obusinge"* as in the outbreak of diarrhea or malnutrition. Various groups and individuals were able to explain what occurred when *obusinge* was broken or missing. Discussions revealed that the conditions of *obusinge* related not to the individual but to the family or community which created a sense of well-being, health, peace, and hope. Thus, an old person living in the comfort of his family could die in a state of *obusinge.*

The health team of Boga zone next took its understanding of *obusinge* to local communities to ask them to determine their priorities in building health. A health needs assessment was also conducted in each of the zone's 15 villages. Earlier, the primary health program had been introduced from above without much

continued

continued from previous page

discussion with the people. Now discussions of how to build *obusinge* along with the needs assessment provoked much discussion and a sense of ownership in the process of establishing priorities. Goals were selected and strategies identified, as well as other measures to achieve the health goals. In due course a set of 10 priorities was identified that embodied *obusinge*. (see Figure 3.1)

1. Peace within the family and between the family and its neighbors.
2. Two to six children with at least two years between each birth.
3. Both parents alive and free from serious chronic disease or disability. They must be living together and capable of caring for their dependent children.

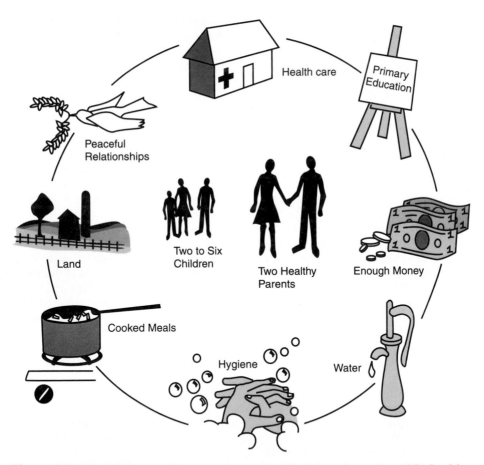

Figure 3.1 The circle of connected determinants of health as drawn by public health educators in the Boga Health Zone of North Kivu, in the Republic of Congo. This represents an application of the traditional concept *obusinge*, "connectedness," to a public health program.
Source: Nickson and Karabole (1992:2).

4. Education to primary level for all children and an opportunity for some of the children to continue to secondary level.
5. Capability in domestic finances, learning and health care.
6. Half a hectare of land or 1.235 acres to cultivate for each family member.
7. Two or more cooked meals each day consisting of at least one staple food and one or more other foods.
8. An adequate standard of hygiene involving use of a covered, deep pit latrine, control of vegetation in the compound, an outside kitchen and maintenance of the house.
9. Easy access to water, within 2,100 meters of the home.
10. Affordable health care within reach of the village.

The story of identifying *obusinge* in northeastern Zaire caught my interest because I recognized the radical of that word, *singa*, as an important Kongo verb meaning to tie, connect, or link together, or *singama*, to support, rest on, or protect. Its noun form, *nsinga*, means string, cord, or underlying connection, as between people. It also has negative connotations, such as to injure, insult, or wish the ruin or death of someone. An *nsingi* is one who is suspected of being a sorcerer. The Boga experiment defines this "connectedness" as the basis of health, hope, and well-being. ■

The Primary Health Care movement evident in the Boga project, alongside the Central African health ideal of "connectedness," will be presented later on page 72 in its original context, as part of the World Health Organization campaign. Before we get to that study, however, it is relevant to this study of culturally particular fabrics of health to take a closer look at modern mainstream health, which anthropologists often call biomedicine.

HEALTH IN BIOMEDICINE: A PHILOSOPHICAL PUZZLE

How can the "health" of biomedicine be culturally particular—specific to setting, place, and circumstance—if by its very claim to validity it is rooted in science, as universal knowledge? This is the philosophical puzzle that this section addresses. Put another way, we might ask in what way is the understanding of the health of biomedicine, the medicine of "science," in any way comparable to the traditions introduced above that are grounded in ancient ideas of balance, purity, social connectedness, and the humors and the elements? To be sure, the balance of humors and temperatures, notions of purity, and the observance of social rules and exchanges are very different from the emphasis put on the sciences of chemistry, cell biology, anatomy, and mathematics which must be studied to gain proficiency in modern biomedicine. By emphasizing the science of modern medicine, we may have a hard time seeing its cultural character. Yet, as we will see, the defining ideas of biomedicine are as culturally particular as those we have just studied. Philosophers of science and medicine and some anthropologists writing about the culture of biomedicine have laid out the thinking by which this becomes evident.

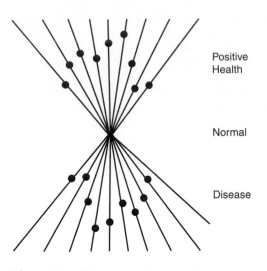

Figure 3.2 Christopher Boorse's depiction of disease and health around a species or cohort norm. Disease represents variance from the norm (*points below the median*), just as does positive health (*above the median*). Although the norm may be statistically demonstrated, the criteria for establishing disease and health dimensions are culturally produced; that is, according to some value or concept of "normal functioning" or "adaptation."
Source: Boorse (1977:571).

The primary definition of health in modern biomedicine is the "absence of disease" (Boorse 1977:550–51). It is thus a negative definition—the absence of—rather than a positive definition such as "balance of humors," the "flow of chi," the "purity of the lineage," or "happiness." A second dimension of biomedicine's understanding of health is in the idea of function and normalcy, or "normal functioning," which stands against the pathological states that are to be removed or corrected. Figure 3.2 illustrates Christopher Boorse's dimensions of health.

Medical historians have usually seen these primary ideas of health in modern medicine as having their beginnings in the 17th-century origin of modern science and the emphasis on direct observation of diseases. The English physician Thomas Sydenham (1624–1689), for example, systematically observed, and recorded, the various kinds of fevers and diarrheas of English people, noting the different phases of some that were intermittent (i.e., malaria), those that were self-limiting, and those that were chronic (Dewhurst 1966). Although Sydenham used humoral ideas in his treatment of these fevers, he considered most physicians to use speculation rather than observation in their work. He was greatly admired by and perhaps inspired the empiricism of philosopher John Locke. This was still in the days before microscopes and the discovery of microorganisms. When that day arrived, in the 18th century, the direct microorganismic sources of common contagious diseases became known, and with them direct cures, leading to single-cause disease etiologies (causal theories) that came to pervade 20th-century medicine.

Because the "absence of disease" definition of health in biomedicine is a fundamentally negative definition, it is not an absolute or general definition. It is a by-product of the focus on disease, the absence of which is the abstract goal to which medicine has aspired for several centuries. It is perhaps a victim of its own success. According to philosopher Christopher Boorse, the biomedical understanding of disease is potentially limitless. For "health" to be the absence of this thing, disease as a general category tends to operate as a creeping expansive category to include not only infectious syndromes such as malaria and syphilis, but also birth defects like spina bifida, growth disorders like cancer, functional impairments like limb paralysis, and all kinds of injuries and causes of death—in other words, all those conditions that in any way impair an individual. The category is inclusive and open-ended to the point that it offers an infinite opportunity for medicine to find new afflictions to "medicalize" any and every condition that in any way impairs or restricts. Aging, fatigue, indeed life itself, may potentially qualify as disease. We are all diseased, in a sense, and lacking in full health by this definition.[4] Anthropologist Arthur Kleinman (1996:28) suggested that the origin of Western biomedicine's singular focus on disease, and especially single-cause disease, reflects Judeo-Christian monotheism and its forceful focus on the identification of sin, which it equated with disease. As time goes on, the effort to overcome disease is joined by the campaign to overcome disability and all pain and discomfort. Health remains an ever-elusive goal beyond the medicalization of life's many special conditions.

To pursue health exclusively as the "opposite of disease, disability, of pain and discomfort" becomes an impossible stance fraught with moral and logical dilemmas (Boorse 1977: 547), for clearly pain does not always indicate sickness; it may be part of a "normal" process as in teething, menstruation, and childbirth. Nor can we say that health as the "absence of disability" is entirely plausible, for some conditions that are disabling (e.g., pregnancy, a baby's inability to do certain acts that adults can perform) are certainly not diseases.

Because of the problematic nature of the "absence of disease" and understanding of health, for all the reasons just given, modern biomedicine has come to also use as the benchmark for its efforts the broad idea of "the normal." What is normal, however identified, is therefore also normative; that is, it constitutes a goal for health instruction, health care, and general norm-based medical work. This designation of health and a goal for medical care is also paraphrased as "functional normalcy," "statistical normalcy," or "instrumental health," the latter of which is really just the removal of particular negative conditions or diseases (Boorse 1977:553), which is not much different from the absence of disease. A number of scholars have studied this functional normalcy definition of health, among them the French scholar of social medicine Georges Canguilhem, whose book *Le normal et le pathologique* (1966) is the most thorough.

Medical practitioners follow several routes to establishing the normal or the normative in health, each of which has been critiqued by scholars. The most straightforward use of the normal is that of statistical normality, identified as the average or mean of all occurring cases being tracked or included. Thus, to take a common index of "normal health," bodily temperature, 98.5 degrees Farenheit is usually considered normal. Or, bodily height and weight by age and gender are often used to identify some kind of normal or norm of growth. Yet each of these measures is problematic for defining health because individuals in a crowd are not alike; they demonstrate a range. There are individuals whose temperature is higher or lower than this "norm" who are obviously not diseased. The cycle of the day finds the bodily temperature of most individuals varying. Normal height and weight are often identified, but clearly many individuals fall above or below the average or mean without thereby being diseased.

Another problem that arises with the use of the concept of the normal as health is that not all that is statistically normal is obviously healthy. If most members of society suffer stress, is that then normal, and therefore healthy? Or if many elderly persons have arthritis, does that make it a healthy condition? Or if a society has widespread malnutrition, is such a statistical norm healthy? Clearly not.

Modern medicine and public health get around the dilemma of using the statistical norm to define health with a "functional account" of health that is specific to a cohort or peer group, for example, young adults, women between ages 20 and 30, menopausal women, or white American middle-aged men. This perspective is inspired by the thinking of the well-known medical scholar Osewi Temkin on "Health and Disease" (1973:395–407). According to this perspective, "normal is natural." After Temkin, "All parts of the body are built and function so as to allow humans to lead a good life and to preserve his kind. Health is a state according to nature. Disease is contrary to nature." In a similar vein, C.D. King (cited in Boorse 1977: 554) said "there is a standard of normality inherent in the structure and effective functioning of each species of organism. . . . Human beings are to be considered normal if they possess the full number of . . . capacities natural to the human race, and if these . . . are so balanced and inter-related that they function together effectively and harmoniously." Boorse accepted this view of health as valid, if it is not taken to excessive lengths, even though it possesses an inherent teleology, or circular "end cause" (e.g., because it is a heart, its purpose is to pump blood, which, if it can perform this function, it's healthy). After all, in biology we can identify the purpose of a kidney or a heart. Biological functions have goals according to their reference class and species design, as illustrated in Figure 3.2 above. Normal biological functioning within a class is to be drawn with reference to age, gender, or other peer sets, so that one may compare, for example, the heart functioning of a given individual with other individuals of the same age, weight, or gender, and establish a norm or at the least a mean for that function. The species or cohort norm is statistically situated where all lines converge; "dimension of positive health" may be imagined to the points above the convergence, "dimensions of disease" to those points below the convergence. Just as disease represents variance from the norm, so does positive health. Although the norm may be statistically demonstrated, the criteria for disease and health are culturally, in a sense arbitrarily, defined. Health then is normal biological functioning ability, just as disease is an internal state that impairs health (Boorse 1977: 562).

But this "normal biological functioning" definition of health is still problematic if it is applied in a setting where there is, for example, widespread malnutrition or diseases of malnutrition. The reference class must be drawn broadly enough to avoid describing a population or cohort healthy just because everyone is equally undernourished. Georges Canguilhem argued that the solution of this problem with normal biological function as a definition of health is to fall back on a broad understanding of adaptation, or equilibrium within an environment within which the organisms must exist and function (1966: 202). But he also warned against using this definition as a way of imposing this in such a way as to coerce individuals to fit a given social situation (1966: 213). The very idea of the normal as applied to health dates to the 18th century in western Europe; it emerged in absolutist monarchies (particularly France and Austria) that were attempting to subject the entire population to particular standards not only in health but in language use and national identity (Canguilhem 1966: 180–83). Since then totalitarian governments have often branded dissidents as mentally ill or deviant, thereby justifying their incarceration in hospital-like detention centers where they are subjected to "reeducation" or "therapeutic correction." In capitalist market-driven advertising campaigns of the late 20th century, entrepreneurs have promoted alluring images of health as defined by their products, to counter diseases or conditions that their commodity can treat or overcome.

All these efforts to identify or define the basis of health reflect the cultural specificity of definitions of health and disease, and the centrality of anthropology in identifying the contours of the ideas or societal techniques that are being used toward this end. We should then not be alarmed or surprised to find that what the philosophers of science and medicine call "positive health" are widely and effectively used in a number of global campaigns in the 20th century that bear further examination. We can also find particular positive health codes at work in local societies rooted in traditional culture, as a vignette in the next section shows.

PRIMARY HEALTH CARE AND REPRODUCTIVE HEALTH

Two campaigns will be examined here for the way in which they embody an idea of health: the **Primary Health Care Campaign** that was often promoted with the World Health Organization's slogan "health for all by the year 2000," and **Reproductive Health,** the phrase that captured several decades of debate and action in family and population planning in the postcolonial, and now the postmodern, world. Health authorities in many countries realized that the Western institutional model of the centralized hospital was neither affordable by many nations, nor would it achieve significant improvements in health for the majority of people. Efforts were made to shift the paradigm of health from high-cost individualized, crisis curative care—the "absence of disease" model of health—to lower-cost, extensive, preventive care. With this in mind the World Health Organization launched its Primary Health Care campaign following a major conference in 1978 at Alma Ata in Soviet Turkestan. The Alma Ata Declaration on health has defined many campaigns of the last quarter of the 20th century, such as the one described earlier in this chapter in Boga, in northeast Zaire. Central to the Alma Ata Declaration was a definition of health, as

> a state of complete physical, mental and social well-being, and not merely the absence of disease or infirmity, [it] is a fundamental human right and that the attainment of the highest possible level of health is a most important worldwide social goal whose realization requires the action of many other social and economic sectors in addition to the health sector (WHO 1978:2).

This definition of health has been the measure of the worldwide emphasis by WHO and other agencies on primary health care as the way of reaching health for all by the year 2000. Although this seemingly utopian goal receded from the realm of the possible in many regions of the world as the year 2000 approached, the programmatic aspects embodied in **Primary Health Care** have improved health in many communities of the world. The backbone of this working definition of health rests on the well-known list of the minimum needs that would provide the means for achieving health as defined by the Alma Ata Declaration. Health for all entails:

> promotion of proper nutrition and an adequate supply of safe water; basic sanitation; maternal and child care, including family planning; immunization against the major infectious diseases; prevention and control of locally endemic diseases; education concerning prevailing health problems and the methods of

preventing and controlling them; and appropriate treatment for common diseases and injuries (WHO 1978:53).

By their own criteria, most societies or cultural traditions have both material and nonmaterial dimensions by which health may be defined and even measured within that setting, or across traditions using one or another definition.

For the "positive health" perspective to have validity within medical anthropology, it is necessary to follow ways in which the benchmarks of health can be identified, researched, and applied within specific settings. In the Boga project the minimal health infrastructural requirements were surveyed in the 15 village communities constituting the zone. Then each community was engaged to define its particular area of priority. These varied from a road in an isolated community in one case, a better source of clean water in another, to the construction of a health clinic in a third (Nickson and Karabole 1992). By the turn of the millennium, the year 2000, it was clear that we had neither utopian nor apocalyptic health conditions. Some of the old diseases such as smallpox have been vanquished, but others remain and continue to plague us as a global community. New variants of old diseases such as vaccine-resistant strains of malaria and TB have emerged after a generation of DDT, quinine, and antibiotics. New strains of old viruses—call them new diseases—such as AIDS and ebola have raised the frightening specter of a slide back to massive old-style epidemics (Garrett 1994). But the wisdom of primary health care in the local community has become the common approach to enhancing basic health. In thousands of local communities, towns, and cities around the globe, the model of Primary Health Care has included, as the basic needs assessment list suggests, a source of clean and adequate water for all; basic housing; land or a source of available, affordable nutrition, especially for infants and children; childhood inoculations against the leading contagious diseases; accessible basic care for common injuries and accidents such as can be provided by local clinics staffed by well-trained nurses, stocked with basic supplies. The world health community has come to see that this simple health infrastructure is only achievable in a social and political climate where social justice exists and where authorities recognize the rights of common people, and among them, the most vulnerable, women and children.

It has taken many decades, however, for health authorities and analysts to recognize and acknowledge that a critical focus of health for all must be the well-being of women and children. **Reproductive health** is a concept that has emerged in the convergence of a number of forums concerning women's rights, population control, family planning, and the Primary Health Care movement of overall health of peoples. The phrase "reproductive health" became a buzzword of the 1994 Cairo U.N. International Conference on Population and Development (ICPD), the successor of earlier conferences going back on the one hand to the Rome Population Conference

(1974), and on the other to the U.N. Women's Conferences of Nairobi (1985), followed by that in Beijing, China (1995). These issues were echoed in scores of regional conferences and coalitions on maternal and child health, women's rights, and related issues such as the Bangladesh Women's Health Coalition, founded in 1980, the Brazil Feminist Health Collective, founded in 1984, and the U.S. National Black Women's Health Project since 1983 (Hempel 1996:74).

In the Cairo conference there appeared to be a breakthrough between the advocates of straightforward population control through contraception, often seen as a First World policy which Third World representatives resented, and the voice of women's rights which included reproductive rights (a voice often dominated by First World feminists). In Cairo, all voices with an interest in the issues of reproduction (the population scholars and policy makers; the feminists of the First World and the Third World; the Vatican; the Islamic clerics; the health nongovernmental organizations) were at the table and after lengthy debates were at least able to agree on the language of resolutions and plans of action (Lane 1994; Garcia-Moreno et al. 1995; Caldwell 1996; Hempel 1996). This degree of unity on so volatile and complex an issue was thought by some observers to be due to agreement over several issues: one, that there are still too many maternal deaths related to unsafe reproductive procedures and conditions (WIN News 1995), and two, the broad realization based on extensive research that infant mortality and fertility reductions are often, sometimes dramatically, brought about through maternal education and empowerment of women (Caldwell 1996:71–72). Some of these issues will be taken up in the discussion of the demographic transition (to lower fertility rates) in the next chapter. Here the focus is on the nature of the concept and practice of health in the notion of "reproductive health."

The Cairo Conference final document reveals its debt to the WHO concept of health in the way "reproductive and sexual health" is defined, as "'a state of complete physical, mental and social well-being' in all matters relating to reproduction" (cited in Hedges 1994: A4). The assumption is now widespread in many circles of health development agencies (whether tied to the WHO, the U.N., or to independent development and church agencies like the World Council of Churches) that women's and children's well-being are a foundation for social prosperity and for the reduction in fertility rates. The concept of reproductive and sexual health has grown out of a better understanding of the need to reduce women's deaths in childbirth, and children's deaths from malnutrition and disease in the first years of life. This is now thought to be best achieved by empowering women, strengthening families, and by the inclusion of women in all levels of policy making (Hempel 1996:74).

The conditions of women's and children's health exist, of course, beyond campaigns. Communities have cultivated their own cultures of care and support. Medical anthropologists have studied these communities to

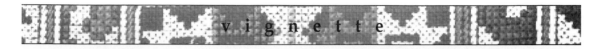

Studying the Health Enigma of Favorable Birth Outcomes in Rio Arriba, New Mexico, in the Light of Unfavorable Indicators

Rio Arriba County in northern New Mexico is a centuries-old Hispanic community whose ancestry immigrated from Spain into greater Mexico long before it was annexed by the United States. Rio Arriba was selected by nurse-practitioner anthropologist Elaine Williams for study because it is typical of a number of Hispanic-American communities in which outcomes in birthing, both in terms of survival of children and welfare of the mother, are better than the U.S. national average. This is particularly interesting in light of this community's low scores on many of the supposed indicators of positive birth outcomes such as prenatal care, income, and formal education. What accounts for these positive outcomes, if not economic standing, formal education of the mothers, and prenatal care?

The national U.S. profile indicates that a pregnant woman with no prenatal care is three times more likely to have a low birthweight baby than a woman with prenatal care in a clinic or center. These rates of late or no prenatal care are comparably higher for minority groups (USDHHS 1990:12). However, among Hispanic women, the incidence of low birthweight is less for infants born to Mexican American and other Hispanic mothers who migrated from Mexico (3 percent and 7 percent) than for U.S.-born Mexican American and Hispanic mothers (14 percent and 15 percent) (Collins and Shay 1994:184). The mothers of Rio Arriba represent an island of Hispanic culture in the United States that is in some ways an anomaly. But Williams hoped that it would reveal some of the secrets of Hispanic culture as it pertains to the preparation for birthing mothers, and would provide insight into the ways that values might affect practices in pregnancy, birthing, and child rearing.

Explanations proposed by researchers for the low infant mortality rates in the New Mexico Hispanic community were a favorable birthweight distribution, good prenatal nutrition, low rates of smoking and drinking among pregnant women, and a high regard for parental roles (Humer, Eberstein, and Nam 1992:1057). However, others (Balcazar, Cole, and Hartner 1992:6) said we really do not know the reason behind this health enigma, and called for research to determine the relative contribution of socioeconomic factors and factors associated with values, traditions, and beliefs that are distinctive in this community and ethnic group. Williams is researching the cultural beliefs and practices associated with positive pregnancy outcomes, with special attention placed on the meaning of children, that are conveyed to pregnant women through social support in the family and community. She is interested in the ways that symbols are the vehicles of meaning, and therefore a vehicle of culture.

Williams worked with 18 pregnant women and their families in Rio Arriba during the course of her research project. Periodic visits over the course of their pregnancy and postpartum period allowed her to trace family dynamics over time and to generate detailed knowledge of how cultural meanings affected social support. In addition, she worked with two key informants from an earlier period of her time as a nurse in the community, women who were mothers and had raised their children in this community. She also administered the Personal Resource Questionnaire to a sample of 32 women in Rio Arriba county, delineating social support networks by analyses of 10 life situations in which the individual needs assistance and seeks intimacy and attachment, social integration, and reassurance of individual worth. Other kinds of

continued

continued from previous page

Photo 3.5 *A float in a local parade features the main points of Rio Arriba's memory and identity, including Spanish explorers and founders* (on the left), *the Madonna* (at right), *and* (between them) *Rio Arriba's young women who represent the community's future.*
SOURCE: Courtesy of Elaine Williams Domian.

data will be collected as well, all in the interest of understanding the meaning given to children.

Williams found a number of cultural practices that seem to emphasize social support of pregnant women in northern New Mexico. (1) Family members reinforced self-care for the pregnant woman by such actions as expressing personal concern through frequent inquiries about the woman's feelings of physical and emotional health, giving advice on self-care and emotional condition, and accompanying the pregnant woman to prenatal and social service appointments. The pregnant woman accepted this advice. (2) Family attitudes toward the pregnancy included public validation that the pregnancy is a "blessed event" that brings joy; even if conceived in an undesirable manner, the family will fully embrace it; the pregnant woman is complimented about her physical appearance; pride for the pregnant woman is verbalized; the family reflects positive rather than negative aspects or stressful situations surrounding the pregnancy, causing the woman to feel positive, hopeful, and excited about the pregnancy; family and friends provide expectant parents with baby clothing, furniture, and other needed items through gift giving.

Regarding the meanings attached to children in these social support behaviors, Williams found the following beliefs affirmed: that women thought they would eventually be a mother; responsibility for children helps the pregnant woman achieve her identity as a mother; pregnancy helps women experience that family is there for them. Beliefs that link children to family identity include: Children continue the legacy of the family through the acquisition of family name and land; respect from children is essential to elder identity. Beliefs that link children to interdependency of family members, include: Children bring happiness, joy, and connectedness to family members; family rituals promote shared responsibility for childrens' welfare; teaching children to respect elders provides a bond among family members; the pregnant woman needs the emotional support and assistance of family during pregnancy.

The pregnant Hispanic female perceives social support helpful to her and helpful to the pregnancy, as demonstrated in a number of statements by women: Family involvement is vital for pregnancy, especially in the promise of the presence of a mother, sister, partner, and best friends in time of labor and delivery; this extends to public health nurses of the area who know and care about pregnant women because they are part of, or know the community.

Finally, this social support results in internalized values of better self-care by pregnant women in areas of diet, nonsmoking, increased rest, nonconsumption of alcohol and drugs, eating right, and not being stressed. The child's needs and well-being are held up as taking precedence to those of the mother. ∎

---

determine what they are "doing right." The story of Rio Arriba reports research on the relationship of birth outcomes to family and community support for birthing mothers, and the values placed on children, in spite of ostensibly unfavorable indicators as defined by government policies of prenatal care in official clinics, and income as defined in terms of the formal economy.

Whether the articulation of "positive health" happens in the context of a campaign of a global agency such as the World Health Organization, or within a particular community, anthropological analysis follows the signs and symbols embedded in conscious and unconscious behaviors, social institutions, and verbalized ideas, just like any other dimension of culture.

THE ECOLOGY OF HEALTH AND THE SOCIAL REPRODUCTION OF HEALTH

Many of the notions of health that have been examined so far are restricted mainly to the human community, reflecting a cultural specificity and subjectivity such that health may mean anything we want it to mean. In an attempt to get beyond this "species" subjective and strictly cultural view of health, medical anthropologists have borrowed the perspectives of biology and ecology. Concern for the environment and the safeguarding of multiple species inhabiting a range of environments—spoken of as biodiversity—has brought the ecological perspective of health increasingly to the forefront of medical anthropology thinking, as formulated in the biocultural perspective in Chapter 2.

At its most inclusive, the ecologist's view of the world is a vast network of energy flowing from the sun to all energy stored in carbon deposits such as coal and oil, and organic matter in topsoil and vegetation that are tapped by living organisms. In this vast and complex network, humans are merely one among many organisms competing for food. Within such a framework, disease and health become highly relative terms. One species' health becomes another's death, its food or host. A human's disease may be another organism's life.

Human health in such an ecological perspective is therefore "species specific" in its definition of whose well-being has the highest priority. Ideally, a harmony with and between organisms is the most generous understanding of ecological health. The ecological perspective enhances our grasp of how organisms compete and adapt within a complex energy network. Thus, some human "diseases" are profiled as organisms that directly invade the human environment or the human organism. Bacteria that cause diarrhea, or the bacilli that cause tuberculosis, would be examples of this form of disease. Any practice or measure that enhances human resistance to such "invasions" would be seen as beneficial to health. Other human diseases are more complex combinations of the infecting organisms and a carrier, often known as a vector. Malaria is a good example of this type of disease. The microorganism that enters the bloodstream and affects the blood corpuscles causing fever and chills is carried by particular varieties of mosquito. Bubonic plague is carried by rodents, usually rats. In the ecological perspective of health and disease, organisms adapt to a niche alongside other organisms or they die out. Examples of adaptation—short term, physiological long term, and genetic mutational long term—abound in the anthropological literature.

The case of the use of DDT in malaria control in the second half of the 20th century is very instructive of the processes of adaptation and the need for a full comprehension of natural and cultural factors in public health measures. Cities, homes, and mosquito-breeding pools were widely sprayed throughout the tropical world in the 1950s and 1960s. The malaria problem appeared to have been largely vanquished. Then, DDT-resistant mosquitoes began to emerge in most places where the pesticide had been used. New strains of malaria made their appearance which were more virulent than those that had been almost eradicated or considerably diminished. Furthermore, DDT, discovered to be a highly toxic substance, had entered the food chain and threatened many other life forms. The end result was much worse than if nothing had been done at all. Human adaptation through technology was shortsighted; longer-term genetic adaptation occurred on the part of the mosquitoes and the microorganisms of malaria. Similarly complex organismic interactions occur throughout the energy chain.

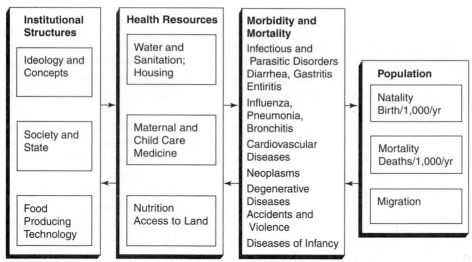

Environmental Factors: Climate, Rainfall, Pollution, Energy Sources

Figure 3.3 A view of the "ecology of health," as the interlocking and interrelated dimensions (*left to right*) of institutional structures, health resources, morbidity and mortality causes and rates, and population dynamics.

Source: based on diagrams in Wellin (1977:56), McElroy and Townsend (1979:14), Cordell, Gregory, and Pichet (1992:45–46), and features unique to this text. The morbidity and mortality column is based on the World Health Organization's Statistical Annual.

Adaptation, one of the concepts of health already mentioned, needs to be focused to be helpful in human terms. Biocultural medical anthropologists have used it because it gives them a good conceptual tool with which to understand the history and diversity of diseases in various environments, and the ways in which the organisms behind the diseases may be handled. René Dubos (1965, 1968) spelled out three types of adaptation in human life. Short-term adaptation is a largely organic reaction to changing conditions or immediate environmental threat. Longer-term physiological adaptation occurs in the conditioning that comes as one becomes habituated to a new environment or situation. The longest-term adaptation is multigenerational and brings into play the most profound of adaptations through genetic change.

However, the flexible adaptivity of human society that comes through cumulative learning and the creation of new ideas reminds us that our capacity for culture is our most unique tool for adaptation and survival. Figure 3.3 depicts culture as a nuanced layering of institutional and pragmatic cushions against "diseases." Ideology and concepts, society and state, and food-producing technology shape the "health resources" such as water and sanitation, housing, maternal and child care, medicine, nutrition, and access to land through which the "energy" in the network maintains human life. The bottom line in this equation is the rates of natality and mortality, and migration, which indicate the level of dynamic continuation or disruption of the population. These population factors, in turn, also affect disease, health resources, and institutional structures. All are seen against the background of the larger environment. Flow charts such as this are not full descriptions of how the world works. Rather, they are suggestive metaphors for the profoundly complex interconnectedness of all of life.

A final cautionary note needs to be voiced against the naturalization of human health. This can occur in the ecological perspective when energy flows, vectors, and demographic rates are allowed to substitute for human faces and political and economic forces. An anthropological perspective of health, as understood in this chapter, should be broad enough to include alongside the factors in the ecology of health the impact of household budget priorities, larger economic factors, and above all social and political institutions and forces. This author and a colleague suggested such a view of the social basis of health (Feierman and Janzen 1992: xvii):

> [T]he maintenance of health is a process that, whether at the household, lineage, community, or professional and national level, requires effective organization to succeed. . . . health, however defined, is not something that "just happens": it is maintained by a cushion of adequate nutrition, social support, water supply, housing, sanitation, and continued collective defense against contagious and degenerative disease . . . [this is] a useful perspective from which to understand why, in settings where state services do not exist, or have collapsed, household, family, or wider network-type supports may to a degree "maintain health."

Anthropologists have sketched the social structures that must be in place to effect what I have called the "social reproduction of health" (Janzen 1992:156–9). There must be sufficient means and management so that the household level, or perhaps even more widely, the economically active adults, or society's productive members, generate sufficient food, medicine, housing, and so on, to support the nonproductive children, the nonproductive elderly, and the sick and disabled (Meillassoux 1981: 33–57; Robertson 1991). The **social reproduction of health** requires the continued survival and effectiveness of the social unit—family, community, networks of support, and the state—within which the well-being of the continuum of generations is assured that includes the elderly, the disabled, the newly born, and the yet-unborn.

CONCLUSION

The "fabric of health" has served here as a metaphor for health and for the widest embrace of the subject matter of medical anthropology. Medical anthropologists study the images, the ideas, the behaviors, the resources, as well as the social patterns and institutions that embody health. The chapter has made the point that health concepts are culturally specific, historically particular, embedded in environments, and social and ideological contexts. This is true not only of classical traditions, but of biomedicine, a tradition of medicine that uses science to legitimize its findings, its measures, and its definitions of disease and cure.

So defined, much of health is beyond the bounds of curative medicine, although public health measures such as clean water, food standards, and inoculations contribute directly to the fabric of health, as do the way people live, or where they live, or the way they think, or eat, or whether they happen to get along with their neighbors and relatives. The Primary Health Care protocol and the ecological formulation of health suggests that health resources—water and sanitation, housing, maternal and child care, nutrition, access to land or other work—and social stability are more essential in creating a fabric of health than doctors, hospital beds, and medicines. But these institutional, technological, and professional resources are a feature of biomedicine's understanding of health as "the absence of disease" or "functional normality" which are as much cultural definitions of health as are positive definitions.

The chapter has also highlighted health research as a field of study within medical anthropology—region, community, ecological niche and adaptive patterns, perceptions, ideas, and behaviors as strategies that medical anthropologists can use in their work. Public health initiatives may be built on these ideas—equilibrium, balance, connectedness—and within the institutions that anthropologists identify as central to life in community.

REVIEW QUESTIONS

1. The chapter begins with two different uses of "thermal" metaphors in health and healing, each stemming from a different major medical tradition. How do we manage to keep them separate and distinctive in North American society and culture? What does this say about the nature and power of culture, or the cleverness of humans?

2. Describe or infer the health concept within a medical tradition or health-promoting practice. For example, explore the local telephone directory for clinics, diet and beauty salons, or other agencies that represent a medical or religious tradition.

3. Are all concepts of health culturally defined, including those of biomedicine and ecology, World Health Organization

"health for all," and "reproductive health"? Answer this question and discuss the issues comparatively with respect to two of these health definitions. To answer this question you will need to reflect on the idea of "in what way is science culture?"

4. What are the major common health concepts in central Africa? Explain what concepts and realities the notion of *obusinge* incorporated in the northeast Zairian health promotion project described in the vignette "Discovering *Obusinge.*"

5. Briefly describe the main points of Eurasian humoralism and related ideas. Does this perspective have any practical health value or is it simply a symbolic reflection of past ideas?

6. How do the notions of "hot" and "cold" in Malay humoralism operate with respect to foods and illnesses? What features make Malay humoralism distinctive within the larger world of thought systems derived from ancient Greece?

Notes

1. See note in Chapter 1 that spells out the way that the term *tradition* is used here.

2. This sketch is based on examination of the Southwestern Bell Telephone directory of Lawrence, Kansas, and an unpublished Guide to Alternative Health Practitioners in the Lawrence Area.

3. Anthropologists and other scholars have taken the Tungu word *saman* and applied it far more widely as a category of religions and therapeutic practitioner, with the attributes described here: trance, mystical travel of the soul, to retrieve souls, and so forth. Although this practice of lifting a word from its context and using it to describe a type of institution, behavior, or cultural feature (e.g., totemism) is common, especially in earlier decades, it is often misleading. It results in the mistaken conviction that if you give something a

familiar sounding name you have identified, understood, or explained it. The results may be especially insidious in the cases of mental illness labeling, handicap stereotyping, and racial and ethnic profiling. For these reasons "shamanism" should not be used as a descriptive label beyond its restricted Asian and American settings.

4. Boorse observed that the range of medical nomenclatures used by the American Medical Association or the World Health Organization's International Classification of Disease (discussed further in Chapter 8), which include such conditions as obesity, foreign bodies in the stomach, or being crushed, seems to be moving toward a total and detailed description of all possible conditions and situations that can possibly impair human life (1977:550–51).

POPULATION AND DISEASE: THE CHANGING INDICATORS OF HEALTH

Photo 4.1 *Scene of the Black Death, or Great Plague, in Leiden, the Netherlands, in the 14th century. In the foreground a physician examines a patient's urine, with the sick and dying all around. Line engraving, unknown artist.*
SOURCE: Wellcome Library, London.

THE MODERN RISE OF POPULATION

Since the beginning of the Industrial Revolution in 1750, when global population stood around 750 million, the population growth curve has ascended almost vertically. The consequences of this growth on a planet of limited resources become central in any discussion of medical anthropology. Global population doubled in the 1800s to 1.6 billion and quadrupled in the 20th century to 6 billion. In the year 2000, the earth saw 90 million persons added to its population. Not until the year 2050, suggest the population experts, will this growth curve level off at between 8 and 14 billion persons (Caldwell 1989; Gore 1992: 308). During the next 50 years, Africa must increase its food production fourfold to meet the need of its growing populace; Asia will need to increase food production by 68 percent, Latin America 80 percent, and North America 30 percent. Only Europe will see a decrease in the need for food production (*Christian Science Monitor* July 23, 1996, p. 2). The environmental impact of this increased demand for food and fuel, and the hazards of environmental pollution and species extinction, are a serious concern.

This modern increase in human population after a relatively steady level of growth since the dawn of human history may be explained by a combination of food production technology, disease patterns, reproductive practices, and human society and economy in the past 10,000 years, but especially during the Industrial Revolution. What does the future hold? On what basis do population experts confidently predict a leveling off of global population by 2050? These issues, of vital interest to medical anthropologists and many others, are the subject of this chapter. They represent a continuity from the previous chapter where the focus was on ideas and patterns of health. Here the focus is on negative health indicators, that is, disease, and the human reproductive consequences (see Figure 4.1).

The study of population is known as **demography.** Anthropologists collaborate with demographers or acquire the training required to collect demographic data and analyze the patterns of population change and reproduction. The number of children born to a couple, the number of children who reach adulthood, the life expectancy, the relative middle age, and elderly—the profile of a society—are some of the issues for which demographers have developed precise formulas and methodologies, a few of which are discussed here. All human populations are dynamic because some of their members die and are "replaced" by the newly born each year. Demographers use the formulas of **birthrate (natality)** per 1,000 population per year and **death (mortality) rate** per 1,000 population per year to describe this process. Thus, they are able to identify the growth, decline, or equilibrium of a population. (Migration is another factor that is usually factored in the dynamics of a population.) Thus, the global population for 1989 (WHO 1990) was 5.2 billion; the birthrate in that year was 27 per 1,000 population; the death rate was 10 per 1,000 population, the difference $(27 - 10/1,000 = 17/1,000 = 1.7$ percent) re-

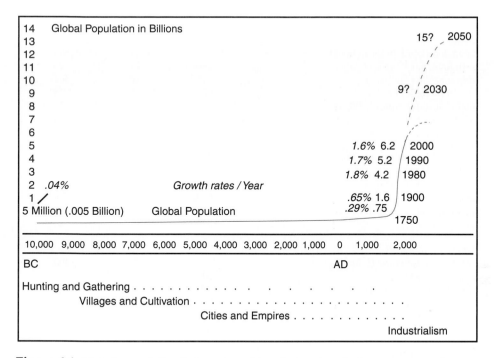

Figure 4.1 Global population in long-term historical and evolutionary perspective.
Sources: Polgar 1975, Boserup 1981, Gore 1992, Richman 1994, and McKeown 1975.

sulting in a growth rate of 1.7 percent per year (See Figure 4.2). The **infant mortality rate (IMR)** is a commonly kept statistic often used as a general indicator of the risks to society's most vulnerable and important segment, its newborns. The technical definition of an *infant,* in demography, is the child from birth until its first birthday; year one of life. The IMR is always given as deaths per 1,000 population born each year. Thus, to illustrate, global society experienced 82 deaths of infants below age one per 1,000 born per year; otherwise put, 8.2 percent of all children born on earth died within the first year of birth in 1989. The **fertility rate** is the number of children born on average to women of reproductive years; sometimes it is recorded as live births of those infants who reach age one. Overall **life expectancy** is another commonly used population statistic that suggests a quality of life, or at least longevity. This figure represents the average life expectancy at birth of infants born in a given year.

A final demographic concept that serves us well in sketching health comparatively is the **demographic transition.** Note that this carries a definite article, thus it refers to a particular transition. As Figure 4.1 suggests and Figure 4.2 shows in the short-term, there have been many demographic transitions in human history, in circumstances such as the shift from hunting and gathering to sedentary agriculture, the loss and rebound

	1979	1989	1998/9
Global			
Estimated Population (millions)	4,222	5,201	5,885
Birth Rate/1,000/yr	29	27	27
Mortality Rate/1,000/yr	11	10	9.2
Rate of Increase/yr	1.8%	1.7%	1.78%
Infant Mortality Rate/1,000/yr	82		57
Life Expectancy	61		66
Africa			
Estimated Population (millions)	436	628	601
Birth Rate/1,000/yr	46	45	54
Mortality Rate/1,000/yr	17	15	16
Rate of Increase/yr	2.9%	2.9%	3.8%
Infant Mortality Rate/1,000/yr	142		57
Life Expectancy	49		49
Asia (without USSR)			
Estimated Population (millions)	2,437	3,000	3,402
Birth Rate/1,000/yr	31	28	
Mortality Rate/1,000/yr	12	9	
Rate of Increase/yr	1.9%	1.85%	
Infant Mortality Rate/1,000/yr	96		
Life Expectancy	58		
Europe (with USSR)			
Estimated Population (millions)	740	782	870
Birth Rate/1,000/yr	*15/18	**15	15/18
Mortality Rate/1,000/yr	11/9	10.7	
Rate of Increase/yr	.0–4/.09%	0.04%	
Infant Mortality Rate/1,000/yr	21/28		21
Life Expectancy	72/70		
*1979 Europe/USSR; **1989 Europe+USSR			
The Americas			
Estimated Population (millions)	587	713	802
Birth Rate 1,000/yr	27	23.6	19
Mortality Rate/1,000/yr	9	7.9	8
Rate of Increase/yr	1.8%	1.6%	.8%
Infant Mortality Rate/1,000/yr	55		
Life Expectancy	68		77/69

Figure 4.2 Global and continental population statistics for the decade of the 1980s.
Source: WHO Statistical Annual, 1980, 1990; World Health Report, 1999.

(or a community's decimation) in connection with epidemics and wars. But "the" demographic transition refers to the constellation of features that include the modern population explosion followed by the eventual leveling off of population growth that is predicted sometime between 2020 and 2050. More will be said later in the chapter about this transition and of the disease patterns that correspond to historical stages or types of cultures, its implications for fertility trends, and why and when it happens.

The pattern of disease in the long term of human history is another element of the medical anthropological interest in health. A most useful approach to mapping changing disease patterns may be borrowed from agencies such as the World Health Organization and the Centers for Disease Control which keep global track of diseases. Tracing the incidence of major categories of disease in given locales over time offers an understanding of the changing health of a society, seen as the relative absence (or increase) of a particular type of disease. The science of **epidemiology** is the basic working tool of public health which tracks diseases, draws correlations with social, environmental, and cultural variables, and thereby offers some idea of the causes of diseases. The major categories are infectious and parasitic diseases (the old contagious diseases such as measles, smallpox, tuberculosis), gastrointestinal disorders (diarrhea, dysentery, cholera), respiratory tract infections (flus, pneumonia), cardiovascular diseases (heart attack, stroke, high blood pressure—that is, hypertension), neoplasms (cancers and tumors), degenerative diseases (mostly diseases of old age such as Alzheimer's, osteoporosis), accidents and violence, and diseases of infancy (WHO Statistical Annual Series). **Morbidity rate** refers to rate of infection, whereas mortality rate refers to death from a given disease or category (both are noted per 1,000 population).

Medical anthropologists need to become familiar with these standardized disease listings and the professionals who create and work with them. The listings have become the global language of health, albeit a "negative definition of health" (see Chapter 3). Many local community health agencies use these formulas for keeping track of population and disease. Standardized formulas indicating population stability and change appear in tabular form in global reports of the World Health Organization Statistical Annuals. Patterns of disease, the decline in incidence of some diseases and the increase of others, as well as the alarming appearance of new diseases, have become instruments that are much depended upon for measuring health and the basis for formulating health policy debates and establishing public health goals.

Medical anthropologists are equally interested in what goes on in a local community, how the patterns of disease are distributed in a community or nation, and whether these patterns are related to sociopolitical and economic conditions and structures. In the perspective of medical anthropology, even the standard population and disease measures are of interest because they are seen as a cultural product of the agencies that define, collect, and analyze the data and publish the reports, and those that determine health policy at local, national, and international levels.

DISEASE PROFILES IN HISTORICAL AND EVOLUTIONARY PERSPECTIVE

Distinctive populational and epidemiological (disease) patterns are evident for each of the broad phases of human food producing and cultural growth of the past: hunting and gathering, the transition to cultivation, intensified agriculture, the rise of cities under the shadow of early empires and trade routes, and the worldwide Industrial Revolution. Some scholars see humanity now moving toward a second-stage Industrial Revolution, also called the postindustrial era, of instantaneous global communication and the greatly increased speed and ease of travel and trade. This too has health and disease implications in new epidemics (e.g., the AIDS epidemic, the global threat of the new viruses such as ebola) and means of communication to pursue global health campaigns.

HUNTING AND GATHERING

Our understanding of the health and population patterns of hunting and gathering societies is based in part on archaeology and in part on research work with contemporary hunter-gatherers such as the Khoisan of the Kalahari, the Mbuti pygmies of the Congo's Ituri forest, the Malay and the Australian aborigines, and some Inuit groups of the North American Arctic. Important insight has come from archaeological research on the physiology, diet, and life settings of the common ancestry of humanity prior to the advent of food cultivation (Herskovits 1989; Polgar 1975; Boserup 1981). Although each historic setting in which hunters and gatherers lived is unique, empirical evidence and analytical inferences allow us to draw some generalizations about the health, disease, and population ratios in their communities.

In the small semi-isolated bands of hunter-gatherers, there were very few of the contagious diseases of the kind that killed later generations in epidemics, simply because the bands were wiped out or were too small to harbor a disease entity that depended upon continual infection in a host for its survival. Causes of death were probably mainly accidents and opportunistic respiratory infections; the latter would have caused a significant infant mortality rate. Otherwise, those hunter-gatherers who survived infancy may have been quite healthy; because of the diet of fruits, nuts, grains, and roots, with some meat, low in sugars and other carbohydrates, yet high in grit, dental caries were very rare (Frayer 1989; Larsen and Thomas 1982). Life expectancies averaged 33 for men, 28 for women (Boserup 1981:38). Accordingly, today's degenerative diseases such as cardiovascular deterioration or cancers were rare, although apparently not unknown among those who survived childhood and reached more advanced years. The fertility span of most women was on average only 10 to 15 years, resulting in three to at most four births per woman (Boserup 1981: 37). Long breast-feeding maintained the spacing between births at around three years (Dummond 1975; Boserup 1981:38). There is ample evidence of other population control measures such as infanticide in many hunting and gathering populations, reflecting the perception that the band society must maintain its mobility and live within its resources; women could not carry two dependent children at once. Survival depended on effective management of human and natural resources, and on a measure of good luck, which was a constant theme in the religion and magic of many hunter-gatherer groups (Koch 1968).

As Figure 4.1 indicates, for the long prehistoric period of human life in this mode, the growth rate of population was on average .04 percent per year, resulting in the total earth population having reached an estimated five million persons by 10,000 B.C., on the threshold of sedentary agriculture (Polgar 1975: 4–7).

THE TRANSITION TO FOOD CULTIVATION: INCREASES OF DISEASES AND FERTILITY

Scholars depict the transition to food cultivation as a reluctant revolution borne of necessity rather than a "great leap forward" (Wright 1991). This transition occurred repeatedly and independently in a number of regions after 10,000 B.C. In the Near East, India, China, the Sahel area of West Africa, Oceania, Mesoamerica, and Peru, distinctive cultivated food crops, domesticated animals, semisedentary ways of life, and societal patterns emerged. The transition was marked by a gradual intensification of collecting wild food, probably because of the growing scarcity of large wild game (Polgar 1975). The resulting food source, gained from intensified collecting and eventually food cultivation, may have been more dependable, but it was not necessarily better. Where resources were ample, hunting and gathering provided sufficient resources to persist in this lifestyle into modern times, even to allow substantial population growth. One example of a "wealthy" hunting and gathering society was the Native Americans of the Northwest coast who had prominent art, large structures, trade, all without agriculture.

According to historian William H. McNeill, whose *Plagues and Peoples* (1976) has chronicled and analyzed the disease impact of this and other transitions, the rise of early food production, and especially the attendant sedentarization of peoples, resulted in a gradual increase of death rates over the conditions that had prevailed in foraging societies. With sedentarization came an increase of animal life in close proximity to the human community, increasing the chance for human infection by some of the diseases that had historically been hosted by the animals. Whether through human coaxing, or through their being attracted to the human settlements because of food or other stimulation, rats, cats, dogs, chickens, ducks, sheep, goats, cattle, horses, and other animals began to live under the same roof and in close proximity to humans. This condition led to the direct transmission to humans of a series of contagious diseases most of which are with us today: chicken pox and smallpox; plague carried by the fleas from infected rodents to humans; malaria transmitted by the anopheles mosquito in breeding pools around tropical settlements to humans; water-borne diseases and diseases carried by the presence of open sewage. All of these are microorganisms which reside in and around human settlements ready to infect their human host.

Not surprisingly, death rates rose overall with the advent of cultivation and sedentary settlements (McNeill 1976). To offset the rising death rates due to infectious diseases, an increase in fertility rates is widely noted as a corollary of the "food revolution." Why should population rise in the face of high overall death rates and periodic epidemics? Some scholars point to intensive agriculture as a social and economic system. Specifically, these scholars suggest, it is the changes in nutritional status, marriage patterns, and breast-feeding practices that shorten intervals between conceptions, that result in the increasing fertility of intensive agricultural societies over that in hunting and gathering societies (Bentley, Goldbert, and Jasienska 1993). Indeed, the religious outlook shifted toward a focus on the desire of heightening fertility, both in crops and children. In the long term, a gradual increase in population density and growth rate has been noted with food cultivation, particularly in the centers of food plant domestication mentioned at the beginning of this section.

EMPIRES, CITIES, LONG-DISTANCE TRADE, AND THE APPEARANCE OF THE BIG EPIDEMICS

As the agrarian centers grew into cities and empires in the Tigris and Euphrates valleys in Mesopotamia, along the Nile, westward to the Niger of West Africa, in the Indus valley of India, the Yellow River Valley of China, the Mayan lowlands, and the Andes, new conditions emerged to affect disease patterns and mortality and fertility rates.

First, contagious diseases that may have been maintained chiefly in animal hosts in agrarian settings, now for the first time had a large enough population pool to permit them to become fully human diseases, spreading from human to human. This was the case with smallpox whose origins may be traced to bovine pox sources. Measles, chicken pox, diphtheria, whooping cough, scarlet fever, the water-borne diseases of cholera and typhus, and a variety of diseases followed this pattern of direct human-to-human transmission.

Second, as such diseases became "partners" to the human community, they developed the oscillating pattern we today associate with childhood diseases. They circulate seasonally or from time to time through schools, playgrounds, and nurseries, with those individuals who become infected and recover developing a lifetime immunity against them. The disease has only the uninfected, newly born young members of the host community to whom it may spread to survive (McNeill 1978: 79–81).

Third, the contagious diseases of ancient cities and empires spread beyond their original homelands to new regions and human communities, along with the influences of these civilizations. What were those mechanisms of expansion? In the case of Alexander the Great (356–323 B.C.), advancing armies extended the reach of his world and his might. But more frequently, contagious diseases spread along trade routes, whether with major transcontinental caravans or across the seas aboard ships.

The type of disease that spread in large-scale epidemics like waves of disaster within big cities, empires, and along trade routes, could have been any one of a number of known contagious diseases (e.g., smallpox or measles). The bubonic plague has a particularly horrendous reputation. Named after the swollen lymph nodes on throats, armpits, and groins of infected individuals, the bacillus of the plague, *Pasteurella pestis,* seems to have been first present in the black rat of India, which early moved from its wild habitat into South Asian cities and houses. From there, this agile climber took to ships and soon landed on foreign shores in Asia, East Africa, the Mediterannean, and Europe, where fleas took care of the spread to humans. McNeill believed the plague was already present in the Roman Empire and was responsible for some of the recorded "plagues," although sources are not clear enough to be certain of this (1976).

The 14th-century spread of the bubonic plague was particularly severe and widespread. Shipping and travel routes between Asia and Europe were so well traveled that news of the epidemic's spread moved ahead of it to inform and terrify those at a great distance. As its terrible progression was followed, cities and regions in its wake did what they could, mostly in vain, to ward it off. Often up to three-fourths of the populace would die, leaving desolation and institutional collapse behind. "The Black Death," as the plague was known because it formed black patches on its victims' skin, was the most feared scourge of late medieval Europe. Barbara Tuchman's vivid account in *A Distant Mirror: The Calamitous 14th Century* (1978), in a chapter titled "This Is the End of the World: The Black Death," lays out the facts as now understood by historians and, more significantly, the terror that the people felt as the Black Death approached, as rumors spread, and then finally, as it reached their cities and towns, to unleash its grim terror. They did not understand its cause: the bacillus, the rat, and the flea.

> By January 1348 it penetrated France by way of Marseilles, and North Africa through Tunis. Shipborne along coasts and navigable rivers, it spread westward from Marseilles through the ports of Languedoc to Spain and northward up the Rhone River to Avignon where it arrived in March. It reached Narbonne, Montpellier, Carcassonne, and Toulouse between February and May, and at the same time in Italy spread to Rome and Florence and their hinterlands. Between June and August it reached Bordeaux, Lyons, and Paris, spread to Burgundy and Normandy, and crossed the English Channel from Normandy into southern England. During the same summer, it crossed the Alps from Italy into Switzerland and reached eastward to Hungary.
>
> In a given area the plague accomplished its kill within four to six months and then faded, except in the larger cities where, rooting into the close-quartered

population, it abated during the winter, only to reappear in the spring of 1349 and rage for another six months.

In 1349 it also resumed in Paris, spread to Picardy, Flanders, and the Low Countries, and from England to Scotland and Ireland as well as to Norway, where a ghost ship with a cargo of wool and a dead crew drifted offshore until it ran aground near Bergen. From there the plague passed into Sweden, Denmark, Prussia, Iceland, and as far as Greenland. . . Although the mortality rate was erratic, ranging from one-fifth in some places to nine-tenths or almost total elimination in others, the overall estimate of modern demographers has settled—for the area from India to Iceland—around the same figure expressed in the casual words of the French chronicler Jean Froissart: "a third of the world died." A third of Europe at the time would have meant about 20 million deaths. (Tuchman 1978: 92–95)

The plague has continued to be present in many rodent populations around the world, and even in the United States a few people are annually infected by the plague as a result of coming into contact with prairie dogs. But the bubonic plague would never again break out on the scale of the Black Death of the 14th century. Perhaps a certain immunity to the disease was given by this initial scourgelike pattern of the microorganism. The association of rats with disease in popular consciousness has generally sufficed to encourage humans to keep their premises free of them.

Epidemiologists have become particularly interested in the extraordinary virulence or severity that contagious diseases such as the plague, the poxes, measles, or influenzas have when they reach a population that has never before experienced it and where, presumably, there is no immunity at all. Even diseases that have become endemic childhood diseases after generations of continued presence in a population may have this original virulence if spread to a fresh population. Epidemiologists and historians of disease speak of "virgin soil epidemics" to describe the initial impact of a new contagious disease upon a population. Usually the impact is severe, resulting in high death rates, because there is little or no immunity against the new invader. Examples of such virgin soil epidemics fill the annals of popular history and histories of medicine alike. The more striking readily come to mind: measles, poxes of various kinds, and common influenza strains brought along by explorers and conquerors after the 15th century. The collapse of Montezuma's Aztec empire in Mexico following the visit by Hernando Cortés was the result of the measles thought to have been carried by one of Cortés's soldiers. Thousands died, leaving an empire unable to fend off either foreign invader or internal dissenters. Measles would continue to course through the Mexican population for many years, resulting in massive deaths and the near total depopulation of the formerly dense Valley of Mexico. Story after story may be told of the conquest of the New World not so much by armed might, but by the silent helper of Old World contagious diseases in virgin human soil (McNeil 1976: 107; Fry 1979).

The opening of the gold mines of the Transvaal and diamond fields of the Orange Free State in southern Africa in the 1870s attracted many fortune seekers. Irish miners, experienced in the deep coal mines of Ireland, came too, hoping to improve their economic well-being, bringing their mining expertise—and their tuberculosis (TB). Historian Randall Packard has presented a long-term research of tuberculosis in southern Africa, and the virgin soil hypothesis, in his 1989 book *White Plague, Black Labor: Tuberculosis and the Political Economy of Health and Disease in South Africa.* The European miners were soon joined by many African workers who migrated on a seasonal basis from the villages of southern Africa. The African workers in the mines were forced to live in crowded dormitories, often scores of men cooking, bathing, spending time, and sleeping together—ideal conditions for the incubation and spread of the tuberculosis bacillus. Equally ideal for the spread of TB were the conditions of work and the periodic return home to their villages where the men would resume intimacies with their wives and spend a brief few weeks with their families and friends. From all over southern Africa—Botswana, Zimbabwe, Mozambique, Namibia, Zambia, Malawi—these workers spread their TB to their home areas. In the late 19th and early 20th centuries the mining companies gave very little care for this new infectious disease; in any case, before the advent of antibiotics there was little they could do. Even after the diagnosis and early treatment of tuberculosis was possible, there is evidence that the mining companies preferred to discharge infected men to return home to die (and spread their disease), rather than treat them in sanitariums. Today, tuberculosis is endemic over much of southern Africa, having entered with Irish miners and spread into virgin soil Africa.

Not only did epidemics of contagious diseases take their toll on populations in and around empires and trade routes. The world's larger cities became repositories of those diseases related to unclean water and inadequate sewage treatment, diseases such as dysentery, cholera, typhoid, and typhus, diseases of the intestinal tract. Until the 19th century, little progress had been made in understanding the cause of water-borne diseases, or the association of some diseases with sewage. Although the Babylonian, Assyrian, Greek, Roman, and other empires often developed clean water sources and supplies, the Roman aqueducts are especially well known for their cleanliness, as are Roman sewers for their systematic effectiveness in evacuating sewage away from population centers. The cities of medieval Europe allowed these aqueducts and sewers to fall into disuse. In 16th-century Manchester, England, for example, the Roman sewers lay buried beneath the city streets through which ran open sewage.

Demographer E. A. Wrigley described preindustrial cities as follows. "Before the industrial revolution had produced the wealth, and advances in medicine and public health techniques, to control or eradicate the causes of heavier mortality in the towns, . . . life in large settlements was apt to be shorter if less solitary than in the countryside" (1969:95). High urban death rates, largely the result of rapid transmission of infectious diseases in crowded conditions, made cities a kind of killing ground whose population could not be maintained by natural increase. Only extensive rural-urban migration allowed the populations of cities to sustain or increase their numbers. Only about 1900 did the tide turn and cities cease to function as "population sumps" dependent on rural immigrants for their survival; they finally became capable of internal growth by a surplus of births over deaths. This was due less to curative medical advances than to public health measures such as improved water, sewage disposal, and better housing (Rosen 1958: 192ff; McKeown 1976).

David Patterson opened his study of the history of public health in Accra, Ghana, in West Africa with the same generalization: "Cities have been able to survive throughout most of human history only by demographic parasitism on their rural hinterlands" (1979: 251). In Accra the installation of a clean water reservoir outside the city, pipes into the city, as well as a sewage system in the 1920s, rapidly improved health conditions and reduced death rates. For the first time the city was demographically able to reproduce its own numbers.

Despite the epidemics of contagious diseases in the preindustrial era, world population grew from 5 million in 10,000 B.C. at the dawn of food production, to 500 million in the 16th century. After each epidemic and war, population densities often bounced back to their previous numbers within a generation or less, if young adults of reproductive age survived.

By the mid-18th century world population stood at about 750 million. The annual growth rate was .3 percent per annum, a figure which masks the somewhat higher growth rates in some parts of the world, and lower rates in others (Polgar 1975). In certain regions of the tropical and newly unfolding colonial world, population levels were in fact experiencing an overall decline because of the importation of new epidemics. In North America, the native population had been decimated to only 10 percent of its estimated pre-Columbian population of 50–100 million (Fry 1979). In western equatorial Africa, peoples were ravaged by the chaos of the collapse of kingdoms in the face of competition for control of the coastal trade, including the slave trade, and the population continued to decline into the 20th century; entire regions became vacant (Sautter 1966). Reproductive goals were high because coastal African peoples feared they were "dying out" (Kusikila 1974). Fertility was emphasized in religious beliefs and medical treatments, as it had been in agrarian societies since the Neolithic revolution. Scourges and epidemics still occur today, in particular during wartime, even though human medical science knows how to avert them or to intervene when they break out so as to control them. The haunting specter of incurable new epidemics such as AIDS or the ebola virus, antibiotic-resistant strains of tuberculosis, new and more virulent kinds of malaria, and the threat of other infectious diseases (Epstein 1996) should lead us to wonder what is the cushion of safeguards and social institutions—the fabric of health—between us and the killer epidemics of old. The vignette on "The Meaning of Cholera" later in this chapter focuses on the outbreak of one such epidemic within the setting of a late 20th-century war.

The Industrial Revolution

The Industrial Revolution, which began in the 18th century in England, the Netherlands, France, Germany, Belgium, and Scandinavia, and in the 19th century in the United States, western Russia, and other European countries, transformed the picture of population trends and disease patterns yet again. The picture that has been painted of epidemics and unhealthy cities unable to maintain their own population base without immigration from the countryside was to continue in the early phases of industrialization. We have indelible accounts by novelists such as Charles Dickens who depicted the squalor and poverty in the new and expanding factory towns in England, as well as the romanticization of life in the countryside that was being abandoned. In the valleys of the Ruhr River of Germany, the class conflicts that accompanied industrialization led to the rapid ascent to wealth of a few capitalists and bankers and the rise of labor unions, the revolution of 1848, and the critical social writings of Karl Marx and Friedrich Engels. The newly found wealth of the industrial powers of western Europe and their control of trade was the impetus for an imperial expansion in the 19th century. They colonized much of Asia, Africa, and South America in the search for raw materials and cheap human labor and ultimately markets for their ever-expanding industries.

The health consequences of the Industrial Revolution generally revealed several phases. First, laborers were recruited into often unhealthy working conditions dominated by the old dynamics of epidemics of contagious diseases. Immigration or compensatory increased fertility offset rising mortality rates. Second, as income and living conditions gradually improved, including nutrition and water and sewage facilities, the decline of mortality rates led to what Thomas McKeown (1976) characterized as "the modern rise of population." Third, fertility rates eventually began to decline, leading finally to a leveling off of the rate of population increase. The population dynamics described here have also been termed the "demographic transition," the subject of the next section.

The transformation to lowered death rates, population growth, and eventually declining fertility has a direct corollary in the pattern and type of diseases of a community. The introduction of improved water supplies and housing led directly to the decline of some contagious diseases, usually those affecting the gastrointestinal tract and the respiratory system. Often these diseases are also those that affect infants and children most seriously. Thus, a decline in these diseases would result in a sharp and direct increase in population; for individuals who survived childhood, the likelihood was much better that they would live to a relatively old age.

The Industrial Revolution is thus associated, in the long run, with a shift from the predominantly contagious causes of mortality to mortality resulting from degenerative diseases and cancers, a shift to what René Dubos (1965) has called the "diseases of civilization."

Although the social, economic, cultural, and health-related context of each industrialization process is distinctive, the transformation that has been described here is general enough to constitute a pattern. Figure 4.3 illustrates this pattern as a changing picture of mortality rates in mid-20th-century South Africa. The table here is a unique composite pieced together by critical scholars David Bourne and Bruce Dick at a time when the government of South Africa had begun to record statistics. Apartheid policy had created the "homelands" as de jure "independent countries," but in reality they were forced labor reserves with some of the worst health conditions not only in South Africa, but in all of Africa; as recently as 1980 infant mortality rates in some homelands were as high as 300/1,000. Figure 4.3 is thus a document of the health profile of apartheid. The categories shown, although given "racial" labels, are really social classes that demonstrate the characteristic profiles of disease and mortality patterns in the course of industrialization in a regime where the class of privilege, power, and control has a sharply different morbidity and mortality pattern from that of the class of oppression, exploitation, and misery. "Black" and "colored" ("mixed" or non-South African blacks and Asians) categories are roughly at the same point in mortality rates in 1970 as the "white" category in 1929. The first three categories of disease (contagious diseases and parasites, gastrointestinal diseases, and respiratory tract infections) generally decline over the period covered, although there are some setbacks and declines (e.g., diarrhea in the colored community, reflecting lack of good water and sewage treatment during the period of forced relocations and resettlements to race-separated suburbs and shantytowns). At the same time there is a general increase, especially in the white classes, of the diseases of longevity and a sedentary lifestyle, cardiovascular diseases and neoplasms. Infant mortality rates show an initial increase followed by decreases in all categories, suggestive of deteriorating living conditions with the advent of strict apartheid in 1948, followed by a slight improvement at the end of the period. The increase of accidents and violence in all categories may reflect the growing social turmoil within South African apartheid society, in particular in the black community, as well as deaths from automobile accidents and other hazards of industrial work. A surprising detail is the relatively low incidence of degenerative diseases, which in other industrializing settings often increases along with the decline in contagious diseases and the rise of cardiovascular diseases and cancers.

Although the onset of industrialization has usually been accompanied by difficult and unsafe work conditions and diseased living sites, later stages of the process appear nearly everywhere to lead to the decline of death rates. Scholars consider this decline of mortality rates in association

	1929	1941	1951	1960	1970
Infectious and Parasitic Disorders					
Black			14.0%	12.8%	13.1%
Colored		25.4%	24.0%	11.1%	7.7%
White	14.6%	8.2%	4.8%	2.1%	1.0%
Diarrhea, Gastritis, Entiritis					
Black			17.3%	15.9%	14.1%
Colored		13.0%	15.0%	22.3%	20.0%
White	7.4%	4.8%	2.2%	1.4%	0.8%
Influenza, Pneumonia, Bronchitis					
Black			19.2%	17.2%	13.2%
Colored		23.3%	17.5%	15.3%	11.6%
White	13.0%	10.4%	8.2%	7.5%	10.8%
Cardiovascular Diseases					
Black			6.6%	7.0%	12.1%
Colored		10.0%	13.7%	15.0%	19.1%
White	17.0%	28.1%	40.1%	42.4%	48.6%
Malignant and Benign Neoplasms					
Black			2.9%	5.0%	5.9%
Colored		2.6%	3.7%	4.8%	6.1%
White	8.0%	12.1%	14.7%	15.7%	15.1%
Certain Degenerative Diseases					
Black			1.9%	2.2%	1.7%
Colored		2.2%	2.0%	1.8%	1.9%
White	6.0%	6.2%	5.1%	4.0%	3.3%
Accidents and Violence, including Motor Vehicles					
Black			8.0%	7.7%	14.0%
Colored		3.1%	3.6%	5.8%	9.0%
White	6.0%	6.1%	6.9%	8.7%	9.5%
Diseases of Infancy					
Black			11.3%	13.1%	7.0%
Colored		4.6%	9.0%	9.9%	7.0%
White	4.0%	4.8%	4.9%	4.8%	3.2%
Unknown Other Diseases, including Pregancy Complications					
Black			11.0%	19.1%	19.0%
Colored		16.0%	10.9%	14.1%	11.5%
White	22.0%	22.7%	13.4%	13.6%	7.9%

Figure 4.3 Proportional mortality for selected causes of death among "whites," "coloreds," and "blacks," 1929–1970, in South Africa. The "causes of death" follow international health agency categories; the death rate trends reveal sharply diverging class differences between white, colored, and blacks, the main group categories used in the government's apartheid policy from 1948 until the early 1990s.
Source: Bourne and Dick 1979: 77.

with industrial society—large cities, industrial workers, mass institutions, the state—to be due to a diffuse combination of improved living standards that come with reliable water supplies and better housing, but also better and more dependable food, and only derivatively as a result of medicine. If medicine is involved, public health measures such as the systematic inoculation of children against the common contagious diseases have the greatest impact.

Where the decline in mortality rates results from the reduction in causes of infant mortality such as contagious infectious diseases and influenzas, the greater life expectancy of most individuals leads to a shift in the causes of mortality to cardiovascular diseases, cancers and tumors, and other degenerative diseases (Polgar 1974; Dubos 1965, 1968). The global picture of the 20th century has been the gradual decline of mortality rates leading to the explosive growth of population outlined in general in Figure 4.1 and in more detail in Figure 4.2 as a slice of one decade, the 1980s, during which overall population rose from 4.2 billion to 5.2 billion and may have reached its maximum growth rate of 1.8 percent per year. By 1989 that rate had begun to descend, at a 1.7 percent increase per year. But the overall population was still rising at a rate of 90 million people a year.

THE "DEMOGRAPHIC TRANSITION" AND THE "HEALTH TRANSITION"

The modern decline of mortality, the ensuing rise of global population since 1750, especially in the 20th century, and the ensuing decline in fertility rates since the 18th century form a pattern that has come to be known as "the demographic transition" (see Figure 4.4), whose stages have been identified as follows: (*a*) a decline of death rates; (*b*) a specific pattern of decline, in at least two stages: in the first (*b*.1) the rate of population growth increases as a result of the growing gap between falling death rates and steady birth rates; in the second (*b*.2) the rate of growth begins to decrease because of the decline of birth rates; (*c*) a new equilibrium of birth and death rate at a lower level (Correa and El Tory 1982:42). This is of course not the first demographic transition humanity has seen, but this one represents a major adaptation to industrial technology, mass society, life in cities, and vast increase in scale of human institutions.

The consistency and variations in the transition may be traced in a number of industrial countries beginning with England in 1745 when mortality rates began to decline, to 1815 when growth rates were at their maximum (i.e., death rates had fallen but birth rates had not yet begun to decline), to 1937 when growth rates leveled off due to a stabilization of mortality and fertility rates (Correa and El Tory 1982: 25).

The same three phases of the demographic transition follow for other industrializing countries of western Europe, North America, and Asia:

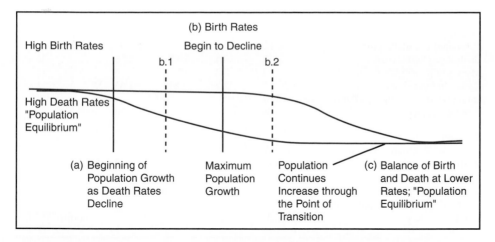

Figure 4.4 Outline of demographic transition that began with Western industrialized societies and has now reached its second phase in East Asian societies as well; sub-Saharan African societies are entering the phase of maximum growth of the transition. Source: Drawing by Author.

France, 1805, 1825, and 1932; Sweden, 1805, 1887, and 1932; Denmark, 1835, 1907, and 1937; Germany, 1865, 1897, and 1932; the United States, 1870, 1875, and 1937; and Japan, 1877, 1927, and 1937. It is noteworthy that the length of the total transition varies greatly from a total of 192 years for England, to only 60 years for Japan; the average length of the transition in all countries that went through this process before World War II is 45 years from the onset of mortality decline until maximum growth, and 44 years for the second phase of the transition—that is, from the time of the beginning of fertility decline until stabilization of mortality and fertility rates (Correa and El Tory 1982: 26). However, as more national societies have gone through this process in the second half of the 20th century, the time span of the transition has declined from a maximum of 192 years in the case of England, to a minimum of a few decades in recent cases of the transition in East Asia (Feeney 1994; Feeney and Jianhua 1994).

Sri Lanka and Thailand both demonstrate the transition occurring from about 1920 until about 1982, a third of the time taken by England (Caldwell 1989: 12). Adult life expectancies rise from about 35 years at the beginning of the transition, to 69 years by 1982; other indicators, shown in Figure 4.5, show the dramatically falling birthrates of the second half of the transition, along with continuing slightly declining mortality rates. Growth rates decline by nearly half, although population doubled in the 30 years from 1959 to 1989.

The causes, corollaries, and consequences of the demographic transition have been debated by many scholars and policy makers. Perhaps the oldest reaction to the prospect of exponential population growth was that of the English economist Thomas Malthus (1766–1834) whose *Essay on the*

	1959	1969	1979	1989	1998
Sri Lanka					
Estimated Population (in millions)	9,625			16,993	18,000
Birth Rate/1,000/year	37	30.4	29.5	22.5	21
Mortality Rate/1,000/year	9.1	8.4	7.7	6	11
Rate if Increase/year	2.7%	2.2%	2.18%	1.65%	1%
Infant Mortality Rate/1,000 births/yr	57				
Life Expectancy	59			70	65(m)//73(f)
Thailand					
Estimated Population (in millions)	21,076			54,916	60,854
Birth Rate/1,000/year	36.6			22.3	17
Mortality Rate/1,000/year	10.3	7	5.7	7	7
Rate if Increase/year	2.63%	2.56%	2.27%	1.53%	1%
Infant Mortality Rate/1000 births/yr	57				
Life Expectancy	59				66(m)/70.4(f)

Figure 4.5 Selected aspects of the demographic transition in Sri Lanka and Thailand. Source: WHO Statistical Annuals 1959, 1969, 1979, 1989; World Health Report 1999.

Principle of Population (1798) predicted that, because population growth is exponential whereas resource expansion is only arithmetic, humankind faced disaster unless reproduction could be checked. Arguments along these lines continue to be heard today by voices such as those of Paul and Anne Ehrlich in *Population Explosion* (1971) and Al Gore in *Earth in the Balance* (1992) who have predicted the planet's environment will collapse under the weight of human population, and as other species and resources become extinct, global warming will result from the increase of burning of fossil fuels, resulting in flooding of coastal areas. Humanity will experience increasing competition for limited good living space, leading ultimately to wars of self-annihilation of the species.

Others, following in the footsteps of Danish economist Ester Boserup in her works such as *Population and Technology* (1981) and *Hunger and History* (1985), have argued that the doomsday prophets have their causality reversed (Horsfall 1992). Population increase in effect stimulates technological innovations for new food-producing methods and substances, prompting new sources of energy and new applications. Increased population produces a greater critical mass of new knowledge and problem solving. Contrary to the Malthusians, the Boserupians and "free market" advocates have argued that population growth is actually a predictor of technological innovation (Simon 1977; Richman 1994). Recent research has documented intensification of agricultural production in several areas of East Africa where there has been rapid population growth (Goldman 1993) and in dryland settings of West Africa (Pearce 1994), but other settings such as nearby Rwanda certainly demonstrate population pressures, eruptions of violence, and massive human dislocation and environmental deterioration.

A third set of voices, prominent in recent decades, has argued that resources and population alone are insufficient indicators to understand the mechanisms at work in fertility regulation. Why do populations, societies, couples, or individuals, move to restrict fertility? Recall that this was done in early times by hunter-gatherers through prolonged lactation, child spacing, and infanticide. The beginning of the modern demographic transition in Europe included mortality decline before the advent of modern medicine, and fertility decline before the advent of 20th-century birth-control devices, whether that be the intrauterine device (IUD), the condom, or the pill. So why did the modern decline in fertility begin, and why does it continue?

One school of thought may be referred to as the "resource and economy" school; the second school of thought centers around worldview, education, and the empowerment of women. The resource and economy argument holds (Boserup 1970; Bourlag 1992) that the modern demographic transition is initiated as a result of improved resources and assured quantities of food, of better lodging that shelters its residents from the impact of excesses of climate (dampness, cold, excessive heat) and protects from rodents and insects, of clean and adequate sources of water, and sewage and garbage disposal techniques. Immunization and the control of catastrophic disease support these measures in bringing down mortality rates. These are characteristics of the first part of the transition which translate into population increases. In this perspective, improved standards of living enable more offspring to survive, and thus parents may imagine making do with fewer offspring; they can envision more economical use of their resources, especially human resources. This "development" model of the demographic transition mirrors the historic pattern of that in the wake of the Industrial Revolution, and would be the current cumulative wisdom on the demographic transition were it not for some recent noteworthy, especially dramatic, declines in fertility in relatively poor societies.

Kerala state in India and Bangladesh have concentrated their efforts on women's education, against the background of political egalitarianism, without there being significant industrialization. These largely agrarian societies now boast lower infant mortality rates and fertility rates than some of the wealthy oil-exporting countries. They are thus held up as a demonstration of the validity of the second school of thought which highlights "worldview, education, and empowerment of women" as the principal driving force behind the second phase of the demographic transition. For John C. Caldwell and his colleagues at the Health Transition Centre of Australian National University and related scholars and policy makers, the question is not what techniques or economic resources are available, but what social, cultural, religious, or ideological realities may account for the conviction, desire, and will to restrict fertility. They have argued that fertility declines are due to the freedom of women to make reproductive decisions and to initiate child care (Caldwell 1989). They see this enablement of women centrally represented in the education of girls. Interestingly, it is not so much the formal content of education as it is their attending school and obtaining the vision that they can act responsibly and freely that is at the core of the link between women's education and fertility decline. The Caldwell school's research on the relationship between girls' (women's) formal education and the mortality rates of women and their children was carried out in Nigeria in the 1950s and in Sri Lanka in the 1960s. Both societies were then in the first half of the transition. Thus, Caldwell and his colleagues were able to study both women with education and women without education, and correlate these with infant mortality rates, which were well over 100/1,000 in Nigeria at the time, and somewhat lower in Sri Lanka.

As infant mortality rates from contagious diseases have receded, attention has shifted, in the thinking of Caldwell and his colleagues, to the overall shifting pattern of health, in what they called the "health transition." This includes not just the demographic transition, but also the epidemiological transition marked by the elimination of major contagious disease. They have become focused upon the social, cultural, and behavioral determinants of health transition.

Although income or access to resources, urbanization, access to energy, adequate caloric intake and animal protein are important corollaries of the transition to low fertility, Caldwell and others argued that it is maternal education, female autonomy, and political egalitarianism that represent the true ingredients of empowerment.

These factors seem to be illustrated by the dramatic mortality and fertility declines seen in Bangladesh, one of the 20 poorest countries on earth. At independence in 1971 the population of the country stood at 80 million, but the leaders committed themselves to a serious effort to control reproduction. National programs of family planning were initiated despite the protests of Muslim clerics. Women's groups were created to do grassroots work with couples. By 1993 the average number of births of child-bearing women had declined from seven to around four. Even so, the national population of Bangladesh now stands at 117 million and is predicted to rise to 200 million before the transition is complete, and birth and death rates stabilize. This case has demonstrated that even in the absence of improving wealth, significant health improvements and reproductive control may be achieved by purposefully bringing women into leadership in this arena of policy and action that affects them and is effected by them (Burns 1994).

These dramatic demographic changes in Asia leave as the main questions to be answered not if there will be population equilibrium, but when will it be achieved, and at what level will the population plateau in a given country. Following from answers to these questions, national planners and governments and nongovernmental agencies need then to determine how to assure adequate food and energy resources, urban infrastructure, and environmental safeguards.

Population scholars and others interested in understanding the diverse forces that lead to a decline in birthrates have turned their attention to

Africa. Most national societies below the Sahara are in the late "first stage" of the demographic transition. Death rates have descended throughout most of the 20th century, although birthrates have remained high. The gap between the two rates has led to population growth of up to 4 percent per year in a country such as Kenya, which translates into a doubling of the population in 25 years, as the increase is geometrical—$1.04\% \times 1.04\% \times 1.04\%$ and so on. In the face of such demands on the productive base of a society and nation, national leaders, international agencies, and researchers alike have been interested in pinpointing the influences that usher in a decline in fertility. The suggestion has been made that Africa is a unique case, unlike industrial Europe or Asia, and that it will not respond as readily in the same way to global industrialization. Another cause for wondering whether Africa will go into the second stage of the demographic transition is the high level of infant and child diseases and deaths. But since the independence of most African nations in 1960, progress has been made in bringing down the infant mortality rates, as the following comparisons from 1960 and 1987 suggest: (U.N. Children's Fund 1989: 88, 94).

Nigeria, 190/1,000 births to 106/1,000 births;

Kenya, 124/1,000 to 73/1,000;

Chad, 195/1,000 to 133/1,000;

Zaire, 148/1,000 to 99/1,000;

Cameroon, 163/1,000 to 95/1,000

These declining infant mortality rates occurred against a nearly even, continuing, high fertility rate of around six children per couple. The achievements by Bangladesh and Sri Lanka in fertility decline and health improvement hold special promise for a region of Africa that is in many cases not building its wealth base with industrialization. A study in Cameroon, featured in the following ethnographic sketch, demonstrates that maternal education does indeed have a direct impact on the well-being of children, and therefore perhaps on the perception that parents may limit fertility, although there is no indication of that in Cameroon nationally.

SOCIAL SUFFERING, WARS, POVERTY, AND DISEASE IN THE MODERN WORLD

The constellation of population and economic factors of human history— overall population increase, decline of mortality rates, transition to lower rates of fertility increase, rising food production—have seemed to suggest a picture of inevitable progress toward a better tomorrow. This section and the next address the problems with such a view of the state of health in the

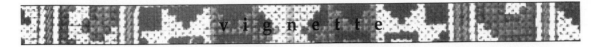

vignette

Signs of Fertility Decline in the Cameroon Grassfields, and the Impact of Maternal Education upon the Health of Infants and Children under Five

Nancy Palmer conducted research in Kitiwum village, Nso kingdom, in northwest Cameroon in 1989–1991 to test Caldwell's hypothesis regarding the impact of maternal education upon the health of infants and children under five years of age, and couples' fertility. Kitiwum is located eight kilometers from the Nso capital of Kumbo where in addition to the palace there is also a commercial center and two hospitals. It is in the region of rich Grassfields art. Regional health initiatives have included local primary health centers, the national public health initiatives in clean water, well baby clinics, and inoculations. Over three years Palmer conducted participant observation as a resident with a local family, speaking mostly Laminso. Her formal questionnaires included a census of 1,235 individuals in two of the four village quarters; a health survey of 104 households (643 residents, 144 children under five); and a bimonthly health interview with 25 mothers (43 children under five) over a period of 14 months.

The context for this study is the mid- to late-20th-century trend of declining death rates

	Mothers with No Schooling				Mothers with 4–12 Years Schooling		
Mother's Age	Mothers' N	Births	Deaths (%)		Mothers' N	Births	Deaths (%)
15–19	0	0	0		3	3	0
20–24	1	4	3 (75%)		14	25	0
25–29	5	27	0		9	25	1 (4%)
30–34	4	26	3 (11.5)		8	37	1 (2.7%)
35–39	14	89	6 (6.7%)		10	57	3 (5.3%)
40–44	10	60	4 (6.7%)		2	9	1 (11%)
45–49	7	40	6 (15%)				
50–54	3	23	2 (8.7%)				
55–59	3	22	0				
60–64	4	25	6 (24%)				
65–79	4	24	7 (29%)				

Figure 4.6 Children born and died by mother's age and education, Kitiwum, Cameroon.
Source: Palmer 1993: 40.

world. Medical anthropologists as well as other scholars are concerned with those sectors of society that do not reflect the scenario suggested by the demographic transition to lower fertility, or by the broader "health transition" of changing disease patterns.

A steady flow of reporting suggests regions, sectors of society, and entire nations in which there has been population and disease "backsliding"—that is, rising mortality rates, worsening health, recurrence of epidemics of tuber-

alongside continuing high birth-rates, resulting in an overall population increase characteristic of the second half of the demographic transition. Since this study concentrates on children, it is pertinent to note that in those few locales where records are available, censuses show exceedingly high infant mortality rates (IMRs) at the beginning of the 20th century. In Lagos, for example, the IMR in 1898–1890 was 450/1,000 births; by 1910, 350/1,000, by 1931, 130/1,000 (Nigerian census 1933).

In the health survey, whose results are tabulated below, mothers age 15 to 44 with four to twelve years of schooling (there are no older women with schooling because schools were only recently introduced) had half as many of their children die as did women with no formal education (3.8 percent versus 7.8 percent). Exactly how formal education affects declining infant mortality rates in this case needs to be interpreted, but Kitiwum data (as shown in Figure 4.6) confirm that it does (Palmer 1993: 40). Mothers with no schooling, shown on the left-hand side of the table, had more children and a greater percent of children die than those on the right-hand side.

Palmer's bimonthly health interviews with the 43 mothers (22 with no formal schooling, 21 with), substantiated the "epidemiological paradox" noted elsewhere, in which children of educated mothers experience more illness than children of the uneducated. In Kitiwum it was more than twice as many (see Figure 4.7).

Palmer's analysis of this paradox is that formally educated mothers are more attentive to their children's health, notice more symptoms and define them as illness more quickly, and seek treatment more often, especially with biomedical treatment. However, even this greater attention does not lessen the most common illness, upper respiratory infections (Palmer 1993: 187). ∎

	Children (N = 22) of Mothers with No Schooling	Children (N = 21) of Mothers with 3–10 Years Schooling
Respiratory	13 (48%)	37 (59%)
Malaria/Fever	0	5 (8%)
Stomach/Nausea	3 (11%)	2 (3%)
Diarrhea	2 (8%)	8 (13%)
Other Illnesses	9 (33%)	11 (17%)

Figure 4.7 The epidemiological paradox: case rates of 43 Kitiwum children in 14 months by mothers' education; percent of type of illness reported or suffered.
Source: Palmer 1993: 187.

culosis, malaria, and other diseases that previously had seemed checked, as well as new diseases such as AIDS. Often although not always this trend occurred in the shadow of war or chronic low-grade conflict.

A group of anthropologists with Arthur Kleinman and Robert Desjarlais coined the term *social suffering* to describe this seeming descent in the modern world into chaos and suffering.

> Social suffering . . . brings into a single space an assemblage of human problems that have their origins and consequences in the devastating injustices that social force inflicts on human experience. Social suffering results from what political,

economic, and institutional power does to people, and, reciprocally, from how these forms of power themselves influence responses to social problems. Included under the category of social suffering are conditions that are usually divided among separate fields: health, welfare, and legal, moral, and religious issues. They destabilize established categories. For example, the trauma, pain, and disorders to which atrocity gives rise are health conditions, yet they are also political and cultural matters. Similarly, to say that poverty is the major risk factor for ill health and death is only another way of saying that health is a social indicator and indeed a social process (Kleinman, Das, and Lock 1996:xi).

These anthropologists are concerned over the tendency to naturalize suffering on a mass scale, or to medicalize and bureaucratize the response to it. They are intent on showing the connection between large-scale suffering and the institutions and power relations that bring about and perpetuate it. A few examples of how this kind of perspective identifies the places of such suffering will be instructive, against the backdrop of the sketched scenario of the "health transition" to a better world.

Nancy Scheper-Hugues, in her voluminous study *Death without Weeping: The Violence of Everyday Life in Brazil,* wrote of "two contradictory epidemiological profiles, one for the rich and middle classes and the other for the poor. It is as if history had bifurcated, producing the expected demographic transition for part of the country, leaving the rest to die the way they always had: of sickness, hunger, and gross neglect" (1992: 282). The onset of military government in Brazil in the 1970s corresponded to an overall rise in infant mortality rates after significant decline in earlier decades. In the big cities such as São Paulo and especially in the northeast, the rise in the IMR was as high as 40 percent, due to malnutrition and related low birth weights (1992: 283). For Scheper-Hugues the pattern of "bifurcating history" in disease and death patterns is the direct result of an unbridled capitalism in Brazil that produces agricultural products such as sugar and extracts raw materials such as lumber from the landscape on the backs of the poor, for the benefit of the wealthy and powerful. *Death without Weeping* documented the resignation that results among mothers who have no hope of caring for their children. (The pattern of mortality in apartheid South Africa shown in Figure 4.3 is a parallel story.)

Robert Desjarlais and Arthur Kleinman saw the pattern of "violence and demoralization in the new world disorder" (1994) as a global condition brought on by the forces of economic and political developments, including the end of the Cold War. Health conditions may be exacerbated not only by the aggressive spread of extractive capitalistic industries in the Third World, but through the character of some states and their relation to the people. Desjarlais and Kleinman spoke of both the repressive nature of some states as well as the collapsed states as conditions that may affect health adversely (1994: 9–10). States may utilize military or paramilitary forces to control and exploit their own subjects. Thus, the day-to-day approach to state affairs may include attacks upon unarmed civilians, arbitrary imprisonment, and the use of rape and torture in the control of suspected resistance in the populace.

Kleinman realized that medical anthropologists like himself, with a close affiliation to mainstream medical institutions, had previously viewed disease and suffering too exclusively within a medical model. His own work on mental health disorders in China led him to revise conditions previously spoken of as "depression," a psychiatric condition, to a formulation as "social suffering" and "resistance" to the oppression of the Cultural Revolution (1995:141–46). Similarly, the application of the medical model of trauma may have disguised outright political uses of violence to control and redefine resistance as disease. The perspective of "social suffering" renders moral what may previously have been defined as medical.

This section closes with an examination of the contexts and immediate causes of gastrointestinal diseases—diarrhea, dysentery, cholera—in the Great Lakes region of central Africa, specifically among Rwandan refugees in Zaire/Congo, and among citizens in Burundi caught up in the low-grade civil war between armies, and between armies and civilians. The obvious implication for medical anthropology, and anyone who will listen, is that while there may be a medical cause to cholera, it is the social condition of war and dislocation that offer the contextual causes of the epidemics and deaths.

On Determinism, Prediction, and the Openness of History

As we have discussed demographic and epidemological patterns, it may appear that we are dealing with "fixed forms" that determine population trends. The process that has been called the "demographic transition" reveals a relatively persistent historical form of fertility and mortality rates that tempts one to project this model on all current and future cases of the transition.

We need to be very careful, as social scientists with a theory of culture, not to read into these patterns the force of laws. While medical anthropology can benefit from the comparative study of disease patterns and population trends, and while there may well be similarities between the cases, we need to be constantly on the lookout for surprising departures from the received historical patterns, or exceptions to the rule. The demographic transition in England required about 150 years from beginning to end. In Southeast Asia it appears to be taking less than half that time. It had appeared that economic development was the basis of the second part of the transition, the decline of fertility. Now, countries such as Bangladesh have shown that fertility may decline because of the enhancement of women's control over their destinies, without extensive industrialization.

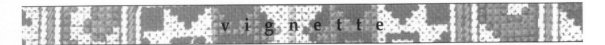

The Meaning of Cholera in the Aftermath of Civil War and Genocide

Epidemics of cholera often break out in the wake of war or intense social chaos or natural disaster. Cholera is the most virulent of a range of intestinal disorders. It is a contagious disease of large and crowded concentrations of people who lack appropriate sewage disposal facilities and whose drinking water is not safe. The bacilli that carry cholera are spread from exposed human feces by way of hand or unclean water to the mouth and ingested. Within a short time severe stomach cramps occur accompanied by violent diarrhea which produces bloody and watery stools. The infected sufferer loses most bodily fluid and, unless rehydrated, may die of dehydration within 24 to 36 hours.

A planned genocide of all Rwandan Tutsi and enemies of the old regime was unleashed after

Photo 4.2 *Rwandan refugees in a camp southwest of Bukavu, Congo, late 1994. This was one of dozens of refugee camps that dotted the landscape in the Kivu region of eastern Congo from mid-1994 until late 1997. Although all camps were under the auspices of the United Nations High Commission for Refugees which coordinated the work of other nongovernmental relief agencies, these camps were sources of continued massacres, disease, and unrest.*
SOURCE: Courtesy of Joyce Martens.

President Juvenal Habyarimana's plane was shot down over Kigali on April 4, 1994, probably by his own hardline "Hutu Power" backers who were opposed to his signing of the Arusha Accords with the Tutsi-dominated opposition Rwandan Patriotic Front (RPF). After the downing of the plane and the unleashing of nationwide massacres by Hutu militia, the RPF launched a conquest of the country to rescue their fellows and to defeat the militia and the army who were in the process of killing all Tutsi and other designated enemies. The militia and many old regime operatives and their families, near two million total, fled across the border into Zaire.

Public health epidemiologists from the Centers for Disease Control in Atlanta and the UNHCR tabulated the incidence of deaths in Mugunga from samples of 150 and 125 thousand respectively during the course of the epidemic. The CDC's statistics from July 14 to August 14, 1994, show that the 530 deaths were due to bloody diarrhea (200, 38 percent of all deaths), nonbloody diarrhea (266, 50 percent), trauma (42, 8 percent), and other (22, 4 percent). Had the epidemic continued unabated at that rate, the entire population of Mugunga would have died out in about 10 months (Swerdlow 1994). By the week of October 23–30, 1994, the UNHCR established the mortality causes and rates as: bloody diarrhea (22, 17 percent), nonbloody diarrhea (42, 32 percent), malaria (17, 13 percent), pneumonia (24, 18 percent), and other (21, 16 percent), an overall mortality rate of 5.4 percent per annum (UNHCR 1994). ■

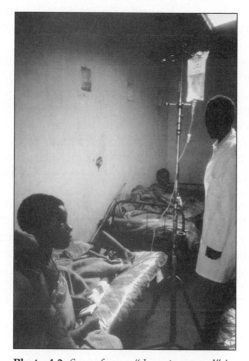

Photo 4.3 *Scene from a "dysentery ward" in Kibimba Hospital, Central Burundi. Low-grade civil war between the Tutsi-controlled army and Hutu-led guerrilla fighters—along the same social lines as the conflict in Rwanda—contributed to the uprooting of many ordinary civilians of both groups. The patients shown here became ill after fleeing their homes and living for some time in forest shelters where sanitary conditions were minimal. They are receiving intervenous glucose rehydration therapy.*
SOURCE: J. M. Janzen.

There is a property to human events that is unlike any other natural phenomenon. The human subject of study and of experience may take notice of the findings, or of the trend that is forecast by past experience, and use that perception as the basis for new action. The very prediction by a scholar may cause the subjects of that prediction to change their behavior and cause the prediction to not be fulfilled. Philosophers of science now suggest that most of scientific observation is like this. It is surely true in the arenas of disease and population. Karl Popper made this fundamental observation years ago in his writing *The Poverty of Historicism* (1964). There he faulted Greek philosopher Plato's *Republic* and some modern theoreticians who believed they could formulate laws of history—"historicists"—and foretell the shape of human society to come on the basis of what had occurred in the past.

Thus, just as the fertility decline and increased food production proved Malthus's dire warnings of future famine to be wrong, so the women of Bangladesh demonstrated that even the demographic transition does not have a "predictable" timetable necessarily "caused" by rising wealth. Caldwell's argument, based on Popper, is that fertility may be "talked down" by research reports, women's movements, and conferences as they gain the ear of national elites and policy-making groups.[1] Medical anthropologists are especially advised to take to heart this caution about prediction and overly tight deterministic models.

A final vignette drives home the lesson of history's surprises. No one, demographer, social scientist, nor politician, was aware that the collapse of the Soviet empire would be accompanied by a huge demographic earthquake. This story situates one community in the larger picture of the collapse, until ethnographies and histories tell the whole story.

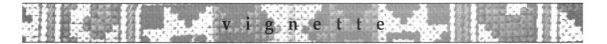

v i g n e t t e

Births on the Baltic, or Overcoming Collapsed Fertility and Rising Mortality Rates of the Post-Soviet Era

Nicholas Eberstadt (1981), a population researcher long interested in the beginning of fertility decline in the developing world, noted that a year or two after the 1989 opening of the Berlin Wall and the subsequent collapse of the Soviet empire there had been a dramatic decline in births in the entire former Soviet realm and that death rates were rising as well. As he wrote in 1994b, "statistics from official agencies not just in Russia but in Eastern Europe paint a portrait of a vast and diverse region seized by a common convulsion. From Leipzig to Vladivostok, birth and marriage rates are plummeting and death rates are soaring. No one—East or West—predicted such violent tremors. Yet these trends are no statistical fluke . . . sudden, precipitous changes in the birth and death rates are compelling indicators of societies in extreme distress—societies unable to cope with health problems that were once routine. From 1989 to the first half of 1993, according to official data, the birthrate fell more than 20 percent in Poland, around 25 percent in Bulgaria, 30 percent in Estonia and Romania, 35 percent in Russia, and more than 60 percent in eastern Germany." Most disturbing were the rising mortality rates for all ages, including infants, an indication of falling supports of health care and standards of living.

In the former East Germany fertility rates declined precipitously after the 1989 opening of the border from the 1988 rate of 12.9 births per 1,000 population to 5.1 per 1,000 in 1993 which, had it continued, would have meant an average of less than one birth per woman per lifetime. Marriage rates also fell in East Germany from 8.2 per 1,000 in 1988 to 3.1 per 1,000 in 1992. Death rates also rose, as they had elsewhere in East bloc countries, for the entire population. Eberstadt noted that in the past, such abrupt shocks have been observed in

industrial societies only in wartime. He suggested that they indicate a society enduring profound uncertainty and anxiety, and severe reductions in material well-being, despite an improving economy (Eberstadt 1994a; 1994b; 1994c).

Photo 4.4 *An ornate 18th-century baroque cherub looks down on the baptismal font in the Lutheran parish church of Rerik on the Baltic Sea coast of northern Germany.*
SOURCE: J. M. Janzen

continued

continued from previous page

At least in eastern Germany, in the small towns along the Baltic seacoast, the trend had begun to reverse by 1995. Uncertain over the future and anxious over work and pay, most couples put off having children. Now, although there is still high unemployment, the reunification of Germany has been completed and new jobs are beginning to appear. The mixed agriculture and tourist business has normalized; nearby Rostock, which has seen some social unrest, is beginning to reconfigure in the new national economy. In Kühlungsborn, a small resort town west of Rostock, where there had been an average of 35 births per year before the 1989 change of government, there were only 5 births per year from 1990 to 1994. Teachers and administrators in local schools were beginning to be concerned with how this populational slump over several years would affect the schools as it worked its way through the system, and whether teachers would need to be laid off (Lassen 1996; Janzen 1996).

By 1995 the number of births on the Baltic coast had begun to rebound, as evidenced by the volume of child baptisms in the Lutheran parishes such as Rerik, where an ornate Baroque cherub looks down on the baptismal font, where here, in October 1995, Jörg and Christine Balssuweit baptized their daughter Marie Sophie.[2] ■

Photo 4.5 *In October 1995, Jörg (left) and his wife Christine Balssuweit pose with their families for a photograph at the baptism of their daughter Marie Sophie, who is wearing a new gown sewn by her mother. The Balssuweits were married just before the 1989 "fall of the wall" and change in East German governments. Due to uncertainty over their economic future they put off starting their family until 1995.*
SOURCE: J. M. Janzen.

CONCLUSION

A central argument of chapters 3 and 4 has been that all indicators of health—life standards, goals of healing, medical traditions, definitions and measures of disease—are themselves cultural constructs and therefore tend to vary from era to era and civilization to civilization. The perspective of medical anthropology which looks at human phenomena through the prism of culture is perhaps easier for the Western student to see with regard to classical Chinese or African medicine than to biomedicine which is grounded in science. Yet precisely here it is important to bring this cultural view of health and disease to the fore, because it translates into the insight that our ideas of nature are culturally formulated. Our relationship with the environment, as a species, is culturally varying and historically particular. Thus, hunters and gatherers act differently and have a different profile of health and disease than preindustrial city dwellers or postmodern city dwellers. Even the "demographic transition," although seemingly a broad pattern of mortality decline and fertility decline that has been replicated in country after country, reveals variations in its time span and its distribution across social classes within single societies. The illustrations of mortality and fertility patterns since the collapse of the Soviet empire indicate that even in the industrialized world long-term mortality and fertility trends are subject to reversal. The cushion of infrastructure—the social fabric of health—that we enjoy in the modern world is not to be taken for granted; it can come undone. The occurrence of civil war, just as the end of empire, can cause broad and pervasive social suffering. Medical anthropology looks at health and disease through the mediation of culture and human experience. Any prediction or patterned regularity can be bent because we humans are thinking, symbol-using creatures, just as much as we are creatures of flesh, blood, and instinct.

These two chapters have explored the broad outlines of health traditions and disease patterns. We turn next to the very particular expressions of the individual life course within the shaping influences of culture and the material forces of birth, living, and dying.

REVIEW QUESTIONS

1. What are the factors that have led to the "modern rise of population" as shown in Figure 4.1?

2. What are the distinctive "health profiles" (in terms of relative birth and death rates, and common disease types) of human societies in the historical/evolutionary phases of hunting and gathering, early food cultivation, preindustrial cities and empires, early industrialization of England, Germany, France, and advanced industrial society?

3. Identify the conditions underlying the outbreak of the 1994 cholera epidemic among Rwandan refugees in

Mugunga camp, Zaire. Do you think such an epidemic could occur in the industrial societies of the Northern Hemisphere? Why or why not?

4. Use the following indicators to describe the "demographic transition" in two national societies of your choosing.

Mortality rates/1000 population

Morbidity rates/1,000 population

Birthrates/1,000 population

Infant mortality rates/1,000 born/year

Characterize diseases in these societies before and after the transition. What factors may affect a society's relatively rapid or slow passage through the transition? What would be the consequences in terms of population growth of the quick and slow transitions?

5. What is your opinion concerning why couples (or women) begin to reduce their fertility in the second phase of the demographic transition? Do you lean more toward the "pessimist" or the "optimist" point of view with regard to the long-term human quality of life and adequacy of food for all (or most)? Why?

6. The decline of fertility is an important feature of the second phase of the demographic transition. What are the key factors cited by Caldwell and his colleagues for the decline? Why does Caldwell not include wealth or socioeconomic status as a key factor in the transition? Do you agree with the Caldwell school of thinking? Why or why not?

7. Is suffering, as presented in the section on "social suffering," more pervasive than a century or two ago? Even if you think it is not more pervasive, why is it important to see epidemics and the consequences of war in more than simply medical terms?

8. What does the material given in this chapter, and the very nature of the subject matter of this chapter, teach us about the social and human sciences as predictive, exact sciences? Is it appropriate to draw predictive models from some cases of the demographic transition in order to apply them to other cases? What are the pitfalls in such an exercise?

NOTES

1. Unfortunately, governments may look at the Bangladesh case and conclude that they can justify withdrawal of funding from family planning programs because of the evidence that fertility can be affected without massive economic expenditure.

2. This story was pieced together by the author who with Mrs. Janzen visited Kühlungsborn in late 1995 to see their daughter Marike, a Fulbright teacher in the local high school. Later correspondence with individuals in Kühlungsborn filled in the details.

THE LIFECOURSE:
BIRTHING, LIVING, AND DYING

chapter

5

Photo 5.1 *"The Stages of Humanity" (Die Stufenjahre des Menschen), German popular print. Captions for each step read: "At five a child, at ten a boy, at twenty a youth, at thirty a man, at forty well-to-do, at fifty stands tall, at sixty old age begins, at seventy an elder, at eighty snow white, at ninety children mock you, at a hundred grace with God." (Below, left to right) "A child with cradle," "to baptism in a carriage," and "to the grave." Color etching by A. Leitner, Vienna, n.d.*
Source: Wellcome Library, London.

115

Our lives are a series of births and deaths; we die to one period and must be born to another. . . I must never lose sight of those other deaths which precede the final physical death, the deaths over which we have some freedom, the death of self-will, self-indulgence, self-deception, all those self-devices which, instead of making us more fully alive, make us less.
    Madeleine L' Engle, *The Summer of the Great-Grandmother*

THE LIFECOURSE PERSPECTIVE

Although the human lifecourse is not a medical topic in a narrow sense—living is not usually considered an illness—the affairs of the course of human life have all kinds of implications for the health of individuals, families, and communities that are appropriate for medical anthropological interest. The individual lifecourse has a biological basis that has to do with conception, birth, growth, maturation, reproduction, physical decline, and death, subjects integral to biological and ecological anthropology. Yet they also need to be viewed through the lens of culture, for many of the social patterns of the lifecourse are culturally defined, having to do with the way particular cultures define childhood, the passage to adulthood, marriage and reproduction, work, families, property, benefits, status, and finally old age and death. The emphasis or de-emphasis on each stage, or even whether the stage is recognized or not, and the timing with which they are observed are matters that, while having a biological dimension, are shaped by culture. This chapter thus logically follows Chapter 4 which looked at how the circumstances of birthrates and death rates affect a population as a whole. It will be followed by Chapter 6 which examines issues that shape personhood and identity across the lifecourse. Special attention is directed there to crises and moments of trauma, ambiguous statuses, and exceptional or adverse health conditions, and to the ethical issues that arise from such circumstances.

The human **lifecourse** as used in this chapter refers primarily to the life of an individual, not in isolation but as defined by society's patterns regarding the rhythms of life for male and female, the constraints and the opportunities. **Life cycle** and **life span** have also been used for these realities, each placing emphasis on a somewhat different understanding of the nature of time inherent in the human life. All three terms may be used in connection with the cycle of a family or a household, a group of individuals related by common social bonds, perhaps by marriage and birth, and by household economic organization.

While use of the term *lifecourse* has been current for only several decades, the focus on time in the life of the individual and in social institutions is well known to anthropology. Early in the 20th century, one way anthropologists looked at the life of the individual in society was in the way special transitions were recognized. Such transitions between life's stages and statuses were called **rites of passage,** a phrase coined by Belgian-French anthropologist Arnold Van Gennep (1908), and which entered common vocabulary in many Western languages. The study of **ritualization,** seen as the use of special symbols and metaphors of these moments of passage—such as "death and rebirth" for all kinds of renewal mentioned by L'Engle—would become a major preoccupation for anthropologists. Household and family cycles were studied to see how the beginnings, crisis points, and transitions were handled in domestic social units (Fortes 1984; Hammel 1984). The question of why certain passages and kinds of circumstances were ritualized yielded much good insight of use to medical anthropologists concerned with the cultural construction of illness. The study of rituals of transition and crisis clearly revealed a society's central values and concepts, as well as its contradictions.

Other disciplines contributed their interests to the development of the lifecourse perspective. Psychology was especially interested in the individual's development. Since Sigmund Freud's interest earlier in the 20th century in the formative influences of childhood in shaping an individual's character, many social and psychological scientists and practitioners studied the ways that society shapes the individual. What was called **human development** grew up around this interest in the lifelong impressions made upon the individual in infancy. Erik Erikson's *Childhood and Society* (1963), for example, sketched the stages of human growth from infancy to death.

In the 1960s a new awareness arose of the growing number of elderly in American and other industrial societies. This new field came to be known as **gerontology.** The elderly were becoming a more powerful political bloc in these societies as well. Much research was done on aging and the elderly, the nature of aging as a biological and a social process, and the search for ways in which these elderly could carry on an unencumbered, useful, and interesting life. One of the now obvious discoveries of this attention on aging and the aged was that all of life was part of aging, as Matilda White Riley explained in her book *Aging from Birth to Death* (1979). There is no single time when one becomes "old"; rather, society's definitions decree that 45 is "middle-aged," or that 65 is old. At the turn of the 21st century many of the social barriers of the elderly are falling, leading to the emergence of the "young old" category in which many individuals in their 60s, 70s, and 80s live independent lives (*New York Times,* "The Age Boom." March 9, 1997).

As the "elderly" became increasingly recognized as just another social category, comparable to "middle-aged" with its "midlife crises," "adolescence" with its distinctive characteristics and needs, childhood and infancy and the special features of this group, the lifecourse perspective (Baltes 1978; Baltes and Brim 1979, 1980) became the umbrella for the many projects and special interests that could be identified as processes in the course of human life. At the turn of the millennium lifecourse institutes, or life span studies, are common.

LIFECOURSE AS SUBJECTIVE EXPERIENCE AND OBJECTIVE REALITY

Everyone has a lifecourse and is involved in the lifecourse of some other individuals. The lifecourse as a human reality and as a focus of study is both subjective experience and objective reality. Time in human life and society is both a very real subjective experience (e.g., looking in the mirror and seeing the first gray hair), as well as an abstraction "out there" to be looked at objectively by studying the general phenomenon of the development of individuals' lives.

Each of us is a self, with a body and an identity. The physiological entity of this self goes through the relentless phases of conception, in utero growth, birth, and then more growth, continuing through recognizable stages: maturing, social responsibility, most likely mating, reproduction and parenting; letting go of children, more responsibility; if we are fortunate, we experience long health and life; if we are less fortunate, chronic disability and perhaps degenerative disease. We all eventually experience death.

The self-conscious identity of each of us is not distinct from our bodies, although that is a heavily culturalized perspective. Just as the body is shaped by our parents' genetic makeup and the nutrients of the surrounding earth, so our conscious self is formed by the mirror-imaged effect of others around us. The self is a child with parents; at some point the self may also become a parent with child. The self that is born is a grandchild, and in due course may become a grandparent; or brother or sister vis-à-vis brother or sister, niece or nephew vis-à-vis uncle and aunt and, similarly, all of the reciprocal ties of human society. The self is a male or female mate vis-à-vis a partner who is the opposite or same gender, with profound consequences for the unfolding of other selves. Toward each of these others the self has rights and obligations, defined often by age or position in society. Every self has multiple others, and is a multiple other in the lifecourse, a condition anthropologists have called the "fractal self."

The reciprocal definition of self and other, subject and object, continues in other kinds of trajectories in the lifecourse. Becoming ill as defined by society evokes a response from others, the definition of the sufferer as sick or marginalized, and the support and care for that sufferer. Chronic illness evokes other responses that sometimes brings family, specialists, or fellow sufferers into close range on a permanent care or mutual support basis. Chronic illness commonly brings with it a major redefinition of self, and this redefinition is usually strongly mirrored in those who are fellow sufferers. (This topic will be taken up more fully in Chapter 6.)

Illness is by no means the only moment of significance that defines the self in relation to the lifecourse. Indeed, most of the time other life events are more defining, that is, they are recognized socially. Launching and achieving a career, coming out as gay, marrying, changing work, moving residence, migrating, deciding to retire—these are points that change the relationship between a subjective self and an objective relationship. Sometimes the moments that bring on a changed definition of self toward others happen quite suddenly, and have far-reaching consequences. Birth and death are the most transforming. Birth represents nothing less than the appearance of a new person and the creation of new relationships. Death is more complex, as a subjective and objective experience. While the deceased may disappear physically, the social person lives on, with the same relationships as before. But the transformed quality of the relationships is such that a death profoundly affects those with relationships to the deceased. Shock, grieving, memory creating, and commemorative anniversaries become the stuff of the relationships. All societies build rituals of these transforming moments in relationships, not just because of the changes that are involved, but because of the emotions that must be expressed. These subjective and objective dimensions of the lifecourse surrounding birth are mirrored on the following pages in the vignette "From the Third Person to the First." Betty Cook, an anthropologist, described the transformations that accompanied the birth of her daughter Emma, Betty and her husband David's first child. Although she remained a "student of birthing," her perspective was vastly enhanced as she also became a "birthing wife and mother."

POINTS OF RECOGNITION ALONG THE LIFECOURSE

Anthropologists have discovered a more nuanced picture of the lifecourse than that formulated by the poet T. S. Eliot in *Sweeney Agonistes* (1932) that "Birth, copulation, and death, that's all the facts when you come to brass tacks; birth, and copulation, and death." Anthropologists have sought to establish which points of change across the lifecourse are very widespread and how they are observed in varying cultures around the world. In his book *The Human Cycle* (1983), Colin Turnbull, long-time student of the Mbuti pygmies of central Africa, compared the lifecourse among these hunter-gatherers with other societies of the world. Trying to bridge the gulf between small-scale forest dwellers and the inhabitants of the industrial West and other societies, often using his own autobiography as evidence, Turnbull saw the stages of life shared by all as childhood, the art of becoming; adolescence, the art of transformation; youth, the art of reason; adulthood, the art of doing; old age, the art of being. An individual in both societies needed to pass successfully through each of these stages to accomplish the "art of living."

". . . One man in his time plays many parts," were the words from Shakespeare's *As You Like It* which Martha and Morton Fried used to refer to the stages of the lifecourse in the opening of their book *Transitions: Four Rituals in Eight Cultures* (1980). First, "the infant, mewing and puking in

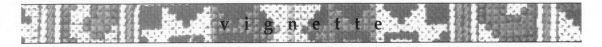

v i g n e t t e

From the Third Person to the First

I didn't believe what the test stick told me. I looked at it very closely. It still read positive. The directions on the box, which I had read at least three times, confirmed my rudimentary lab technique. I showed my husband David. "You're pregnant, honey," he said. He had such faith in take-home technology. I felt a funny dread start up my spine. I was pregnant? At that moment, I changed completely, from an anthropologist who studied birth to an anthropologist who would give birth. It was the distance, fairly large, from the library to the cold metal tables of gynecology and obstetrics. I wasn't totally sure I wanted to place my child and myself into those hands, but I was very sure I was not going to be able to simply read my way through labor. I would need assistance. That is, assuming I was really pregnant. Fearing the take-home technology had failed me, I went to my nurse-practitioner for confirmation through sonogram.

As I moved down and placed my knees in the knee stirrups, I was once again reminded of the many things in the room that signaled that this was a medical event. The light had been dimmed for a better view of the sonogram screen, therefore giving the room the hushed feel of a church. There were latex gloves, cleaning fluids, a sink, a standing lamp, and a woman in a white coat looking between my legs. She used a form of sonogram called a vaginal probe, which is placed in the vagina and sends its sound waves through the cervix, rather than through the abdomen. "There it is," she said, "I see fetal heart tones, so you're about seven weeks."

She turned the screen toward David and me. We saw a series of black-and-white lines. In the middle was a black smudge barely 4 centimeters long (see Photo 5.2). Part of the smudge flickered back and forth. I was watching my child's heartbeat. David and I looked in awe. In unison we both responded with a breathless "Wow!" We were completely mesmerized.

Neither one of us noticed that I was on my back, with a piece of technology in my vagina and a medical technician in a white coat showing us the previously hidden and private world of our developing child. We watched our daughter like we watched a particularly good special effect in a movie. Like the true video children we were, we only believed I was pregnant when we saw it on TV. The subjective experience of a lack of menstruation and enlarged breasts was now objective. The entire experience was very disturbing. I remembered what I had read in Brigitte Jordan's *Birth in Four Cultures* and Robbie Davis-Floyd's *Birth as an American Rite of Passage*. I did not want a hospital birth. It was most assuredly because of the writing of these two women that I searched for, and found, a midwife to assist me in a home birth. If other women could birth at home, so could I.

A friend of mine had a friend who had a home birth. When I finally met Brenda, my midwife, she told me almost all of her referrals are from word-of-mouth. It seems that midwifery was illegal in Missouri and had an ambiguous status in Kansas. Pending when I found her was a lawsuit, expected to go to the Supreme Court, testing the legality of midwifery in Kansas. She explained that I wasn't breaking the law by birthing at home. This was legal in all 50 states. It was of ambiguous status as to whether she could help me without being charged with practicing either medicine or nursing without a license. What was really ambiguous here was whether this was a medical, or a natural, or a family, event. As a scholar I could clearly see the lines that we attempted to draw between what was culturally a part of Western biomedicine and what was not. I could also see the attempt, by many levels of individuals, to control this event. As a woman attempting to birth the way I wanted, I simply felt oppressed. What I was doing was profoundly political.

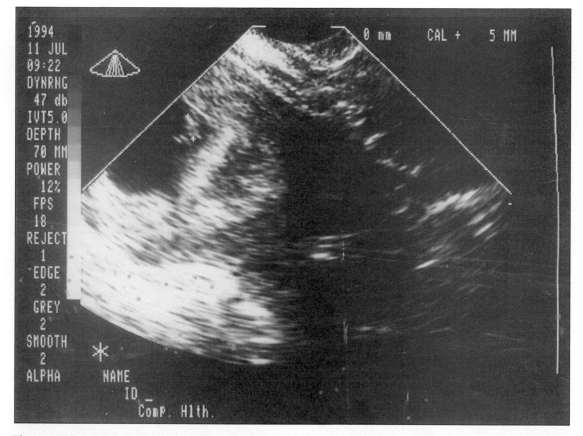

Photo 5.2 *Sonogram of a seven-week fetus. See the small "+" mark in the black cavity in the upper left of the scan.*
Source: Courtesy of Betty Cook.

The birth itself began with my daughter tearing the bag of waters that surrounded her at approximately 12:00 P.M. on a Saturday night. The next 30 minutes or so were spent with David and me attempting to determine whether this was, indeed, amniotic fluid. As it continued to flow, however, I determined that it was, and our wait for "real" labor began. By 6:00 A.M. Sunday morning I began having regular contractions. At 12:00 noon the same day everyone who was to accompany me on my 36-hour journey to motherhood had arrived. They were: my mother, my husband, my midwife, and her apprentice. While my contractions were still relatively low intensity, we began the search for a videographer. We had waffled back and forth about whether we wanted the technology to interfere with the birth process, and were still ambivalent as I went into labor. Finally, it was agreed that the apprentice's husband would do this for us. His participation served a dual purpose. He had never seen what his wife was learning to do. My birth would allow him to understand what she was doing when she was gone those long hours. I had always liked the idea that while I was reproducing a human being, I was also helping to reproduce another midwife by helping to train Brenda's apprentice.

continued

continued from previous page

By Sunday evening I was in "serious" labor. I had been awake for nearly 24 hours, and I felt most of the labor pain in my back, though I was not really having "back" labor. "Breathing through" my contractions was much more difficult than I had thought it would be. In fact, labor was much harder than I thought it would be. I began to wonder why in the world I had wanted to do this without medication, although I never had a second thought about birthing at home. At one point I looked at the digital clock in my bedroom and could not discern whether it was 5:00 in the morning or at night. My midwife continued to try to help me walk, and she gave me herbs to help my contractions come stronger and closer together—in short, to stimulate labor. Finally, at 1:00 P.M. on Monday afternoon I was told I could push. What followed was a comedy of errors. I attempted to find any and all positions in which to push. I tried to make a "C" by pushing on my side. I tried the toilet. Finally I birthed the way women have birthed all over the world since time began—I squatted beside my bed, supported on one side by David, and by my videographer on the other. At 6:00 P.M. on Monday night, I screamed, grunted and pushed my daughter into my midwife's hands.

I had birthed in a similar way to most other women in the world. Within my own culture, however, I was part of only two percent of women nationwide. I had birthed without medical intervention or a hospital. I had also moved from understanding this process from speaking in terms of "she" to speaking in terms of "I." I had moved from the third person to the first person. As I watched my husband cut the umbilical cord, a common ritual in home birth, I was struck by the intimacy of what we had created. I completely understood why anthropological researchers might be excluded from studying another person's birth. It would have felt odd to have had anyone observing this

event. Simply by being part of birth as a researcher, I was involved in an intimate family moment. I will always remember this as I continue my work in studying women and birth. I will also always remember David, Emma, and myself falling asleep together in bed in our home after she was born. I was sure in the fact that no nurses, doctors, lab technicians, or family members were going to come through our bedroom door in the next few hours. That time was ours as a family, alone.[1] ■

Photo 5.3 *Betty Cook, her husband David, and daughter Emma.*
SOURCE: Courtesy of Betty Cook.

the nurse's arms," followed by "the whining schoolboy," who will turn into "the lover, sighing like a furnace"; becoming a soldier, "bearded like the bard [poet]." Then comes the justice, "in fair round belly with good capon lined"; the sixth age is one of shrunk shank, and a voice "turning again to childish treble." It all ends in second childhood, slipping into oblivion "sans [without] teeth, sans eyes, sans taste, sans everything" (1980: 13). Casting about for the most diverse of societies in which to explore the basic phases of the life course, the Frieds looked at the !Kung hunter-gatherers of Namibia and Botswana, the Muslim Hausa of northern Nigeria, the Chinese of Taiwan, the Pacific island society of the Tikopia, the Tlingit Indians of Alaska, and three socialist societies: the then Soviet Union, Cuba, and the People's Republic of China. Despite the extreme range of societies, the common stages and transitions between them that all observed were birth, puberty/adolescence, marriage, and death.

It is an article of faith of the anthropological perspective of the lifecourse that the biological or physiological fact of birth, maturation, reproduction, aging, and death are recognized and patterned distinctively in each human society. "Aging" itself is culturally constructed by many innuendos and attributes given it (Backett and Davison 1995). Not everywhere is it associated with the end of productivity (retirement), loss of authority (senility), or isolation, as it tends to be in the West. The pronounced disjuncture between physiological events and their sociocultural recognition leads anthropologists to proceed with a cautious comparison of the general picture, looking as much for contrasting as similar cases (Mageo 1995), as is illustrated in the following cases.

Biological birth occurs everywhere in human society. But the recognition of social personhood in the timetable for naming and social membership is remarkably varied. In North American society parents are expected to have names ready for a newborn infant upon delivery, and these names—first, middle, and surname—are inscribed in the birth register of the hospital or clinic and transferred to the nearest state record-keeping office. The newly born individual is considered to be a social individual at birth, a member of his or her family, and a citizen of the nation. This may seem "natural" to most North Americans, but the timing of all this, and the collective bodies into which the new person is assigned membership, are quite unique procedures.

In other times and places, there was no nation-state to keep account of its members by birth, or, as in ancient Athens, some individuals became citizens whereas others did not. In !Kung bands of the Kalahari Desert, as in other hunting and gathering societies studied by anthropologists, those offspring who came too close in age to their next older siblings were killed by adults other than the parents in the band before the parents were able to give them a name. Physiologically born, they were denied social personhood.

The distinction between, and the relationship of physical growth to social maturation, is nowhere more evident than in the dual process the

Frieds called puberty/adolescence, the first being the physical process, the second the social process. The two are everywhere juxtaposed in some way, but their synchronization varies from society to society. In Western society physical maturation is often accompanied by a turbulent social "coming of age," filled with many informal stages some of which recognize the changing obligations and opportunities of the individual. However, in other traditional societies which have had a chance to formalize social patterns over many generations, the transitions to social adulthood may be more clearly articulated in uniform initiations for boys and girls in which all participate under the direction of authorities, followed more or less directly by entry into social adulthood. Some of the physical signs that demarcate these passages include circumcision, tattoos, or shaving of hair. These temporary or permanent markings may, however, come very early or very late in relation to the physiological changes of puberty. Thus, the transition to social adulthood is timed differently from society to society.

The point of change brought on by mating and reproduction is also recognized by most societies as a physiological transition that corresponds to the entry into that important social role of parenthood. Marriage is in many societies a legitimation of children born to the union of a man and a woman, as much as it is a formal recognition of their sexual rights to one another. However, sexual activity is per se not often given formal social recognition unless the couple and their families are in consent with the union. In today's society a great diversity of social forms exists to acknowledge the identity of a child and the pedigree of the child's parentage.

Death is everywhere a climactic finale to the dual passage of the physiological and cultural lifecourse. Here, too, the cultural timing of transition is carefully coded, in keeping with notions of personhood, and may or may not coincide strictly with biological death. The very notion of biological death is so culturally constructed that modern medicine itself does not have a "natural" definition, but must depend on a carefully constructed working definition that has physiological, legal, social, and religious parameters. In Kongo society, wailing often begins when family members believe that an individual will die, thus already beginning the death ritual. In political structures of sacred kingship, the physical death of the king may not be announced for a while, and a pretense of continuing life is maintained until the king's handlers are ready to deal with the public and political aspects of the transition of power, which they see as a very dangerous time.

As will be shown in Chapter 6, the concept of the person often determines the notion of life's beginning and life's end, as well as the boundaries that articulate one person from another and spell out the terms of relations between them.

Other thematic motifs and patterns that reflect a society's dominant values may be evident in points of transition across the lifecourse. These are often the same cues that are picked up to think about and socially define sickness, although it is important to separate them conceptually in

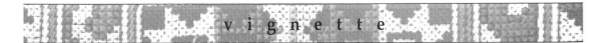

v i g n e t t e

The Lifecourse of Cornelius and Helena Voth of Central Kansas

When the Voth family migrated from southern Russia to the prairies of central Kansas in 1874, Cornelius was 49 and Helena 45. Their nine children (two were stillborn or died at birth) ranged in age from infancy to 19. The Voths and many others in the Kansas group benefited greatly from homestead provisions and reasonable land purchases through the Santa Fe Railroad which had arranged their journey. They were part of a Mennonite migration of 18,000 to Kansas, Nebraska, and South Dakota and Manitoba and Saskatchewan in Canada. In each area they were surrounded by many thousands of other immigrants from Europe and the eastern and midwestern United States who were part of the expanding American frontier. Although they were members of the large Alexanderwohl Mennonite congregation that came as a unit to the prairies of Kansas, the Voth family

Photo 5.4 *The family of Cornelius and Helena Richert Voth (center, front row), 1885, eleven years after their migration to Kansas from the Ukraine.*
SOURCE: Courtesy of Mennonite Library and Archives, Bethel College, North Newton, Kansas.

continued

continued from previous page

approached the transitions and crises in their lifecourse with self-reliance, a great deal of mutual assistance, good sense, and faith.

Cornelius and Helena Voth were able to nearly double their land acreage in Kansas from what they had owned and farmed in the Ukraine, thanks to the sale of their farm in the Ukraine and to good land prices in Kansas. They further mortgaged some of the land they bought in order to expand their holdings in the years when their children were growing up and able to work for their parents, marry, and establish their own households. The Voths paid off their debts by the time Cornelius was 66 and Helena 62. Their youngest daughter, Suzanne, lived with them at home through that time. As her marriage approached, the family discussed financial and land arrangements, as well as the children's role in caring for their aging parents. When Suzanne married, daughter Helena and her husband Peter P. Schmidt sold their farm in Oklahoma and moved in with the parents. At the same time the parents began to build a retirement home nearby. The Voths helped their children, but always in equitable terms. If one received land, all others (sons and daughters) received an equivalent sum of money. This strict version of "partible inheritance," along with neolocal household residence of the small nuclear family, constituted important features of the social structure in this Mennonite tradition.[2]

A consistent application of these rules of inheritance, even though some of the children experienced financial problems, permitted the Voths to continue as a close family, offering each other considerable mutual help, especially in times of sickness and disaster. For example, when son Henry's wife died in Arizona, his children returned to Kansas to live with the grandparents and other relatives for a while. When son Johannes, still unmarried but living on his own farm, experienced a terrible tooth abscess which was "lanced inside and out," his mother, sisters, and brothers-in-law took turns caring for him and his farm.

The second photograph of the Voth family was taken about the time of their "Golden Wedding," or 50th anniversary, in 1905. This was an important marker of their successful marriage, family, and effective financial management. Two years before this anniversary, the elder Voths moved to the little house on the farm. Helena died in 1909, Cornelius in 1912. The Voth family cycle represented the typical pattern of family support for one another and for the elderly before the advent of retirement homes. In their community, the Bethesda Home for the elderly and indigent was founded in 1906 for those who lacked adequate family support.[3] By 1960 in this community, most elderly unable to care for themselves lived in such retirement centers rather than with their children. ■

---

medical anthropology. For neither birth, puberty/adolescence, marriage, growing old, nor death are enhanced by defining them as a kind of sickness, to be medicalized and somehow "cured." They are normal experiences that indeed demarcate the "art of living."

The stages of life of individuals and the transitions between them are eminently socialized and socially recognized. They are never merely acts of autonomous individuals. To some degree in all societies the individual moves through preexisting social roles and institutions, fulfilling society's expectations for an individual or individuals of that age and gender set. The subjective lives of individuals become interlocked lifecourses, demonstrating their objective character within society's order, which itself may change in a rhythm still different than individual lives. This interlinked life

Photo 5.5 *Cornelius and Helena Voth (front row, third and fourth from left) at their 50th wedding anniversary in 1903, with grown children and children-in-law. He was 75 and she 71 years old. The family includes farmers, a banker and businessman, ministers and teachers, a part-time jeweler, and a missionary-ethnologist. The support of these children was crucial in the parents' retirement. He lived to be 84, she 77.*
Source: Courtesy of Mennonite Library and Archives, Bethel College, North Newton, Kansas.

of individuals within society is shown in the vignette of the Voth family of late 19th-century Kansas.

Time, Identity, and the Ritualization of Passage

Anthropologists have been particularly interested in the moments of transition in the lifecourse, as recognized and commemorated by society—Arnold Van Gennep's "rites of passage" (1908). Here, amid the celebrations and rituals, the values and implicit understandings of a society are most profoundly revealed. The remarkably similar social markers that identify rites of passage and those that identify sickness require us to lay out here some of the insights anthropologists have learned about **ritualization,** why it happens, and what its effects are in human social life.

Van Gennep suggested that the life of the social person over a lifetime was analogous to an individual walking through a house that had multiple rooms, rooms representing the formalized stages of the individual's life. To get from one room, or stage or social role, to the next, one needed to leave the previous "room," cross the threshold in the door, the "limen," and enter the next "room."

For Van Gennep, each of these passages—at birth, adolescence, adult life and parenting, occupation or career entries, death, and others—are made up of three rites: separation, transition, and reintegration. In the first, the "rite of separation," the individual is separated symbolically from a previous role, status, or place, indeed his previous personhood. A recurring symbol of separation is the veil or shroud, or graduation tassel, facial painting, or other special costumes and markings of initiation, that figuratively renders the ritual subject distant from his or her former peers. Physical separation often accompanies this visual separation. Imagery of death and grief is commonly used at this stage by those who feel separation and loss.

For Van Gennep, the second phase of a rite of passage is the all-important "threshold," the actual passage, during which one is in a kind of no-man's-land, "betwixt and between," or liminal space. Individuals in this part of the **rite of passage** are often neither what they were, nor yet what they will become: They are nonentities or strange figures in limbo. Imagery of this phase often includes role reversals, obscenity, license, and a scrambling of what normal life keeps right. Hazing and sensory deprivation are common at this stage as well. The impact of such symbolic and identity scrambling is to further loosen the individual from comfortable associations of the prior role, and to prepare him or her for entry into the new role. Because of the frequent mixture of unrelated associations in this stage, learning may be heightened, as many initiations suggest. Threshold passage is often traumatic to the social person in transit, because of the disorientation and sense of loss.

Van Gennep called the third stage of the rite of passage a "rite of reintegration." Here the individual in transit returns to society, but now in a new role or status. The veil is lifted, the tassel is moved aside, the white or black of **liminality** is replaced by the color of conventional society.

Some recurring symbols have identified rites of passage in societies around the world. Veils, masks, associations with death and resurrection, going under water (or land) and reemerging, association with color and no color, body painting during the liminal phase, and association with spirits have all commonly been used in rites of passage to "move" the individual from one stage of life to the next. Madeleine L'Engle captured this identification of life's growing edges, change, loss, and renewal, with symbols of passage in her book *The Summer of the Great-Grandmother:*

Our lives are a series of births and deaths; we die to one period and must be born to another. We die to childhood and are born to adolescence. . . to our highschool selves. . . our college selves into the "real" world. . . our unmarried selves and into our married selves. . . If I am to reflect on the eventual death of her [great grandmother's] body, of all bodies, I must never lose sight of those other deaths which precede the final physical death, the deaths over which we have some freedom, the death of self-will, self-indulgence, self-deception, all those self-devices which, instead of making us more fully alive, make us less (L'Engle 1974:52–53).

Rites of passage often grab onto concrete and bodily symbols to depict the changes, the losses, and the new situations because the underlying ideas of time, our origins, our mortality, and our destiny, are abstract and unfathomable, paradoxical, and contradictory. They are filled with emotions difficult to verbalize. Therefore, images of growth and fruition in nature, of peculiar actions in the animal world, the cycles of the seasons and the heavenly bodies, mechanical metaphors such as clocks, lines, and oscillating pendulums, all represent what we feel deeply at a time of change. Rites of passage allow these feelings and permanent changes to be publicly acknowledged and accepted. The permanence of change and perhaps loss is easier to accept if all around us share in it.

At least two contrasting concepts of time are in evidence in life-change rituals: one is linear, the other cyclical. To the first, we assign number sequences such as years; in the second, we emphasize the sameness, the repetitiveness, of our lives, and the lives of our parents and our children and others. Time in these differing forms of embodiment may thus move linearly "forward" (in the straight line of aging chronologically year by year), "backward" (in the return to youthlike appearance or feeling), "cyclically back to the same point" (in the repeated ritual of celebrating spring, the renewal of the world, or divine conquest over human mortality). Anthropologists have rightly noted that the very notions of the lifecourse, life span, and life cycle embody these contrasting senses of time, and therefore are simply yet other cultural constructions with which we make sense of, and try to conceptualize, the mysteries of change (Ostor 1984: 281–302).

It should not surprise us to be told then that religious thoughts and symbols often are statements about the same enigmas of time and life. In the great monotheistic religions of Judaism, Christianity, and Islam, chronological years mark the time since the appearance of the divine in the human: Moses, Christ, Muhammad. Individual identity or personhood, once named and announced, persists for eternity. In Eastern religions there is a stronger sense of the cyclical recurrence of life either in reincarnation or the absorption of individual identity into the "nothingness of Being." Both in their way try to come to terms with the ineffable powers of time and being, as the following vignette shows.

vignette

Representations of Time and Being

The relationship of time to the individual life cycle is often represented in mortuary art, either as a unique named individual, or as generic human being in relation to the prevailing cultural or religious understanding of time. Here such depictions are shown from a European, an African, and an Asian setting. The first is from a ruling family of 16th century Italy (Photo 5.6), the second from a contemporary Kongo peasant

Photo 5.6 *Tomb of Giuliano de' Medici, Medici Chapel, Church of San Lorenzo, Florence, Italy, completed 1534. Sculpture by Renaissance master Michelangelo (1475–1564).*
SOURCE: Alinari/Art Resource NY.

lineage community in central Africa (Photo 5.7), and the third from a mid-20th century Chinese Buddhist community (Photo 5.8).

The depiction from 16th century "Renaissance" Italy is that of the tomb of Giuliano de Medici, the "Duke of Medici," in the family chapel of the Church of San Lorenzo, in Florence, Italy. The sculpture, by Italian Renaissance master Michelangelo, carries an identifying text that reads *Il tempo che consuma tutto*—Time that consumes all. This elaborate tomb sculpture renders an allegorical depic-tion of Night (left, female) and Day (right, male) to illustrate the power of time. Night is accompanied by her symbols: a star and crescent moon on her tiara; poppies which induce sleep; and an owl under the arch of her leg. The huge mask at her back may allude to Death, since Sleep and Death were said to be the children of Night. According to Michelangelo's notes, "Day and Night speak, and say, 'we have with our swift course brought about the death of Duke Guiliano De Medici'" (Hartt 1969: 488–89). Even the mighty Duke of Medici depicted in his prime could not overcome the power of time and change. Although the mighty duke is depicted as a realistic full scale portrait, he is still subjugated to the powers of nature, of mortality. Yet, in typical western form, his memory lives on as an individual.

In Central Africa, the individual lifecourse is also identified with the course of the sun. The tombs in the north Kongo region (Photo 5.7) are decorated with the half cross-like "life of the person" symbol that is an analogy of the "course of the sun around the earth." Two show the half-circle of the sunrise (birth), noon (adulthood), sunset (death) of the sun/person; others show the entire cycle that adds midnight (being ancestor). Cement trees and sculpted portraits in the nearest tombs are meant to depict the life of the ancestors that is similar to life of the living.

Photo 5.7 *Tombs sculpted of cement, near Sundi Mamba, north of Luozi, in the Manianga, Lower Congo, Democratic Republic of Congo.*
SOURCE: J. M. Janzen.

The cemetery is itself on an old village site near the village of the living (*in background right*), suggesting a cycle of life shared by the living and the dead. Although individuals are named, and remembered in their lineages, they are thought in the course of time to become submerged with the light of the sun, and part of a collective spirit. Although there is individuality in naming and genealogy reckoning, time moves like a vast spiral as individuals are lost from memory to merge with the spirit world, and as new individuals are born.

The Chinese Buddhist *Samsara,* or the "wheel of rebirth," introduces the idea of multiple rebirths or reincarnations into the world. All life is eternal, but its contemporary manifestation may take any number of forms, as Photo 5.8 depicts. According to Li Jian (Personal communications, September 1999), the King of the "wheel of rebirth" palace (*upper right*) documents every act of every living being, in particular humans. Individuals (*left*) enter the "wheel of rebirth" where the shape and type of being of their next life is determined. The painting depicts them being born as insects, rodents, larger mammals, slaves, peasants, or pilgrims to the sky palace (*shown at top left*), the final goal of human aspiration.

continued

continued from previous page

Distinctive representations of personhood in time are shown in these three examples of mortuary art. They suggest a range and a continuum from highlighting individuality to negating it, and from depicting the individual within linear time to the individual within spiral or cyclical time. ■

Photo 5.8 Samsara, *the wheel of rebirth in Chinese Buddhism (identified by Li Jian September 1999). Paint on cloth, Kauffman Museum, North Newton, Kansas. Gift of Lloyd Kauffman, ca. 1940s, from Taiwan or mainland China.*
SOURCE: Courtesy of Kauffman Museum, North Newton, Kansas. Gift of Lloyd Kauffman, from Taiwan, 1940s.

ALTERNATIVE GENDERED LIFECOURSES

The influence of gender upon the lifecourse is like the other issues that have been raised in this chapter. Although the biological and material forces of maleness and femaleness are givens, the way particular societies and cultures define these forces are constructed in a variety of ways. Anthropologists and other scholars use the term *gender* to describe the culturally constructed realities of maleness, femaleness, and other gender definitions. Gender and health issues have held a prominent position in medical anthropology in recent years; this brief section can only sketch the general direction of these works as they pertain to the lifecourse.

Although some of the basic differences in lifecourse trajectories of men and women are obviously shaped by their different roles in reproduction and child rearing, anthropologists who write about this stress that women should not be exclusively identified by just reproduction and how society (i.e., mostly men) relates to this (Lock and Kaufert 1998). The culturally constructed nature of reproduction issues is evident in the cross-cultural variations around such matters as ideas of conception, the place of child-bearing women in society, the role of fathers in responsibility for children, the meaning of menstruation and menopause, masturbation and semen, placentas and maternal milk, and a host of other questions at the core of how men and women live together in society, much of which is viewed with at least a coloring of gender, that is culture.

One of the most significant gender differences in the lifecourse is the economic and social position in household work and child rearing. Monica Das Gupta, an Indian anthropologist, examined some of these themes of gender, independence, and control of one's life, in a study of Indian women (1995). She was interested particularly in the impact of gender inequality in the reproductive years upon birthrates and birthrate changes. Peasant societies of preindustrial northern Europe emphasized the conjugal bond while intergenerational bonds were weak. The reverse is true in contemporary northern India. As a result, greater potential exists for the marginalization of women in society. The combination of low autonomy due to early marriage and gender difference means that women's autonomy is at its lowest point during the peak of childbearing years, and subject to manipulation by husbands and other men. As a consequence, there is a greater opportunity for poorer child survival, slower fertility decline, and poorer reproductive health.

Margaret Lock, in *Encounters with Aging* (1993), conducted a comparative study of menopause in Japan and the United States. She discovered very different cultural meanings of this basic change in women's physiology. In the United States menopause is seen almost as a diseaselike condition beset with all sorts of symptoms: Hot flashes, loss of bone substance, "drying up," and social marginalization are all "treated" with medications (e.g., estrogen replacement). Menopause is culturally structured in the United States as diametrically opposite to the prevailing emphasis upon youth and beauty, especially in women. In Japan, by contrast, menopause is regarded as a natural occurrence for which there are very few "treatments" because it is culturally seen as a transition to a freer, broader life of women, a second stage beyond family and household responsibilities.

Other studies of differential gender in the lifecourse, drawn from psychology, gerontology, social epidemiology, and social psychology, tend to assume that the setting of their findings is Western industrial society, although this is not usually stated. An important, and contrasting, characteristic of anthropological work on the lifecourse is to specify the cultural and the historical context.

Chloe Bird and Catherine Ross (1994) traced a study of the differential perceptions of health by men and women in the United States throughout the lifecourse. They noted that men report better health than women, but that gap closes with age. Women report more stress and fewer subjective work rewards than men. They suggested that gender inequality in paid and unpaid work and the subjective experience of inequality disadvantage women, whereas lifestyle—smoking, obesity— disadvantages men. By age 59, however, women's health perceptions are equal to, and even surpass, those of their male counterparts.

As a result of these kinds of findings, Barbara Barer (1994) concluded that American society shapes the "aging" process differently for men and women. In Western personhood, it seems, "freedom" and "control" over the determining factors of life are held to be significant and highly desirable. Men have fewer limitations on their ability to act; they are more independent and exercise more control over their environment than women. This is true because of financial and social structures in American society. Men, however, find themselves less able to come to terms with widowhood, care giving, and relocation—all dimensions of longevity—than their female counterparts.

Individuals' ability to remain flexible toward these gender-defined constraints and characteristics, as well as those defined by other age-specific social terms, tended to most enhance lifecourse adaptation (Katz and Ksansnak 1994). Independence, freedom to define one's personhood, and flexibility to adapt to life's changes, are generally considered positive in these studies of the lifecourse.

This emphasis on independence, flexibility, and self-control as factors enhancing and improving health and "psychological functioning" throughout the lifecourse (Pulkkinen and Ronka 1994) was reinforced by the findings of a social-epidemiological study in which researchers found a positive correlation between "volunteerism" in work settings and lower cancer rates among a group of 391 German men in a study that controlled for smoking, asbestos exposure, and socioeconomic group membership (Becker et al. 1995). The exact mechanism of these relationships is not understood, but the findings seem to corroborate the importance of one's overall long-term outlook to health throughout the lifecourse.

Many other insights of gender and personhood within the social body across the lifecourse have been identified, some of which are perhaps "commonsensical" or "intuitive." Thus, friendship enhances the quality of life across the life span and especially among the aged (Brinthaupt et al. 1993); the importance of "emotionality" rises with age (Carstensen and Turk-Charles 1994); persons with a religious outlook are healthier and happier than those without (Chatters, Levin, and Taylor 1995). Nevertheless, the ideas here form the basis for an important understanding of how the crisis of illness is socially defined and structured, and how personhood is affected in the process.

CONCLUSION

The lifecourse perspective is integral to anthropology and to medical anthropology, even though much of what it outlines is neither illness nor healing. Rather, it is a way of visualizing the life of individuals in society over time. Although human life is given in biological individuals who are born, mature, reproduce, are adult, become old, and die—all in the normal course of things— the ways in which life is understood, interpreted, and experienced occur only through the signs and symbols of culture. The highlights and transitions of society are marked by culturally articulated rites of passage. But what is articulated may differ among groups within a single society, as well as differ from one society to another.

The moments of life's passages that are ritualized are also of interest to medical anthropologists because they structure the way that a society deals with other kinds of transitions, life events, and crises that are less predictable. The onset of illness, for example, may be marked by the same symbols as those used in a major transition; indeed, illness is often symbolized as a rite of passage out of which one might hope to pass back into society. Yet because the outcome is often uncertain, feelings of ambivalence, anxiety, and fear on the part of individuals who become sick are often ritualized. For its part, society may put those who are marginalized, stigmatized, or who become chronically ill into similarly ritualized, or liminal, positions. This is the topic of the next chapter.

REVIEW QUESTIONS

1. What are some of the points of the human lifecourse that are likely to be recognized by most human societies? Can we be certain that these points will be recognized by all societies? Why or why not?

2. How is the reality of culture manifested in the way that the episodes or events of the lifecourse are recognized and played out? Is the concept of "aging" an objective description of the human individual or is it a culturally colored concept and term? Discuss the meaning of this term in anthropological perspective?

3. If birthing is a natural process, why is it so highly ritualized in most cultures? Define "ritualization" and illustrate your answer with a comparison of several accounts of birthing, either given in the text or elsewhere.

4. What are the basic features of the "rite of passage" as described by writers such as Arnold Van Gennep, Colin Turnbull, and Madeleine L'Engle? Illustrate the notion by applying it to a particular transition and to a sickness experience. How is a person's identity changed by going through a rite of passage?

NOTES

1. Written by Betty Cook, PhD candidate, University of Kansas, who went on to conduct research on midwifery and the construction of pain in the Netherlands and in the United States.

2. Partible inheritance and the neolocal family is part of a widespread northern European tradition that emphasizes the economic viability of each and every family and the transfer of family assets (i.e., dowry) in advance of the death of the parents.

3. The Voth cycle was researched as part of a National Institute of Aging project among Mennonites of Kansas and Nebraska (NIA AG01646–03) carried out by scholars at the University of Kansas and members of the community. It was reconstructed from the extensive personal correspondence of Henry R. Voth with members of his family during his years of missionary and ethnographic work in Oklahoma and Arizona, and other records. Mary Becker Valencia, Jeff Longhofer, Jerry Floersch, Jill Quadagno, and the author contributed to this work (Quadagno and Janzen 1987).

chapter 6

Personhood, Liminality, and Identity

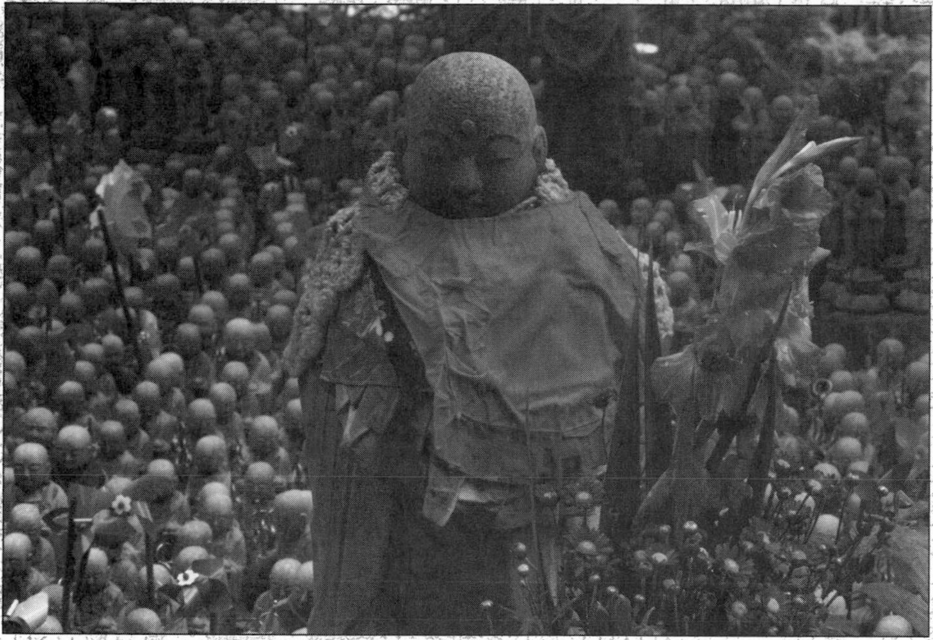

Photo 6.1 *Effigies of aborted fetuses in a* Mizuko jizo *shrine in Japan.*
Source: Gary Braasch/Corbis.

The effigies in the *Mizuko jizo* shrines of Japan and Korea commemorate and mourn the interrupted lives of aborted fetuses (see Photo 6.1). Their bodies were destroyed, yet they were accorded personhood by their mothers, fathers, and families and by East Asian Buddhist theology. Barely having begun their lives, their souls were sent on for further cycles of life on the wheel of *karma* (see Photo 5.8). They are a remarkable illustration of **liminality;** that is, an ambiguous status that is neither one thing nor another, a condition that is betwixt and between two states. Similarly paradoxical, contradictory, painful, and chronic conditions are of great interest to medical anthropologists, for they are at the interface of sickness and health, society and religion, science and folklore.

Extensive work by anthropologists on dimensions of liminality and personhood in health and sickness shows how the ritual symbols and metaphors of the life cycle are often extended to come to terms with ambiguity, contradiction, paradox, crisis, and chronic illness. Victor Turner, a leading scholar of these themes, saw that these conditions often led to the permanent transformation of a person's identity—in a kind of unfolding liminal redefinition of self (1969: 102–111). The basis of a society's definition of the person profoundly affects not just the lifecourse of an individual, but also the individual's fate in sickness and whatever extraordinary situation may affect an individual. We therefore need to develop a fuller understanding of **personhood,** with all that it implies concerning the value of life, rights and obligations of persons, determinations regarding which transitions are recognized, and by whom, and how society determines who should be cared for and who ignored, and ultimately, who should live and who should die.

This chapter builds on the longitudinal view of a life in society that was considered in the previous chapter. It explores anthropological approaches to personhood, exceptional—liminal—conditions, and identities of persons in sickness, ambiguity, and crisis.

PERSONHOOD AND THE SOCIAL BODY

It is useful at the beginning of this section to clarify terms that are often used interchangeably. *Individual* means a single human being. *Person* is reserved for the social characterization of the individual human being. *Self* is used to designate the conscious "self-concept" of such an individual. *Personhood* is really "social personhood," society's understandings and laws regarding how an individual will be represented and treated, the degrees of autonomy or dependence he or she will possess throughout life; when individual life will be considered to begin and end, or whether it will be seen as part of repeated cycles over time, or whether it will be considered to live on once it has come into being. All of these issues, anthropologists believe, may be illuminated by studying a culture's concept of the person.

French anthropologist Marcel Mauss studied the makeup of this social person both in its Western sense and in comparisons with non-Western civilizations. The word "person" from which we derive such diverse appliations as the theatrical persona, personhood, personality, and many other uses, has its etymological roots in Greek and Etruscan. From the early beginnings of these cultures, personhood was more than just a biological, even legal or social entity. It referred to something that was unique and more than the sum of its parts. Like a mask or player in a theater, the person had a kind of "value-added" quality that Mauss tried to capture by calling it "a moral fact" (1960: 350–56); it cannot be dissolved by technical or legal considerations. It is this Greek idea, generalized in Roman law (but extended only to Roman citizens), and embraced by the religious traditions of Judaism, Christianity, and Islam, where the person who once identified by name, became a unique and inviolable eternal being. Readers will also recognize here the foundations of ethics with which we try to sort out some of the tangled issues in modern medicine.

Western philosophers and theologians built upon these early ideas to produce doctrines that systematized this notion of the person. For Aristotle (384–322 B.C.), the potentiality for humanness made all attributes and parts of the individual essential to being human among the many kinds of creatures (Burke 1996). That is, any body part or attribute—semen, the heart, the soul—was defined by its potential as an integral part of the human being. For St. Thomas Aquinas (1224–1274), an important Christian thinker, the individual was a member of a more inclusive category of humanness; the relationship of personhood to humanness was like that of genus to species (Moreland and Wallace 1995). Personhood was therefore a given if you were human, a status that was not always assumed as Europeans explored other continents in the 15th century. Debates raged over whether the inhabitants in newly discovered lands had souls and were human. These early doctrines of humanness, whether defined by potential or by inclusion in a species, were important forerunners of inclusive perspectives of human rights. Later philosophers and thinkers went beyond formal definitions in search of a more dynamic understanding of personhood, understandings that we recognize as closer to that which we use and embrace, although some of our modern dilemmas surrounding organ and tissue transplants, surrogate parenthood, abortion, and euthenasia are rendered problematic by newer formulations of personhood, as will be seen below. The ability to freely author a life characterized essential personhood for Immanuel Kant (1724–1804) in the 18th century (Gowans 1996). René Descartes (1596–1650) emphasized the segmentation of personhood into body and mind by stressing the cognitive part of human functioning. John Locke (1632–1704) de-emphasized inherent qualities of character, stressing an individual's unique experience as the basis of personhood. These writers anticipated modern trends in the definition of personhood in the contingent—that is, the experienced—realm rather than in any absolute quality, which opens the possibility of some aspects, or circumstances of individual experience being outside of the inviolable human being of Aristotle or Aquinas (Moreland and Wallace 1995). For example anthropologist Lynn Morgan suggested that we "produce persons through our actions and rhetoric. . . . Personhood and relationality can be better analyzed as dynamic, negotiated qualities realized through social practice" (1996).

Marcel Mauss thought the "moral fact" of the person was universal and could be identified in all cultures. Generally, anthropologists have adhered to the premise of a universal human nature spelled out by Edward Tylor (1958 [1871]: 1), resulting in many studies of personhood in particular cultures and of comparative studies of personhood or "selfhood" in non-Western societies. A late-20th-century ethnography of personhood illustrates this anthropological genre. Anne Taylor's study (1996) of experience and representation of the self in Jivaroan Achuar culture in the Amazon observed how the sense of self of these people is rooted in a progressive fusion of a generic, given bodily form and its human attributes, which is progressively "singularized" by memory of affective moods experienced in daily social interaction. But this self, so defined, is susceptible to states of weakness and uncertainty (categorized as illness) as well as states of enhancement (brought on by communication with spirits). The anthropologist requires basic concepts as well as thorough contextual knowledge to consider such indigenous ideas. These analytical approaches to the comparative study of personhood are all needed to address adequately some of the conceptual and ethical challenges that modern medicine and global citizenship have put before us.

CONCEPTION AND PERSONHOOD

Ideas of life and personhood often occur in their most profound form around birth and death because these are the most critical moments where definition is required. Anthropologists interested in identifying such organizing ideas in a culture find they are most accessible in the area of "conception," or how the person is believed to be constituted. Even though some of the ideas about conception that anthropologists report from far and wide seem far-fetched to those trained in current biology and reproduction, they nevertheless reveal the makeup of the social person. Underlying ideas about conception often survive the introduction of genetics and more thorough teaching of reproductive biology.

The widespread association of sexual intercourse with conception does not mean that all peoples have held to modern biological ideas of reproduction. Just what comes together to produce a person is the stuff of ideas that, while at variance to modern ideas, are nonetheless entirely plausible and based on empirical evidence. One such idea is that the fetus is formed from congealed menstrual blood, a view very widely reported in the Pacific islands, Africa, the Americas, and Europe (Hanson 1970: 1444–47). Pacific islanders on Rapa (in French Polynesia), studied by Hanson, explain one variant of this view. Conception is most likely to occur in the three or four days following menstruation, as semen enters the uterus and coalesces with the blood. Menstruation ceases after conception because all the blood goes to building the fetus. Sexual intercourse is beneficial after pregnancy to nourish the fetus. In the Rapan version, there is no understanding of ovulation, eggs, and their fertilization by sperm. According to Hanson (1970: 1444), Rapans were frustrated with the ineffectiveness of their attempts to limit births by refraining from sexual intercourse immediately following menstruation. But these ideas are similar to those held by ancient Greek gynecologists and more recent 19th-century European writers, who in discussing contraception are quoted as recommending abstinence in the days during and immediately after menstruation to avoid pregnancy (Hanson 1970). Indeed, the notion of the thermal humors is significant in Western ideas of mammalian readiness for conception: "coming in heat" is associated with menstruation.

Although notions of congealed blood and semen may be replaced by those of ova and sperm, or recombinant DNA, the person's make up in terms of social belonging, ancestry, and presumed social rights that come from belonging to a family or to a society or nation are not changed. In Kongo society, the individual acquires rights to his or her mother's lineage land and group rights at birth. Social belonging is thus automatic. One's father is thought to contribute to the intellectual endowment of an individual. Father, who is usually a friend and not a disciplinarian, is interested in these things. With such a "bilateral" identity of the individual in place, the name of a Kongo individual does not usually reveal clan or lineage membership; it is distinctly individual. The social identity of an individual is so clear that an individual needs only to mention clan, lineage, and home community to be perfectly well situated. Personal names may be amended or changed at will on a whim or on the occasion of a significant lifecourse change.

ETHICAL CHALLENGES SURROUNDING PERSONHOOD

Comparative personhood studies are wide-ranging and intriguing, revealing a variety of concepts of conception, as well as the social belonging of the person. Most of the received theories of personhood of the world's cultures are, however, challenged by global medical techniques and innovations such as invasive surgery, blood transfusions, organ and tissue transplants, fetal monitoring and amniocentisis, reproductive technologies such as in vitro fertilization, and surrogate parenting. How does the inviolable core of personhood now get drawn? The new medical and reproductive technologies have opened up realms of knowledge that were previously shrouded in mystery (e.g., in the area of fetal monitoring). The extension of civil rights into the arena of reproductive rights has pitted the vested interests of the mother against those of the fetus. The same debates are being waged at the other end of the lifecourse between those who uphold the sanctity and inviolability of the individual person and those who claim the "right to die" with the help of a physician. In the middle of the lifecourse, debates rage over the "ownership" of human organs and tissue, and the control of genetic blueprints for research.

How do we now define the contours—beginnings and endings—of life? What is the threshold of Mauss's "moral fact" of personhood? Who has the right to determine the end of physical life of an inviolable eternal person? In many Western countries this issue is being tested in demonstrations, political campaigns, and courts.

Thus, the U.S. Supreme Court, in the landmark *Roe* v. *Wade* decision in 1967, ruled seven to two that a pregnant woman has the right to make the decision over the fate of the fetus, and that the in utero fetus is not yet a person (Tompkins 1996). How was this determined or justified? Two principles were involved. One was grounded in the Fourteenth Amendment to the U.S. Constitution which guarantees personal liberties. The second hinged on the definition of the person as personhood is construed in U.S. law. At the time of the ruling, there was no precedent, the court ruled, with which to identify the fetus as a person. Only as it grows toward viability and reaches the point where it can survive on its own outside the uterus, in this reasoning, does the fetus acquire personhood. Until then, it is not a person, and can be aborted legally within the greater freedoms and rights of the mother.

However, this double definition of the person—the mother's freedoms, the fetus's emerging personhood—is precarious. For one thing, fetal monitoring has made it possible to "see" and "know" far more about this emerging pre-person than ever before. Gender, hereditary predispositions to disease, and other characteristics are now easily determined through the testing of the amniotic fluid surrounding the fetus and through sonograms. With genetic engineering and in utero transplanting, at least the promise exists of "designer children." The outcomes of birth are increasingly guaranteed, in theory at least, so that prospective parents can literally shape their offspring and time the event of the birth. However, most of the opposition to the U.S. Supreme Court definition of the person, and the ensuing legal consequences, comes from those who oppose abortion in the name of sanctity of all life. They personify the fetus by calling it "a baby," and by labeling doctors who perform abortions "baby murderers."

The United States is not the only society to have collectively agonized over the issue of the personhood of the fetus. The denial of personhood to infants born too soon among the !Kung has already been mentioned. But another comparative approach to the dilemma of personhood and unwanted pregnancy comes from advanced industrial societies such as Buddhist/ Shinto Japan and Buddhist Korea (see Photo 6.1). There abortion is popular as a contraception owing to a kind of radical Asian Cartesianism that separates the spiritual from the material life of the fetus. *Mizuko jizo* rituals at memorial parks filled with rows of little statues to the "Bodhisattva of the water-babies," represent aborted fetuses, and allow the mother to express any grief or guilt she may feel. These statues, which are sometimes clothed and given gifts, perpetuate the fetus's identity and the mother-child relationship, as shown in the depiction of a contemporary Buddhist shrine in Japan (WuDunn 1996). The fetus's soul is encouraged to seek rebirth in another body at another time (Oaks 1994; Tedesco 1996; Lee, Midori, and Osaka 1995; La Fleur 1992).

At the other end of life the same debate occurs surrounding euthanasia, and the right of individuals to take their own lives or to have a doctor-assisted suicide. Here as well, the issues range around the coming together of concepts of the person, on the one hand, and the rights and duties of others toward the individual, on the other. Just as there is no clear-cut agreed-upon understanding of when the person begins, so there is no clear definition of when death occurs. The absence of consciousness, breath, or heartbeat, while all highly important constituent parts of personhood and life, may each be missing without a person being considered "dead." Medical procedures also allow life to be sustained in the absence of one or more of these, and other, criteria of the vital signs of life. An uneasy working compromise exists at the turn of the millennium between those who would perpetuate life at all cost, and those who would allow some form of willful termination of life. "Living wills" prepared by the individual in question, authorizing medical care teams "not to resuscitate" or giving designated family members "medical power of attorney," provide a way for those surrounding a dying and suffering individual to make decisions in the face of conflicting principles (see Kaufman 2000).

It should be apparent by now that many issues surrounding personhood in our society are most highly charged at the beginning and ending of the lifecourse. It is here that ritualization is most elaborate as well because of the ambivalence and contradictoriness of opposing principles of life and competing rights. Furthermore, such ambiguities and ritualizations are evident in many societies in recent human history, which does not lessen the ethical dilemmas that individuals and families and practitioners must face.

PERSONHOOD IN THE SICK ROLE

The sickness experience, being ill, has many of the characteristics of a rite of passage, as already noted. A simple reflection on what happens to one's image of self in sickness may be helpful in understanding issues of social status and ritualization. If you, as reader, recall the last time you were sick with the flu, you may remember how you decided to accept your illness. When you could hide it or ignore it no longer, you decided to "be sick." Perhaps you announced to your family, or roommate, that you "are sick." You may have called your place of work where such episodes are adjusted according to a sick leave policy. Your announcement, and society's acceptance, of your being sick set in motion socially determined rules. Once recognized as sick, you gained the right of staying at home from your work and other obligations, of perhaps soliciting the help of your family, friends, or roommates. The signs of distress you gave off were accepted as legitimate, bringing on a series of appropriate social responses. Like the first stage of a rite of passage, you became symbolically separated from your normal social role.

The middle phase of the sickness, akin to the liminal phase of a rite of passage, will be characterized by reversed expectations, scrambled realities, and all kinds of ambiguous messages. You dress differently, you eat special foods if you are capable of eating at all, and you may not abide by your regular schedule. In your misery you lose your sense of time, or time seems to stand still. You may seek metaphors that give definition to your special condition. If your flu or condition is of the type that runs its course, the day arrives when you feel that you are well. Socially, you are still sick. Then comes the moment when you decide to "be well." You may take a good bath, get dressed, and prepare to rejoin society. As you get up, rejoin your family, go to class, work, or appear in public, those with whom you relate most commonly, who know you have "been sick," may recognize your transition and greet you with words such as "good to see you back" or "You're well again? Hope you're feeling better." These are the rites of reintegration.

The "sick role" is how social scientists once characterized this passage from and back into society at the time of sickness (Parsons 1951: 428–47). Writers in this tradition noted the shift in rights and obligations that occurred during socially accepted sickness, as with beginnings, endings, and moving through other conventional social roles. However, they also recognized that not all sickness experiences were equivalent. There was variance over the degree of seriousness of the illness, and whether they were contagious and dangerous to others. Some types of illnesses (e.g., various flus, well-known contagious diseases such as measles, chicken pox, or a condition like heart attack) were "legitimate," whereas others were "stigmatizing" (Freidson 1970: 224–43). The latter, of which sexually transmitted diseases, mental illnesses, and cancer were the foremost mentioned, evoked fear and dread on the part of the sufferer, and a reaction of embarrassment, silence, and avoidance from others surrounding the sufferer. Sick role theory generally situated sickness within the sociological perspective of an understanding of deviance, along with crime, and the way in which society reacts to those considered deviant. Ideas of ambiguity, liminality, and ritualization are also helpful in evaluating the shifting basis of personhood in sickness.

Trauma, Chronicity, and New Identity

The transformation of a sickness experience into that of a condition which becomes chronic brings other dimensions of social and moral judgment into play that are not covered in applying the simple analogy of the rite of passage or that of the sick role. The affected person's very identity is now in question, requiring others to make shifting and long-term adjustments in their dealing with him or her. The experiencing of trauma in childhood, as a spouse, in war or other violence, or forced migration from home may quite literally scar an individual, resulting in a kind of social paralysis that consumes and overwhelms that person's identity, at least until the trauma is resolved or "healed."

Sue Estroff analyzed the ailments to which we, in American English, attribute an identity of "being" as opposed to "having." Her focus is on schizophrenia, a chronic condition that results in the sufferer "being a schizophrenic," just as we speak of being an alcoholic, a hemophiliac, a diabetic, an epileptic, a manic-depressive, or being retarded, blind, deaf, paraplegic, and anorexic (1993:258). By contrast, one "has" multiple sclerosis, osteoporosis, cystic fibrosis, arthritis, and heart disease. What is the difference? The first set is perceived in our cultural construction to be an identity-transforming affliction, whereas the latter is not so pervasive. This sharp dichotomy between the two belies the often gradual change toward more all-consuming identity change as the chronic condition progresses or becomes worse and more persistent.

Chronicity is not just a condition of those who live longer in advanced industrial societies, and suffer from degenerative diseases of various types. It is a familiar circumstance in the developing world, in societies that are only entering the disease profile of modernity. For the 8 million chronically disabled adults in the United States at the end of the 20th century, there were 500 million in the developing world (Estroff 1993:148). However, in the latter setting "chronically disabled" includes those who suffer from recurring infections, infertility, one or another handicapped condition, and a variety of ailments attributed to human society and the spirit world. Whereas illness types are often culturally specific, chronic ailment is universal. In international health agencies such as the World Health Organization, the terms *disability* and *handicap* have been increasingly applied to chronic ailments in an attempt to reduce the identity-transforming character from these conditions. Entire vocabularies and typologies have been generated to free these conditions from their identity-pervasive status or stigma, as the case may be (Hamonet 1990). Such efforts at destigmatizing these conditions may work in some cases. In another very widespread pattern, however, the ailment identity is accepted and becomes a creative force for forging an alternative identity and life. In other words, the affliction becomes the center of a new identity, reinforced by a support community whose members often share the same condition.

The best-known example in the Western world of this type of new identity associated with an ailment/condition is that of Alcoholics Anonymous (AA), a self-help order that dates from the 1920s and has spread worldwide. Recovering alcoholics join to lend one another support in overcoming their debilitating condition of dependency on alcohol. AA embraces its identity-transforming condition in its principal article of faith: that each and every member must acknowledge "I am an alcoholic." This is the first step toward rehabilitation. However, the basic identity is never lost.

Many support communities following the model of AA have arisen around other conditions. The list is nearly endless, including Weight Watchers, Parents Anonymous (for abusive parents), cardiac sufferers, Parkinson's disease sufferers, parents of murdered children, couples suffering sterility. Almost any condition regarded as chronic or disabling may be organized into this model of the cosufferers joining to support one another in their common suffering.

The model of Alcoholics Anonymous may have arisen independently in the West, but it corresponds to many groups in other parts of the world. In central and southern Africa a widespread uniquely African tradition of healing cults has been known since the 1960s to scholars who began to call them "drums of affliction" after the use of drumming, rhythm, and dancing in the rites that accompanied the gatherings of groups of common sufferers (Turner 1968). They have covered conditions as varied as gynecological disorders, hunting difficulties, disorders caused by spirits of European people, the ravages of contagious diseases, or generic mental disorders. These conditions are recognized in Africa as having been sent by ancestors or other kinds of spirits. The afflicted individual is typically diagnosed as being possessed by the spirit. To be able to live somewhat normally, although never entirely cured, the sufferer needs to come to terms with the afflicting spirit. Often this involves learning a particular form of dance or song which embodies the unique character of the spirit who is someone who may have suffered from the same condition.

In his later writing, Turner generalized his findings from these "cults of affliction" on the southern savanna of Africa to other societies around the world. The continuing liminal status of these sufferers, around their common affliction, transformed into a kind of continuing community. Turner spoke of this kind of state of a public or a group as **"communitas"** (Turner 1969). Within communitas there prevailed "anti-structure" in contrast to the "structure" of corporate society; equality rather than inequality or hierarchy; a tendency toward anonymity rather than systems of nomenclature; sacredness rather than secularity of symbols and roles; acceptance of pain and suffering rather than avoidance of pain and suffering (1969: 106–107).

Common to both the Western and the African versions of these self-help communities is the support given to the sufferer of the chronic condition by fellow sufferers and family members. The role of this support cannot be underestimated; it is critical to the sufferer's ability to come to terms with a chronic condition and the new identity that grows out of, indeed is defined by, the affliction. Where a chronic condition has become the central identity of personhood, it has become the principal shaping force of the life of the individual. The most significant others of such an individual are those who have gathered together as cosufferers to support one another. Often cosufferers or former sufferers of a condition are the only ones who really understand the emotions of the condition.

Lifecourse studies also recognized the significance of this combined identity and support structure in the shaping of individual lives. They spoke of the "convoy of social support" that maintains persons with chronic and debilitating conditions (Kahn and Antonucci 1980). Individuals who could marshal, or have marshaled for them, such meaningful support when they needed it, were likely to fare far better in their affliction or special conditions than those who lacked such support. Family, friends, cosufferers, and professionals could all step in to constitute the "convoy of support" across the lifecourse.

CONCLUSION

One of the common themes of the life-course in a range of societies is the idea of personhood, the self-conscious yet social identity of individuals. Personhood defined socially becomes most sharply visible in the way the beginning of life and the end of life are defined. The idea of personhood, widely recognized and highlighted in rites of passage, emerges again in the way illness and trauma are experienced, both in time and in transformations of identity. Most illnesses that are self-limiting are like rites of passage;

they are transitory and the person returns to the prior state. With chronic illness or disability, and in the aftermath of unresolved trauma, identity changes permanently. The illness or disability, and the trauma, become the centerpiece of personhood.

In this chapter illness identity is seen as a special case of social identity. In the next chapter we turn to the sickness experience as a transformation in its own right, full of rich signs at all levels of existence and experience.

REVIEW QUESTIONS

1. In light of the varied concepts and definitions of personhood, self, or the social individual presented in this chapter, can you see your own concept or traditional notion of the person mirrored in them? Write about your sense of self in society, and compare it with another sense of self that seems very different, either one taken from the text or another source.

2. The many ethical ambiguities that confront us around the beginning and at the end of life, as well as in between, require more than a culturally relative reading of comparative examples of personhood. Discuss the moral and ethical issues surrounding abortion, infanticide, life support, and euthenasia.

3. What is the difference between "being sick" and "having a sickness" in Sue Estroff's study reported in this chapter? Is the way we construct affliction a peculiarly American cultural feature? Or is there something more widespread and universally human at work here? Consider some comparative cases in widely differing traditions such as the United States and central Africa, Asia, or elsewhere.

4. What are the ways that society "recognizes" sickness and legitimizes it, from "sick leave," to special care from the family, to disability benefits, and self-help groups?. What is the evidence that such "social support" affects the well-being of the recepient? Cite evidence and examples.

THE TRANSFORMING SIGNS OF SICKNESS AND HEALING

Photo 7.1 *Rembrandt Van Rijn.* Christ Healing the Sick. *Rembrandt combines in one image the many instances of Christ's healing ministry (many examples of which are found in the Gospel of Saint Luke), thus capturing a particular role of Christ—Christus Medicus, Christ the Healer—that received major emphasis during the Middle Ages and through the 19th century. Rembrandt shows the range of people who come together around Christ, poor and rich, women and men, children, lepers, beggars, cripples in wheelbarrows, all scrambling for a fleeting glance at the luminescent savior, a figure of light or radiance, like a sun, source of hope and new life. His gesture is one of blessing, embracing, accepting, lifting up. The etching is worth study by medical anthropologists in order to appreciate and understand the power of anticipation, hope, and faith in healing.*
Source: Wellcome Library, London.

149

Pain too has a present, immediate, uncategorized, and prereflective aspect to it. But this "Firstness" of pain is overwhelmed by what Peirce calls "Secondness"— the experience of radical otherness in which ego and non-ego are precipitated out against each other in unique and absolute opposition . . . "Thirdness" is Peirce's phenomenological category of mediation, mainly through language and culture. It is in Thirdness that semeiosis resumes its continuity, its movement. Thirdness is the domain of meaning.

E. Valentine Daniel, *Charred Lullabies*

. . . [M]y point is that illness is *not* a metaphor, and that the most truthful way of regarding illness—and healthiest way of being ill—is one most purified of, most resistant to, metaphoric thinking.

Susan Sontag, *Illness as Metaphor*

The sickness experience, in whatever cultural setting, and its entry into therapy with the anticipation of healing, is at the heart of the focus of medical anthropology. The quotes from Daniel and Sontag introduce the concepts that will be developed in this chapter: to provide a language of signs with which to capture the depth and complexity of sickness, healing, and related experiences.

Sickness is the subjective experience of a condition that disrupts ordinary life and causes suffering. Where individuals are part of stronger group identities, sickness may be shared more fully by several persons together. Sickness may not everywhere be as individual an experience as in the Western world where the individual person is given great autonomy (Hahn 1995: 5–6). Wherever the locus of the subjective experience of suffering lies, there the experience of sickness is defined. **Illness** is the culturally embedded, subjective definition given to suffering by the patient, and to the behavior in which it is expressed. **Disease,** on the other hand, is the objective condition or pathology as determined by a medical professional. In recent years, however, the illness/disease dichotomy has been criticized because medicine and its professionals have been seen increasingly as part of the culture in which they live. Nevertheless, the illness/disease dichotomy is a useful tool to differentiate what the patient feels from what the physician sees.

Suffering has come to hold great interest for medical anthropology in recent years. Broader than sickness, suffering is the existential experience of many who live lives of hardship and difficulty. Suffering may or may not lead to healing; it often becomes a permanent human condition and is, therefore, like sickness, often accounted for in religion and wisdom literature.

Healing is used here in a general sense to mean both the sufferer-defined resolution of the sickness experience, as well as the medically defined transformation of the disease or disorder. In some cultural traditions the term for healing is derived from **wholeness;** thus healing is the restoration of wholeness.

However, these terms are really little more than commonsense words picked from the English vocabulary and given semitechnical definitions.

Their uses and meanings have changed as the theoretical perspectives of authors have shifted. The role of culture in illness and healing has continued to be raised, even in the nature of disease. Medical anthropology has sought approaches that can include both "causality" and "interpretation." At the core of medicine defined as a science lies the conviction that precise disease causes can be identified and cures developed. The model for scientific investigation that is held up as ideal is the single cause or, failing that, the probable cause, gained through the testing of a research hypothesis. The sharp either/or dichotomy that pits causal explanation against interpretation is also a problem because most circumstances of sickness and healing fit somewhere in between. Yet in many cases sickness is due to multiple "causes" or risk factors, and the model of precise cause is misleading.

For medical anthropology several scenarios and issues are more appropriate for understanding the transformation of sickness and healing. (1) Why does infection occur to some and not others given that all individuals in a room or family are exposed to a bacillis or disease condition? What role might immunity, genetics, or stress play upon susceptibility? (2) How is pain experienced individually and defined culturally? Is some pain (as in athletic competition or exercise) "good," whereas other pain is "bad"? How is episodic pain (as in childbirth) defined as opposed to chronic pain that must be endured without likely relief? (3) How does a culture interpret suffering, the fate of individuals, groups, and entire societies? Is it unmitigated "evil" or is suffering, as pain, sometimes good, redemptive? (4) What is the relationship of suffering to healing? What are the implications of the fundamentally different outlooks on pain and suffering that lead to their being, in some contexts, aggressively attacked for elimination, and in other contexts considered to be a necessary prerequisite for becoming a healer (all healers need to have suffered sickness to be effective in their calling)?

This chapter seeks to present some of the leading medical anthropological approaches to the cross-cultural, cross-healing traditions, study of sickness and healing, and some of the conclusions that may be drawn for understanding the "art of healing" and the clinical process. The chapter closes with a reformulation of the unitary approach to the subject that is afforded by semiotics, the doctrine of signs.

SIGNIFICATION IN SICKNESS

Sickness always occurs in time, just as do "illness" (the sufferer's subjective perception), and "disease" (the condition objectively defined by laboratory tests, a specialist's diagnosis, or other signs). The process of a sufferer becoming and being sick, by which the signs of sickness are given signification, occurs over time, at many levels of signification, and between individuals. At the close of the previous chapter the social signification suggested by the "sick role" was introduced, as well as the extent to which a condition transforms the sufferer's identity on a temporary or a permanent basis (whether it is a condition for example, of "having" heart disease or of "being" a diabetic).

Within these broader social conventions, however, the individual experience of becoming and being sick is marked by a range of feelings, dawning subjective realizations, and self-images that are of interest to the medical anthropologist. In the words of anthropologist E. Valentine Daniel at the opening of this chapter, the experience of pain begins with "a present, immediate, uncategorized, and prereflective aspect" (1996:152). Perhaps this is the evidence of organic signals of biochemical and hormonal messages and meanings of which the individual is unaware. Perhaps it is a sign of one's organic processes going about their business; thus, as Charles Peirce expressed it, one is feeling "life."[1] For Daniel, such "firstness" may give way to "secondness," an experience of "radical otherness in which ego and non-ego are precipitated out against each other in unique and absolute opposition." That is, the subjective experience becomes one of consciously reflecting upon pain or some other sensation, and either identifying it as something known or wondering about its nature, and depending upon these possibilities while being filled with curiosity and possibility, or confusion, fear, or dread. This stage of realization of a condition raises questions about signs and symptoms that may or may not be given voice with regard to whether the signs and symptoms constitute "being sick."

A third phase of the sickness or pain comes, for Daniel, when the dawning subjective experience is shared with others or, more forcefully, is taken over by culture and language. The individual feelings, thoughts, and images are subsumed to society's prevailing categories and are given a name. This transformation may occur in the hands of family or other close kin, or it may occur in the hands of a professional practitioner who divines or diagnoses the official meaning of the signs and symptoms. "Yes, you have chicken pox, schizophrenia, cancer, AIDS," and so on, or "you have nothing, those are just 'growing pains,' 'your heart beating,' or 'the tests are normal.' " In central Africa the interpretation might be that "yes, it is the ancestors, or spirits," or "no, it is just an ordinary sickness for which you can go to the healer or hospital." In Hmong society of Southeast Asia or the United States the diagnosis might be "indeed, it is soul loss" or "you are suffering from fright," as Anne Fadiman described so dramatically about a Hmong girl in California in her work *The Spirit Catches You and You Fall Down: A Hmong Child, Her American Doctors, and the Collision of Two Cultures* (1997). Such formal labeling of a condition by family, physician, healer, or diviner may then create even more powerful significations that invoke all the culturally sanctioned values and powerful symbolic codes of the condition's danger, seriousness, and stigma.

In Western biomedicine the official diagnosis of a subjective condition is given the full signification of natural disease, as established in "objective" testing by scientifically educated specialists using powerful scientific instruments that can see inside the body, organ, cell, or atom (Kevles 1997). The prevailing biomedical diagnosis usually ignores the subject's own feelings in the categorization and labeling, and tries insofar as possible to remove the subjective dimension from the results of the tests. Objectivity is the goal of biomedical testing. Even the hint of subjectively influenced bodily changes is minimized in favor of autonomous physical or material reality. Body is separated from mind.

Although they do not reject disease, medical anthropologists are interested in the ways that biomedicine's object is shaped by subjective and cultural influences. Although some diseases like children's chicken pox occur in a quite predictable time frame, many other conditions vary in time span, severity, and occurrence. Even in these cases of relatively routine childhood diseases, the anticipated natural history of the disease is not a sure predictor of the experience. There are variations of severity and complication. Some individuals may be exposed and not catch the disease or become infected. Not everyone infected gets a cold. Not everyone exposed to the Black Death in the 14th century died of it. The exact extent to which a disease may shape its social and cultural response varies according to severity, understanding, feelings, genetic predisposition, a mixed set of other factors that the medical community speaks of as "risk," and other ingredients of a complex reaction. The disease shapes sickness, but usually through a blanket of mediated personal, physiological, and cultural filters. Sometimes, too, medicine creates side effects that become like disease and sickness where none previously existed.

Other conditions like the adult degenerative diseases of Parkinson's or multiple sclerosis not only vary in time of onset but differ in the severity and character of the disability, with a corresponding ambivalent set of social reactions and the ability of sufferers to deal with the condition of being sick. As sickness turns chronic, it comes to affect identity, subjecting the sufferer to many new conditions: social, physical, emotional, and spiritual. Some of the features of the second phase of sickness such as an individual's being "liminal" or "other" may become part of this permanent identity, with all the implications of losing the conventional moorings of reality, sense of self, time, and social context. This is particularly true in the case of an illness whose outcome is uncertain, as one awaits a defining diagnosis or the impact of a treatment. Questions may be raised about the seriousness of the affliction. Is it terminal? Am I going to live or die? Here, too, the official diagnosis may strongly affect the subjective course of the sickness experience. The prognosis, based on objective data, may affect the outcome by virtue of its influence on the subject of the sickness experience. Whether the "condition" of the sufferer shapes the process of being sick and becoming well, or whether it is the social process of becoming well that affects the prior condition of sickness, remains an open question subject to much discussion and interest by medical anthropologists.

The "Biography of Medicines," the "Placebo Effect," and "Voodoo Death"

Just as the experience of sickness has been studied in medical anthropology with a view to understanding the cultural content of signs, symptoms, and symbols, so the practices of healing have been closely examined for their cultural dimensions. Medical anthropologists have studied non-Western healers as well as biomedicine. They have also brought many explanations to healing in order to decipher what healing is and how it can be understood. This section looks at three examples of such studies that have contributed to the overall understanding of culture in healing. The first is an extended study led by Dutch anthropologist Sjaak van der Geest of the power of medicines, especially of pharmaceutical products, in the contemporary world. The second is by American anthropologist Daniel Moerman of the widely known placebo phenomenon in drug testing and surgery. The third is a series of studies of the now recognized instances of death resulting from curses, otherwise known as "voodoo death." All three of these examples of transformation in sickness and healing represent previously intriguing research problems that seemingly defied explanation but which, upon careful study, yielded answers. They are presented here as puzzles whose theory-yielding solutions are presented in the next section. Together the three show the outlines of a distinctive anthropology of healing.

The Biography of Medicines

Anthropologists have long studied medicines, especially non-Western medicines, which had a mostly magical reputation (Van der Geest, Whyte, and Hardon 1996), although herbal medicines were acknowledged to sometimes operate as empirically effective substances. Theories of magic were put forward by early anthropologists such as James Frazer and Bronislaw Malinowski, but these theories attributed beliefs of wonderful and superstitious workings to the makers and users of these medicines. These magical medicines were substances of the mind and culture, rather than biology and body. There was a complete gulf in anthropological thinking between the medicines of magic and the medicines of science.

But in recent years medical anthropologists have discovered that pharmaceuticals—that is, industrially manufactured drugs—have not just their chemical efficacy but also other social, symbolic, and religious attributes given them by their users. The studies by Van der Geest and his colleagues Anita Hardon and Susan Reynolds Whyte offer special interest for the insight they brought to the combination of biochemical and cultural attributes of medicines.

Medicines are substances, Van der Geest and his collaborators suggested, which by definition have the capacity to change the condition of a living organism (1996:154). Most people—globally—attribute to medicines the significance of being able to cure illness effectively. The secret of medicines and their attributed power is in their concreteness (1996:154; Van der Geest 1989). Medicines are tangible, usable in a concrete way for a particular problem. They can be swallowed, smeared on the skin, or inserted into orifices, all activities that hold the promise of a physical effect. The application of a "thing" transforms a vague condition of sickness into something which can be concretely affected, changed, resolved. "Practicing medicine . . . is the art of making disease concrete" (Van der Geest, Whyte, and Hardon 1996:154).

The "biography of pharmaceuticals" approach to understanding medicines and their significance looks at all aspects of medicines over the course of their particular use in individual cases and their popularity in general. The stages that are studied thus include (1) preparation, whether in a raw handcraft type of medicine, or in a manufactured "high-tech" setting; (2) the marketing of medicines to storekeepers, pharmacists, or retailers, whether by private firms or through state institutions; (3) their acquisition by consumers, either through prescription or direct purchase; then (4) the use of the medicine for the purpose of restoring, improving, or maintaining health; and finally (5) the "afterlife" of the medicine, its considered effect on the person who took them (1996:156). Each stage has a fairly distinctive cultural context and signification.

The preparation of medicines is defined by how the marketers or manufacturers believe they may make a living from their products, and what kind of product they believe they are promoting. The culture of medicine making is usually given an aura of contributing to the social good. However, producers also usually know that medicines can have deleterious or lethal effects if not used correctly, or perhaps used intentionally for antisocial purposes. The process of production of medicines is thus often shrouded in secrecy, subject to governmental regulation, and stringent testing and control. The marketing phase of pharmaceutical products highlights the economic significance of medicine in general, and raises the specter that this activity has other than humanitarian purposes. It also demonstrates the economic and political power of pharmaceutical manufacturers, especially in today's global marketplace. Even in traditional societies the power of the healer and herbalist deserves study by anthropologists, along with the political role of the healer as societal authority. The rhetoric or "spin" of promotion that is put on the medical product reveals the marketer's understanding of the user's desire or belief in the product, or the marketer's pitch that the product will sell successfully. Anthropologist Bronislaw Malinowski was insightful when he compared Melanesian gardening and beauty magic to modern advertising, both with their artful phrases and lilting tunes lauding the wonders of the product or technique (Malinowski 1965:236–39). Anthropologists have also compared the fetishes of "primitive" societies with the "fetishism of capitalist products," a Marxist insight. Medicines seem to fit both.

The stage of a medicine's prescription for use—that is, the authorization by the healer—carries further numerous functions (Van der Geest, Whyte, and Hardon 1996:158–59). It has psychological effects, it is a means of communication, it shows power and facilitates social control, and it produces income and has symbolic significance. Prescription or recommendation is the gate-opening step toward authorized access. What does prescribing mean to the prescriber and to the user? Is dosage a factor in this bargain? The right to prescribe gives practitioners significant authority over their clients, and recognition with each other. Often traditional healers incorporate commercial pharmaceuticals into their materia medica, a step that increases their power and influence. Reasons for prescription among professional physicians in biomedicine may include dimensions other than the simple medical treatment. As we shall see shortly, prescription is a social act that becomes one of the main elements of the doctor-patient relationship and the trust that exists between them. The reasons for the use of placebos—ostensibly neutral substances but in actuality symbolically active—in a clinical setting deserves careful anthropological scrutiny for what it suggests about the element of trust and faith in healing. By the same token, refusal to prescribe may also challenge the doctor's ability to maintain trust because he or she must persuade the patient that no medication is warranted in the face of the patient's good reasons for consulting the doctor in the first place. Usually prescription of medicine functions as a legitimization of the sickness that has been agreed upon between doctor and patient (Van der Geest, Whyte, and Hardon 1996:161).

Over-the-counter pharmaceutical purchase and marketplace buying of medicines—and we might as well add mail-order and Internet purchases—represent a relatively new phenomenon in the global proliferation of medicines to the mass public. Faith in the doctor is replaced by a faith in medicine itself or the message about it, and in one's own ability to understand the application of the medicine for the particular condition. Anthropologists have studied this commodification of medicine and health care and its impact upon other community measures often associated with public health. One suggested outcome is the "medicalization" of health and life. At the same time others have suggested that the access to medicines in the market is beneficial since increasing numbers of people have access to powerful drugs. Yet the proliferation of some medicines such as antibiotics and their incorrect use leads to the mutation of diseases into more resistant strains.

The next stage in the biography of medicines is the actual taking of the substance, whether at the hand of the physician or healer, or in self-medication. Self-medication seems to be the most widespread and commonplace mode of taking medicine, especially in many communities of the non-Western world where broad-spectrum antibiotics and basic medicines for malaria, worms, and diarrhea are available, and in the Western world where over-the-counter drugs are widely promoted as well (Van der Geest, Whyte, and Hardon 1996:165). This pattern of nonprescription usage reflects the ideas and assumptions of popular medical culture about illness cause and cure, and economic means. In Central America pharmaceuticals are often subsumed into the hot/cold dichotomy; in East Africa they are put into the triadic ritual color code (1996:166). Professional opinions of such popular usage of medicines is that it is excessive, wrongly taken, and harmful, and that it undermines the authority of the professionals. "Noncompliance" is the key word of the medical profession which assumes the doctor's authority is supreme, when in fact most people who do not follow the prescription do so not out of disrespect or misunderstanding of the doctor, but because of their own ideas on what should be taken, and different interests. In mental health care, the most common reason that patients do not comply with prescriptions is that they deem the side effects to be worse than the illness being treated, or they believe that the medications so dull them that life is not worth living. The advent of newer drugs to treat psychoses has brought down the level of noncompliance because of their greatly reduced side effects (Staiano 2000).

The final stage of the biography of medicine is the assessment of the efficacy of that which has been taken, and its considered effectiveness. The power of medicine "extends far beyond the chemical or physical realm, . . . the effects of medication are social, cultural, psychological, and even metaphysical" (Van der Geest, Whyte, and Hardon 1996:167). Not everyone shares the pharmacologists' belief that their healing power is an inherent part of the substance. In many medical traditions of the world, the power and efficacy of medicine is considered to be conditioned by such things as the personal authority of the healer, the rituals that accompany the administration of the medicine, the words spoken, and the predisposing circumstances of the one who received the medicine. Also medical anthropologists generally do not limit the efficacy of a medicine to its chemical properties working in a vacuum; they study the symbolic and cultural aspects of expectation, connotation, and meaning that accompany the entire process of medication. Many of these features are subsumed in the placebo effect of medicines, to which we turn next.

THE PLACEBO EFFECT

The importance of the cultural context in the anthropological understanding of medicine is nowhere more important than in the **placebo effect.** The current meaning of placebo derives from the medieval Latin reference to singing vespers for the dead, specifically to the Latin version of Psalms 116:9: "Placebo Domino in regione vivorum" (I shall [be pleased to] walk before the Lord in the land of the living) (Shapiro 1968, in Brody 1977:9). This meaning of placebo has been taken up in the medical vocabulary to refer to at least two other dimensions, and the negative connotation the word has in medical usage (Schonauer 1993). The first of these is to the therapeutic use of an inert substance in which the physician wants to give the expectant patient something "to please." The second and more recent is the use of a supposedly inert substance in clinical drug trials to contrast to the active drugs being tested (Brody 1977:9–10). The negative connotation of the first use in medicine comes from the assumption that the placebo, being inert, is unethical trickery on the part of the practitioner. It is, in any case, illegal in the United States without the patient's consent.

The placebo effect has attracted the interest of anthropologists because in a number of cases where ostensibly neutral substances are used in drug or clinical trials they have been demonstrated to effect the cure as well as the active substance against which they are being tested. There is a paradox here. Either the tests are inaccurate or wrongly designed, the placebos have a therapeutic power they are said not to have, or there is a placebo reaction in the recipient that produces an independent therapeutic effect. In any case the "efficacy of the placebo" has presented a mysterious challenge to medicine and to anthropology. The accompanying vignette features research by anthropologist Daniel Moerman on the efficacy of the placebo in double-blind pharmaceutical and clinical trials.

Two other medical anthropologists, Robert Hahn and Arthur Kleinman (1983), analyzed the placebo effect. They suggested that it was part of a wider power of society and people upon each other and their bodies not just for healing but for harming, which they called the "nocebo" effect. The two together represented a generalized field within which internal and external forces operated to contribute to sickness and healing from a range of causes not perceptible in a "disease" in the strict sense. However, both explanations, while they could affirm or document the presence of sickness and healing, or even model it, did not explain how it occurred, how a placebo might effect healing, how a curse might effect silent death, or how stress might effect long-term organ damage.

VOODOO DEATH

One of the areas of interest to Hahn and Kleinman, and other anthropologists, was the previously unexplained phenomenon of "voodoo death" in which persons who believed themselves cursed or otherwise doomed, died for no apparent physiological reason as determined by attending physicians. Hahn and Kleinman thought that if these negative effects of suggestion could be understood, then the positive effects of placebo might also become transparent. Physician-anthropologists Walter Cannon (1942) and Barbara Lex (1974) reviewed the cases on record having some good medical documentation in which individuals had been ostensibly killed by curse. They suggested that the fear of curse resulted in systemic "shock," and that the deaths were caused by hormonal hyperactivity. This explanation will be taken up in the discussion of Hans Selye's general theory of stress in the next section. The vignette to follow presents the historic

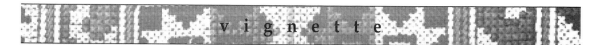

The Placebo Effect in Ulcer Medication and Coronary Bypass Surgery

Anthropologist Daniel Moerman and associates studied the placebo effect in the outcomes of a series of clinical trials for the ulcer drug cimetidine (1983) in several European countries and in North America, and in experimental coronary bypass surgeries (1985) to determine exactly what the agent of healing or pain relief might be in the placebo. The anthropological fieldwork in this case consisted of archival research into the published accounts of drug tests and clinical trials, and cultural research of societal values and clinical conditions that might account for the placebo effect in the published studies.

In each case of the cimetidine tests with ulcer sufferers, the new drug was given to one group and the control group received a neutral "placebo." The attending physicians did not know which group was given which substance. Moerman noted that in the published results of these drug trials the resulting rate in reduction of symptoms was 63 percent among the active drug recipients, whereas the rate among the placebo recipients was 48 percent, on average, a surprisingly high rate which seemed to confirm the efficacy of the drug. But when the researchers scrutinized the individual tests, they noted that the results of placebo efficacy varied greatly, from a low of 10 percent in Italy to as high as 90 percent in some German tests, where the placebo had an even higher success rate than the active drug! Moerman analyzed this remarkable range by suggesting that factors other than the medicine effected the healing of ulcers. Perhaps it had been the client's faith in the doctor, or in medicine itself. The drug manufacturers and the physicians doing the tests continued to isolate the "active" ingredient in the drug itself and to eliminate any other factors that might be responsible for the supplemental efficacy of the treatment.

Moerman and associates also studied heart surgery trials, specifically coronary bypass ligation for relief from angina pectoris, the severe symptomatic pain that accompanies arteriosclerosis and damaged heart muscle (1998:312). Accepted traditional treatment of angina pectoris for over a century has been small doses of nitroglycerin dissolved under the tongue, often followed by dramatic but temporary reduction in pain. The drug's effectiveness is thought to be due to its relaxing impact on the blood vessels, allowing the blood to flow more freely to the heart, and oxygenation to resume.

Coronary bypass surgery began to be developed in the 1940s. The first type of surgery used the internal mammary (thoracic) arteries that arise from the aorta and descend in the wall of the chest. Some of these arteries were surgically redirected (ligated) to the heart muscle to redirect blood flow and supplemental oxygen to the heart. Because the arteries redirected to the heart were relatively shallow in the chest wall, this surgery was possible with only local anesthesia. Surgical tests in the late 1950s were reported to provide symptomatic improvement (reduction in pain) in 68 percent of the first 50 cases with several months follow-up, leading to growing popularity of the procedure (1998:313).

It was during the early stages of coronary bypass surgery in the 1950s that surgical teams conducted double-blind trials on the procedure. In several such studies one of the two research teams performed the full bypass surgery, the other team carried out a sham procedure with the same operation except that the arteries were not ligated. Follow-up examinations were conducted by cardiologists unaware which patients had undergone the arterial ligation. In both studies that were performed, the sham surgeries produced the same extensive relief as the full

continued

continued from previous page

surgeries (in the actual surgery, 67 percent of 21 patients reported substantial relief, 33 percent slight relief; in the sham surgery, 83 percent of 12 patients reported substantial relief, 17 percent slight relief). The efficacy of the sham surgery— that is, the long-term reduction of angina pain— led the researchers to conclude that the actual internal mammary artery ligation was not an effective treatment, and it was abandoned.

In the 1960s, however, coronary surgeons began to treat angina pain with the use of arteries from elsewhere in the body, grafting them directly from the aorta into the coronary arteries beyond their blockage (1998:313). Today such coronary bypass surgery is a multibillion-dollar-a-year business, although the operation is still controversial. Many surgeons believe that reoxygenation is the reason for its effectiveness. This is at least the understanding in the biomedical community. Yet studies have suggested that the surgery does not increase the long-term survival rate of patients beyond those who receive medical treatment (77 per-cent versus 70 percent survival after 5

years, 58 percent versus 57 percent survival after 11 years) (1998:314). Reports accompanying this more direct type of ligation procedure have circulated which indicate reduction in pain in some cases even though all or most grafts are clogged. Even to some medical authorities it is clear that there is more going on here than merely the increase of blood flow to the heart. But what exactly is going on?

Moerman pointed out that the medical community continues to adhere to the reoxygenation theory of coronary bypass surgery's efficacy because it fits the mechanical model of the body. The surgery works, but not only for the reasons the surgeons suggest. He argued that the surgery itself and the relationship of the patient to the physician, and the patient's faith in both, represent a powerful metaphor whose action brings about the reduction in pain. Thus, the symbolic power of medicine is just as important in healing in biomedicine as it is in shamanism and other traditions. ■

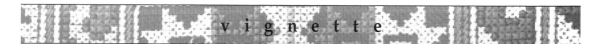

v i g n e t t e

Driving a Wedge of Anger into Mister MaKongo

In historic Kongo culture of equatorial West Africa, the wedge represents a widespread technique for social control and healing. It is very likely the origin of this aspect of Haitian and other New World voodoo. But the historic Kongo rationale for the wedges is different and more nuanced than the North American stereotype of the doll whose intent is thought to be to kill an enemy by using a pin to pierce an effigy of the person in question—the "voodoo doll."

In Kongo the wedges driven into the statues are called *mfunya*, "anger." They were driven into humanoid figures by the healers to which they belonged and wrapped with string to "tie up" the forces of conflict in order to quiet the dangerous consequences of anger between individuals in society. The figure shown here was named Mister MaKongo, Nakongo, or MaKongo Mpanzu. It was used for cases of the affliction the Kongo knew as *mpanzi*, or *lubanzi*, cramps or spasms of the side, back, neck, and head, which one translator called "stitch-in-side" and we might call tension headaches or neck aches. Today these sharp stabbing pains are still considered by the BaKongo to be the sign of interpersonal antagonism, due to a recent argument or fight, or presumed to come from a forgotten incident or an unknown assailant. Left unresolved, such anger was (and is) believed capable of making the antagonist ill, or even of leading to his or her death.

A client with this *lubanzi* or tension stitch-in-side went to the healer, who went about his work in the following manner. First, he administered tranquilizing drinks, massages, inhalation therapy with pungent incense, or plant medications rubbed into small skin cuts, to sooth the symptoms. If these measures were not effective, then, in standard Kongo therapeutic procedure, the underlying cause, the conflict and its "anger," were addressed. The wedges, driven into the statue with dramatic pronouncements,

Photo 7.2 *Mister MaKongo (or NaKongo), late 19th-century Kongo* nkisi *figure, Western Equatorial Africa. There is no good English translation of* nkisi, *so the KiKongo word is used here.*
SOURCE: Courtesy of Fowler Museum of Culture History, UCLA.

were intended to "wake up" Mister MaKongo so he would "see" the hidden links of hostility and loosen them. The pointed objects—the anger wedges, *mfunya*—are seen to have been bound with string or rags signifying the manner in which Makongo Mpanzu or its doctor "ties" (*kanga*) the force of anger, tension, or envy. If an assailant was identified, Mister MaKongo would

continued

continued from previous page

be verbally charged to return the aggression back onto him.

In these rituals of healing, we may imagine the full scene. The doctor of Makongo Mpanzu used the statue, in public performance, to address the relationship, to protect the client, to dramatize the pain or its source, and to send the pain back upon its source. In the process—songs, chants, driving the wedges, wrapping the wedges, spitting on the figure, and conversing with it— the statue was said to "have come to life" and acquired a character and a personality all its own. It became a highly charged icon, symbol, and metaphor of the environment around the sufferer

and his or her kin and community, the healer, and the entire society.

The technique described here was also applied by healer-judges to resolve conflicts between two neighboring groups with the threat that if they did not end their antagonism, Mister MaKongo or another statue like N'kondi would threaten to make the antagonists sick or to strike them with some other misfortune if they continued their aggressive activities toward one another. The vigilance of consecrated figures like MaKongo and N'kondi was credited with keeping the peace, especially in regions where centralized authorities were not common.[2] ∎

Kongo tradition from which the idea of "voodoo" killing originates, but it is not as simple as the North American stereotypes of sticking pins into a doll suggests. The historic practice illustrates the placebo and nocebo effects in a traditional Kongo form of treatment, suggesting that we have much to learn from comparative study of healing around the world.

THEORIES OF HEALING IN ANTHROPOLOGY

These examples of transformations in sickness and healing—the meanings of medicines, the placebo effect in drug trials and heart surgery procedures, "voodoo death," and the Kongo treatment for anger—illustrate the powerful forces at work in therapeutic manipulations of the body. These forces include medicinal substances and surgery as understood by mainstream medicine but, as is abundantly apparent, they include the dynamic and less well understood force of something more. While modern rationalist and positivist medicine has tried to isolate medicine and surgery from these other forces, anthropologists are interested in the entire holistic perspective of healing. We have used the term *culture* to refer to this something more that is involved in healing. The terms *placebo* and *nocebo* have been added, as have been metaphor and symbol. *Voodoo* is nothing more than a exotic word from West Africa used by many Westerners to refer to something sinister and mysterious for something that we do not understand or in any case do not believe. We may as well also introduce *magic*[3] here, another term commonly used for that which we do not understand, or which anthropologists have sometimes used to speak of workings of techniques and words that are believed to have a special power over the material world and persons.[4]

Medical anthropologists have approached the analysis of illness and healing with perspectives that go well beyond simplistic labels. Here, three such approaches will be presented that arise from the previous materials. The first of these is the theory of personhood, already introduced in the previous chapter on the lifecourse. The second is the approach of embodiment, presented in the second chapter on theory. The third is the general theory of stress as introduced to medicine by Hans Selye, and to the generalized medical theory of endocrinology, or psychoneuroimmuniology. Anthropologists have adopted and adapted these theories to account for and to de-exoticize some of the accounts like the placebo effect and voodoo death.

The "theory of the person" is used by some anthropologists to account for the ways in which humans use symbols, that is, learned representation of experience in the material world. This theory, as propounded by Howard Brody (1977:77ff), holds that humans, as animals, exist in physical space and their physical being obeys the laws of chemistry and physics; some of their behavior can be explained with such laws. However, to the extent that animals are goal oriented in their behavior and are conscious of it, they are able to choose alternative goals. To pursue a goal is common to many animals, but to reflect upon it and to select alternative goals, is a uniquely human capacity. Representation of such goals and alternatives is symbolic; that is, it is learned and reflects in previous experience. When such learned awareness of alternatives to goal-oriented behavior comes to be shared in a community, the symbols are shared and are part of culture. Language is an example of shared meaningful experience. The individual animal who participates in such a shared culture is a person.

For proponents of person theory, the relationship between the physical realm and the mind of the person is not a dichotomy but a hierarchy of capacities, such that the ability to self-consciously use symbols and mind are not opposed to the physical, but are in a sense part of it, or at least in constant interaction with it. These theorists reject the idea that there is a "mind" separate from the "body." Rather, the person is both and simultaneously mind and body, that is, being. In any event, the placebo effect, to which phenomenon Brody applied the theory of the person, argues that we need to use all capacities of the person to account for effects in any single realm of being (1977:82–84). Rather than to limit explanation of physical phenomena to physical and chemical theories, where these are not adequate to account for phenomena, other theories from symbol and culture must be incorporated. We may even need to speak of sociosomatic illness (Kleinman 1973, cited in Brody 1977:84). Anthropologist Daniel Moerman, who has done much of the anthropological research on the placebo effect, argued that the role of diagnosis in illness is crucial in human healing because it renders inchoate disease meaningful and controllable (1998:317). Likewise, in the treatment of illness as performance, medical metaphors are able to "move" us, to manipulate physical predications, in the process we call healing. Thus, the physical is affected not only by the physical and chemical of medicine, but also by symbol, metaphor, meaning, and hope.

Other anthropologists of the late 1980s and 1990s have used not personhood but the body as the central metaphor to formulate a holistic perspective on sickness and healing. They have sought to resolve or at least reformulate the observer-observed and subject-object dichotomies in anthropology, as well as to transcend the mind-body dualism of mainstream medicine and thought.

In their pathbreaking article on "The Mindful Body" (1987) Nancy Scheper-Hughes and Margaret Lock suggested that the existential experience of suffering had been overlooked in much medical anthropological writing. Their new metaphor "the mindful body" integrated the lived experience of the sufferer with a number of levels of observation: the lived self (the personal body) as a phenomenological reality, the social body of symbols and structures, and the body politic of power and control. These levels of the body metaphor may be read in correspondence one to the other, just as in experience the one shapes the other. Thus, sickness is a form of communication that may convey contradictions in life. Often contradictory sentiments and social states are metaphorized back into the body (see Lock 1993 on "*nerves*"). Medical care may itself be an exercise of power that contributes to ill health. Some medical constructs are themselves metaphors of political ideologies, as Donna Haraway suggested in her writing on the immune system as a metaphor of the Cold War (1993).

At least one author, Thomas Ots, while sympathetic to their effort, suggested that Scheper-Hughes and Lock had still not escaped the mind-body dichotomy (1991). He argued that they had prioritized the mind by making the body mindful; the mind is still the subject, and the body its object. Ots would reverse the emphasis, suggesting that one must look for the "embodied mind." Along with Scheper-Hughes and Lock, and Kathryn Staiano (1992a, 1992b), Ots, a physician, lamented the emphasis on single signs and symptoms of much medicine. Even where multiple signs and a range of subjective states are indicated in connection with a condition, biomedical thinking idealizes the elevation of one leading sign and one cause for one disease treated by one therapeutic method (1991:44). Ots does not dismiss out of hand this focus on the singularity of cause and effect in medicine; rather, he finds fault with the manner in which diagnosis and nosology have become totally dependent on the objective signs produced by instruments and tests, at the expense of a more complex somewhat intuitive traditional understanding. His interest in the role of emotions such as anger, anxiety, and depression in producing physical signs of distress led him to argue for a cross-cultural approach that can identify these connections that are often held to be true in traditional therapies. Biomedical thinking constructs its object through a monocausal etiological ideal; it discovers diseases on the basis of leading signs. Yet, said Ots, "the 'facts' we 'discover' depend on the ontological definitions of our disease constructs" (1991:44).

It will not do, Ots argued, to replace this monocausal model established by objective signs with a totally symbolic model of medical knowledge and the human being, as much current medical anthropology advocates. Rather, we need to understand the "lived body" of the human individual as subject (1991:45). For Ots the problem is not the mind-body dualism, but our society's prevailing view of an inert, intentionless body controlled by mind. This we must reject. In its place we must recognize a perception of a living, intention-capable, organism-body. Western thought, particularly 20th-century social sciences, has tended to dismiss biology and the logic of the natural world in favor of a human, thought-controlled, interpretation of things in which human rationality—that is, culture—controls and is all that matters. "The contempt of the social sciences for biology and the refusal of biomedicine to deal with culture are two sides of the same coin" (1991:49).

Ots therefore called for "a phenomenology of the 'lived-body'" (1991:46–48), which he applied to his study of Chinese traditional medicine. This phenomenology is filled with all sorts of emotions and feelings, affects, and sensations that both have a conscious dimension yet extend into unconscious or not verbally articulated realms of being. In a lengthy recital of all these sensations, feelings, impulses, and thoughts, Ots portrayed a rich fabric of subjective life that ranges from the urges of hunger and thirst, lust and feeling temperature, to pain, sense of body-self, to understanding of time, joy, speaking, feeling about others, to being moved—the range of human actuality and potentiality. A great deal of this activity is "pre-cognized," that is, it is perceived, felt, but not really thought through. Sickness and healing thus occur largely in this "lived body" realm of the feelings and senses where our physical being and our conscious being interact.

The most long-lasting theory of healing (and sickness), which has been used in anthropology to account for placebo, voodoo, and a host of other matters, is the mid-20th-century work of Montreal-based Hans Selye on the "stresses of life" (1956). We owe to Selye and his associates the notion of the "fight or flight syndrome" in reaction to danger, and to the "general adaptation system" whereby our beings either adjust to stressors or, failing to make such adjustment, eventually succumb to local or generalized breakdown. The research on laboratory rats was conducted well before the popular notion of "stress" entered our vocabulary as a popular cause for many ailments; it contributed to its spread, however. Selye's research was later extended to humans (1976; 1977; Taché, Selye, and Day 1979), with wider implications for our understanding of the role of perception and environmental factors in health, disease, and healing.[5]

Selye defined *stress* as the introduction of noxious agents, stressors, into an organism: in effect, too much or too little of practically anything (1956:109–17). In his experiments with laboratory rats, he injected toxic substances into their skin to create stress. He was interested in the short-term and the long-term consequences of these stressors in the body of the rats, and in the implications of these reactions for the overall picture one could gain of resistance and adaptation to any stressor.

The short-term impact of the stressor was localized inflammation and an increase of white blood cell production as the body sought to overcome the irritant. Selye spoke of this as the "localized adaptation syndrome" (LAS). If the irritant was maintained over a longer time period, the local inflammation receded and a more generalized reaction set in. Selye was interested in the nature of the "generalized adaptation syndrome" (GAS) because it more appropriately characterized the many types of human stressors such as worry, fear, pain, and physical irritants (1956:109–12). This longer-term continuation of stress implicated most organs and areas of the body in ways that were complex, cumulative, and unpredictable for a given individual. In other words, the unresolved stressors could contribute to breakdown in individually varying ways and timetables.

The long-term continued production of hormones could lead first to increased activity of the affected organs, and then eventually to their exhaustion or damage. Selye defined this process in terms of three stages of adaptation (1956:118–24). The first was that of "alarm reaction" in which mechanisms were mobilized to maintain life as the reaction spread to more extensive regions of the body. In a second stage, the "stage of resistance," a spatial concentration emerged to focus the adaptation on the most appropriate specific channel of defense. But continuing stress could lead to a third stage, the "stage of exhaustion." Reaction would spread due to wear and tear in the most appropriate channel of defense. At this point hormonal production would rise, but life could only be maintained until auxiliary channels were exhausted. Lesions or organ breakdown could occur from this process (1956:121). Only removal of the original stressors would "cure" the chain reaction of responses, although damage might still have been done.

The mechanism that Selye considered to produce this three-staged reaction to stress was the combined hormonal response of the thalamus and the hypothalamus, affecting the limbic system, the trigger of emotional receptors and responses. These affect the pituitary gland in the lower brain and the autonomic nervous system in all mammals. On the one hand, the process could excite the sympathetic nervous system; alternatively, it could relax the parasympathetic system. Both types of actions, working singularly or together, affect a range of organs such as the thyroid gland, adrenal cortex, liver, kidneys, blood vessels, and tissue throughout the body.

Selye was interested in the big picture in which all of the parts cohered and interacted. His shorthand explanation of hormonal responses to stress or stimuli suggested that "mineralo-inflammatory corticoids" generated a range of defensive actions. Initially the adrenal medulla produced adrenalin or *norepinephrine* to increase the heartbeat rate and to constrict blood vessels, thereby increasing blood pressure. This reaction decreased the secretion of digestive juices while increasing the secretion of blood sugar; it allowed the liver to produce glucose to activate the pituitary to increase water retention. This was the well-known fight or flight reaction. The continued production of these inflammatory corticoids could lead to exhaustion and damage, and ultimately death.

By contrast, the alternative response of the autonomic nervous system acting upon the parasympathetic system would have the effect of decreasing the heartbeat rate, relaxing the blood vessels, and in general leading to an overall increase of the anti-inflammatory corticoids within the body; in other words, the "natural healers" that we may imagine are activated with widely varying therapies of song, massage, meditation, drumming, even surgery and ingesting medicines, or seeing a highly reputed doctor.

Selye's understanding of these antagonistic hormonal activities was not just that prolonged adrenal-inflammatory corticoid activity produces breakdown and that anti-inflammatory corticoid activity produces healing or immunity, but that the prolonged or excessive activity of both systems, working against each other, has a deleterious impact on the body in that it produced raised blood pressure and had other long-term damaging or dangerous effects. Intense hormonal activity over a prolonged period can damage the organs in question, especially the thyroid, kidneys, and liver. In a sense, all organs and tissue are damaged in the long run by excessive hormonal "struggle" and are healed by the resolution of the sources of such struggle, whence the importance of meaning and social support in healing.

Narratives of Sickness and Healing

Medical anthropologists have also devoted much attention to the study of the narratives of sickness and healing, in an attempt to understand the conscious or semiconscious concepts of illness and healing. Although narratives of patients and healers have often been studied from a culturally "clean" perspective, the approaches introduced so far encourage us to look at these narratives in the context of a more fully embodied holistic approach. This section reviews a number of recent projects in medical anthropology that have researched narratives of sickness and healing. Although much of the work on narrative in medical anthropology adheres strictly to the formal characteristics of text, such narratives may also be read with an eye toward their "motivated" use to seek an understanding of how indeed narrative may afflict or heal the whole body and person. A vignette at the close of this section reports on this author's research of a widespread central and southern African form of healing ritual, *ngoma*, that includes narrative "song-dance," thereby engaging a range of sign types to seek an expression of affliction and the achievement of wholeness.

Researchers of "illness narratives" approach their subject with the premise that the experience of sickness may be told as a story, with all the properties of story: a plot, characters, a timeline with a beginning, an unfolding, a point of maximum tension or conflict between alternative forces and outcomes, and finally a denouement. "Therapeutic emplotment" (Mattingly 1994; 1998) may be developed by the sufferer, possibly together with others, including the clinical staff or healer, and gives meaning to both the suffering and the therapeutic actions by putting them within a larger story or framework. Such plots are never completely preordained, although with some stories the outcome is strongly suggested. Improvisation and revision are often evident; complete closure may not occur until after the illness has ended, if then, as the experience is retold.

Published illness narratives often show one of their most important features to be the elucidation of alternative outcomes of inherently ambiguous emotional, moral, and therapeutic situations. No life situation is more excruciating than that of an expectant mother and father to learn, through fetal testing, that their child is impaired. A study by Linda Jones and Margarete Sandelowski, "Healing Fictions: Stories of Choosing in the Aftermath of the Detection of Fetal Anomalies" (1996), described how these parents constructed subtly different accounts of pregnancies continued or terminated that located the moral agency for affecting these pregnancy outcomes either in themselves or elsewhere. Through their stories the parents were rehearsing the painful decision they would have to make to live with either outcome. The researchers identified five "emplotments of choice": nature's choice, disowned choice, choice lost, close choice, and choice found.

Jones and Sandelowski drew the conclusion from their research that such constructions of choice made by parents after a clear determination of fetal diagnosis helped to promote either psychological recovery, in case an abortion was chosen, or optimal parent-infant interaction in the event of acceptance of an impaired child.

Cancer sufferers experience many of the same dilemmas of uncertainty, dread, and the need to make life- or death-affecting decisions about therapeutic intervention. Costs are usually a consideration as well. A group of narrative researchers found that the time horizon of oncology clinicians and their patients was significantly shaped by the approach they took to the composition of their stories (Good et al., 1994). In the United States where an attitude of hope is culturally encouraged, which suggests a longer or indefinite time-horizon outcome, the uncertainty and apprehension of clinicians often betrays the cultural ideal. These clinicians often avoid the long-term view; they focus on a nearer time horizon. Thus, despite the "discourse of hope" in much of American cancer treatment, the subscript is often similar to that in cultures where the truth is kept from cancer sufferers.

In another study of cancer narratives among black women in North Carolina, in which the sufferers, their kin, and friends were listened to closely (Lannin, Mathews, and Mitchell 1994), the stories were found to serve the purpose of bringing together knowledge from a variety of sources—indigenous models of health, popular American notions about breast cancer and treatment—to gain for themselves an understanding of the nature of their disease in the face of conflicting information, and to clarify for themselves what their options were. The "cancer stories" are by no means limited to sufferers and their kin. The same dilemmas and constraints that affect sufferers may engage narrative development among clinicians and medical professionals in order to clarify options and outcomes. Linda Hunt found that practicing oncologists in a provincial Mexican setting pitched their stories around themes of remaining professional and working effectively under severe financial constraints by seeking moral vindication for their work with the poor (1994).

Chronic disease and pain sufferers, like the parents of impaired babies and cancer sufferers, have experiential ambiguities that give rise to clear narratives of illness. Above all, theirs is the dilemma of finding meaning in the face of mysterious and intractable frustration and misery. Sufferers of chronic pain have been assisted by the Rashomon approach in which a therapist-interviewer raises a series of questions that permit them to configure future experience, thereby hopefully turning the experience into a meaningful engagement of self-therapy (Jackson 1994). In other instances therapists may help a sufferer relate a chronic condition to existing cultural models shared by others, with whom they may further share their own experience and understanding (Garro 1994). In a project with Turkish epileptic sufferers, researchers found narratives by sufferers and families incorporating "subjunctivizing tactics" of story to justify continued care seeking and to maintain hope for positive, even "miraculous" outcomes. The subjunctive mode of story—"if this, then that"—provided alternative plots about both source and outcome of illness, thereby offering sufferers and families a strategy of possibility and continuity in the quest for healing (Gelisen et al. 1994).

The foregoing accounts of illness narratives deal with the story's power to effect meaning and to clarify perceived reality in difficult decision-making situations. These researchers, for reasons of theoretical concern, avoided directly imputing narrative with healing power. Others, however, focused their research not only on narrative, but on its role in healing. For example, Greg Gutfeld and Marty Munson (1993) demonstrated that stroke victims have a 65 percent better chance of improving cognitive functioning within six months if kin or others are present who listen to the sufferer, than those without next of kin or close others.

Personal observation suggests how being able to tell one's story might enhance recovery from stroke. In a visit to my wife's uncle, Wolfgang, a retired physician who had suffered a stroke which left his right side partially paralyzed and his speech slurred, it was apparent that he had not lost his mental acuity and was seeking to overcome not only his paralysis, but especially his depression over having been so disabled and curtailed in his functions. After weeks of physical therapy, he could not write and could walk only with leg braces, a cane, and close supervision. But as a consummate lifelong storyteller, whose wife and family were also storytellers and indeed usually discussed their world in storytelling form, Wolfgang needed to tell us about his stroke, his hospitalization, and his slow recovery. In his story to us, which did not need to be elicited but which sounded as if it was still in the formative phase of becoming a story, he told of having "woken one morning not being able to get up . . ." and of then "having been walked to the hospital." We noted that this was not so much a slip of grammar, but an attempt at an ironic joke about his invalidity. He talked about needing to relearn many physical functions and of his speech therapy which consisted of talking so much that he was hoarse, for which he apologized. Later, when we went to the restaurant in the rehabilitation clinic, where his wife and daughter began to tell stories, he was able to match with his own, which brought general laughter and good feeling to all, especially Wolfgang. I can imagine that he will develop a more complete story of his ordeal as time progresses, and that this will have helped him to come to terms with his disablement. In this setting, story not only lends coherence to a condition of suffering, but it may set into action some of the ineffable symbolic and biochemical forces that heal life and limb through mechanisms that Selye and others have explored.

It is a short jump from the narratives of illness reviewed so far, to narrative prayers, long held by believers to be efficacious in healing. In recent years the medical community has become increasingly interested in the power of prayer in healing and coping with disease. Clinical trials that conform to standard experimental procedures have demonstrated improvements by those sufferers involved in prayer, or for whom prayers are said, compared to those for whom this is not done. In a noteworthy experiment with 393 cancer patients in San Francisco General Hospital in 1988, half were prayed for by charismatic healers in different U.S. cities, and half were not. The patients were not aware of the prayers. Those prayed for needed less treatment than those who were not prayed for (Marquand 1995). Harvard Medical School cardiologist Herbert Benson, who is founder of the Mind-Body Medical School Institute at Deaconess Hospital in Boston, suggested, with regard to a relaxation response technique he developed, that "when a person engages in a repetitive prayer, word, sound, or phrase, and when intrusive thoughts are passively disregarded, a specific set of physiologic changes ensues" (Benson 1996). Benson believed that these techniques and powers could account for a substantial decrease in peoples' medical needs, in particular those that are due to anxiety and stress. Of the cumulative set of more than 200 clinical studies since the mid-1980s on the effects of religious ritual and activities, 160 showed positive, only 15 negative, effects on health (Marquand 1995). Not surprisingly, a 1995 editorial of the

Journal of the American Medical Association asked, "Should physicians prescribe prayer for health?" (Marwick 1995). Marwick suggested that physicians should explore the connection between prayer and healing, especially with patients with religious beliefs. The effects of religious belief should be measured, especially among patients with chronic and disabling diseases who tend to handle their situations better if they hold religious or spiritual beliefs. There are, apparently, many voices within the medical community that practice, or have an open mind toward, the power of prayer in enhancing healing. But they prefer demonstrations of this fact be clothed in and confirmed by proper experimental form.

In settings outside orthodox medicine and controlled trials, the voices advocating prayer in healing or as a primary therapy for healing are less hesitant. Women's therapy groups studied by Barbara Kazanis and Ellen Kimmel (1995) believe that women's groups are able to honor and reclaim the "feminine principle" for their exploration of goals beyond the self. Using "storytelling as prayer" they focus on stories of medicine, teaching, and power in order to find healing, development, and transformation.

In another setting, bibliotherapy, the recitation of scriptural texts pertaining to healing, is described as efficacious in the empowerment of rehabilitation clients (Byrd and Byrd 1993). Christ's identification with the chronically disabled, as seen in a series of biblical stories, becomes a source of great strength. John Carroll (1995) offered an interpretation of how this identification with a supernatural figure might lead to actual physical healing (see Photos 7.1 and 7.2). In his review of New Testament references to sickness and healing, he pointed out that Christ's healing and exorcism expresses the sovereign rule of God and victory over the dominion of Satan. In both Christ's sayings and in stories of his healing the reader encounters the fundamental conviction that God wills the wholeness of human beings.[6]

The dichotomy of drugs versus words, or surgery versus prayer, which seems to dominate in Western therapeutic thought, is, however, transcended in many non-Western therapies. In the vignette of *ngoma* healing from southern Africa, a striking range and continuum of representational media are used (Janzen 1992). A short list would need to include songs sung by individuals and by the entire group; prayers or prayerlike invocations to ancestors, to God, or to the surrounding group; rhythmic shaking of rattles, rhythmic body movement, dance, drumming; bodily decoration with medicines, color-coded and ritually signified objects such as animal skins, colored beads, and interesting things taken from daily life; blankets and commercial clothing donned and taken off at particular times in the rituals. But *ngoma* healing ritual is not reducible to its constituent elements in order to test whether the "active agent" is song, rhythm, or the medicines used. Rather, the reality of the transforming signs of sickness and healing is that they are part of a totalizing whole. Their signification and efficacy are accessible only through rich ethnographic accounting of the authentic setting in which they are used and experienced.

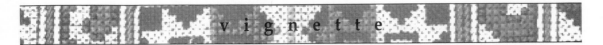

"Doing ngoma*"*, *Call and Response Song-Dance*

One of the central features of *Ngoma* ritual healing across central and southern Africa is the use of song in connection with divination of a sufferer's misfortunes, and intensive, physically demanding dancing-singing performances such as that shown in Photos 7.3 to 7.6. At periodic gatherings in the homes of healers or novice-patients, participants in these sessions who are both patients and healers "confess their dreams" and pour out their

Photos 7.3–7.6 *Doing* ngoma, *Guguleto, Cape Town, South Africa, "Doing* ngoma" *is a good translation of the Zulu and Xhosa phrase* sa ngoma.
SOURCE: J. M. Janzen.

agonies to the others present. The confessor will then break into a song and the others will respond, after which musicians enter with shakers or drums and the tight circular dancing-singing goes on until the song is spent, and another "takes up the song." *Ngoma* is a word with many meanings that include, literally, drum, but also song, singing-dancing, as well as the network of healers and novice-patients. In some regions it also includes the sense of divining the cause of misfortune and figuring out the solution.

The young man had been to a Cape Town psychiatric hospital but was not helped, so he was brought to the ngoma healer. His song was addressed to his ancestors, "Ka Ngwane, hear me!" The response by the others was a song reference to a mediator in nature: "Sing and clap for the crab alongside the water. . ." They also sang a second song which dealt with his being pent up: "He Majola, come out of jail . . . We have news of your house . . ." He was being invited, prompted, to come out of himself, to hear the news about his house.

The woman in her daily life was a single mother who worked in a home of upper-class whites in Cape Town. She was near graduation in her life as an *ngoma* healer. In the *ngoma*

convention, therapeutic initiation is indicated by a call from the ancestors or spirits who come out in song and dance. The long years of counseling and initiation serve as a time for self-clarification, for reaching peace with the spirits and those around the individual. Ideally, the patient-novice discovers in dreams a song or songs that tell his or her story. This self-story is rehearsed, sung by others, and eventually spread abroad where it may become a popular song known to many. These personal songs often tell of a historic figure such as an ancestor, or of a particularly traumatic event in the person's life, or of a difficult time for his or her people. Initially, a sufferer-novice's song may be a fleeting single phrase. After much repetition and affirmation through collective singing-dancing, the song is longer and more fully formed and nuanced. The growth of the personal song is accompanied by strong singing and self-presentation. The body costume of the novice close to graduation is more elaborate. At first only white beads and a few strands of goat hair mark the "whiteness" of the novice. Later, color is added, and elaborate beaded, furred, and blanketed costumes are created. The leader of the session is shown here with the beginnings of a colorful beaded costume.[7] ∎

THE "ART OF HEALING" AND THE CONSTRUCTION OF CLINICAL REALITY

The perceptive reader will wonder at this point where the Western clinic fits into this unfolding picture of the panoply of comparative cases of sickness and healing. Certainly many of the themes that have been raised—the course and significance of suffering, the meaning and use of medicines, the placebo effect, the place of narratives of sickness and healing—are part of the clinical experience in medicine. Anthropologists have spoken of the Western medical clinic as ritual or performance (Helman 1990:192–213), as a special kind of reality (Kleinman 1980), and as "reading a narrative" and reflecting on it (Hunter 1996). One dimension of Western medicine is commonly called the "art of healing."

Some anthropologists and medical doctors with anthropological training have seen the striking similarities between the clinic and rituals of healing and life transition. Cecil Helman, a medical doctor at University College London, regularly asks his interns to consider their own and their patients' rituals (1985). These include the white coats and stethoscopes worn to give themselves professional identity, the phases of hospitalization—admission, changing clothes, reemerging as treated or well—that are similar to the rites of passage discussed in Chapter 5. Rituals of affliction use the same symbols as rites of passage except they may become permanent markers of identity if the condition becomes chronic. Observers of the medical scene have noted the ritualistic (i.e., charged symbolic meaning) character of medicine's technology itself (see Moerman 1998 on coronary bypass surgery; Davis-Floyd 1992 on birthing).

A favorite anthropological approach to understanding the clinic is that originally proposed by psychiatrist-anthropologist Arthur Kleinman (1978, 1980, 1996), which considered primarily the **Explanatory Models** of physician and patient in the shaping of **clinical reality.** This is a largely cognitive approach that is usually restricted to the "cultural construction" of the reality of the clinical encounter. It is much favored by medical professionals who seek to bring anthropological analysis into their work and teaching (Helman 1990), although it has been applied to nonbiomedical healers such as the *tang-ki* shaman in Taiwan (Kleinman 1980) and Central African trance healers (Friedson 1996). The explanatory model of each party, or sometimes of a range of different specialists (Helman 1985), is examined in terms of the concept of disease, diagnosis of cause, nature of the treatment, and other related aspects of information. Because it is a cognitive cultural model, focused upon the ideas and concepts, it veils a commonly powerful medical establishment and extensive power around the physician. The doctor has authority over the patient for the most part (although courtesy and the popular rights movement suggest that the physician should listen to the patient's concerns), and the doctor knows what scientific medicine understands about the disease, whereas the patient is held to usually have only a folk model or a subjective sense of "illness" surrounding his or her condition. In other words, the physician's view is based on "disease" (an objective condition), whereas the explanatory model of the patient is based on "illness" (a subjective condition). The physician makes the diagnosis and the plan of treatment, not the patient, and certainly not the family or kin. Their independence from the line of reasoning of the physician is considered to be a "lack of compliance" to the expected "compliance."[8]

Distinctive about clinical reality is its synthetic, negotiated character. This quality of "reading" and interpreting the signs, of reaching decisions about next steps, and evaluating them with the patient and the patient's kin and confidants, and again interpreting them, has been compared to the practice of reading literature, of storytelling (Hunter 1996) as seen in the previous section. Physicians draw on case narrative to store experience and to apply and qualify the general rules of medical science. Clinical medicine, like reading, stimulates the moral imagination through retrospective construction of a situated, subjective account of events. Narrative, as clinical medicine, provides provisional truths that remain situated, particular, and uncertain, open to further comparison and reinterpretation.

The narrative quality of the clinical process is of course identical to the "narratives of sickness and healing," in which the concept of "therapeutic emplotment" (Mattingly 1994) is used as a way of understanding the importance of words to express suffering and to engage symbols in healing, and to give the combined group of healer(s), patient(s) and family some measure of guidance and articulation in their common experience.

If narrative is recognized as an important part of clinical reality, all of the symbolic and emotional qualities of sickness and healing may be incorporated, including the power of metaphors for disease (or disease as metaphor), and the importance of the healer as symbolic agent in healing. *The Lancet,* a leading British medical journal, editorializes (1995:1449) that the profusion of publically accessible medical information cannot replace the practitioner because the greater the mass of available and often contradictory material, the more someone will be needed to personalize, synthesize, and interpret it.

The practical importance of narrative in clinical medicine is evident in research on the extent to which medical doctors are able to speak with their patients about diagnoses, causes, and other issues pertaining to sickness and healing. A recent study by Wendy Levinson of clinical encounters in Colorado and Oregon suggested that those physicians who can talk easily with their patients, spend more time with them, and who demonstrate compassion toward them, are sued less often or not at all, even if their medical decisions formally differ little from those of their colleagues who are sued more often (1997).

The "art of healing" that is the medical clinic combines a variety of types of knowledge and practice, and many kinds of symbols, toward the end of transforming the suffering of individuals. A clinician or a healer must identify the precedent cases that resemble the case before him or her from among the many known. Although science may supply medicine's "gold standard," knowledge exercised in the care of patients is, like moral knowing and compassion, a matter of practical reason (Hunter 1996; MacNaughton and Sullivan 1996). Clinical judgment is required that cannot be reduced to rigid codes. Although working with patients requires keeping abreast of the relevant literature, it takes more than memorizing data from evidence-based medical trials in the latest research. This open-ended and personal nature of the clinical encounter makes it a rich human setting for the anthropologist to consider.

THE TRANSFORMATIONS OF THE SIGNS
OF SICKNESS AND HEALING

This chapter concludes here with an attempt to spell out and illustrate a more refined and unified approach—based in sign theory, semiotics—to understanding the nature and role of culture in the often perplexing realms of sickness and healing that anthropologists have studied in the placebo effect, voodoo death, the magic of medicine, narratives of healing, touch therapy, Christian healing, *ngoma* song-dance, and clinical reality. Such a unified approach seeks to transcend the various dichotomies that have plagued medicine and medical anthropology: culture and nature, mind and body, causality and interpretation.

The most basic feature of a sign is the relationship between an object and its representation. The object may be a thing, a process, an idea; that which represents it can be anything that is perceptible by the senses—in sound, touch, taste, smell, or sight.[9] A third feature of the sign is the interpretation of the relationship of the object to the representation, its significance, meaning, the feeling it conveys, or the consequences it may convey for immediate or future action. The triadic sign as presented here is the foundation of the most adequate rendering of the sign for medical anthropology. Its proponents have been identified at the close of Chapter 2. In the specialized vocabulary of Charles Sanders Peirce, the three poles mentioned are called the **representamen,**[10] the **object** to which it points, and the **interpretant.** The representamen identifies the experience as having a sensory pole, something like a pain, feeling, or perception. This sensation points to an object, which may be the source of pain (an infection, the sting of a bee, an injury, a threatening person in the foreground, anything). Third, there is in this formulation of the sign the interpretant, that is, a thought, intentional reaction, or name for the representamen and its object. As an experience unfolds, the triadic sign of one moment gives way to a new triadic formulation. The sign is never static; the representamen of one moment itself becomes an object to be represented and interpreted. The interpretant of one moment may be reinterpreted at the next. This process of ongoing signification is called **semiosis,** the endless unfolding of the "fluid sign" (Daniel 1985).

What medical anthropology needs, then, is a formulation of the sign—a semiotic—that can describe the range of those remarkable connections of "body" and "mind" seen in examples of sickness and healing such as the stresses of life research of Selye, the strange and persuasive power of will in the voodoo deaths, the careful reading of the role of the placebo in ulcer drug tests, the impact of touch therapy, of spoken prayer, the shaman's sung journey, as well as surgery, medication, and biomedicine when it effects cures as intended by the book. Theories of personhood, embodiment, and psychoneurology all contain dimensions that bridge causality think-

Sign Type	Relation of Sign to Object	Embodied In	Relation to Cognition	Examples
Signal	Compulsive Necessary	Organic and Material Expression	Usually Unconscious	–Immune Response
Symptom				–Sensation of Fever
Icon			Usually in Consciousness	–Fever Equated with Infection
Index				–Diagnosis: Fever Results from Infection
Symbol				–Redness of Disease Is Cultural Code for Danger
Name				–"It's the Hong Kong Flu…"
Metaphor	Arbitrary	Language		–Disease Is "a Curse from God"

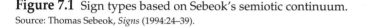

Figure 7.1 Sign types based on Sebeok's semiotic continuum.
Source: Thomas Sebeok, *Signs* (1994:24–39).

ing with interpretive thinking, but a rendering of sign theory offers the greatest range and diversity.

For our purposes it is sufficient to look to a sign typology put forward by Thomas Sebeok, dean of late 20th-century American semioticians (see Figure 7.1).[11] This scheme shows signs ranging along several axes, depending upon (1) the degree of compulsion in the relation of sign (representation) to object, (2) the sensory vehicle in which the sign is embodied (language or not), (3) the extent to which the sign is "in consciousness."

For Sebeok, the **signal** is "a sign which mechanically (naturally) or conventionally (artificially) triggers some reaction on the part of a receiver" (1994:22–24). One of the most commonly experienced signals is the system of green, yellow, and red traffic signals at the basis of our orderly pattern of going, proceeding with caution, or stopping when driving a vehicle or crossing a street on foot. The message of these signals, although culturally learned, is worldwide. The most useful aspect of the signal for the purposes of medical anthropology is the sense of it as operating "mechanically, or naturally, that is, without human consciousness," in Sebeok's terms. It is in that sense that the term *signal* is used by scientists to describe the impulses in neural transmitters, the messages between cells, the production of pain, or any sign which triggers an automatic reaction on the part of the receiver. This meaning of signal is used in the following sentence from a scientific abstract about a DNA splicing experiment to control *E. coli,* a bacteria sometimes found in food poisioning. "Plasmids containing the full-length virus sequences, placed under control of the cauliflower mosaic virus 35S promoter and the nopaline synthase termination signal, were stable and easy to amplify in *E. coli* if one or more introns were inserted into the virus sequence" (Johansen 1996). In other words, the ideal of the perfectly predictable experimental reaction was reached in this case. It is important to recognize that what medicine calls "natural" is a sign that may be situated in the same scheme as those signs that are "cultural."

The **symptom,** Sebeok suggested, is a "compulsive, automatic, nonarbitrary sign such that the signifier is coupled with [that which is] signified in the manner of a natural link" (1994: 24–28). A strong sense of co-occurrence is indicated between a symptom and its referent, either in a temporal sense (as in co-occurring), in a logical sense (they are part of the same underlying thing or process), or in an identificatory sense (they are one and the same thing; the symptom is part of its object). This feature is part of the original Greek meaning of *symptomat,* a happening or attribute which indicates the presence of a bodily disorder, subjective evidence of disease, or physical disturbance. Symptom conveys the sense of a feeling, conviction, or physical attribute that indicates the referent object, in this case the disease or injury. The symptom is the subjectively felt encounter by the individual sufferer of the sign or signal of a condition. A cluster of symptoms becomes a syndrome. In scientific and medical research, syndrome is a rule-governed configuration of symptoms with a stable and predictable designatum, which gives it a societal connotation that it might not have unless it forms part of a medically recognized condition.

The **icon** is a sign that contains its meaning in its very form and nature, according to Sebeok. It has a formal similarity between a signifier and that which it denotes (1994: 28–31).[12] We may associate the icon with the Eastern Orthodox Church's painting of a saint and the belief that the painting literally is the saint, or has attributes of the saint making the painting sacred. Or we may associate the icon with the little pictures on our computers which convey to us by direct association a particular software or function. The icon of Microsoft Works or Word Perfect is that system. A small picture of a printer, when pressed, initiates the printing function on the computer. In the strict sense of the term *icon,* the sign has a very direct identification with its object that Sebeok calls "topological similarity." In the realm of illness and healing there are many examples in which the meaning of the sign lies in its form and nature. A cataract—the film that forms over the eye—is the affliction; the spirit that possesses an individual sufferer in the *ngoma* songdance is the object of affliction and sometimes identifying it becomes the source of the cure of the affliction that it brought on. Diseases such as cancer or AIDS often evoke direct imagery of an iconic sort having to do with the meaning of the appearance of the sufferer (e.g., thin, sallow). In healing rituals the iconic dimensions of rhythm or sound patterns are independent of the verbal meaning of words and may affect their therapeutic efficacy or structure the way in which they heal (Wimsatt 1996). Rhythm, music, or the beat of recitation may have a signification separate from the meaning of the words spoken, sung, or commented.

The **index** is another important type of sign whose "signifier is contiguous with its signified, or is a sample of it" (Sebeok 1994:31–33). Contiguous here has the sense of being close or identical to, actually accounting for, the object. The index sign has sometimes been called the closest of the signs to a "scientific fact." Examples of an indexical sign include the footprint Robinson Crusoe found in the sand as evidence of some kind of being on the island, or the waggles of honeybees to convey to their fellow bees the location of pollen. In the vocabulary of signs of disease, we may think of fever as an index that is "contiguous with" (i.e., the hard evidence of) an infection or condition of disease of some kind. We speak of "health indicators" such as mortality rates and birthrates, epidemiological profiles of disease, and positive indicators such as clean and adequate water, good food, housing, and the rest of the checklist of the primary health movement.

The **symbol** is "a sign without either similarity or contiguity, but only with a conventional link between its signifier and its denotata" (Sebeok 1994:33–37). This means that there is no intrinsic or formal relationship between this kind of sign and its object. The association of a symbol with its object is usually an accident of human history that can be accounted for only by figuring out the range of meanings it has and the origins of these meanings in earlier human events. The symbol's relation to its referent is thus arbitrary rather than necessary. Language is of course the best example of symbolic activity, and the prototype of all symbolic activity, in that the means of expression have no relationship to the meaning, as in the case of indexical or iconic signs. This property of the symbol establishes an important distinction between it and the symptom on the one hand, and the signal on the other. Whereas the signal is a supposed objective or natural mark of a condition, the symptom and the symbol exist in the felt and thought perception of the subject, the sufferer, and those around the sufferer. Symptom and symbol open the way for an insinuation of culture into the sensate realm of sickness and healing without losing touch with the immediacy of the signs of the physical world such as indexes and icons.

The **name** is for Sebeok a sign that refers to a single example of a class, which allows us to identify uniqueness and singularity to something. It is a verbal symbol in language but, unlike most culturally shared symbols, a name suggests a class of objects or beings to which it refers (1994:37–39).[13] In the realm of sickness and healing, we know the significance that is given to a set of vague feelings and conditions when they are named and placed within a category of causes and associations. Naming the condition is an important part of diagnosis; it is the first step of healing of an illness.

Naming goes well beyond tagging; it brings cultural definition to an experience of being sick, to a scattered syndrome of signs and symptoms. Such a definition may be a matter-of-fact description of some functional insufficiency, defined normatively, as in the case of "lactose intolerance," meaning that one cannot digest animal milk products. Naming also carries with it the particularity of an individual sufferer's condition, as when it is announced that Joe Blow has a serious case of diabetes.

The names of many illnesses do more than simply describe the deficiency or pathology. They may carry a set of powerful cultural definers full of stigmas, connotations, and social expectations. The kinds of illnesses mentioned in the previous chapter that redefine existence by describing the victim as a state of being (as in "being an epileptic," "being a schizophrenic") are among the most illustrious examples of this type. Names such as this are really metaphors because they bring additional identifiers, which have an independent identity, into association with the condition and the sufferer.

Susan Sontag has studied the metaphors of illness, using Aristotle's definition of **metaphor** as "giving a thing a name that belongs to something else" (1988:5). Based on her own experience with cancer in *Illness as Metaphor* (1977), she explored the powerful connotations generated around that disease, as well as tuberculosis in the 19th century. To be diagnosed with CANCER was tantamount to receiving a social death sentence. Other individuals around the sufferer, even family members, tended to avoid the afflicted individual. In her *AIDS and Its Metaphors* (1988) Sontag explored the more recent powerful connotations quickly assumed by this illness name, transforming those identified with it into society's stigmatized outcasts. To have identified a condition "TB" in the 19th century, "cancer" in the mid-20th century, or "AIDS" at the turn of the 21st century, clearly went beyond descriptive labeling to construct a metaphor of powerful connotations. Often such disease metaphors are extremely negative and mystifying, leading Sontag to campaign to demystify and dispel them by arguing that "illness is not a metaphor." But of course it is not the affected individual that makes such a judgment; rather it is society or other individuals using society's conventions. For our purposes Sontag made the important point that metaphors of disease are supernames that draw from the disease to provide culture with imagery, and bring from cultural imagery the stuff of naming, meaning, and emotion with which to define disease.

This continuum of types of signs, as presented by Sebeok, moves from the "automatic" or "compulsive" levels of the signal and the symptom, to the more specific realms of the icon and index which are still governed by necessity although the form may be particular, to the arbitrariness and particularity of the relationship between form and content found in the symbol, the name, and the metaphor.

This range of significations and other attributes of sign types (see Figure 7.1) establishes a continuum much more nuanced than a simple division between causality and interpretation so often thought to divide the natural sciences from the social and cultural sciences. It also facilitates our understanding of the ways that the entire gamut of significations flows together and are part of one semiosic process—within and across the signal, symptom, icon, index, symbol, and name/metaphor. The "engine" of this motion of the sign process is the triadic sign within the settings of firstness, secondness, and thirdness, all of which are integral in Peirce's semiotics.

Such a semiosic process is evident, and transparent, in the illustrations offered earlier in this chapter of the biography of medicines, the placebo effect, and voodoo death or "driving wedges of anger into Mister MaKongo," or of various narratives of healing. A fairly narrow spectrum semiosis is involved in the effect of drugs that operate at the level and in the way signaled by chemical processes. However, who is to say—and double-blind placebo studies suggest—that broad semiosis across the spectrum of signs is not indicated in drug efficacy. To believe in the power of a medicine (or healer, or technique) that is chemically powerful brings at least signals, symbols, names, and metaphors into action, a process ranging from firstness to thirdness.

Over time in the experience of illness and healing, the vague signals and symptoms in what Peirce called a quality of "firstness" whose "sign's character is in itself," may give way to the beginning of recognition of the object of disease (Peirce 1955:97). In the case of malaria the victim may wonder, "Do I have something? I feel vaguely achy and sick." Then with the onset of the fever and chills it is clear that this is malaria. Peirce attributed the quality of "secondness" to this recognition phase. Icon and index may also be a part of this dimension of semiosis, in the way the fever and chills are identified with the sickness. "Thirdness" is a type of knowing which was reactive and conscious, represented by the third part of the sign Peirce called the interpretant: concepts and language, perhaps a theory of causation, names for the parts of the disease. Firstness, secondness, and thirdness are really ways of knowing that correspond to the sign types. In philosophical terms, they are three kinds of epistemologies: Firstness is characterized by vague feelings signaled by bodily processes; secondness is characterized by embodiment with some consciousness; thirdness is characterized by conscious schemes articulated with conscious cultural models and language.

Peirce's triadic sign is certainly more intricate than the dyadic sign in which there is a signifier and a signified, a sign and an object, or a sign and a referent. The advantage of the triadic sign in medical anthropology is that we can overcome the paralyzing dichotomies between body and mind, fact and symbol, cause and interpretation; even that distinction between illness and disease now appears to be in trouble because the object of the sign, whatever it is, is constantly being rerepresented and reinterpreted, which in turn influences its very ontological character. The direction of semiosis moves not only from the signal and symptom to the icon and symbol, and from firstness to thirdness, but also in the opposite direction, suggesting that relationships, thoughts, and words may affect our inner feelings as well as our well-being. It is a way of saying that although the "natural" course of disease may run its course quite predictably, all those other influences of the immune system—the mind-set, the presence of others and their mind-sets—may also play a role in shaping the course or its outcome. Rather than to simply attribute this shaping to mystery, magic, coincidence, or the placebo effect, we now have a language with which we can describe the process.

Thomas Ots suggested (1991:50–51) that a semiotics like that presented here can grasp and model the intelligence and intention of organisms, including those of disease as well as those of the human "lived body" and all its complex actions and reactions. Organisms can and do learn; they store information, have a memory, and respond to their immediate environment. It is not possible to differentiate between subject and object in this view of the lived body. Rather, following the work of Thomas Von Uexkull and W. Wesiack (1988:131), Ots suggested that we need to adopt a semiotics that includes the actual signs and their combinations (syntactics), the meaning and interpretation of the signs (semantics), and the clues for action or nonaction (pragmatics).[14]

CONCLUSION

The study of the experience of sickness and healing in medical anthropology has gravitated around the distinction between a subject (of consciousness, of action) and an object (of study, of being acted upon). An oversimplification of this distinction has led to the so-called mind/body problem which has often been blamed on Western thought or on René Descartes or modern biomedicine. As has been seen here, however, various formulations of sickness and healing and the nature of the human space have allowed a far more nuanced perspective of these issues. Approaches to sickness and healing as reviewed and discussed here—Selye's general adaptation system, the placebo/nocebo model of Hahn and Kleinman, the "mindful body" of Scheper-Hughes and Lock, the "embodied mind" of Ots, or the clinical trials of narrative therapies—have all suggested that medical anthropology can formulate a holistic approach to a range of traditions and practices.

The sign continuum allows us to imagine the transformations of the signs of sickness and healing as a somewhat fluid, or at least flowing, series of signification enactments, which at one end are compulsive and automatic—those that are in consciousness although perhaps not willed—and at the other end those that are intentional, reflexive, and verbalized. But the logic of this continuum must not be seen as a series of contrastive oppositions, but as a progression with neither end claiming priority.

"Voodoo death" has been in the anthropological spotlight for a long time as a set of exotic stories from around the non-Western world. As it turns out, the stereotypes of voodoo are wrongly oversimplified, especially when traced to their African origins as the vignette on Mister MaKongo does. However, even with a more sophisticated reading of this use of metaphors of anger driven into a human-like sculpture at the bodily place of the pain, the underlying interpretation of those interested in voodoo death proves useful. In the Kongo case, anger in social relations is taken seriously as a cause of affliction, even in the late 20th century long after the wedges and statues have been abandoned. The insights of the power of symbols and metaphors in conceptualizing illness and healing may then be applied to areas of our own medicine. The demystification of the placebo as a "symbolic specific" standing for the patient's belief in medicine, the doctor, or a cure, reveals the pervasiveness of culture in all medicine.

Even more inclusive is the song-dance of *Ngoma* in exercising the entire gamut of signs. "Getting out the words" and continually exchanging songs in a charged rhythmic, emotive, danced rite releases sources of energy that are said by those involved to heal. I have argued elsewhere that we must not isolate the rhythmic drumming and dancing as a kind of iconic reductionism in trying to analyze these therapeutic rites. Nor would it be right to say that the verbal component is "more important" than the dance. Clearly *Ngoma* "plays" the entire spectrum of signs in their distinctive and combined potential for healing transformation.

A knowledge of the spectrum of signs in sickness and healing might be of assistance to the medical anthropologist or health practitioner in looking across healing traditions to see practices in pluralistic health systems. How, in the other tradition, are the symptoms expressed? How are the icons, metaphors, and symbols of illness couched and expressed? How are words and names used to give powerful connotations? Are those words directed back into bodily signs? Do they transform health?

The knowledge of the spectrum of signs would also be of help in looking for cultural signification beyond the spectacular practices and rites of healing in the very ordinary practices of food preparation, bodily rituals such as bathing or not bathing, the meaning of bodily fluids and excreta, and the way these are mirrored in social relationships. Something as innocent as a request to boil drinking water or to wash one's hands with soap, in the interest of public health, may have extensive symbolic and emotional implications. At their most general level, the transforming signs of sickness and healing remain one of the most fascinating and challenging areas of medical anthropology.

REVIEW QUESTIONS

1. Can there be illness without disease? Disease without illness? Offer some examples.

2. Can you think of some ways in which sickness and suffering are culturally defined, that are different in national or religious traditions?

3. What are the ways in which medicines have meaning in Van der Geest's review of the "biography of medicines"?

4. The placebo is a seeming anomaly in modern medicine, yet it is an important example of the fusion of the "physical" and the "symbolic." What role is it supposed to play in the double-blind test in pharmaceutical research? Why does it not always "behave" as in the cimetidine studies? Or in the coronary bypass studies? What accounted for the wide range of variance (10 percent to 90 percent) in the efficacy of the placebo-treated groups in the cimetidine studies? What are the implications of "placebo

efficacy" for understanding illness, healing and ritual?

5. What are the neurophysiological processes that commonly occur in the "fight or flight" alarm reaction? What happens to the tissue or organism or the entire person in the longer-term alarm/resistance/exhaustion sequence in Hans Selye's general adaption syndrome (GAS)?

6. Apply the Selye GAS to a negative "fight or flight" syndrome that results in exhaustion such as migration, getting a cold, experiencing grief or war, a major change, so-called voodoo death, or any other similar stressor. Can you similarly find a positive example of the GAS that results in a healing outcome?

7. "Embodiment" theory has had a major impact in medical anthropology. How does this perspective influence the interpretation of illness, personhood, culture, the reading of emotions, and relationships? Review

the application of this perspective to health, illness, and healing material.

8. What is the reason for the change in the discourse on cancer in the United States in the past 10 years, according to Mary-Jo Delvecchio Good, from keeping the diagnosis a secret to telling it with hope? What does this reveal about the assumptions of the physicians of the emotional causes, or at least contributing causes, of cancer?

9. Illustrate the place of story in both the expression of suffering and in the therapeutic process. Describe a particular circumstance or published example of the role of narrative in sickness and healing. How might one analyze the power of story, of words, in these circumstances?

10. How does the construction of clinical reality help determine the efficacy of a therapy carried out in that reality?

11. Why do the physicians who speak easily and frequently with their patients have a lower rate of being sued for malpractice (according to Wendy Levinson's study) than their counterparts who don't, even when there is little or no appreciable difference in the content of their clinical care?

12. What are the distinctive features of the points of Sebeok's sign continuum that include signal, symptom, index, icon, symbol and name (including metaphor)? Can you illustrate most or all of these types of signification in one and the same sickness experience, either simultaneously, or at successive stages of an experience.

NOTES

1. For Peirce, such firstness was described as "existence" without awareness or, as he phrased this in one of many passages that might be quoted, "existing independent of anything else" (Peirce 1955:322).

2. This vignette was summarized from much more technical research and writing on Kongo min'kisi by the author (see especially Janzen 1982b), Wyatt MacGaffey (1991), and Karl Laman (1962:142–148). Makongo, Nakongo, and Mwe Kongo are more or less synonymous appelations translated here as Mister MaKongo, although in particular circumstances one or the other name would be used for this nkisi to treat stitch-in-side or related conditions. Specialized applications of this type of nkisi gave rise to second names such as Makongo Mpanzu, Makongo Banga, Makongo Mbongo, and Makongo Mbu (MacGaffey 1991:179–181).

3. The term *magic* derives from the Greek adoption of the Persian *Magus,* originally sorcerer, or wise men, *magi.*

4. Anthropologist Malinowski distinguished magic from religion on the one hand, and from science on the other. Magic is practical acts and words used in "domains of the unaccountable and of adverse influences, or the unearned increment of fortunate coincidence," whereas religion is the adoration of unseen beings; science, like everyday common sense, is the art of the empirical, of well-known conditions, the natural course of things (1948:29). He was particularly interested in the way language was used in magical formula, and spoke of the "meaning of meaningless words" in the efficacy of magic to lend cohesion to social relations and cultural values otherwise called into question or threatened by misfortune,

the unknown, and the dangerous (1965, vol. II, 213ff). The relevance of such understanding of "magic" in healing, in the face of uncertainty and death, is clearly apparent.

5. Selye's work has been followed by a host of research in psychoneuroimmunology, the "fight and flight" syndrome and stress. This literature is too vast for the present space and setting.

6. Ironically, this enthusiastic near single-minded identification on scriptural and spiritual healing is given a reality check by Lutheran theologian and church historian Martin Marty (1994), who urged caution in the face of these newly discovered, yet ancient, Christian practices. The holism that is sought, he wisely suggested, will only be found by also ministering to physical needs with the best of modern medicine.

7. This research was conducted in 1982 and 1983 in Kinshasa, Zaire; Dar es Salaam, Tanzania; Swaziland; and Cape Town, South Africa, with a Senior Research Fellowship from the Fulbright-Hays Commission.

8. Kleinman, however, has recently expressed his own misgivings about the "politically blind" application of the Explanatory Model approach to understanding clinical reality through a kind of insular doctor-patient relationship (Kleinman 1994: 8–9). The model overly formalizes, and overly simplifies, the context of medical decision making. It ignores the power relationships of the context of therapeutic activity. He has favored a more ethnographic approach to describing the context of suffering and healing.

9. In biosemiotics, such representation may also occur outside human perception, in the reception of any organism to a stimulus.

10. Some versions of sign theory used by anthropologists rely on a diadic sign constituting a "signifier" and a "signified," roughly equivalent to the object and the combined representation and interpretation. The representamen in Peirce's scheme is roughly the same as Ferdinand de Saussure's signifier; the interpretant the same as Saussure's signified. The diadic sign of Saussure is derived fully from a linguistic basis of culture and lacks the independent object of the Peircian scheme.

11. Sign "grid," "hierarchy," or even a "sign kaleidoscope" would most accurately describe the "world perfused with signs" visualized by Charles Sanders Peirce, who in one scheme suggested 32 different types of signs, and elsewhere thousands!

12. The original reads: "topological similarity between a signifier and its denotata."

13. The original reads: "has an extensional class for its designatum."

14. The terms *syntatics, semantics,* and *pragmatics* were first used in this combination by Charles Morris (1971:38).

MEDICAL KNOWLEDGE

Photo 8.1 *Tanzanian healer Mahamoud Kingiri-Ngiri of Dares Salaam reads to a woman who is suffering from irregular menses. His practice is a combination of Swahili African medicine, Islamic "Medicine of the Prophet" as articulated by Abdul Fattah of Egypt, and the local version of Sufism, one of the major denominations of Islam that emphasizes mystical union with the supernatural.*
SOURCE: J. M. Janzen.

WAYS OF KNOWING, TYPES OF KNOWLEDGE

This chapter examines the ways anthropologists have approached the subject of knowledge about health, illness, and healing in a range of societies and traditions. What is medical knowledge? Let us begin with that which is most familiar from the perspective of students of medical anthropology. In the Western industrial world, science is considered to be the source and standard of medical knowledge. Science is commonly understood to be knowledge that is somehow systematized, orderly, and established through widespread empirical observation, laboratory research, or experimentation under specially controlled conditions through which the investigators may arrive at generalizations based on propositions or hypotheses that account for the facts. Every year Nobel Prizes are awarded for the most significant research breakthroughs in the discovery of treatments for major diseases, or for the most insightful advances of fundamental understanding of human functioning. Is this not how medical knowledge is established and advanced in the modern industrial world?

Although scientific procedures as described are certainly central to medicine, brief reflection will demonstrate that there are indeed other kinds of knowing that must be included in an anthropological—that is, holistic, inclusive—picture of "medical knowledge." The knowledge a physician has of his or her patients is of a different sort, more personalized, than that gained from the laboratory or from clinical trials. The "art of healing" and the persona of the doctor as considered in Chapter 7 may well be as important to effective care as the memorized knowledge of the research literature. Common sense about health on the part of private persons is a kind of medical knowledge. These several kinds of knowledge, even within modern biomedicine, are qualitatively different, but each contributes to the whole of what we call medicine.

If we open the scope of our investigation to the study of worldwide healing traditions and their historical backgrounds—a must for anthropological consideration—then we recognize an even greater range of types of knowledge. We may approach this subject as if there are different types of knowledge used in medical settings (e.g, common sense, traditional understandings, empirically tested knowledge, including a vast lore of medicinal plants, the techniques with which to use them, and other materia medica); classical texts, both written and orally transmitted, that couch the wisdom of learning and practice in canonized form; dream- or trance-derived directives from spirits, the findings of diviners; understandings of emotional states and collective symbols, including those bound up in stories and performances used by ritualistic healers often called shamans.

At this broader scope of coverage, knowledge in health and medicine usually centers around theories or concepts of disease or illness, their causes, consequences, and implications, the substance of symbols, and the power of healers, techniques, and materia medica. Questions of how knowledge is constituted, legitimated, tested or critiqued, and transmitted are part of the context of knowledge that interests anthropologists.

Much of the vocabulary we use in the Western world to discuss medical knowledge comes from the ancient Greek term for knowledge, **gnosis.** The derivation of common medical terms is readily apparent. **Diagnosis** is the recognition of a disease by its signs and symptoms; **prognosis** is the foretelling of the outcome of the course of a disease or peculiarities of a case on the basis of the diagnostician's understanding of the case in the light of other prior cases; **nosology** is the discipline of classifying medical knowledge around the symptoms and signs of given conditions of distress. These arrangements of signs and symptoms are sometimes referred to as a **taxonomy** (from the Greek for "arrangement" as in syntax, order of words, or taxidermy). How we know these signs and symptoms of disease—by observation, by theoretical deduction, by some other means such as dreaming or spirit possession, and so forth—is called **epistemology,** a branch of philosophy that investigates the origin, structure, methods, and validity of knowledge (Runes: 1959:94). In a recent project on medical knowledge in the major traditions deriving from ancient Greece, ancient India, and China, two concepts were set forth in order to review and compare these major classical traditions that have informed much of the world's medicine since then: the "gnostic" and the "epistemic" (Bates 1995:3). In the first, knowledge is centered on the knower, on the process of learning, experience, or initiation. In the second, knowledge is centered on the constituted body of knowledge, its theories, its methods and substance which in medicine would deal with diseases and how to heal them, and how it may be known. These initial ideas provide an opening profile of concepts and tools that anthropologists often use to discuss the ranges of knowing and classifying understanding about health and affliction around the world.

The classical medical traditions of Asia, Europe, and Africa are often associated with founding—historical or legendary—figures to whom central ideas are attributed. Ancient Greek medicine is often traced back to dynastic Egypt, and the role of culture hero Imhotep, the vizier, architect, and physician of King Djoser who united Upper and Lower Egypt in 2600 B.C., and was later identified by the Greeks as Aesculapius, patron god of healing (Steuer and Saunders 1959; Westerndorf 1978:141). About a dozen manuscripts survive from this early period of Egyptian medicine, indicating the degree of its development of an understanding of pathologies that were given pragmatic explanation or considered to be caused by spiritual or magical forces (Janzen and Feierman 1992:196). Later, Greek medicine would come to be identified with the writing of Hippocrates (ca. 460–377 B.C.) and Galen (A.D. 129–ca. 1999) who would explain and codify the basis of the humoral perspective that would persist for over a millennium, within Islamic learning in North Africa and the Middle East.

The Chinese medical classic *Nan-Ching* (also known as the *I-Ching*), which scholars trace back to either the fifth or eighth centuries A.D., presents 81 "difficult issues" that lay out the basis for a coherent view of the complementary cosmic forces yin and yang with reference to all known medical conditions, the organs, their diagnosis, and therapeutic practices, including the use of medicines, dieting, and acupuncture (Unschuld 1986:33). The *Nan-Ching,* like some other ancient medical texts, carries a pedigree of sponsors or authorities who have successively held to this teaching, or who have commented on or amended it. Two thousand years of Chinese medical learning has provided perhaps the most complex classical tradition known, one that continues to be mined and studied by scholars and practitioners alike.

In India the situation is very similar, where the classic teachings of Ayurveda are contained in two nearly 2,000-year-old Sanskrit texts by Caraka (the *Carakasamhita*) and Sucruta (the *Sucrutasamhita*), thought by modern scholars to be the systematization of earlier legends and teachings (Mazars, in Huard, Bossy, and Mazars 1978:20–21), often attributed to the god Brahman. These texts spell out the details of surgery, medicine of the throat and eyes, general therapy, toxicology, demonology, obstetrics and pediatrics, tonic medicine, and aphrodisiacs (1978:20). As in China, the Indian texts have had many commentators over the centuries who have amended and interpreted the ancient teachings. In addition to the basic teachings of Ayurveda in India, the healing arts of Yoga and Siddha must be added, each of which has its classic texts as well. French anthropologist-historian Francis Zimmerman (1982, 1985, 1995) has devoted much of his career to the study of how generations of Indian medical scholars have transcribed and commented upon the classic texts over 2,000 years. A "high tradition" based upon Sanskrit learning fuses with more vernacular texts in other languages that in turn reflect oral "folk" traditions maintained by thousands of healers and priests in Indian villages and towns.

A similar combination of local or regional practice and more widespread textual knowledge is presented by the Tanzanian healer Mahamoud Kingiri-Ngiri, shown in Photo 8.1 reciting from a text attributed to Egyptian Abdul Fattah. Kingiri-Ngiri speaks of himself as a *waganga,* the Swahili term for doctor, yet he avoids some of the African ritual practices, using in their place Sufi Islamic ceremonies and practices. The text by Abdul Fattah is grounded in the Medicine of the Prophet tradition that includes elements of classical Greek medical learning along with Islamic mysticism and the tradition of the prophet Muhammad.

Classic texts may also come in nonwritten form, notably in societies and civilizations in which the discipline of memorization and performance are even more highly cultivated than in literate societies. Numerous examples of healers using such texts exist in a variety of traditions. Chapter 7 refers to African song-dance healing in the Ngoma tradition whose core features extend throughout central and southern Africa (Janzen 1992). In her book *Taming the Wind of Desire* (1991), Carol Laderman published a transcription of two lengthy healing texts by Malay *main peteri* shaman Mat Daud bin Panjak. The emphasis on performance in these oral texts suggests that music, perhaps dance, and the entire emotionally laden setting is as much a part of the knowledge as the words. Anthropologists have emphasized the broadening of the concept of "text" to include much of the "context."

If what we call "medical knowledge" is opened to such a diversity of modes and formulated in a variety of types of social settings and media of articulation, can we still speak of this knowledge as "progressing" cumulatively as we do with scientific knowledge? Or must we accept that there are multiple types of knowledge, all culturally shaped and contextualized, and that each has its unique modes of being constituted and validated? In other words, is medical knowledge in some sense absolute or is it relative? These questions are not only part of the anthropology of medical traditions, but also they are debated within the philosophy of medicine and science. If medical knowledge is to be cumulative, the forms—types of arguments, concepts of cause—in which it is formulated need to be constant. In this view, truth is truth, no matter what era; we can learn, and are inheritors of the work of the ancients such as Imenhotep and Aesculapius, Hippocrates, Galen; the authors of the Nan Ching; Carnaka and Sucruta; Malay shaman Mat Daud bin Panjak; and many more healers.

In the face of precisely such diversity of medical knowledge within and across medical traditions, an alternative view that is widespread in the philosophy of science is that what has been called "normal science" is governed by **paradigms,** that is, assumptions and working practices. In his widely known work *The Structure of Scientific Revolutions,* philosopher of science Thomas Kuhn defined paradigms as "universally recognized scientific achievements that for a time provide model problems and solutions to a community of practitioners" (1970:viii). Kuhn suggested that scientific work itself may frequently point out the contradictions within an existing ruling paradigm and, as the established theorems and assumptions fit decreasingly well, a new paradigm or paradigms may take the place of the preexisting one. Soon scholarly knowledge is evaluated in terms of the new paradigm, and the previous paradigm becomes history; it is no longer valid, it does not explain reality. Consider what occurred to the understanding of malaria ("mal aire," bad air of the swamps) once the transmission of the malaria protozoa from mosquitoes to the human bloodstream was discovered. The old humoral view of bad air was overthrown, for these and other reasons, by the view of disease as an intruding organism.

If Kuhn is right, it means that anthropologists of health, illness, and healing may look at all kinds of knowledge as culturally constituted views of reality. What then happens to the idea of cumulative knowledge? And to the claims to truth of science? In a sense the debate of the nature of scientific, and presumably medical, knowledge is between Aristotle and Kuhn (Beyley

1995; Gillett 1995). On the one hand, the defenders of Science, or medicine as science, have suggested that the notion of "heresy in science" be reintroduced to defend science from practices or ideas that depart too far from orthodoxy of a cumulative science (Wolpe 1994). On the other hand is the perspective that knowledge is made up of "incommensurate world views." In this perspective, to hold to the view of singular truth is a "reflection of unproblematized power. . . [and of the] agency of persons living in society who shape this knowledge. . . " (Legge 1995).

THE SHAPE OF MEDICAL KNOWLEDGE

Having opened so many options to medical knowledge may seem disconcerting to the student of medical anthropology. Yet at another level it is possible to recognize a few clear substantive themes at the center of most healing traditions, regardless of the type of knowledge in which they are couched. These are (1) the identification of cause and cure of affliction, (2) the scale, scope, and focus of such concepts, and (3) the situation of the person within this framework.

IDENTIFYING CAUSE AND CURE
One of the most readily visible attributes of medical knowledge is the manner in which cause and cure are articulated, that is, the notions about what causes disease and how it is manifested in signs and symptoms. Another term often used for the cause of disease is **etiology.** Generally a corresponding cure will be based on the way the notion of cause is understood, and the wider underlying ideas about the way elements and forces in the world act upon one another. Efforts by anthropologists to create global summaries of cause and cure have, until recently, been summarized in George Peter Murdock's *Theories of Illness: A World Survey* (1980). In his attempt to create a rubric for comparison, Murdock has contrasted "natural" from "supernatural" causation theories. The first includes theories of infection, stress, deterioration, and accident. The second includes theories of mystical causation (fate, ominous sensation, contagion, mystical retribution), animistic causation (soul loss, spirit aggression), and magical causation (sorcery, witchcraft). Other anthropologists, having looked at the same material, have formulated the range of cause and cure ideas to exist worldwide in medical thinking as revealing, in pure or blended synthesis, a basic distinction between "naturalistic" and "personalistic" causal regimes (see, for example, Foster and Anderson 1978).

Such generalized catalogs may be helpful for broad identifications and comparisons, but they do not explain how the theories of health, illness, and healing come together as complex ideas, especially in the major classical medical traditions of Asia and Africa, and how these are often blended within specific disease contexts. They also do not seem to accommodate the historical changes of these medical traditions, including modern biomedicine, which usually brings several causal notions to bear on single illness and healing situations. The basic notions of these classical traditions may be reviewed here, as they were introduced earlier in Chapter 3.

Soul loss is the leading etiology of affliction in the Asian and American traditions associated with shamanism. Retrieval of the soul, the protection of the soul, or the creation of harmony between souls in the universe, are the fitting therapies for soul loss. A different kind of etiological idea widespread in Old World traditions, and echoed in New World traditions, is the **imbalance** of elements in the body or the universe such as blood, bile, and other fluids, or forces such as wind, water, fire, and air. Thermal ideas of disease are very widespread, according to which disease is caused by excessive heat or cold, or contact with those substances or forces that promote one or the other, causing the affected person to become excessively influenced by one or the other, therefore sick. Our ecological theory of disease and health represents a kind of imbalance/balance theory of disease, as does the idea of an immune system that somehow protects the health of organisms because all the parts are in balance.

Another kind of disease cause has to do with the **intrusion** into the body or personal space by an agent or substance which is believed to injure the host. Spirits, witchcraft, dirt, or germs have at various times been seen in this way to cause disease. The "germ theory of disease" is based on the intrusion of the pathogen. Curing consists in either effective protection against harmful outside agents through ritual purity, cleanliness, antibodies, or other shields and defenses, or through driving out, cutting out, or destroying the intrusive agent. In a sense, our view of cancer has until recently been based on the intrusion view—"the cancer is in my liver, or stomach, or brain." Appropriate cure of a disease object which has "intruded" is to suck it out, cut it out, zap it through radiation, or remove it in one way or another. As medical ideas of the "cause" of cancer have shifted to other theories, treatments have shifted as well to reflect new understandings such as various internal or systemic causes including stress, environmental and nutritional pollution, the breakdown of the immune system, and most recently, genetic markers and inherited predisposition. As a better understanding of the immune system was reached, treatment such as the weakening of the immune system became the cause as well as the effect of new diseases such as AIDS, "*a*cquired *i*mmune *d*eficiency *s*yndrome," although the HIV+ designation still was framed in terms of the intrusive virus.

SCALE, SCOPE, AND FOCUS

A second dimension of medical knowledge that may be noted is the scale, scope, and focus of these notions of illness and healing. A part of the presence of culture in medicine is that scale, scope, and focus of ideas of illness and healing are not always automatically fixed upon the individual and the body. The range of scale, scope, and focus is so great that adherents of one profile of concepts may not even recognize those of the other as belonging within "medicine." A few examples will illustrate the extent of variation here.

Late 19th- and early 20th-century biomedicine may have been the most narrowly focused of all medical traditions, and, indeed, one direction of the development of medical research continues to study increasingly minute elements and units of the body, finding the microcosm of life within organ, cell, atom, molecule, and gene. At the same time current biomedicine, or its internal critics, find new links between organisms, cells, atoms, and genes of a broader ecology of health. The preoccupation of the single cause and single effect model of biomedicine may be located within a certain historical period that begins with the invention of the microscope, the discovery of several bacilli-based diseases (e.g., smallpox by Edward Jenner), and the discovery of corresponding vaccines using the diseases as antidotes. This "paradigm" of the narrow focus of knowledge of disease cause continues even with the search for genetic information that marks the predisposition to disease. However, there is now a greater realization than before of the importance of other factors such as diet and the environment.

The classical medical traditions of Asia and Africa mentioned in Chapter 2 and earlier in this chapter all emphasize the broader forces of the universe, whether "cosmic," "natural," or "social" that encompass the individual. The African notion of the "human cause" of misfortune couches the physical specifics of disease within this broader framework of harmony in the social or even the natural realm. The Chinese concept of the harmonization of the yin and yang principles widens the framework to cosmic forces. Perhaps nowhere is the framework of human health and ill health, fortune and misfortune, as broad as in some North American native cultures where some situations of distress in the human community can only be resolved by "world renewal" ceremonies that include all of life, whose harmonious relationships are necessary for the human community to prosper. The scale, scope, and focus of ideas of cause and cure thus constitute an important dimension of medical knowledge without which the anthropologist cannot make sense of what people may be doing or expect to have done for health to be restored.

SITUATION OF THE PERSON

A third dimension or perspective that shapes medical knowledge may be outlined in the situating of the **person/body** within the first two dimensions of medical knowledge. This third dimension of course has to do with the way that personhood and body are defined, as was seen in Chapter 6, and the manner in which the first two dimensions—ideas of cause and cure, and their scale, scope and focus—play upon the person/body. Just as social personhood is negotiated and defined in society—defined by laws, court cases, and religious beliefs—so the shape of medical knowledge revolves about definitions of personhood and body. Much has been made of the influence of the "mind-body" dichotomy in Western thinking and culture, and especially in the moral elevation of thought over the emotions and bodily functions such as sexuality. The apostle Paul of the early Christian church and French philosopher René Descartes are often blamed for this Western mind-body dualism. Although there are countervailing tendencies in Western thought, such as the holism of the Hebrew (as opposed to Greek) view of the person in the Bible, the works of some later medical writers such as Paracelsus (1493–1541), and right up to psychosomatic medicine, it is apparent that the Western division of mind and body has been very pervasive and has affected Western medical thinking.

The concept of the person, however defined, remains an essential component of the shape of medical knowledge. This includes establishing the boundaries between persons, the way relationships are defined and the inner person is divided (or not divided) into complementary attributes, parts, and functions, whether they are given positive or negative value, and their temporal status in the sequence of life events. The following vignette summarizes research by Narcisse de Medeiros (1994) on the juxtaposition of West African, South American, and biomedical ideas of cause, scale, scope, and focus, and the situating of the person.

THE POWER OF CLASSIFICATION IN KNOWLEDGE CREATION

One of the most active and readily accessible aspects of medical knowledge has been *nosology,* the operation of categorizing and classifying signs, symptoms, and syndromes of affliction in order to identify diseases. This is a supremely semiotic process (Corin 1989a:463); signification is established as the signs, symptoms, and syndromes are selected and associated, whether loosely or tightly, with named diseases entities. The process literally brings into being a "body of knowledge." We are all affected by this process which occurs each time a doctor considers vague signs and symptoms we bring as a patient, and these are put through a diagnosis and several laboratory tests until finally a name is pronounced. You then have a disease, or are diseased.

Nosological work is at the center of medicine in current industrialized societies of the world. Several well-known examples will be reviewed here to illustrate the process and to establish a comparative basis to show that this creation of classifications is the same type of activity that has gone on in world cultures for a long time. Anthropologists study cultural classification

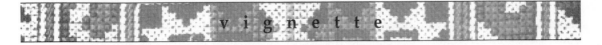

Blending Popular and Academic Medical Knowledge in Ouidah Television[1]

Early in the 19th century a number of Brazilians actively involved in the trans-Atlantic slave trade created a colony named Ouidah on the Slave Coast near Abomey in the African kingdom of Dahomey. The main purpose of this colony was to take advantage of the opportunities of open trade in slaves and other commodities between the New World and the interior of West Africa. A significant portion of the people of Ouidah were of mixed Portuguese-Brazilian and Afro-Brazilian origin, in particular those of Yoruban ancestry. The distinctions between slave and slave trader often became blurred over time; that is, the ancestry of particular individuals extended back into both groups. Today, over a century after the end of the slave trade, and nearly 40 years after the demise of European colonialism, Ouidahians retain their distinctive Portuguese-Brazilian-Yoruban identity within the modern nation of Benin.

Narcisse de Medieros is a physician of this Yoruban-Brazilian-Ouidah-Benin background. In the late 1980s and early 1990s, he undertook research in ethnography and communications to identify the popular medical knowledge of the people of Ouidah and wider Benin society concerning the causes of some common illnesses. His project was undertaken to inform a health promotion campaign by the Ministry of Health. He studied the responses of a selected number of households to televised "spots" that depicted scenes of health-related dramas around several well-known and preventable diseases, including sexually transmitted diseases, tuberculosis, and water-borne diseases which cause diarrhea, dysentery, and cholera. Although ownership of television sets is limited to the middle and upper-middle classes in Benin, television is quite influential because many people view it in the houses of extended lineage families, or they watch it in public sites like bars. Medieros's sample consisted of several dozens of these extended households which served as focus groups. Pilot health-related spots were produced and broadcast, depicting scenes and discussions about the diseases that were targeted for attention.

The impact of the health spots was surprising. It was established that a high number of the respondents to the TV spots in the study were well aware of the biomedical explanation of the diseases depicted, the causal agents involved, and consequent requirements for their prevention. However, a significant number also attributed these "germ"-based diseases to attributes of broader transmission through dimensions of the individual's relationships to a kin community. In other words, the Benin "person" seemed to be broader, more inclusive, and subject to wider influences in the minds of Benin respondents than in the minds of medical researchers. The implications of the televised health campaign were that the promotion of a "narrow" idea of cause around a single individual did not persuade the audience to abandon their broader causality that allowed for sorcery and witchcraft, as well as community support, in their view of disease and health in society. ■

---

for what it can tell us about cultural order and, more specifically here, medical knowledge.

The most widespread example of medical classification is the **International Classification of Disease** (ICD), developed by the World Health Organization, which is in its ninth edition at the time of this writing. The ICD has become the bible of medical nosology and is used by biomedical practitioners the world over. A second classification of wide interest is the *Diagnostic and Statistical Manual* put out by the American Association of Psychology. It too has received continual revisions, and is in its fifth edition at the time of this writing, known as DSM-V. The third example of current medical taxonomy has arisen around disabilities, such as the **International Classification of Impairments, Disability and Handicaps,** also sponsored by the World Health Organization in collaboration with other organizations seeking to develop attention toward the disabled or the handicapped.

Summary examination of an earlier version of the ICD (WHO 1957; College of General Practitioners and Research 1963) demonstrates how such a medical classification is put together. It is organized into 19 classes that cover the known universe of diseases, related signs, symptoms, and syndromes or general conditions, as follows:

1. Communicable [contagious] diseases.
2. Neoplasms [tumors, growths].
3. Allergic, endocrine system, metabolic and nutritional diseases.
4. Diseases of blood and blood-forming organs.
5. Mental, psychoneurotic and personality disorders.
6. Diseases of the nervous system and sense organs.
7. Diseases of the circulatory system.
8. Diseases of the respiratory system.
9. Diseases of the digestive system.
10. Diseases of genitourinary system.
11. Deliveries and complications of pregnancy, childbirth, and Puerperlum.
12. Diseases of skin and cellular tissue.
13. Diseases of bones and organs of movement.
14. Congenital malformations.
15. Certain diseases of early infancy.
16. Symptoms and ill-defined conditions.
17. Accidents, poisoning, and violence.
18. Prophylactic procedures.
19. Administrative procedures.

Each of the classes, except for 18 and 19, are set up listing numbered, known "diseases" first, followed by descriptive signs, symptoms, and descriptive conditions that are often clustered around body parts or regions or organic functions. Category 1, communicable diseases, begins with such well-identified diseases as tuberculosis of the respiratory system (1.001–008), other forms of tuberculosis (1.010–019), syphilis (1.020–029); there follow such diseases as dysentery (1.045–048), chicken pox (1.087), scabies (1.135). The first category is the oldest category of the ICD, reflecting the earlier preoccupation of infectious and communicable diseases. Neoplasms (category 2) is divided between malignant neoplasms situated by location or organ (2.140–207) and benign neoplasms (2.213–229), and followed by signs and symptoms such as ascites (158), pleural effusions (519.2), and other symptoms, signs, or incompletely diagnosed diseases in this group (1963: 208). As the ICD of 1957 progresses, the category is increasingly filled out with vague descriptive terms rather than diseases. This is especially true of those categories dealing with mental, psychoneurotic, and personality disorders (5), deliveries and complications of pregnancy, childbirth, and puerperlum (11) and accidents, poisoning, and violence (17). Category 11 includes complications of delivery as well as puzzling categories such as "delivery without complications" (11.660) and "normal delivery" (11.Y.06). Category 16 is a list of conditions like headaches, coma, fever—signs and symptoms which cannot be attributed to a specific cause; Category 17 describes such extremely varied incidents as fractures, lacerations, burns, alcohol poisoning, including "motion sickness" (17.N989), as well as "symptoms, signs, and imprecisely determined conditions in this group" (College of General Practitioners and Research 1963: 216).

The International Classification of Disabilities should be appreciated by students of medical classification as an effort to create a comprehensive list of known afflictions so that they have a scientific, uniform global listing of conditions which, as physicians, they must treat. For the World Health Organization, this listing provided the basis for a comprehensive and global record of diseases, the first of its kind. Since its creation, it has been adopted by most nations and international organizations. It is reflected increasingly in medical research and writing, including disciplines such as medical anthropology (see Chapter 2).

Classifications such as the ICD have become indispensable in a variety of areas. The documentation of worldwide diseases, especially epidemics, is done by the World Health Organization and agencies such as the U.S. Centers for Disease Control in Atlanta for public health purposes. Classifications have also become key instruments for use by government health agencies, health insurance companies, and health management organizations (HMOs) in the control of "third-party payment" regulation and coordination such as every health insurance company makes to medical practitioners or their clients. In health care systems in which the state pays for medical interventions, classifications play the same role. In an era of managed care, as for-profit agencies serve this function of monitoring care and payment, the classification provides the instrument for regulation of expenditures and reimbursements. Specified conditions are given specific reimbursement levels. Peer review groups or quality assurance committees monitor the practitioner's diagnosis, providing a secondary oversight on behalf of the health care providing company. The classifications of symptoms, syndromes, signs, and diseases or conditions represent an attempt to codify for practitioners those conditions whose diagnoses and therapies are deemed legitimate for reimbursement. The aura of reality given to a cluster of signs and symptoms when they are named as a disease is strengthened if this naming legitimizes the payment of funds for treatment by medical practitioners and institutions.

Medical anthropologists and medical historians look at these official classifications and note a certain similarity between them. Each contains an epistemology of lesion (way of determining the injury), based on some theory of the person, scale, cause and cure, meaning, and, implicitly or explicitly, in the background, a notion of what is normal functioning. Anthropologists are accustomed to recognizing that all cultures organize knowledge in those areas where there is much activity and where there is otherwise considerable attention. This is the well-known cultural phenomenon that results in the Inuit and other northern peoples having dozens of words for snow and icy conditions. Similarly, pastoral nomads have detailed schemes and terms for the anatomy and habits of their livestock. Herbal-based medicinal traditions of the tropics have well-organized classifications of medicinal plants and their appropriate applications. Anthropologists have examined many such disease classifications that exist entirely outside of the world of the ICD, the DSM-V, and the International Classification of Disabilities.

Anthropologist Charles Frake, working in the 1950s and 1960s, and using the then popular methods adapted from descriptive linguistics, which were known as "componential analysis" or "ethnographic semantics," studied the classification of skin diseases among the Subanun of Mindanao in the Philippines (1961). He was interested in understanding both this particular domain of classification, as well as the general process of cultural classification. He had a hunch that this realm would be a good focus for such a study, because the Mindanao talked a great deal about medicinal plants and diseases such as those affecting the skin. When the Subanun mentioned an instance of being sick and named a condition, Frake's basic question would be, "What kind of illness is that?" The answer would reveal the disease category (1961:115). Following through with this approach, he constructed an elaborate Subanun conceptual scheme based on answers to a series of questions about diagnostic categories (i.e., the conceptual entity which classifies particular instances of being sick); the disease name involved in the instance, the single reference to "being sick"; the diagnostically significant responses to questions about the origin of illness and prior diagnostic condition (what he called the "prodromal criteria"), symptomatic criteria (diagnostically significant responses to questions regarding attributes of illness currently perceptible to patient or observer), and finally the etiological, or causal, criteria (what caused the disease, and why, through divination). This scheme pertaining to skin alone (1961:116) included 132 diseases with unique distinctive labels, and 186 disease categories, some of which may be translated into English as familiar conditions such as rash, eruption, inflammation, sore, ringworm, and itch (1961:118). Writing about the Subanun classificatory activity in realms such as disease and plants, Frake concluded that "conceptually, the disease world like the plant world, exhaustively divides into a set of mutually exclusive categories. Ideally every illness either fits into one category or is describable as a conjunction of several categories. . . the conceptual exhaustiveness of the Subanun classification of natural phenomena contrasts with reported situations of many other peoples" (1961:131). In other words, Frake thought the Subanun were more rigorous in their classification of the natural world than many other human communities.

Critics and later observers who tried to replicate this method of ethnographic study eventually discovered that most people, when asked, could create similarly exhaustive classifications of their illnesses and other cultural realms. Most of these schemes looked curiously like the pyramidal classifications of academic biology or the disease classifications of the ICD. Many anthropologists who tried this method concluded that it had the potential to produce a classificatory scheme that was an artifact of the method used unless exercised with caution.

Other anthropologists tried Frake's and similar approaches to study disease and treatment classifications, often with good results. Dennis Warren amassed in great detail the classification of diseases and cures among the Techiman-Bono, an Akan people in Ghana, as part of a longer-range project to bring this classification to the attention of health workers ((1979; 1982). P. Stanley Yoder (1995) followed similar techniques to elicit the categories of differentiation that mothers of infants in Shaba, Zaire, made (in Swahili) of their babies' diarrhea. He also studied their treatment interventions. The overall purpose of his work was to launch a public health education program for more effective home use of oral rehydration therapy to bring infant diarrhea, the number one killer of children globally, under control. Among the many studies of indigenous classifications of illnesses or treatments that have been made by anthropologists, one needs to mention physician-anthropologist Gilbert Lewis's systematic research of disease classifications among the Gnau peoples of the Sepik River in New Guinea (1975, 1976), or the work by Susan Dawson and her colleagues on the place of acute respiratory infections in illness classification among the Boholano of the Philippines (1995).

Anthropologists and medical historians who study cultural classification emphasize that particular realms of classification like disease categories, appropriate treatments, or types of plants are subject to change over time, even within the same society and healing tradition. Also they note that the same cultural realm in two different societies is very likely to be seen relatively differently in each setting. In other words, although cultural classification may follow somewhat similar procedures of generalization toward categories, on the one hand, and particularization toward unique experience, on the other, the cumulative culture of a society—its knowledge—is a reflection of its distinctive historical experience and central values. Anthropologists have brought home some of their discoveries about cultural classification the world over. They are taking a closer look at this aspect of the culture of biomedicine and the way it creates its medical knowledge. Several examples of ongoing changes in the ICD reflect heightened awareness of special areas of health concern. Thus, the role of nutrition-related diseases has recently come under close scrutiny because of the resistance by third-party payment groups to pay for foods prescribed by care givers as the best treatment for protein-energy malnutrition. The American Dietetic Association recommends revision and amplification of that portion of the ICD pertaining to malnutrition (Babineau et al. 1996). Similarly, the growing attention to the ethical dilemmas of the end of life, and the conditions of death and dying in the late 20th century and early 21st century—no doubt driven by the rising costs and increasing numbers of the very elderly in the United States—has led to a realization that the ICD needed a category for the terminal condition apart from every disease. Dying was finally recognized as a part of life, rather than as a disease. In its ninth revision (1994), the ICD included a code for terminal care that was different from any disease classification (Cassel and Vladeck 1996).

This recognition of the manner in which a disease classification reflects the historical changes of society is not surprising to anthropologists and medical historians. The very rooting of modern disease classification in a particular historical era and as part of the mind-set of that era is more remarkable, but should not surprise us either. This is precisely what French rehabilitation physician and anthropologist Claude Hamonet has done in his scholarly and practical medical work with disability. As the related vignette demonstrates, he places Western medical classification squarely within 18th-century cultural history, more precisely to Swedish naturalist Carolus Linnaeus (see Photo 8.2). Reflecting the Enlightenment worldview that the created order was God's handiwork, therefore orderly, Linnaeus used a scheme of inclusive and exclusive categories to create a pyramidal universe of plants and animals that is still used today. Discrete yet interconnected species, genera, classes, and orders describe this view of the natural world, a scheme that many consider reality.

Although this classification scheme continues to be applied to the botanical and biological universe, its application to human society in the 18th and 19th centuries, in an analogy of the natural species, gave rise to human racial classes, consisting of physical traits such as skin color, facial shape, hair, and believed geographical origin. These racial classifications fueled virulent racism and atrocities in the 20th century. The anthropological perspective of cultural relativity, the doctrine of culture as learned rather than inherent, and the discoveries of genetic science in the blueprinting of thousands of physical traits have completely invalidated the former racial theories derived from a Linnaean classificatory scheme of the natural order. Nevertheless, once created and absorbed within many national societies, the "races" persist in popular thought.

Nowhere has the anthropological study and critique of medical classification been more energetic than on that portion devoted to psychiatric

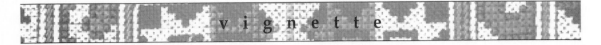

The History and Power of Medical Classification, seen in Claude Hamonet's Classification of 'Handicaps'[2]

Western efforts at systematic disease classifications derive from the tradition of the 18th-century Enlightenment when natural philosophers sought to describe the full range of the universe of species, races, and all phenomena. Claude Hamonet has

Photo 8.2 *Carolus Linnaeus (1707–1778), Swedish naturalist, as a young man. He is shown here with books, a plant he may be ready to examine, and collection bags hanging from his waist. His influence is still felt today in the phrase "Linnaean taxonomy," to refer to the way natural orders are classified.*
SOURCE: Wellcome Library London.

demonstrated a direct "genealogical ancestry" in 20th-century French medical classifications from 18th-century classifications by Swedish naturalist Carolus Linnaeus, the first modern thinker to systematically organize nature— species, genus, class, and so forth—along the lines we now often hold to be "natural." Hamonet, a French rehabilitation physician and anthropologist, set out in 1980 to develop a classification of disability (handicaps) for the World Health Organization that would place this field, yet unrepresented, within or alongside the International Classification of Diseases. As Hamonet worked on his anthropology disserta- tion and for WHO, he was drawn increasingly to the history of medical classifications. Tracing the history of French medical classifications led him back to the work of Jacques Bertillon (1912), then Philippe Pinel (1802) (see Figure 8.1), and Boissier de Sauvages (1761) and ultimately to Linnaeus (1735).

This retrospective view of the history of disease classifications, and thus of the identi- fication of the scientific object of medicine, was very useful as a way to situate the concept of handicap in relation to that of disease. Parallel to Hamonet's work was that of Michel Foucault (1963, 1972) who, in his research on "the archae- ology of medical thought," found French author Boissier de Sauvages's *Nosologica metodica* (1761), which transferred Linnaeus's classification of the natural order directly to the classification of diseases.

With this understanding of the historical construction of natural classifications in a genealogical line from Linnaeus to the late 20th-century disease classifications of the World Health Organization, Hamonet set about to create a classificatory approach to disability

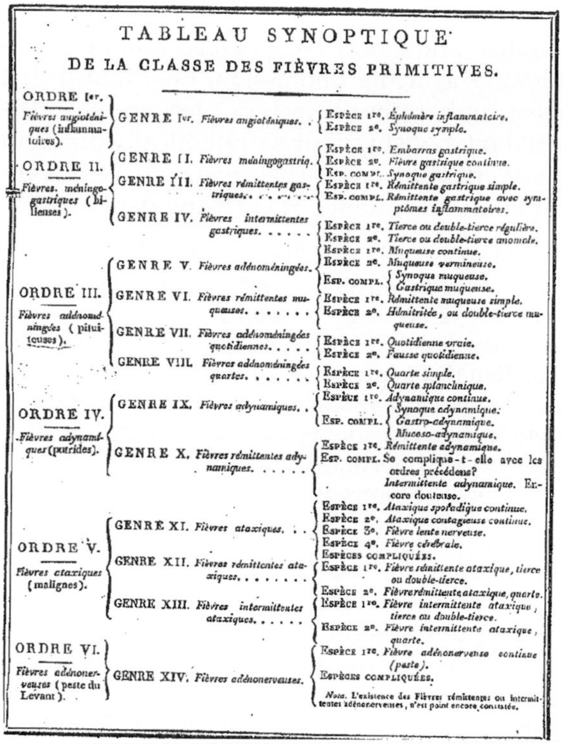
TABLEAU SYNOPTIQUE
DE LA CLASSE DES FIÈVRES PRIMITIVES.

ORDRE Ier. Fièvres angioténiques (inflammatoires).
GENRE Ier. Fièvres angioténiques. — Espèce 1re. Éphémère inflammatoire. Espèce 2e. Synoque symple.

ORDRE II. Fièvres méningo-gastriques (bilieuses).
GENRE II. Fièvres méningogastriq. — Espèce 1re. Embarras gastrique. Espèce 2e. Fièvre gastrique continue. Esp. compl. Synoque gastrique.
GENRE III. Fièvres rémittentes gastriques. — Espèce 1re. Rémittente gastrique simple. Esp. compl. Rémittente gastrique avec symptômes inflammatoires.
GENRE IV. Fièvres intermittentes gastriques. — Espèce 1re. Tierce ou double-tierce régulière. Espèce 2e. Tierce ou double-tierce anomale.

ORDRE III. Fièvres adénoméningées (pituiteuses).
GENRE V. Fièvres adénoméningées. — Espèce 1re. Muqueuse continue. Espèce 2e. Muqueuse vermineuse. Esp. compl. Synoque muqueuse. Gastrique muqueuse.
GENRE VI. Fièvres rémittentes muqueuses. — Espèce 1re. Rémittente muqueuse simple. Espèce 2e. Hémitritée, ou double-tierce muqueuse.
GENRE VII. Fièvres adénoméningées quotidiennes. — Espèce 1re. Quotidienne vraie. Espèce 2e. Fausse quotidienne.
GENRE VIII. Fièvres adénoméningées quartes. — Espèce 1re. Quarte simple. Espèce 2e. Quarte splanchnique.

ORDRE IV. Fièvres adynamiques (putrides).
GENRE IX. Fièvres adynamiques. — Espèce 1re. Adynamique continue. Esp. compl. Synoque adynamique. Gastro-adynamique. Muqueso-adynamique.
GENRE X. Fièvres rémittentes adynamiques. — Espèce 1re. Rémittente adynamique. Esp. compl. Se complique-t-elle avec les ordres précédens? Intermittente adynamique. Encore douteuse.

ORDRE V. Fièvres ataxiques (malignes).
GENRE XI. Fièvres ataxiques. — Espèce 1re. Ataxique sporadique continue. Espèce 2e. Ataxique contagieuse continue. Espèce 3e. Fièvre lente nerveuse. Espèce 4e. Fièvre cérébrale. Espèces compliquées.
GENRE XII. Fièvres rémittentes ataxiques. — Espèce 1re. Fièvre rémittente ataxique, tierce ou double-tierce. Espèce 2e. Fièvre rémittente ataxique, quarte.
GENRE XIII. Fièvres intermittentes ataxiques. — Espèce 1re. Fièvre intermittente ataxique, tierce ou double-tierce. Espèce 2e. Fièvre intermittente ataxique, quarte.

ORDRE VI. Fièvres adénonerveuses (peste du Levant).
GENRE XIV. Fièvres adénonerveuses. — Espèce 1re. Fièvre adénonerveuse continue (peste). Espèces compliquées.

Nota. L'existence des Fièvres rémittentes ou intermittentes adénonerveuses, n'est point encore constatée.

Figure 8.1 Classification of types of fevers in the "Tableau Synoptique" (1802) by French medical scholar Philippe Pinel (1745–1826).
Source: Courtesy of Claude Hamonet.

that would not stigmatize the object/person, so that a handicap would not overwhelm the identity of the individual. He was aware that societies often marginalize those with chronic disabilities, making them into "lepers" or outcasts. As the head of a large unit at the Hôpital Henri Mondor in a Parisian suburb, Hamonet was particularly concerned to avoid this process of marginalization through cultural categorization. He was aware that the French language does not use the word "disability" (*deshabilité*), a negative term, but uses "handicap" instead to describe impaired physical functioning. He researched the origins of the term *handicap* and discovered its sports origins, where it means that certain competitors are provided an extra advantage to equalize their chances of winning. In his work on classifying impairment, he stressed the handicaps, the methods of providing "head starts"—that is, rehabilitating those who needed it—rather than to classify on the basis of disability. As a physician and an anthropologist, Hamonet was able to create the culture of handicap so as to avoid some of the negative stereotypes that would come from simply transferring a taxonomy of nature, and disease, onto disabilities, with all the reification and stigma that this implies. ■

conditions, as contained in the *Diagnostic and Statistical Manual* (DSM) of the American Psychological Association. There has been widespread tension in this field between those practitioners and scholars seeking to establish a scientific medical basis for psychiatry as a universal branch of medicine, and those who see it as a field of syndromes and conditions that vary due to the experience and cultural context of the sufferer, or to unique historical conditions. Anthropologists, or clinicians trained in anthropology who have studied this field closely, are wary of the process of diagnosis, prognosis, and treatment that simply applies the DSM labels onto individuals and puts them through a regimen of care based on that condition. At the root of this unease with the DSM is the question of whether the diseases it describes are really entities, rooted in some universal biological property, or whether they are **culture-bound syndromes,** specific to a particular community, society, or cultural tradition.

The case of "depression" is instructive. Although a gathering of anthropologists and psychiatrists (Kleinman and Good 1985) agreed that there is a hormonal basis for what we identify as acute depression, they found that dysphoria—sadness, hopelessness, unhappiness, lack of pleasure with the things of the world and with social relationships—has dramatically different meaning and form in different societies (1985: 3). The organizers of this investigation reported some examples of this difference in "being depressed."

> For Buddhists, pleasure in the world and social ties is the basis of suffering; dysphoria is the road to salvation. For Shiite Muslims in Iran, grief is a religious experience, associated with recognition of the tragic consequences of living justly in an unjust world; the ability to experience dysphoria fully is a marker of depth of person and understanding. The Kaluli of Papua New Guinea value full and dramatic expression of sadness and grieving; Balinese and Thai-Lao, by contrast, "smooth out" emotional highs and lows to preserve a pure, refined, and smooth interior self. Members of such societies vary not only in how they express dysphoric emotion; they seem to experience forms of emotions that are not part of the repertoire of others. (1985: 3).

The authors argued that since there are no constant universal symptoms and values for depression, one must face the possibility that ultimately there is no disease known as depression. The role of culture which establishes the values of dysphoria determine whether the condition will be considered a virtue or a negative state, a disease.

Some psychiatrists and anthropologists have therefore tried to bring culture into the *Diagnostic and Statistical Manual,* so that the culture bound syndrome is recognized, even though it is not universal. Thus, in the DSM-IV revision, where such lobbying by culturally attuned anthropologists and psychiatrists was substantial, some culturally specific syndromes were included. *Koro,* a Malaysian and East Asian condition producing "sudden intense anxiety that sexual organs will recede into the body and cause death," was included (Goleman 1995); as was *Qi-gong,* a Chinese psychotic reaction described as "a short episode of mental symptoms after engaging in Chinese folk practice of *qi-gong,*" or "exercise of vital energy"; as was *Taijin kyofusho,* a Japanese "intense fear that the body, its parts or functions displease, embarrass or are offensive to others" (Goleman 1995). But the DSM did not include many other culturally specific conditions considered to be real to their sufferers, but limited to a non-Western cultural reality. Some of these include: "Running amok" (Malaysia), "a brooding followed by a violent outburst, often precipitated by a slight or insult; seems to be prevalent only among men"; "ghost sickness" (American Indians), "a preoccupation with death and the dead, with bad dreams, fainting, appetite loss, fear, hallucinations"; *publoktoq* (Arctic and subarctic Eskimo), "extreme excitement, physical and verbal violence for up to 30 minutes, then convulsions and short coma"; or *susto* (Latino groups in the United States and the Caribbean), "illness tied to a frightening event that makes the soul leave the body, causing unhappiness and sickness."

Arthur Kleinman, psychiatrist-anthropologist who has promoted the recognition of these culturally specific syndromes or conditions into standard psychotherapeutic procedures and classifications, argued that many psychiatric nosologies are culturally constructed. Some of the common conditions or disorders in the United States which we believe to be diseases are limited to middle-class westerners. For example, anorexia nervosa is a culturally specific disorder in a society where thinness is highly valued; it was until recently unheard of among American Indians (Kleinman, in Goleman 1995). No matter how persuasive the anthropologists' argument of the cultural construction of illness may be, medical specialists perceive it as an erosion of their claim to scientific authority. Byron Good commented on the implications of the difficulty with which culture was incorporated into the DSM-IV.

> Cultural concerns are represented in a significant manner in the text of DSM-IV—in the Introduction, in the introduction to the multi-axial structure, in the text associated with particular categories . . . and in the "outline for cultural formulation" appearing in Appendix I. On the other hand, many of the substantive recommendations made by the task force—the wording of particular symptom criteria, variations in duration criteria, the inclusion of new or revised categories (a mixed anxiety-depression category, culturally distinctive forms of dissociative disorders, neurasthenia as seen and diagnosed in many Asian cultures), significant revisions of the definition of personality disorders—were not incorporated into the body of the manual, in spite of strong empirical data from the cross-cultural research literature. The primary trust and philosophic commitments of the DSM-IV remained largely impervious to the empirical and ultimately political claims of those at the cultural margins of American society (Good 1996:128).

The emergence or construction of a psychiatric syndrome for war trauma, studied by medical anthropologist Allan Young, is one of the best documented psychiatric "new diseases" of the 20th century. Young's work illustrates that culture is part of disease classification at the heart of current Western therapy. In his initial interest in post-traumatic stress syndrome (PTSS) or post-traumatic stress disorder (PTSD) among Vietnam War veterans, Young was led back to what had happened to soldiers in World War I. Veterans of that war were often plagued with bad dreams, trouble sleeping, and difficulty getting on with their lives after the war. Investigators of this scene, including the early medical anthropologist W. H. R. Rivers, recognized "shock" as a consequence of experience in battle. However, this label had become so generalized by the Vietnam War that it was not adequate as a description of what veterans hospital physicians were finding. Thus, they adapted an already existing diagnosis, post-traumatic stress syndrome, to the condition of the Vietnam War veteran's common reaction to battle. Young's ethnography and analysis in *The Harmony of Illusions* (1995) documented the stages from the time Vietnam veterans were in Veterans Administration hospitals with a variety of conditions, to the wholesale use of "post-traumatic stress disorder," which in effect created a disease identity for the Vietnam veterans based on the conditions in the official *Diagnostic and Statistical Manual*. Backed by the Veterans Administration and the American Psychological Association, PTSD is a legitimate psychiatric condition whose care and treatment is reimbursed by health insurance companies and the U.S. government. Young was clear in stating that he did not believe that PTSD is a single disease; rather, it exists as a taxon in the classification. Therefore, for all intents and purposes, it is real, culturally real. Young's work attested to the power of cultural classification already seen in Hamonet's work on disability, or handicap. It behooves those who create and redefine the classifications of diseases and conditions addressed by medicine to realize that a name given to a cluster of signs and symptoms is a first step toward creating a reality.

THE CONSTRUCTION, CONTROL, AND TRANSFERENCE OF MEDICAL KNOWLEDGE

Wherever specialized medical knowledge is codified and practiced, it is protected by rules, procedures, and ethical norms. It is also taught to new practitioners. This holds whether one is considering shamanism, African or Asian healing, practitioners of the classic medical literary traditions of Asia and Europe, popular ideas of health and healing, or current professionalized, academic, and bureaucratized biomedicine. In each case there is some agreement by those within concerning what is regarded as common knowledge (which includes a view of reality), who should or should not use or have access to this knowledge, and what should be taught to those destined or designated to acquire it for future use. Some of these issues concerning the control of medical knowledge will be considered more fully in the next chapter on the institutional context of medical thought and practice, and the enormous difference made when such knowledge comes to be held and practiced by a trained elite which makes its professional living from such knowledge.

One of the most widespread modes of control and instruction of medical knowledge has been the apprentice form of initiation. Understudies, disciples, favorite followers, or however they are designated, assist and learn from a master practitioner or scholar the basic secrets, teachings, and practices of the tradition. This form of teaching is reflected in the genealogies, or pedigrees, that accompany texts in classical medical traditions, much like source citations in modern scholarship. Practitioners or learned scholars may certify their practice by invoking their teacher, and the teacher's teacher, and so on back to the master. This "genealogy of knowledge" also exists in many orally transmitted traditions of learning, such as the Malay *main-peteri* shaman or the African *ngoma* diviner-healer. Sometimes the named source of the recitation, song, or recipe is a human ancestor or a spirit. Important in such usage may be that the source of knowledge is outside oneself, in the sacred otherworld, safe from questioning rivals.

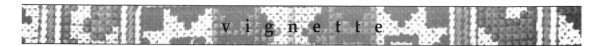

Transmitting Medical Knowledge at Harvard Medical School

Byron Good and Mary Jo Delvecchio Good, medical anthropologists, undertook to contribute to a medical anthropological understanding of biomedicine's "medical knowledge." In the light of other studies that have been conducted of medical knowledge, biomedicine in particular, they were persuaded that this could only be done meaningfully by doing a situated, contextualized, and ethnographically rich portrayal of a cross-section of one setting. They studied three groups in the class of 1990 at Harvard Medical School who were involved respectively in the traditional curriculum, the "New Pathway" curriculum, and the health sciences and technology curriculum. They interviewed the students several times, attended classes and clinics for first-year students, and interviewed faculty and administrators about the new curriculum. Some ethnographic observation was also done. By concentrating on the training of physicians, they believed they could discern the "phenomenological dimensions of medical knowledge, on how the medical world, including the objects of the medical gaze, are built up, how the subjects of that gaze—the students and the physicians—are reconstituted in the process, and how distinctive forms of reasoning about that world are learned." (1993: 83–84).

The findings of this inquiry are given in accounts of several thematic premises that pervade medical training, as follows:

1. **Medicine is science, especially biochemistry.** The first two years of the curriculum are emphasized as being science, above all, because medicine is science. Science is based on facts and is value-free.

2. **The person is a body.** The object of medicine is the individual person, but above all, the body. This is made clear in the way teaching is done through case histories of individuals afflicted with particular diseases or conditions. These individual cases suggest that disease results from organisms or toxins trespassing the boundaries of the body or an organism.

3. **Medicine is about "entering the body."** Through the case histories and in lab exercises, it is made very clear that medicine is nothing if it does not get inside of the body. The microscope of the histology lab provides entry into the world of the cell and all the mechanisms and communications and transports across and among systems of the body. The anatomy lab and the cadavers bring the student into physical touch with the inside of the head, torso, feet, arms, muscles, skeleton, and organs of the cadaver. The radiology lab provides another entry into the body, through X-ray, CAT scan, nuclear magnetic resonance (NMR) images, sonograms, and other sectional images that represent the internal joints and tissues.

4. **This "medical gaze" and its view of the body reconstitute the person as object.** The many exercises within the person-body, but especially the dissections of cadavers, result in a very different, detached manner of seeing the human patient. Not surprisingly, the dissection of cadavers has often been forbidden because it violates the central tenet of the mystery and sanctity of the body. In medical training, the student is reconditioned to hold this conventional view in suspension, and to relearn an alternative view of the person-body, that of anatomical, organic, biochemical system.

5. **The "medical gaze" reconstitutes the subject, in this case the student.** Many medical students have suspected that they are suffering many of the diseases they study. With discipline, they are able to learn

continued

continued from previous page

the alternative perspective and must then juggle their objective gaze with society's conventional view of the person-body.

The juggling act between the objective body-intrusive perspective learned by the medical student and the conventional view of the human person result in the medical curriculum carrying a dual, and often contradictory, message. The Goods represent the two emphases in the curriculum as "the dual discourse of **"competence"** and **"care."** Competence is about learning, knowing, and doing the science part of medicine. This part of medicine is given priority, because it is the presumed basis of medical practice. But it is also an essential ingredient of the professional self-worth of the physician, as the boundaries of specialties are negotiated and become the grounds for compensation. Care, the second emphasis, remains relatively undifferentiated in the mind of the student; it is often part of the original rationale for entering medicine. It focuses on listening, relationship, and the worth of the human patient. In some students, the Goods noted, care becomes subverted to competence such that "to care" means doing something intrusive because that is what has been learned as medicine.

The most transforming dimension of learning medicine, suggested the Goods, is in learning to handle the transgression of boundaries that normal conventions would consider violated if one did what physicians do routinely. ∎

More complex institutional forms of teaching and practice create a cushion of legitimacy around medical knowledge. It is less important to couch one's knowledge in an exclusive genealogy. Often rulers, holding wide political power, could patronize medical knowledge. The identification of the Egyptian physician Imhotep with Djoser, the ruler who united Egypt, is an example of such patronage. Medical knowledge, like other knowledge, often receives the protection of the state because it is considered valuable but also dangerous. Its practitioners are at risk because they may be regarded as sorcerers for their powers. More will be said about this process of legitimation of knowledge in the next chapter.

The anthropological study of a modern medical curriculum, such as that provided by Byron Good and Mary Jo Delvecchio Good, illustrates many of the themes of the study of medical knowledge touched on in this chapter. It is clear how this knowledge is specialized and special, and that it requires distinctive methods to transform the students' thinking and emotional makeup into mature physicians. Not mentioned by the Goods is the extensive institutional support from university, profession, and the state which this unusual medicine requires to maintain and protect it. We so take for granted highly specialized professions that we rarely consider how they are maintained. Such a perspective needs to deal with power and control, because not all knowledge is equal. That which is harbored by a professional or political elite is a reflection of the dominant class's view of its world that it seeks to promote usually as the "natural" way of seeing. But it may not be the view of the rest of society. The social control of medical knowledge, however, gets us into the subject for the next chapter.

CONCLUSION

The study of knowledge is of course not an exclusive domain of anthropology. Quite the contrary, anthropologists have borrowed from other disciplines most of their tools for the study of knowledge, as in this case the specialized domain of medical knowledge. As was clear at the outset of this chapter, terms from medicine and medical history—Western medical history, in particular—such as gnosis, diagnosis, prognosis, nosology, taxonomy, and epistemology may be adopted for this discussion. Anthropology's helpful contribution to the analysis of medical knowledge comes when this domain is opened up to comparative perspective, both to other medical traditions and to multiple ways of knowing. Some of the questions asked by philosophers of science and of medicine are germane. However, anthropologists have contributed the revolutionary (to medicine) view that all medical knowledge, including science, is shaped by social and cultural context. This negates the view that science is somehow natural and apart from culture.

This chapter has identified some of the ways in which medical knowledge is culturally constructed. This occurs in the articulations of "cause and cure," "scope, scale, and focus," and "situating person/body"; in classifications of diseases; in clinical practice; and in passing on the knowledge to the next generation of practitioners. Such a way of viewing cultural content does not, however, mean that medical knowledge is unreal, or that diseases whose identity is classified with a certain set of signs and symptoms is not "out there." But if the ideas of medical knowledge—including science—evolve and change, then we know that such knowledge is not definitive as the final truth.

Such a perspective is helpful in looking at the debate between cumulative "single truth" knowledge and incommensurable worldviews; in its exaggerated form, that scientific truth is absolute versus it is relative. This issue may never be resolved since there is some validity to each perspective. An observer of this debate has written that there will never be closure on scientific discovery because the more we know as time passes, the more new issues arise that need study and resolution (Loevinger 1995). Hamonet has shown that while we cannot deny the impaired functioning of some people, according to cultural definitions of normalcy, the classifications we create and the way we compare them to disease, crime, and marginality have the power to shape reality and to hinder the handicapped from full participation in society. This is brought out as well in the recognition of the social reality of violence, and the truth of the terminal condition that calls not for false hope but for comfort in the face of inevitable death. We have the power to shape medical knowledge in ways that will either negate human dignity, or enhance it.

Review Questions

1. What are the different types of medical knowledge mentioned early in this chapter? How do they differ? How are they legitimated by society?

2. What does Thomas Kuhn mean by "paradigms" in his discussion of changing ideas of reality in science over time? Can you offer an example of a change of paradigm in Western medical knowledge? What were the circumstances that caused a prior paradigm to go out of fashion? What replaced it?

3. How would identifying a set of medical ideas with a famous founder like Imhotep, Aesculapius, Galen, Hippocrates, Caraka, Sucruta, and so on, give those ideas greater authority? How is this authority different from that gained in a replicated experiment by unknown researchers in a medical university?

4. Can you identify your own or someone else's "shape of medical knowledge" by applying the three kinds of criteria discussed in the second section of this chapter: cause and cure, scale, scope and focus, and the situation of the person?

5. What are some of the common characteristics of the classification of diseases or disabilities in medical knowledge, both of modern medicine and other traditions? How might the process of classification create reality and thus give the schema's author great authority. What might be a disadvantage of a rigid classification system for something like disabilities?

6. Explain the competing discourses in medicine that the Goods speak of as "caring" and "competence," in the vignette on curricular reform at Harvard Medical School.

Notes

1. This vignette is based on Dr. Narcisse de Medeiros's dissertation (1994), his doctoral defense at the University of Montreal in which I was an external examiner, and personal conversations with him at that time.

2. This vignette is based on Dr. Claude Hamonet's published work (1985, 1990, 1992) as well as an unpublished manuscript prepared while he was a visiting professor at the University of Kansas. The author and Hamonet held many conversations on the substance of his research and problems of culture and disability classifications during this time.

chapter 9

Power and Organization in Medicine

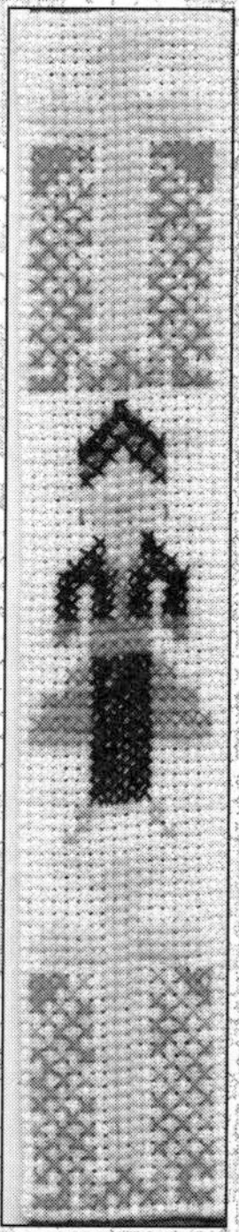

Photo 9.1 *Hmong embroidery on a bookmark, made in the Kansas City Hmong community. Compare this adapted embroidery with Hmong traditional and Christian motifs to the traditional* paj ntaub *piece on the cover of this book.*
Source: J. M. Janzen.

The ability to heal, the knowledge of therapeutic techniques and health solutions, and the wherewithal to health from whatever source constitute a kind of intrinsic **power** in medicine. Earlier chapters identified aspects of this understanding of power without explicitly calling them that. Chapter 3 sketched the basis ideas and practices underlying health and healing in a number of the world's grand medical traditions. Chapter 7 identified ways in which the signs of sickness and healing are constructed and transformed (as signal, index, icon, symbol, and metaphor). The power in medicine and healing may be compared to other "raw" materials such as foodstuffs, fire, earth, water, and air. They are transformed through domestication, controlled or at least coordinated, and also exploited for gain; they are converted into wealth, status, and political influence. One source of such coordination in medicine and healing, as we saw in Chapter 8, is the cultural process of classifying diseases and conceptualizing what healers do and the powers medicines are believed to have. Michel Foucault's view that knowledge is power (1980a; 1980b), just as sex and madness have a kind of power, is critical to the understanding of how the "raw power" of healing and medicine are controlled and organized. Similarly, for Paul Unschuld (1975b) the "primary resources" of medicine and healing—the skills of healers, the medicines, the knowledge—become "secondary resources" as they are researched, licensed, institutionalized, commercialized, and otherwise given shape by society.

This chapter examines further ways in which medical anthropologists and related scholars have contributed to the study of how this basic power in medicine and healing is controlled, coordinated, and transformed by society. It will include such topics as the following: how the basic coherence of a medical "tradition" is recognized; how the primary resources of a tradition are controlled and coordinated through decision making by practitioners and clients; how techniques, practitioners, and bodies of knowledge are given authority—that is, made legitimate—and how they are incorporated as groups and institutions; how practitioners organize as professionals; how sovereign states further organize and control medicine and healing, or encourage the agents of the market to use medicine to make wealth; and how we may interpret the shape of medicine that results from such political control or lack thereof. Without such control, sponsorship, legitimation, or organization within institutions, the power of medicine and of healers is often seen as dangerous to others and is associated with witchcraft, sorcery, or evil that is threatening to ordinary humans or, in the contemporary setting, is seen by critics as excessive "medicalization."

The power of medicine and healing, and the ways in which control of it is sought, may be illustrated from a number of comparative, historical, and contemporary examples to make the subject of this chapter more vivid. The manner in which spiritual healing has been controlled and organized is especially illustrative. Spiritual healing in historic China was controlled by the emperor who claimed healing power for himself through direct contact with spirits and ancestors. Later, healers of this type, who are now identified as *tang-ki* shamans, were banished from the empire, yet they persisted on the margins or in times and places where there was major upheaval and social change (Unschuld 1985). Today shamanism persists in modern industrial centers of Asia away from the mainland Chinese state, in places such as Taiwan (Kleinman 1980), Hong Kong, and Korea (Kendall 1985). The same is true of *ngoma* and other trance healers in central and southern Africa featured in a vignette in Chapter 7. Historically, kingdoms and states sought to subordinate these healers to their sovereign authority, sometimes banishing them beyond the borders because they threatened the rulers' authority. They have thrived best in decentralized societies or on the margins of powerful states, and in changing, industrialized, urban Africa, notably in such places as Kinshasa, Dar es Salaam, Swaziland, Johannesburg, and Cape Town (Janzen 1992).

The perspective of this chapter on the control and coordination of health care is also apparent in the way in which modern governments of industrializing and industrialized states have tried in the 20th century to create comprehensive centralized health systems. Until recently, this model seemed the general trend. Today, however, increasingly in market-oriented Western countries and in the former Soviet Union and its former satellites, the tycoons of big business are moving to control and organize the powers of medicine and healing—the drugs and the miracle techniques, the institutions, and the physicians themselves—in the name of serving society while making a profit. The shape that medicine takes in society is thus in large part due to the way it is controlled, legitimized, and promoted.

SOURCES OF COHERENCE IN MEDICAL TRADITIONS

One of the first ways that medical anthropologists have looked at organization in medicine is to explore the prevailing patterns within a broad **tradition,** that is, cultural features that remain recognizable over time and territory. This perspective was adapted from the anthropological study of civilizations as patterned cultural traditions. Applied to health and healing, this perspective suggests that such a tradition would "reveal characteristic ways of identifying and classifying disease, organizing treatments, and expounding teachings" (Feierman and Janzen 1992:163). This approach was applied to Asian and Mediterranean traditions of medicine by Charles Leslie and his colleagues in the 1970s (Leslie 1976), to the study of Latin American medicine (Fabrega 1973; Foster 1978), and later to the study of African medical traditions (Feierman and Janzen 1992).[1]

Medical anthropologists emphasize the need to associate the ideas and practices—that is, the recognizable coherence at the core of a tradition—with the social context in which it arose, flourished, is carried on, and practiced today. Does the tradition in some sense continue to live through the ideas and actions of practitioners and people? If so, how and by whom is it carried on and practiced? Or, does the "tradition" exist in a scholarly community totally apart from the healing of the sick or only in ancient manuscripts? The ideas of a tradition may be in peoples' minds, but have no immediacy or salience to them because other sets of ideas are becoming more important. This was the situation among the Maguzawa Hausa of northern Nigeria studied by medical anthropologist Murray Last (1992). He observed that the Hausa beliefs in spirit-caused sicknesses were waning in the face of Islamic religion and medicine and modern biomedicine. To the Maguzawa Hausa the beliefs in spirits no longer seemed to matter. Similarly, we might look at the place of humoral ideas of ancient Greek medicine in today's Western world. These beliefs are found in folk sayings such as "chills cause colds" or that "hot chicken soup helps ward off a cold." But we tend to take such truisms halfheartedly. The sum total of such beliefs, practices, and technical knowledge pertaining to health and healing, both of which are vital as well as those which are there but no longer vital, Murray Last called the **medical culture** of a society (Last 1992), the broadest common denominator of anything identifiably medical, with no particular regard for institutions, roles, or structures. Later he would speak of **national medical cultures** and **international medical cultures** (1990:351).

In a similar vein, the medical anthropologists who began to study Western establishment medicine—variously called cosmopolitan medicine, Western medicine, allopathic medicine, then biomedicine—picked the phrase **"the culture of biomedicine"** to describe its core ideas, techniques, assumptions, institutions, and practitioners (Rhodes 1990; Hahn and Gaines 1985). This identification of the culture of mainstream medicine was intended, and some authors said so explicitly, to include Western biomedicine in the set of all those medicines that had previously been called **ethnomedicine.** Another way of saying this was to suggest that "biomedicine is an ethnomedicine."

A persistent trend in the medical anthropological study of medicine as culture is to describe the cross-section of practices, types of practitioners, and organizing ideas within a single society or region as elements, themes, or values. Thus, David McQueen's account of medicine in the United States (1978) begins with a description of five seemingly very different types of medical traditions: mainstream biomedicine, the most widely practiced type, which he called allopathic medicine; osteopathy; chiropractic; Christian Science; and faith healing. This is not intended as a comprehensive listing of medicines practiced in the United States; rather, it is a cross-section to demonstrate the thematic method. Without minimizing their differing natures and the sources of their knowledge, McQueen pointed out that all share certain fundamental themes about human nature and disease that reveal their embodiment, in medicine, of the values of

American society. These themes are (1) the individual (rather than the collectivity) is the focus of treatment; (2) emphasis is on somatic or physical illness and treatment and acute (rather than spiritual or chronic) affliction; (3) the sick or deviants are to be institutionalized; (4) they all share a mechanicanistic metaphor of the body—the body is a machine that may be repaired or receive replacement parts; (5) medicine is predominately attuned to a "single cause" etiology (McQueen 1978:73–74). Lynn Payer (1988) undertook a similar study of the dominant values in national medicines of four countries: the United States, England, West Germany, and France. Payer offered a glimpse of the legal and political organizational backdrop of different branches of medicine in the countries she compared. In Germany, where 19th-century ideas of Romanticism and a back-to-nature movement were very influential, she described the insurance system that allows multiple modes of healing, from allopathic hospitals and clinics to health spas and homeopathic establishments, to coexist. The chapters on England and France are suggestively titled "Keeping the Upper Lip Stiff" and "Cartesian Thinking and Terrain," respectively. American medicine— described in a chapter titled "The Virus in the Machine"—is premised, for Payer, on an emphasis on intrusive disease agents (e.g., viruses, germs) and invasive, curative medicine. The body is essentially a machine which can be adjusted, fixed, or have its component parts replaced. The coherence shown in these projects that focus on themes, values, or elements is similar to the more recent work in medical anthropology which shows how medicine is "culturally constructed."

In the early years of medical anthropology—that is, in the 1950s and 1960s, and even into the 1970s—the labels of "system" and "structure" were easily applied to what has just been called "tradition" and "culture," as the 1976 title *Asian Medical Systems* suggests. This was the heyday of the theoretical dominance of the orientation known as "structural-functionalism," when society itself was understood to be a well-ordered system whose integral functional parts could be analyzed and understood. The comparative study of **medical systems** presumed that if a cluster of practices, ideas, and roles could be recognized, they represented a subset of the social system (Janzen 1978a; Janzen and Prins 1981) or of the cultural system (Kleinman 1978). That view of society and medicine gradually came under attack for overemphasizing (or reifying) static idealized models of a systematic society and culture. Above all, some of these projects presented a view often blind to the exercise of power and the forces of historical change in the ways that reality and social institutions were shaped.

Other medical anthropologists seeking to describe the social context of health and healing adopted the **sectors of health care** approach that situates each and every health care practice as "popular," "professional," or "folk," a schema originally introduced in the 1970s (Leslie 1976; Kleinman 1980; see also Helman 1990, chap. 4). The "popular" sector of health care is characterized by being lay, nonprofessional, and nonspecialist, in which illness is first

South Asian (Indian) Medical Pluralism

India is a rich and complex region with its own classic medical traditions: Ayurveda, foreign Greek medicine (called Yunani, from "Ionian" in Arabic), as well as several branches of modern medicine introduced in the 19th and 20th centuries. All of these traditions, and the specialists who work with them, continue to exist alongside each other in contemporary India. Anthropologist Charles Leslie set forth in the 1960s to describe and conceptualize the world of South Asian medicine (Leslie 1976:361). Based on field work and archival research, Leslie sought to understand particularly the revivalist movement among professional Ayurvedic and Yunani practitioners. He visited their medical colleges and studied the political climate in postindependence India in which these medicines were part of the identity of Indian nationalism. He also documented the practitioners of folk and popular culture medicine. Figure 9.1 shows the relative distribution of each type of practitioner and the situation of each subtradition within that larger scheme and occupational type. Leslie demonstrated that the majority of medical practice is in the hands of part-time folk, homeopathic, and religious specialists; most of the modern physicians are full-time professionals, as are most but fewer of the Ayurvedic and Yunani physicians. There are a few full-time learned doctors of Ayurveda and Yunani medicine who are full-time scholars rather than practitioners.

The contrast between folk and popular, and between professional and learned medicine and culture categories in Figure 9.1 is intended to be impressionistically representative of the number of each type of practitioner and type. ■

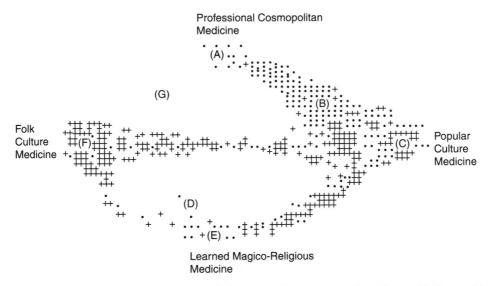

Figure 9.1 Charles Leslie's depiction of South Asian medical pluralism, along lines of full-time (•) and part-time (+) practitioners, folk versus popular, professional versus learned scholars, within each tradition. A = physicians of biomedicine with MD degrees (Leslie called them physicians of cosmopolitan medicine); B = professionalized Ayurvedic and Yunani physicians; C = homeopathic physicians; D = learned traditional culture Ayurvedic and Yunani physicians; E = religious specialists with unusual learning and healing powers; F = folk practitioners; G = classic Ayurvedic and Yunani text descriptions of medicine.
Source: Leslie 1976:361.

defined and in which most of the illness episodes are managed (Kleinman 1980:50). For Kleinman, much of what occurs within the family as perceiving and experiencing symptoms, labeling and valuating the disease, sanctioning a particular kind of sick role, and deciding what to do about it, is found within the sector. The "professional" sector of health care includes all activities that are in the charge of practitioners who make their living at medicine, and are usually part of a well-organized professional association such as the American Medical Association. Clinical practice often is bureaucratically organized within hospitals or health care organizations, within which the payment formula is predetermined and covered by an insurance or other third-party payment. The "folk" sector of health care in this schema is a residual category that includes everything not covered by the first two. In Kleinman's original work on Taiwan, it includes shamanism, ritual curing, and other forms of herbalism, traditional surgery exercise, and other sacred and profane medicine. By definition, folk healing is not bureaucratically organized, nor do its practitioners make their living from their practices.

The three-sector perspective of health care does identify some of the defining social contexts of medicine and the differing kinds of issues, constraints, and characteristics that is the overlapping nature of the sectors. The ambiguity that one meets in tracing the status of particular therapies or practitioner groups over time, and comparing them from one setting to another, renders this approach problematic. To understand how or why a particular therapy may be folk at one time or setting, popular in another, and highly professionalized in a third, one needs to look at other aspects of coherence in the medical tradition. Particularly, dimensions of power and organization need to be addressed. Charles Leslie's depiction of medicine in South Asia remains a useful attempt to combine several approaches presented here. Later (1992) he would revisit this material and speak of the blending of biomedical (or cosmopolitan) medicine with Ayurvedic medicine of India in an attempt to make it presentable alongside state-sponsored biomedicine. He spoke of this blending as "syncretism."

RESOURCE CONTROL AND DECISION MAKING

Although the thematic, cultural, element, or core idea approaches just summarized are good at identifying the basic intellectual coherence of a medical tradition, they tend to ignore the significant economic, political, and ideological underpinnings that society often puts into health and healing. These vested interests and pressures certainly help determine which ideas, techniques, and practitioner types will become dominant or become marginalized, which will become the leaders, and which will become socially invisible or even illegal. Medical anthropologists and related analysts have put forward a number of perspectives to identify the ways in which vested interests—political, economic, ideological—affect medical practices and ideas. These issues have been addressed by medical anthropologists at both the large-scale level of national or global institutions, as well as at the very small scale, intimate, level of clinical decision making and the social processes around individual cases. The first has been called "macroanalysis," the second "microanalysis." But the issues are really the same.

Although there are many lines of analysis of the political and economic shaping of medicine, that referred to as the "resource model" is helpful here (Unschuld 1975b, 1992; Crandan-Malamud 1991). As primary medical resources (i.e., medical knowledge, materia medica, and the skills and techniques practitioners use to address health needs) are controlled and coordinated, they translate into secondary medical resources of economic and political influence, the infrastructure of professions, salaries, clientele, and institutions. Unschuld originally identified this scheme in his study of medical authors in the Tang dynasty in the seventh century A.D. He noted the ways that the kingdom both enabled and controlled the practitioners of Chinese medicine (1975:18–19). Later he would apply the scheme to the 20th-century setting of competing medicines in China. From the seventh to the 19th centuries in China, some paradigms of medicine and their respective practitioners were backed by the court, whereas other types of medicine, particularly shamanism, were repressed, or at least driven to the margins of kingdom society. One of the central tools that court physicians used to gain control over the practice of medicine in the wider society was a code of medical ethics. With this, the medical elite of dynastic China was able to sanction all opponents by imposing its ethics upon a limited field of practitioners, and by forbidding access to all those who did not conform to their concept of ethical medical practice. Some of these issues of state and professional power and control of medicine will be taken up later in this chapter.

At the intimate scale of clinical decision making, where practitioners and their clients meet, the interplay of primary and secondary resources also becomes very apparent. Medical anthropologists have studied the process of clinical decision making to determine how knowledge, techniques, practitioner skills, and medicine are coordinated and controlled by the vested interests of patients, their families, professional groups, the forces of the market, and the state.

Other medical anthropologists have directed their interests a little more closely to the social context of therapeutic decision making, the negotiations of alternative or varying viewpoints, the process of decision making and medical reality in a setting where there is no dominant model with dominant professionals, but rather multiple or pluralistic medical settings. Control of the "primary medical resources" may even be in the hands of nonhealers. Such a medical setting was studied by this author in Kongo society of central Africa (1978b), and is featured in the accompanying vignette. In a setting of perhaps extreme decentralization of authority in so-

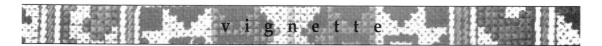

Therapy Management in Kongo Society

The management of therapy in kinship-centered society was the focus of study that was published in *The Quest for Therapy in Lower Zaire* (Janzen 1978b). Kongo society of western equatorial Africa in the 1960s was the kind of society that anthropologists spoke of as "decentralized" or "segmentary." Chiefship that had existed earlier in some regions of Kongo society had been undermined or destroyed by the forces of colonialism in the early 20th century. The newly independent Democratic Republic of Congo continued to use many of the laws of the Belgian colonial government, but the central institutions of this new state did not much affect local health care. Indeed, there was much debate and ambiguity over the laws that governed the practice of medicine. African practices of herbalism, divination, purification rituals for persons and groups, and symbolic therapies which had been persecuted by the colonial government were once again practiced in the open, and their practitioners sought support from the new political leaders. At the same time institutions such as clinics and maternity hospitals of Western-introduced biomedicine also sought state support and legitimacy. In the absence of any health insurance or government-supported health care and in the face of ambiguity over who controlled healing, sufferers and their kin became the main decision makers, the effective managers of healing.

In the decentralized Kongo setting depicted in the case studies of *The Quest for Therapy*, therapy managers are parents and mother's brothers, those who hold general social rights over the sufferers, children, and matrilineal descendants (Kongo is a matrilineal society). Often the diagnosis of a case needs to be negotiated by these kin, and it is they, or a designated individual from among them, who accompanies the patient to a diviner, healer, hospital, or clinic. Because of the kin therapy managers' control of the process of therapy seeking, payment or reimbursement is not made to a healer until the therapy has been deemed successful and effective. Much to the consternation of medical personnel in Western-oriented clinics and hospitals, patients under the guidance of a kin therapy manager may also be taken from the wards for alternative treatment at an African medicine doctor without the consent of the attending staff. A close ethnographic coverage of case studies revealed a pattern of "shuttling" between types of therapies.

The therapy managing group is constituted of those who participate in the diagnosis, decision making, and care of a patient (or related group of patients). This always includes someone or some social group who is sick (households, lineages, entire communities may be considered "sick"). It normally includes a next of kin. But at the time of uncertainty and crisis within the kin community, it also includes the diviner who is consulted. It may also include for each episode or string of related episodes, appropriate healers or medical personnel, including biomedical practitioners (who are usually unaware of the structure of the therapy managing group). ■

---

ciety such as the Kongo cases represent, the primary medical resources of knowledge, techniques, and materia medica are largely controlled by the same forces that control any resources of whatever type. Medicine is embedded within the structures of general society, in this case largely kin-based. Healing is often subject to the conflicts and limits of other resources such as land, food, and precious and desired states of being within the same social institutions that govern all other social processes. It becomes a situation of "struggle for control" of the primary resources, as another medical anthropology and history scholar of East Africa has noted (Feierman 1985:82–83).

The related concepts of **therapy management** and of **therapy managing group** were coined to describe the process of negotiation for control of therapeutic resources, and the group of people who share in the decisions and care giving (Janzen 1978a, 1978b, 1987). Although these concepts were developed in a particular setting, they appear to have wider application especially where there is not an exclusive control of medicine by a professional elite, but where the resources of health and healing are part of the overall resource base of a community, or where medicine is "pluralistic" and family or others around the sufferer must diagnose, negotiate, and reach decisions about what to do next.

Medical anthropological approaches to decision making in care giving have included an even greater emphasis on the process of therapy. French anthropologist Marc Augé and colleagues have used the phrase *itinéraire thérapeutique* (**therapeutic itinerary,** or course) to describe a process much like therapy management, to describe the "totality of processes involved with their detours and curves in a quest for therapy, going from the appearance of a problem to all its steps, institutional or not, where diverse interpretations may be identified (divination, rumors) as well as cures, in a pluralistic medical context" (Sindzingre 1985:14). All of the perspectives around medical resources and therapeutic decision making that have been mentioned reflect the idea of the **hierarchy of resort** (Romannuci-Ross 1969), a sequence of different consultations with medical practitioners or therapies in an unfolding case. However, the idea of a predetermined hierarchy is not implied in therapy management or in the therapeutic itinerary. James Young, in his book *Medical Choice in a Mexican Village* (1981), applied a decision-making model to household economies as well as to the distribution of medical traits used in care.

Decision-making models have been used for a wide range of studies of how the knowledge and reality of illness experience shapes care seeking and care giving. In recent years, however, anthropologists have shied away from exclusive emphasis on rationalistic decision making or formalistic aspects of these decisions, and have instead emphasized the recognition of wider political and economic realities in shaping medicine, as well as the emotional dimensions of the experience of suffering and undertaking healing.

FORMS OF CONTROL AND LEGITIMACY IN MEDICINE

Anthropologists and other social scientists have long made the point that much power—that is, control—is exercised with the consent of the controlled. Some writers make the distinction between **power,** the sheer ability of some to manipulate others or to control them, and **authority,** the consensual exercise of power in a legitimate manner. This distinction is helpful in understanding how the resources of health and healing may become the focus of tremendous influence in society, both by those who have or are reputed to have skills of healing, and those who manage somehow to transform those skills into influence, wealth, and fame, or to control others with such skills. Related to this is the process by which medical paradigms, discussed in Chapter 8, and the institutions and practitioners who represent them, are accepted by the public. Thus, the authority of medicine in Western industrial societies may be taken for granted because it is said to be based on scientific truth; it is conducted by certified, licensed practitioners; it is protected by professional codes of ethics; and it is regulated by state laws, all of which are supported by the public or professional groups. This has not been the case everywhere nor for all times. It should still be slightly amazing to us that people would give their life savings to someone who carries out an invasive procedure on them (e.g., open heart surgery, brain tumor surgery, or bone marrow transplant) that stands a fifty-fifty chance of killing them. They do this not because they are coerced, but because they consent to having the procedure done on them. They have given the physicians the authority to conduct the procedures.

It might appear to belabor the obvious to insist that practitioners need to be given the authority to practice medicine by the people on whom they practice. However, not everywhere, nor at all times, have medical practitioners been able to even practice openly. Sometimes they have been considered witches or demonic if their work is unusual or not well understood. Even today in Western industrial society, lawsuits against physicians are common, resulting from mistrust or fears of abuse by practitioners who normally carry extensive liability insurance coverage, but the demand for medicine is at an all-time high and budgetary outlays are huge. An inquiry into the basis of medical authority therefore needs to look at the general basis of authority.

The German sociologist Max Weber (1864–1920) had much to say about authority and legitimacy, and these ideas can be applied to the question of what makes a particular profile or body of knowledge convincing, true, or authoritative, protecting those who practice it as legitimate (1964:324ff.). Weber identified three types of authority: traditional authority, rational-legal authority, and charismatic authority; of course, these types may overlap in real human society and may, to some extent, all operate in one and the same context.

Traditional authority is evident in most medical traditions and is identifiable by the simple phrase "we've always done it this way," or "we do this because our forebears have done it." Traditional authority, according to Weber, rested on established belief in the sanctity of immemorial traditions and the legitimacy of the status of those exercising authority under them (1964:328). Users of favorite medicines may vouch for the efficacy of a treatment by invoking ancient secrets or revealed insight from spirits or textual sources. One of Weber's hallmarks for traditional authority is the presence of a "chief," that is, an authoritative figure whose command or word is truth. In medicine this would be a master teacher or healer whose disciples or apprentices offer complete and unflinching loyalty and trust. His words become "imperative," his teachings "truth" (1964:342ff). While this type of authority frequently carries economic advantages for the faithful, this is not always the case. Later, a former novice may often be able to invoke the pedigree back to his teacher and teacher's teacher as the legitimacy of therapeutic practice. In research or academic circles, even today, one often hears reference to having "studied with so-and-so." Scientific referencing echoes this practice as well. Classical medical texts carry a measure of traditional authority on their own, but a living master may enhance his or her legitimacy by linking personal practices to ancient texts. French medical anthropologist Francis Zimmerman has illustrated this in demonstrations of how masters of Indian Ayurvedic medicine use ancient texts (Zimmerman 1982, 1989, 1995). Weber suggested that traditional authority is often embodied in gerontocratic, patriarchical, and personalistic modes of social control, thus conservative and repressive, which may be why tradition often has negative connotations in science-legitimized medicine.

In Weber's view, **rational-legal authority** is in many ways the opposite of traditional legitimacy. It is impersonal, rational, and based on explicit laws or rules rather than customary ideas. Rational-legal authority rests on a belief in the legality of rules and the right of those elevated to authority under such rules to issue commands. Its claim to exact obedience from subordinates is due to its identification with a corporation or a government, thus a bureaucracy. But these rules are of an abstract kind, intentionally established by governing bodies to be carried out not by slaves or serfs, but by "staff" who obey only insofar as they are members or employees of the bureaucracy (1964:329–30). The administrative staff of the organization is held to be completely separated from ownership of the means of production of the corporation. Employees hold their offices by appointment, due to their technical qualifications, not their family identity or popularity in society at large. The bureaucracy is strictly hierarchical, thus bestowing on the organization—be it a manufacturing company, a state, or a medical clinic—a degree of specialization to carry out its goals with supposedly unprecedented efficiency.

It is evident how Weber's picture of rational-legal authority and legitimacy might transform medicine and healing in a society where this mode is prevalent, namely our own. Healers must have specialized skills and are hired by larger agencies because of those skills, not because of other reputations. They are trusted to carry out their medical duties, even as complete strangers, because they have met the rational-legal criteria society has laid out for those tasks: They must have honestly passed their exams and obtained their degrees with integrity, not bought them or received them by influence (which would be a legally punishable crime), and they must have been certified in the specialty which they practice. If the rational-legal mode of legitimacy of the medical office is intact, sufferers will come to the bureaucratic practitioner, who may be a specialist stranger, because of their full trust in the system.

Charismatic authority, in Weber's view, is set apart from traditional and rational-legal authority by its high degree of focus on a remarkable individual who is endowed with supernatural powers and qualities (1964:358ff), a picture of the healer that would surely fit shamanism and trance behavior (both of which are mentioned by Weber), faith healing, leaders of certain therapeutic movements, and less dramatic but just as real instances of belief in a doctor or healer like those manifested in the placebo effect (discussed at length in Chapter 7). Weber made it very clear that the authority of the charismatic person lies not in that person's inherent powers, but in how "the individual is regarded by those subject to charismatic authority, by his 'followers' or 'disciples'" (1964:359). For this reason there is usually a mass or collective aspect to charismatic authority; the charisma is shared within a community. Therein lies its power, even if this is elusive. Weber called charisma the greatest revolutionary force, one that is often born out of suffering, conflicts, or enthusiasm, a view that surely must be taken into account by medical anthropologists who look at the misery of many human situations, including war (1964:363). Charismatic authority is outside the realm of everyday routine and the profane sphere.

Many of the medical or therapeutic examples of charismatic authority that come to mind would seem to fit aspects of the classic traditions of healing (e.g., Asian and South American shamans, African trance healers, diviners, and famous medical leaders of the past). As defined by Weber, however, charismatic authority would surely also characterize the popular belief in specialized diets, "miracle" cures for cancer, New Age therapies, or faith healing as practiced by some Christians.

Charismatic authority is notoriously fickle and short-lived, Weber suggested. The extraordinary, the supernatural, seems invariably to lose its power. Over time it tends to become routinized which is its kiss of death. Followers defect or the leader explains away the lost touch with a turning away of the gods that inspired the power in the first place. Central to the medical anthropologist's regard of charismatic authority and legitimacy of those symbols, products, and techniques generated by charisma is that it lies in the attitude of the disciple, follower, or user.

THE INCORPORATION OF MEDICINE

Although much of the best analysis by medical anthropology in the focus of this chapter—namely, power and organization—has gone in the direction of studying the subtle forms of control and influence couched within signs of the body and self, and away from a focus on the formal, official institutions, these have obviously not vanished. We still find hospitals, more and larger medical associations than ever, and research establishments such as university hospitals, departments, and institutes. Outside the modern industrial world's institutions of health and healing, there remain midwives' guilds, networks of shamans and healers, and therapeutic cults of many kinds. The last of these has often taken on the trappings of modern institutions, forming into national associations or research institutes and universities. Although anthropologists usually look behind the official organization or in its internal cracks, medical anthropology students do well to have at their disposal the basic criteria of what constitutes corporate organization. With this they may identify the sources of rising political and economic influence of a medical group or set of practitioners and their followers, or the relative strength of several groups vis-à-vis each other.

It is necessary here to simplify the discussion on corporate organization to a few key concepts by several of the many scholars who have addressed this subject. The idea of a **corporation** is older than modern industrial companies to which we tend to apply this term today. Indeed, this term arises from ancient Roman law and the Latin term *corporatus,* from the verb *corporare,* to organize into a body (Maine 1960). The embodiment of things therapeutic in a social body—social embodiment—is what gives persons, ideas, and techniques in the realm of health and healing their coherence and power.

Corporation theory applied to recent comparative studies globally has been reviewed most effectively by Michael G. Smith in his *Corporations and Society* (1974). Smith distinguished between corporate category and the corporate group. **Corporate category** is an identifiable, named, group of individuals following some common criterion (e.g., blacksmiths, heart attack victims, all Joneses in Ohio, or medical practitioners). The individuals of a corporate category need not be aware of their commonness to constitute such a category. However, one step toward their becoming a **corporate group** is consciousness of their common affairs. A corporate category becomes a corporate group as it meets to conduct business around these common interests, and to elect officers (or somehow designate a leadership) who officiate in such business and represent the group to outsiders. Such a **corporation aggregate** takes on its own personhood—that is, a legal status as a being—but unlike the individual person, the corporation, once created, continues in perpetuity unless dissolved by the members (Smith 1974:94; Janzen 1978a:126–27). Smith's analysis of the corporate group is truly global; with it he evaluated a wide range of social entities that includes hunter-gatherer bands, lineages, secret societies, healers' guilds, trade unions, churches, multinational corporations, and all-inclusive nation-states. The criteria of corporate category and corporate group allow us to analyze the degree of political organization that a given corporate group has at its disposal.

One aspect of corporation theory that is very helpful in our understanding of power and organization in medicine is that of governing relationships between two or more corporate groups. They may of course be of equal and independent character. But often two corporate groups will have some relationship of asymmetric interdependency, such that one is given its corporate strength by another, more inclusive group. We see this most frequently in the way that a corporate group gains its legal status by registering with the state, which is a more inclusive, indeed sovereign, corporation. The incorporation of medicine often entails such nestling of one group within another more inclusive, more powerful group, such as a local hospital which belongs to an association of hospitals, or a local physicians' organization that belongs to a state or national organization.

A further aspect of corporation theory of great use to medical anthropologists interested in the power and organization of medicine is the manner that transformations occur from corporate category status to corporate group status, with all that this entails in the gaining and losing of rights. A series of illustrations to close out this section will demonstrate the applicability of corporation theory to our subject.

The relationship of ancient kings and emperors to healing is an intriguing one that illustrates the power of medicine and the need to come to terms with it as the corporate organization grows. Centralized power has either co-opted the power of healing or it has marginalized it. As already hinted above, in the very early Shang dynasty in China, according to medical historian and sinologist Paul Unschuld, the emperor was the principal healer and mediator with the spirit world, competent to treat everything "from headache to crop failure" (1985:24–26). In later dynasties, shamanism was eventually marginalized because of the threat it posed to the emperors, although it remained widespread among the lower classes (Unschuld 1985). Other paradigms of medicine evolved and their practitioners became the court-supported, dominant medical authorities. Shamans rarely are well organized, because if they were, they would constitute the sovereign power with a powerful charismatic legitimation.

Other illustrations of the corporate character of healing and medicine, closer to the here and now, demonstrate the consequences of organization (or the lack thereof), and the transformation in corporate organizations or their relationships to each other. These examples come from the relationships of healers to European colonialism in Asia and Africa, and from the fate of midwives in the United States and Europe.

In 19th-century European colonial regimes of Asia and Africa, traditional healers were usually suppressed or closely supervised because of the threat that colonial authorities believed they posed to public health and, incidentally, to the fledgling operations of colonial doctors trying to bring under control infectious diseases of malaria, sleeping sickness, yellow fever, and a host of water, food, or sewage-borne diseases such as cholera, typhoid fever, typhus, and dysentery (Vaughn 1991; Curtin 1992). Wherever healers' organizations had been, they were destroyed or the activities of their members severely curtailed. In some colonies, healers were prosecuted under clauses such as "practicing medicine without a license," without taking account or considering their own types of corporate categories or groups. Yet as independence came to these British, French, Portuguese, and Belgian colonies in Asia and Africa, medicine often became a focus, as well as a vehicle, of nationalistic revival (Leslie 1976b). Healers and indigenous medicine practitioners sought to organize, or reorganize, to form associations to emancipate themselves to the level of respectability of their counterparts who had trained within colonial (i.e., biomedical) medicine. The new political leaders needed to juggle this medical scene of now competing claims for medical authority, by sorting out and reforming laws regarding the practice of medicine. In some newly independent nations, indigenous medicine was emancipated and given a status alongside biomedicine. In other settings, it was tolerated without legal status; in still others, it was systematically defamed and repressed in a continuation of colonial policy. Yet in countries like India and Zimbabwe, where indigenous medicine practitioners achieved national associations, they were able to promote their own interests, gain acceptance with the state, and regulate the practice of their own arts.

The fate of midwifery in the United States and western Europe illustrates both rising and declining corporateness in medicine, depending on the particular national story. In the United States midwives were widespread and common in the early 19th century; they were well-reputed women who knew their communities and who were widely known. They attended most births, which took place in the homes of the delivering women. Midwifery, however, had the status of a "corporate category." The midwives were a known group of individuals, and they knew who they were, but they were not organized. The situation was very similar across western Europe. However, with the coming into being of physicians' organizations in the United States and Europe around 1900, the status of midwives would be totally transformed. In the United States, for a variety of reasons that included a desire on the part of the birthing women for pain medication in connection with birthing, obstetrician-physicians began to perform births in hospitals where they could oversee the administration of risky but effective pain-deadening medication such as ether (Leavitt 1986). Obstetricians also began to use forceps in difficult births and other surgical techniques which required the support services of the operating room. The well-known Flexner Report of 1910 recommended a series of regulations and openly antimidwife recommendations by the physicians. By the 1940s, 70 percent of American women were birthing in hospitals; by 1950, 98 percent. Midwifery nearly vanished as a practiced art in the United States. Laws regulating birthing vary from state to state. In some States midwifery is outlawed if practiced without the accompanying presence of an obstetrician-physician; in other states, while not outlawed, it is effectively curtailed because midwives may not solicit their services, or they may not "perform medicine" which is left vague in regard to birthing (not technically a disease). They risk being prosecuted for "mistakes" or "accidents." The near demise of midwifery in the United States is due to the failure of midwives to organize at a time when the now powerful physicians' organization, the American Medical Association (AMA), formed and gradually "co-opted" birthing. A string of legislative enactments sealed the power of the AMA and the physicians with regard to birthing (Cobb 1981).

In Great Britain, the Netherlands, and Germany, in contrast, midwives have continued to operate, either within obstetric-gynecological departments of hospitals or as independent teams which make home calls in mobile units that contain many of the modern medical services needed in an emergency. In these countries midwifery is a viable profession. The difference in the picture of midwifery here and in the United States may be traced to the history of the midwives assuming corporate status through national associations before, or while, the physicians were creating their professional associations. These associations were able to represent the interests of midwives, improve their use of techniques for the protection of the mother and child, and negotiate rights before state legislative bodies that created modern health and medical practice legislation. Physicians in these European countries normally intervene in birthing only in emergencies. Midwives are in charge of birthing in all other cases.

The story of midwifery is not over in the United States, where lay midwives continue to work unofficially in some states, often under suspicion from local physicians and state regulators, whereas in other regions they are thriving and accepted. Home birthing and midwives' lobby groups and associations have formed to promote their interests. But these recently created corporate groups must now wage their campaigns against deeply entrenched powerful corporate organizations that have a century of professionalization and legislative action behind them.

These examples of the incorporation of medicine or other practitioners demonstrate the importance of corporation theory and analysis for medical anthropology. This body of theory is often held appropriate for formal organizations and is thus sometimes criticized for reifying formal organizational properties at the expense of a more subtle understanding of the "power of the margins and cracks" of society. But if corporation theory includes the conditions of the corporate category, and the relative corporateness of several groups which may have very uneven degrees of incorporation such as those illustrated above, then corporation theory becomes a helpful tool for the analysis of the social context of health and healing in all settings.

PROFESSIONALIZATION AND THE STATE

The emergence of a group of professional practitioners in a medical tradition, and the state's embrace of these professionals and their organizations, represent the ultimate incorporation of medicine. The state's legal endorsement of a medical group, as well as the action of that group's own internal codes of behavior upon its members, provide a powerful combination of forces by which such a practicing elite becomes the establishment. Alternative contenders are pushed to the margins of reality and legality. Each of these forms of incorporation has its own dynamics that can be discussed before bringing them together to understand their impact upon medicine.

A **profession,** in the sense that it will be used here, refers to the full-time pursuit by an individual of a specialized skill, usually for pay by customers or by an agency that buys the skills of the professional (Freidson 1970:185–87). For purposes of this discussion on the incorporation of medicine, it is useful to make this definition collective, with medical anthropologist Murray Last and medical sociologist Gordon Chavunduka (Last 1990:350; 1986:6), to suggest that professionalization occurs within a body of such specialists who

- are aware of themselves and their place among other specialists;
- have defined criteria of membership through licensing, certification, or registration;
- have the right to regulate themselves independently of clients or employers;
- have an expertise (which is more than a craft) over which they seek primary control;
- possess an ideology of service or code of ethics governing relations between the professional and the client, and limiting competition between professionals; and
- have a body of esoteric knowledge with a theoretical basis, developed and held by them, the "experts," which they may protect, formulate, and pass on to their membership.

These criteria fulfill those of a corporate group, but designate medical practitioners as a particular type of group, with a powerful hold on practice and knowledge.

All these criteria characterize the physicians of the American Medical Association, the German midwives' association, and the traditional doctors of postindependence Zimbabwe. It does not hold true for the mid-wives in the United States, the healers of colonial Africa, nor the barber-surgeons of the United States in the 18th century, the precursors of today's physicians.

One of the most important aspects of a profession in medicine is the internal control of standards of practice among its members, both the purely technical kind and the ethical kind. This process of internal control usually begins with the training of the practitioner, but it continues in the even more important step of certification, or licensing, of the practitioner. The gatekeeping function of licensing is all important for the maintenance of a standard of recognition by the consumer as well as for the recognition and endorsement on the part of the state. Sometimes the state takes over these controls or standards from the profession; at other times they are developed independently. Such controls or sanctions work not only upon members of a profession. They also may be directed against those who are not part of the professional association or who are not certified by the state-endorsed license. The threat of prosecution as a criminal offense for the practice of medicine without a license is the ultimate sanction a profession with the backing of the state may have against an uncertified competitor or alternative practitioner. The positive side of state certification of professional medicine is of course the protection from charlatans operating with impunity. Also, we are the recipients of vast protection from government agencies such as the Food and Drug Administration through their testing and authorization of substances and their determination of food standards, and that which the National Institutes of Health and other governmental agencies offer in the way of research on critical issues of national health.

But this sketch of the double incorporation of a profession and the state would not be complete without mention of the possibility, with such powerful forces organized, that the profession can become an instrument of the state's impulse to control its citizenry. While one hopes that this would not occur in an open democratic society, it has been known to occur in totalitarian states.[2] Michael Foucault's extensive writing on the birth of the prison (1979), the asylum (1973), and the hospital (1975), and the use of technologies of control in Western societies, give us reason to believe that the potential is at hand for the sophisticated tools of medicine to be manipulated toward the excessive control, even persecution, of the wayward citizen. Several examples may be cited of the uses of medicine in the hands of the state to control its citizens.

Medical experiments by Nazi doctors upon their victims represent the most notorious of such examples in the annals of Western medicine. In order for German medicine to go down the road of collaboration with the Nazi regime, the independent professional identity and power of the physicians needed to be destroyed. The National Socialist regime systematically abolished German medical societies and replaced them with a state organization for Aryan physicians. At least half of all physicians became members of the Nazi party, and many participated in unethical experiments. Eugenics and sterilization of undesirable persons and social categories became part of the medical curriculum (Seidelman 1996).

Another example of the state use of medicine to control citizens comes from the Soviet Union where psychiatric institutions were used to incarcerate dissidents who were diagnosed as "mentally ill." The Soviet prison system, which was known as the "Gulag Archipelago"—an entire archipelago of concentration camps—and described by Aleksandr Solzhenitsyn (1991–2) in a book by that title, classified its prisoners as political and criminal, and put the latter in charge over the former, who were often branded as mentally ill. Such was the distortion and control of medicine in this totalitarian society.

MEDICINE, THE STATE, AND THE MARKET

Attention to the social contextual sources of coherence in medical traditions would remain incomplete without the inclusion of the economic dimension of medicine. For surely, just as the form of medicinal services and institutions is shaped by preferences and controls of interest groups and political cliques, so its availability and access are determined by economic forces. The economic dimension of medicine is inherent in Unschuld's resource model of medicine (1975b). Medicine's "primary resources" of techniques, knowledge, skills, and materia medica are certainly highly valued and carry a price, or may be traded, bought and sold, or given away through the good graces of the donor. Medicine's "secondary resources" of institutional infrastructure, the financial or in-kind support of government, associations, and communities allude to the economic field within which the primary resources are distributed and made available to society. The specific form these secondary resources of medicine may take, however, is exceedingly varied.

Medicine, the primary resource, has been structured by as many types of socioeconomic arrangements (the secondary resource) as there have been human communities. It has existed in societies in which basic goods are gained through subsistence collecting or exchange rather than through money, perhaps something available to each person as energy and reach allow. Yet even in such societies, living as hunter-gatherers or as basic subsistence cultivators, healers have been recognized as persons with special gifts that cannot be bought and are not remunerated. The idea that the healing is a gift freely received and therefore must be freely given persists to this day.

With the advent of centralized empires and long-distance trade, medicine became a realm of specialized knowledge but also a commodity to be bought and sold in the marketplace. As has been noted, this much sought after resource of medicine—the knowledge and the goods—was controlled by rulers in ancient China and Egypt, and no doubt elsewhere. As practitioners' guilds and associations arose, medicine—again, the knowledge and the goods—tended to be controlled by the combined elite of the profession and the state. In the absence or reluctance of the state, the resource of medicine is held by either the professional elite or by the open market of popular demand.

The annals of the history of medical economics of the future may look back at the 20th century as a peak of government control and sponsorship by the bureaucratic state. A few comparative studies of national health plans like Guy-Pierre Cabanel's review of "nationalized" and "liberal" medical policies throughout the world (unfortunately available only in French, 1977) or Murray Last's portrayal of national and international **medical cultures** (1990) provide an invaluable basis for analysis to the medical anthropology student with an interest in national health care systems. A sketch of this material is all that is possible in this textbook.

The complete socialization of medicine—that is, the state-sponsored "free" services model of health care, which we associate with socialist or communist dominated political systems—was initiated by 19th-century Prussia under Chancellor Otto von Bismarck, Max Weber's home society where modern "rationally legally legitimized" bureaucracy reached its zenith. This model of bureaucratically centralized medicine was taken over and instituted in the Soviet Union under Stalin, and copied by other communist or socialist dominated societies such as China, North Korea, East Germany, and other post–World War II Soviet bloc countries. Medical services, research, and control became part of the larger centrally planned, "command" economies. Western social democracies beginning with Germany, but later including Sweden, the Netherlands, Great Britain, France, and Canada, achieved systematic national health care coverage as complete as that under communist governments, although the economic "engine" of these societies remained corporate capitalism. In the United States health care legislation enacted in the 1970s gave nearly complete state coverage to sectors of society such as the elderly (Medicare) and the poor, indigent, and elderly (Medicaid). But an attempt in the 1990s by the Clinton administration to extend health insurance to all through a comprehensive national health care plan failed amid much opposition from the American Medical Association and the political opposition. Although there was a good deal of "politics" in this opposition, an underlying reason for the defeat may well have been the fear that such a plan would extend the national deficit. The collapse of the Soviet Union and its Eastern European allies, 1989–1991, revealed that these command economies had essentially gone bankrupt long before they collapsed politically. Following the reentry of these countries, after 50 years, into a free market economy, state-provided health care needed to be radically cut back. In many cases this transformation was accompanied by severe health crises, demographic shock (see Chapter 4), and a chaotic resurgence of a multitude of types of medical providers. It will be years before the former communist countries regain some sense of stability in health and medical economics.

The United States continues to reflect a mixture of economic approaches to the structuring of health care services. While many government programs instituted in the 1960s and 1970s continue, with some reform, a sea change appeared to be occurring in the 1990s in health care organization and financing. In part this transformation was driven by cost-cutting concerns on the part of consumers, in part by the forces of technological and information changes. In part it reflected the worldwide shift from centralized national economic control to private (some small, others very large) corporations, as the primary institutional mold for organizing and delivering a service, in this case health care. "Managed care" was the favorite term in the late 1990s and the early 21st century.

The most common vehicle of managed care is the for-profit health maintenance organization (HMO). This term dates to the founding in the 1950s of the ancestral prototype in California, Kaiser Permanente. Kaiser grew out of a now defunct automobile manufacturer's concern for its workers' health. Physicians were hired by Kaiser to offer a number of services for a set fee shared by the company and the worker which included not only curative care, but also health planning and health education. The rationale behind this approach was that health care services would cost less if the clientele—workers and their families—paid some attention to their own health, including periodic checkups and reminders about basic hygiene. Other HMOs came into being across the country during the 1970s and 1980s until eventually most employees of companies large and small, employees of cities and states and the federal government, and residents of most metropolitan and some rural areas had HMOs which they could join for a flat fee.

Then, in the 1990s, powerful and aggressive for-profit HMOs emerged bearing names like Humana, Oxford Health Plans, United Healthcare, and Columbia, who began buying up hospitals and other smaller HMOs in a manner similar to corporate takeovers in other sectors of capitalism as we know it. These companies have become the most aggressive at setting ceilings on the payments they will make for set services. These cost-cutting and advance-estimate decisions are made by batteries of bureaucratic physicians who work for these companies poring over the invoices or charges as they come from clinics. Health insurance companies, those that survive, have begun to operate like the for-profit HMOs. The impact of this corporate revolution on the practicing health care worker is that "productivity" and "profit" now tend to be driving forces. Not surprisingly, monopolistic tendencies have appeared. The largest of the HMOs tend to be least efficient and slowest in their payments to contracted physicians (Freudenheim 1997). Concerns for the quality and equity of care are raised. Questions are asked by critics over the huge—million-dollar—salaries of

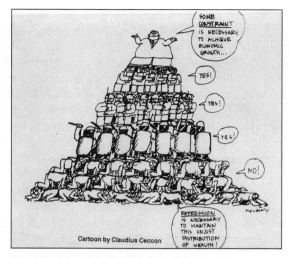

Photo 9.2 *Cartoon by Claudius Ceccon.*
Source: Courtesy of *Contact,* a publication of the World
Council of Churches.

the executives of these companies. The specter has been raised of a society
in which the true costs of this system of health care are paid by those individuals who are not in these plans, are unemployed, or unfit to work. In
other words, a kind of triage exists in which the most fit are covered, while
those who are costly are preselected not to be covered. On the other hand,
nonprofit HMOs have also emerged, many launched as church-related organizations. Others are nonprofit by virtue of their charters (e.g., Blue
Cross and Blue Shield). In the mixed model of American health care, usually one or another program offers something for everyone. The growth of
publicly funded programs for the poor, such as Medicaid, or the increasing
practice of just showing up at an emergency room where care would not
be refused, has become the medicine of an increasing number of Americans. The cartoon by Claudius Ceccon, illustrates the reasons for the failure of many primary health care programs (see Photo 9.2). It is also an apt
illustration of the consequences of unregulated health care for profit in a
class-divided society.

MEDICAL PLURALISM, OR THE LIMITS OF COHERENCE

Rarely has medical incorporation been so uniform and complete that a single paradigm has ruled supreme in a given time and place. The image
some Westerners may hold of medicine as being synonymous with what

their doctors do in a local hospital or university clinic, and which is normative of all medicine, is surely atypical. As suggested above, it does not even hold in the United States. More common, worldwide and historically, is the image of the delivery of medicine as in a marketplace, with stalls in the medicine section offering goods from a wide variety of sources, representing most of the major therapeutic traditions on earth, the good and the bad, the benign and the dangerous. If the market offerings reflect national or state health service regulation and certification, customers may complain of a conspiracy to limit the drugs available or to withhold the best and most powerful cures. Such "wonder" drugs will be available from some unofficial, possibly even illegal, source by mail or through peddlers operating semisecretly. In some countries they may be available from the very officials who might be getting rich from bribes or are directly involved in the traffic of unregulated medicines. That this condition is not new is evident from George Cruikshank's 19th-century satirical etching of "The Sick Goose and the Council of Health" in which every huckster offers his special remedy (see Photo 9.3).

Medical anthropology has used the notion of **medical pluralism** to describe the coexistence of ideas and practitioners from several traditions occupying the same therapeutic space in a society. Charles Leslie's picture of medicine in India suggested this notion; other scholars have since used the term. The uses of the term have masked several types of "pluralism," rooted either in different ideas of health, illness, and healing, or differential incorporation of their adherents and practitioners. These kinds of medical pluralism may constitute at least the following three types.

In a first view which reflects the centers of mainstream medicine, there is but one medicine: medicine as it is practiced in mainstream hospitals and clinics. All else is "alternative." Medicine is institutionalized, official, legal, and professional; alternative medicine is peripheral, unofficial, sometimes illegal, and rarely professionalized. Murray Last identified this type of medical culture as an "exclusivist system" exemplified by the former Soviet Union and, to a lesser extent, France (Last 1990:355). Interestingly, these so-called alternative medicine practitioners and advocates accept this designation, as indicated in the name of the Office of Alternative Medicine of the National Institutes of Health. This reveals a type of asymmetrical pluralism because there is clearly a dominant versus subordinate rank difference between these representatives of different medical traditions that is reflected in their differential incorporation.

A second type of medical pluralism—from the viewpoint of professionalization, incorporation, and state legitimation—is more symmetrical. Here the representatives of different medical traditions are ranked equally in society, are given equal status before the state, and are either equally unincorporated or equally incorporated. Last called these "tolerant systems" which are exemplified by British and German medicine (1990:357–59). The coequal representation of **homeopathy** and **allopathy** in German pharma-

Photo 9.3 *The Sick Goose and the Council of Health, a satirical cartoon by G. Cruikshank (1792–1878). A large group of doctors deliberate around a patient, represented by figures bearing the characteristics of the cures they are prescribing surrounding a goose. A bottle says: "I think the poor goose requires a little of Godfrey's cordial"; Another bottle says: "A bottle of balm of Gilead would revive him." A water pump is suggesting: "I should recommend him to sleep in wet sheets and drink three gallons of pump water daily." A pill says: "Let him have a dozen boxes of Blair's gout pills, and put his drumsticks in hot water." A bottle of ointment says: "His case is exactly like the Earl of Aldborough's so nothing can cure him but Holloway's ointment and pills." An old man says: "Parr's life pills I see are the only things that can save him." Another bottle of pills replies: "Life pills! Vegetable pills you mean, let him be well stuffed with Morison's no. 1 and 2." A minute man on top of a book titled "Homeopathy" says: "It's cholera clearly and I should prescribe a little unripe fruit—the millionth part of a green gooseberry."*
SOURCE: Wellcome Library London.

cies shows such a symmetrical pluralism. Parallel associations for biomedical practitioners and African medicine practitioners in Zimbabwe likewise show such a symmetrical pluralism.

A third type of medical pluralism has little differential or parallel incorporation of the medical traditions, but distinctive ideas and therapies are still recognized as deriving from distinctive traditions. Here we might speak of this as a kind of thematic pluralism, or as "integrated systems" (Last 1990:359–60) exemplified in some Asian and African settings (Janzen 1978:223–29). With little differential incorporation, practitioners of historically recognized distinctive traditions may begin to borrow and adapt techniques, ideas, and practices, a circumstance that some have called "medical syncretism" (Leslie 1992).

The notion of medical pluralism possibly reaches a point of diminishing returns when practitioners lose the conviction that what they are doing is distinctive, and they are not organized around that distinctiveness. With medical practices and ideas, as with every other domain of culture, change and new incorporations occur regularly. When an American buys a Japanese car, is he a "pluralist" consumer? Does a Japanese orchestra performing Beethoven become "pluralist"? Human culture is itself very synthetic. Medicine is one of the most dynamic and synthetic areas of human culture, and we should regard it as such and not be amazed if members of a society adopt practices from their neighbors or foreigners, right alongside "their" culture. The vignette of Hmong medicine by Lisa Capps demonstrates the latter type of pluralism. All medicine is in some sense pluralistic. As the outcome of conquest, globalization, and the difficulty or inability of professional and state authorities to control healing, medicine reveals the power of healing that generates an infinite number of new ways to address human suffering.

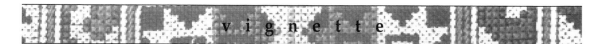

Hmong Medical Culture in Kansas City[3]

At the close of the Vietnam War, and especially after the fall of Laos to the communists in 1975, the United States government allowed thousands of Hmong people to immigrate to the United States. The Hmong, at home in the hills and mountains of Vietnam, Laos, Thailand, and Burma, had been recruited by the U.S. Central Intelligence Agency to form a counterinsurgency army to fight against the Viet Cong and Laotian communists. When the United States withdrew its support and the tide turned, the Hmong fighters and their families were targeted for reprisal and fled to refugee camps in Thailand from where they were airlifted to the United States. From special army camps in Arkansas they were dispersed in small groups throughout the United States. Yet within a short time many of these scattered Hmong had regrouped into larger communities in U.S. cities, of which the Kansas City Hmong became one.

Lisa Capps, a nurse practitioner in Kansas City, Missouri, and an anthropologist, having met the Hmong in her practice and wishing to know more about their background and health beliefs, decided to study the Kansas City community of 650 persons. Photo 9.4 shows her, notebook in hand, conversing with Bee Yaaj of the Kansas City community. She also spent several months in northern Thailand with Laotian Hmong to gain a better picture of their health beliefs and practices prior to reaching the United States. But it was not possible to make many generalizations about Hmong culture, despite their self-conscious worldview, because the numerous Hmong clans, scattered throughout Asia and the Western world, have been on the move for many centuries as slash-and-burn cultivators. The many streams of Hmong reflect slightly different cultural practices. According to Hmong memory and scholarly research, they were displaced from earlier home sites in China by the Han dynasty as early as 2,000 years ago, and gradually moved southward from the Yellow and Yangtze rivers until in recent centuries they became highland farmers in south China, Burma, Thailand, Vietnam, and Laos. Further divergent streams developed as some Hmong became Christian, others Buddhist. In the early 21st century Hmong are found in all the Asian countries mentioned, as well as France, Canada, French Guyana, Australia, and the United States. After some adjustments and more moves, most of the Kansas City Hmong were Protestant, constituting in particular congregations of Baptist and Christian and Missionary Alliance (CMA), from the time of their conversion as early as the 1940s and 1950s in Laos.

In conversations with the Kansas City Hmong such as Kang Her at a home party (see Photo 9.5), in community and church events, in mediation work with the Hmong and Kansas City clinics and hospitals, and in some direct care, Capps was able to discover the outlines of what she called Hmong "medical culture." She used this term rather than system or structure because Hmong ideas and practices did not seem to constitute a logical or meaningful whole. Rather, they were like a mirror of the Hmong historical experience whose strands included a background of shamanism (which had been officially abandoned), a vigorous life of group prayer meetings in the CMA context; a belief, held by many, of "fright" or soul loss; bits of Chinese medical ideas (as reflected in the use of pressure points by a few healers, an understanding of the uses of acupuncture, some notions of humoral balance between hot and cold; but no awareness of the doctrine of *ch'i*); acceptance of most aspects of biomedicine, hospitals, clinics, and their therapies (with some exceptions, including a

continued

continued from previous page

Photo 9.4 *Lisa Capps, nurse-anthropologist, with Hmong interviewee in Kansas City.*
SOURCE: Courtesy of Lisa Capps Padesky.

reluctance to give blood); high natality, with large families, organized as named patrilineages with reverence for patriarchs. Although the Kansas City Protestant Hmong had assimilated the world of spirits and ancestors to the Christian notion of the Devil, who might still send illness but could be overcome by prayers to God and Jesus, fright and soul loss represented genuine concerns for the Hmong. On several occasions Capps witnessed diagnoses of soul loss and therapies deemed appropriate to this condition, most often massages, accompanied by prayer.

Capps wrote that although there was no single element in Hmong medical culture that could be called unique to them, their strong sense of identity led them to identify certain illness as

Photo 9.5 *Lisa Capps with Kang Her at her home party with children, Kansas City Hmong community, 1991.*
SOURCE: Photo courtesy of Lisa Capps Padesky.

"Hmong" and related therapeutic practices—such as fright (ceeb), prayers twice a week to be protected from malevolent spirits by Jesus and the Holy Spirit—helped them to maintain a strong Hmong culture.

One could say that the image in Photo 9.1 on an embroidered bookmark has become an indexical sign of Hmong identity in the same way as fright illness. When the Hmong reached the United States, many of them gave up their distinctive clothing for American clothing. But one of the first desires of Hmong women was to purchase beads, yarn, and cloth with which to continue weaving distinctive Hmong patterns and images, like the one shown on the cover of this book. The evolving Hmong self-definition in illness, therapies, and religion, as in artwork, shapes a continuing Hmong identity as it has for centuries since they left their original homeland in Asia. ■

CONCLUSION

This chapter began with a definition of the two sources of power in medicine—"raw power" and the control of medicine—then introduced a series of dimensions of medicine that showed ever greater degrees of coherence or control over the original power of medicine. Each of these was accompanied by pertinent studies or theories and methods in medical anthropology and related disciplines. The first was the simple establishment of coherence within medicine, even if that was merely the "culture" of medicine. That was followed by a look at how resources of medicine are allocated or claimed in therapeutic decision making. The different types of legitimacy that have given authority to medicine, its ideas, or practices, were then studied. These considerations set the stage for a review of the many ways in which medical practitioners and controllers may be incorporated—that is, organized as corporate groups to command and direct medical resources. The process of incorporation was followed to the most powerful medical corporations of all, professional associations, the state, and private market-oriented corporations.

The underlying issue of this chapter has been the extramedical sources of control and power that shape the product or the process we call healing. Those extrinsic forces tend to pull one way and another at the ideas and techniques of medical practice. If the social context is well ordered, there may be a monolithic unity to the appearance of that medicine, especially if the state or a royal court sponsors medicine the way it sees fit. However, most of the time there are contradictory pulls upon medicine—as upon other institutions of the arts or knowledge—resulting in a contradictory or complimentary set of ideas and bodies of practitioners. Then too there may be the hand of history in the medical traditions represented in a community, revealing different layers and centers of knowledge and practice, a state of affairs we call medical pluralism—the rule rather than the exception. The case of the Hmong in the United States and other countries of the Western world, and of their health and healing practices, represents an intriguing example of this kind of pluralism in culture and medicine. An examination of power and organization in medicine offers insights for both the further comparative research of medicine, as well as a grasp of some of the ways that health problems may find practical solutions, which is the topic of the next chapter.

REVIEW QUESTIONS

1. Name five factors that play a role in giving a medical tradition or order its coherence—socially, cognitively, logically. Describe these factors and cite authors who have written or spoken about them, with reference to a particular medical tradition.

2. What is "medical culture" as considered in the writing of Murray Last and those who have borrowed this idea?

3. Identify the "primary resources" and "secondary resources" of a medical tradition, as put forward in Paul Unschuld's useful perspective on the ways that medicine is controlled and becomes a tool for control in society.

4. How does the therapy management group get constituted in Kongo cases of illness and healing, and what does it do? How are the above processes or concepts embodied in its practice? What are the criteria in Kongo thinking that differentiate an etiology of "human caused" from "God caused"? What are the consequences of this in therapy?

5. Using the notions of "authority" and "legitimation" of Max Weber, and of "incorporation," assess the relative fates of allopathic medicine and midwifery in the United States in the first half of the 20th century. How have aspects of legitimation such as academic research, the place of founders and their fame, professionalization, legislation, advertising, and popular demand been used to shape, control, and influence other medical traditions such as chiropractic, acupuncture, psychiatry, and so forth?

6. What accounts for the continuing popularity of shamanism in many countries of the world? Using a particular instance, how does one explain this in the rapidly industrializing settings of South Korea, Taiwan, Malaysia, and Hong Kong?

7. Compare the meaning or character of "medical pluralism" in India, Kongo, Malay, and contemporary U.S. society. Are all medical cultures "pluralistic"? Is the medical pluralism of the Hmong of Kansas City different from, or mostly like, other cases of medical pluralism?

8. What do you understand by the phrase "culture of biomedicine"? Lorna Rhodes spoke of biomedicine as "contingent" (i.e., shaped, affected) in terms of (*a*) the assumptions it reveals about its historical context, (*b*) how social meaning is embedded in biomedical categories, and (*c*) the daily practice of clinicians. Can you think of illustrations of the culture of biomedicine in each context?

9. Despite their very great differences, what are the themes that allopathic medicine, homeopathic medicine, chiropractic, and Christian Science healing in the United States have in common, according to David McQueen?

NOTES

1. See note 2, Chapter 1, for further comment on this use of the idea of "tradition" as a living, changing reality.

2. Kathryn Staiano, who has worked in a state Medicaid agency, suggested several ways that the U.S. government actively controls its citizenry. "The national governmental funding agencies decide what kind of research they're going to fund; state programs (such as Medicaid) interfere in decision making at every level deciding what conditions will be treated and which won't; they institutionalize the mentally ill (which is basically removing a person from society's view because they are disruptive or disturbing); state pharmacy boards and the

Board of Medical Examiners control prescriptions that can be dispensed and how much can be dispensed; the Congress is about to pass the "Pain Relief Act" which may define who is terminally ill, and so on. Look at recent Supreme Court decisions which allow the state to continue to keep someone in prison (probably in a forensics unit of a prison or a state hospital forensics unit) who has committed crimes of sexual abuse, has served his sentence, but is predicted to commit the same crime in the future. The state can hold such a person indefinitely. For some time, Medicaid and Medicare programs would not pay for a transplant of a liver into a patient who was an alcoholic and continued to drink. Legal action changed that." Personal communication, September 16, 2000.

3. This vignette is based on the writing of Lisa Capps (1994), many discussions with her about her work, and several visits with her to her fieldwork site in the Kansas City Hmong community.

Shaping the Fabric of Health

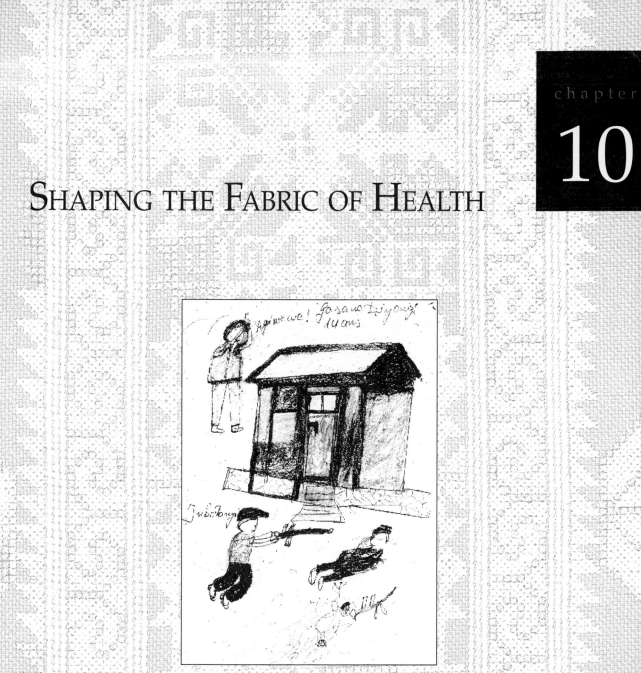

Photo 10.1 *Rwandan child's drawing of his traumatic experience in the genocidal war of 1994.*
Source: J. M. Janzen.

Throughout this book the "fabric of health" has been used as a metaphor for life-enabling means such as food, clean water, shelter, significant others of family, friends, and community, as well as concepts, medicinal substances, therapeutic techniques, and institutions and behaviors with which to come to terms with health problems and to seek healing. The book's title has highlighted the social dimension in the fabric of health, however, because it is through relationships, social practices, economic conditions, and institutions that health may be significantly transformed. In terms of this metaphor, then, where the fabric of health has frayed, where it has been torn or cut, it may be repaired, or patched. The ancient threads of social arrangements, ideas, and signs in the fabric may be extended to cover new applications. New arrangements or ideas—new, synthetic, flexible threads—may be expanded to address unique new problems. This chapter is about the perspective of anthropology and the role of anthropology in the ongoing shaping of the fabric of health.

Throughout this book, perspectives, ideas, and illustrations of medical anthropology have laid the groundwork for this chapter's sketch of some ways in which medical anthropology may be used to shape the fabric of health. Chapter 3 demonstrated the connection between classical healing traditions and innovative health campaigns of primary health care and reproductive health. Chapter 4 sketched the historical profiles of population and disease and then identified some ways in which current health and reproduction patterns around the "demographic transition" are subject to public policies and campaigns for family planning. Chapter 5 covered many ways that the lifecourse is punctuated by significant moments that are widely shared across cultures, some of which may be open to shaping by anthropological understanding and advising. In Chapter 6 the definitions of social personhood provided the basis for the understanding of identity, and this in turn may offer insights into the ways that personal transitions and chronic illnesses may be handled. This chapter also explored some of the ethically contested area of personhood, such as how a person is defined in conception and how life is defined at death. Chapter 7 examined the manner in which signs of illness and healing are transformed by the way we recognize suffering, and the way that the power of healing may be understood with those signs. Anthropologists have helped understand pain, suffering, and the symbolic dimension of medicines and therapeutic techniques, and the power of language in healing. Chapter 8 showed how knowledge is constructed and made legitimate, and Chapter 9 continued the presentation of how knowledge and the power of healing are wielded and controlled. These processes must all be understood if anthropologists, or others, are to effectively shape health.

Most medical anthropologists would heartily support the proposition that the knowledge they produce in their studies and the analyses and writing that result are beneficial to human communities. Different labels have appeared in anthropology to identify those anthropologists or anthropological projects that explicitly seek to bring learning back into the shaping of health. The most common term that has been used is simply **applied an-**

thropology. A focus on health issues has then been called **applied medical anthropology**; when it has a special focus upon the context of healing, it has been called **clinically applied (medical) anthropology.** Other anthropologists who work with the communities they study to solve problems or otherwise bring about directed change have drawn a further distinction between applied anthropologists and **action anthropologists.** The latter emphasize that they work only at the request of the community, on problems and issues selected by the community, and not for an administration, industry, or outside agency. Other anthropologists have called themselves **practicing anthropologists,** to differentiate themselves from academic anthropologists. Most recently the term **public service anthropologist** has been used. However, much anthropology may have an impact on the setting in which it is done because of the knowledge that is generated and can be brought to bear on issues of whatever kind. An insightful monograph or research project, as we have seen in the vignettes featured in this book, may illuminate issues and bring insights applicable to a wide variety of situations. In this sense, all medical anthropology has potential application.

Five "applications" of medical anthropology follow in this chapter; they represent a cross-section of the many ways in which anthropology has been brought to bear on shaping the fabric of health.

Understanding New (and Not So New) Diseases

The book opened with a case study of kuru, a viral disease that raged among the Fore of New Guinea in the 1950s and 1960s. Medical anthropologists working with other scientists finally identified the mode of transmission of this disease: the cannibalistic "drinking" of bodily fluids of the deceased by close kin women and children. This same ability of anthropologists to "see" the obvious, by participant observation and cultural analysis, makes them uniquely helpful in identifying and understanding risk behaviors and modes of transmission and in developing educational strategies for combating such new diseases. Despite the hope and reality of the demographic transition and the seeming disappearance or decline of many of the old contagious diseases from our health landscape, some old diseases such as cholera are ever ready (as in war) to bound back. Laurie Garrett, in *The Coming Plague* (1994), has detailed on a global basis the specter of new diseases that faces humankind unless we are vigilant in preventing the conditions that spawn them, and understand their causes and consequences when they break out. Robert Desowitz's *Tropical Diseases: From 50,000 B.C. to A.D. 2500* (1997) followed the same subject of returning old diseases as well as new diseases which have their main hearth of active life in the tropics but which may be readily and quickly brought into the Northern Hemisphere by travelers.

The ecology of disease and adaptation is essential to an understanding of the emergence of new diseases and the resurgence of old diseases. Increasing numbers of disease organisms have developed a resistance to medication that was once powerful enough to control or eradicate them. Tuberculosis was long treated effectively with a regime of penicillin, and was thought in the decades after the invention of this antibiotic to have disappeared from the list of human health problems in Western industrialized countries. After 1980, however, new strains of tuberculosis were discovered in these same settings that were more virulent than those before, and were resistant to most antibiotics. It is now apparent that tuberculosis bacilli never disappeared and that they reacted to penicillin and successively more powerful antibiotics by adapting and developing more resistant strains. In this case the organism humans labeled a "disease" did the adapting to its environment, in the process becoming more "healthy" and resistant. (See Randall Packard's research on tuberculosis in southern Africa in Chapter 4, and Paul Farmer (1999) on new TB outbreaks.)

Many other diseases have, like TB, made a return in a more virulent form that has overcome and developed resistance to the chemicals used in the second half of the 20th century to combat them. One of the most widespread of these resurgent diseases with major consequences is mosquito-borne malaria. The reason for its resurgence is directly the result of widespread spraying of DDT in peoples' homes and over the cities of the tropical world several decades ago. This was done to kill mosquitoes directly in these homes and cities. But this practice, while temporarily effective for months or a few years, never killed all the mosquitoes, and it did not eradicate the malaria parasite from pools of water. Today malaria is widespread in the same areas as 50 years ago, only it is more dangerous; the mosquitoes are bigger and "better."

Learning to cope with more resistant known diseases is one thing, but quite another is the appearance of entirely new disease entities like AIDS, ebola, and Legionnaires' Disease. In contrast to TB (a bacterial organism) and malaria (a microorganism living in the blood of mosquitoes and humans), AIDS and ebola are viral diseases which affect the cells directly by causing them to grow in abnormal ways, or to self-destruct. Acquired immune deficiency syndrome (AIDS) weakens the immune system, allowing all sorts of other diseases to infect the body opportunistically. AIDS has no known cure although a combination of drugs taken intensively may suppress the virus that causes it. Therefore, much attention has focused on the high-risk behaviors that transmit AIDS: unprotected sexual intercourse, the sharing of needles with an AIDS or HIV-positive person, and of course a blood transfusion. The infant of a woman infected with AIDS has a high chance of being infected, unless the pregnant woman receives the same medications that AIDS patients receive, specifically AZT.

Medical anthropologists have been deeply involved in the study of AIDS risk behavior and the cultural context of its development as they look for the why, wherefore, and what of risk behaviors, education strategies, and dealing with the consequences of the disease. AIDS, a virus like ebola and kuru, creates the opportunity for collaborative work with virologists and epidemiologists. Anthropologists can make a distinctive contribution by studying the ways that people think of these diseases and understand them within their worldview. Anthropologists can then work with others to create culturally and contextually appropriate solutions. Paul Farmer's *AIDS and Accusation* (1992) looks at AIDS in Haiti, at a time when the very first case appeared in the community he was studying. Farmer, a physician-anthropologist, had the unique opportunity to study the unfolding image of this disease, as well as to study the early North American cultural stereotype that AIDS was a "Haitian" disease. He situated the larger image of AIDS within the global political economy and culture of the United States and Americans' tendency to blame others—in this case Haiti, a poor black country—for the scourge. Just what would constitute "applied" or "action" anthropology in the face of AIDS is not so clear, especially since no cure was known.

Where both cause and cure of a disease are known, one might at first think that it would be a simple thing for health personnel to explain to the affected people what they must do to avoid becoming diseased or what they must do to become well. But in a disease that is this well understood, and yet persists, other factors enter in to make it so. The many and varied entities or conditions that medicine and society call "diseases" may be exceedingly different—bacterial organisms, viruses, genetic predispositions, nutritional complications, allergies, physiological insufficiencies, weaknesses, and the consequences of the life cycle itself. The vignette that follows is about a "disease" that is related to the predisposition of some persons' metabolic processes to be unable to generate enough insulin to digest and synthesize sugars and fats. This "disease" is called diabetes. But even within this category there are at least two types of conditions, depending on whether the symptoms of diabetes are related to insufficient insulin secretion or not. The latter is called "non-insulin-dependent diabetes" (NIDD). The long-term possible consequences of both forms are the same: damage to kidneys and tissue, the tendency for extremities to lose their blood circulation and to develop gangrene, and loss of vision due to deterioration of the eye tissues. This disease, although well known, represents a gradually ascending crisis in the lives of those who develop it. The vignette describes anthropologist Christina Loehn's work with a community where NIDD reached epidemic proportions.

For medical anthropologists, one of the most important issues of understanding how a community may come to terms with a resurgent or

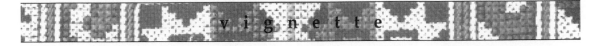

The Epidemic of Non-Insulin-Dependent Diabetes among the Southern Cheyenne, and Its Control: An Example of Action Anthropology[1]

Christina Loehn, a licensed physical therapist and medical anthropologist took her interest in health issues among Native Americans to anthropologist Karl Schlesier. Schlesier has practiced **action anthropology** among the Southern Cheyenne of Oklahoma for several decades, basing his research on priorities set by them. Schlesier had studied with Professor Sol Tax at the University of Chicago, founder of the action anthropological approach in work in Chiapas, Mexico, and among the Fox Indians of Illinois. Among the Cheyenne, Schlesier worked in particular with the Arrow Keeper and his group, who represented the traditional religious interests of the Cheyenne, and who conducted a variety of ceremonies such as the Arrow Renewal and the Sun Dance. One project Schlesier conducted with the Arrow Keeper was to organize the traditional religious leadership within the framework of U.S. and Oklahoma state law so they could become part of the effective tribal government. For over a century the traditionalists had been outsiders to the Cheyenne-Arapaho Council, because they had resisted involvement with the United States when their people were defeated militarily and forced onto reservations. Now involvement of the traditionalists in government affairs was helpful in bringing the Cheyenne together to deal with their common problems and affairs.

When Christina Loehn, through Schlesier, approached the Arrow Keeper's court in 1991 and asked which health issues she might help them with, their unambiguous answer was that she should assist them in figuring out why diabetes had become such a problem for the Cheyenne, and what they could do about it. One of the last acts the aging Arrow Keeper took before he died was to sign the letter authorizing Loehn to conduct her study among them and to help them with diabetes control. He was succeeded by his

son Bill Red Hat with whom Loehn then continued to work. Loehn prepared three field statements for her research: on Cheyenne history and traditional concepts and practices of health and healing, with Schlesier; biomedical and anthropological research on diabetes, with a diabetes specialist in a Medical School; and on applied and action anthropology programs in health issues among Native Americans, and the reasons for their success or failure.

Christina Loehn's research focused on non-insulin-dependent diabetes, which has become a serious problem in many Native American societies. The technical definition of diabetes is to have a higher blood sugar level than that somewhat arbitrarily established by medical authorities. Later-stage complications of the disease include kidney dysfunction, blindness, and loss of peripheral limb blood circulation, leading to gangrene, the terrible treatment of which is amputation. Once not present at all in Native American communities, it is now many times more prevalent there than in white mainstream society.

But above all the Arrow Keeper had asked Loehn to draw up a series of recommendations about what they could do to prevent and control diabetes. Recommendations were to be couched in the context of the history of Cheyenne diet and physical activity. As the hunting life had ended with reservation status, the intake of fresh fruits and foods dropped off, as did the active physical life required to forage for food. In their early years on the reservation, the Cheyenne had tried to live off their land as sedentary people; they still grew vegetables and found some wild plants. But since the 1940s and 1950s, and the advent of government relief food—dried and packaged cheeses, milk, beans, and other foods obtained from nearby markets, and drinks such as pop and sugared cereals, candy, and so on—in the context of welfare checks, the level of refined sugar had skyrocketed and the level of exercise had dropped. Many informants did little or no active exercise. Loehn found some understanding of this correlation of exercise and diet to diabetes, as well as a residue of traditional beliefs about being pure and in touch with nature. Some Cheyenne individuals with whom she spoke were willing to undertake efforts to change their diet and exercise behaviors. But she also found some who knew of the bad effects of obesity—a diet high in sugar and fat, and a sedentary lifestyle—but who were unwilling or unable to act on this knowledge.

In a few other Native American communities, in particular the Pueblo societies of the Southwest, public health programs have promoted the importance of a healthy diet and active exercise. Sports competitions are sponsored in the schools for children to introduce the idea of the need for a physically active life. Some of these already-existing and apparently successful programs were included in Christina Loehn's eventual recommendations to the Arrow Keeper and to local health centers for implementation. ■

new disease is how cultural knowledge relates to actual behaviors. Thus, for example, the question arises, "What behaviors contribute to contracting the disease?" In the case of non-insulin-dependent diabetes among the Cheyenne, why were some individuals in the high-risk group of Cheyenne willing and able to change their diet and exercise behavior, and others not? In general, what predicts or guides the ways people will change their behavior toward a disease. In American society at large, many similar questions can be raised; for example, "Why do some Americans eat high sugar and high fat diets, and become obese, or smoke, even though they know of the risks to their health?" Medical anthropologists who have extensive experience in public health programs, health education programs, and primary health care programs, suggest that it is necessary to look at more than the stated belief of individuals to predict behavior, or change existing patterns of behavior (Yoder 1997). The social context of eating, drinking, working, sexual relations, and playing and images of self in public are all involved in looking at health-related ideas and behaviors. In the language of the sign, icons of personhood embody deeply held feelings, rhythms, and motivations in connection with certain behaviors, some of which may be disease inducing. Such behavioral icons may be at odds with the thoughts expressed in spoken form. Such complex contradictions in culture, society, and health may be effectively studied by anthropologists using distinctively anthropological methods of participant observation, looking for sign systems that give meaning to behaviors and relationships, and understanding powerful feelings in relationship to health-promoting, or health-destroying, behavior.

PLANNING HEALTH CARE DELIVERY

This subject has been described in various ways throughout the book. "Health care delivery" is the usual phrase used in medical and public health circles to describe the institutional frameworks for delivering "health" to people, although this phrase carries a clear connotation that health is what the ministries and professionals "deliver" to the people. Accounts in previous chapters of primary health care and the campaign of reproductive health (Chapter 3), the incorporation of medicine in institutions and medicine related variously to professional groups, the state, or corporations (Chapter 9) have all been topics that bear on the ways and the issues surrounding health care delivery. Anthropologists may not be the first professionals that health care planners think of when they go about designing institutions or reforming entire systems of health care delivery. But anthropologists have been involved in these matters and may be able to effectively analyze and interpret some of the perplexing issues that defy logic. For example, just as many people, against their rational judgment, continue to act in ways that jeopardize their health, so societies and nations pour money and resources into health care structures that may not be effective or may be inefficient. By way of illustration, the United States has a pattern of putting huge sums of money into crisis medicine for those who are at high risk, compared to the relatively smaller sums that are spent on public health or preventive care.

Health care delivery institutions and patterns are constantly changing. Due to the competition over scarce resources and the wrangling of administrators and politicians over the most appropriate institutional forms through which to incorporate medicine, health care delivery structures are constantly changing or intentionally being reshaped. The World Health Organization's Primary Health Care campaign for the medically undersupplied world was described briefly in Chapter 3. As Chapter 9 suggested, centralized state control and source of revenue, once the goal and mainstay of every nation, began to decline in the late 20th century due to financial or ideological and political reasons. A picture of triage—having to choose who will survive because of limited means—has emerged, in which by default or by design scarce resources are allocated to only some of the needy or those desiring services. Many different models are being explored. The two vignettes that illustrate this process are from the United States and from central Africa. They make an interesting and instructive comparison. The first portrays the work of anthropologist Kathryn Staiano, whose long-term position in the Oregon State Medicaid program gave her an exceptional position from which to see the policy shifts and experiments in health care delivery in the United States. She described the dynamic interaction between the state, the legislature, the people, and the professional care providers.

The second example of the retreat—"collapse" is a more apt term—of the state from health care is in one area of Congo, formerly Zaire. Pakisa Tshimika, a Congolese MD and public health official, described what happened to a model Primary Health Care region as the state collapsed, and how local agencies stepped in. This region is Bandundu, and the city is

Kikwit, where ebola broke out in 1995. Ebola "was only the tip of the iceberg," said Tshimika. In other words, it was as much a symptom of deeper and pervasive problems having to do with the collapse of the social infrastructure, the fabric of health.

These two vignettes are rather lengthy because they contain much background information on the societies, governments, and the histories of health care programs. Health care delivery systems, or care programs, never occur in a vacuum; they are situated in particular historically shaped cultures. Therefore, it is never possible to begin with a clean sweep, to start afresh. Furthermore, there is never enough money on hand to meet all the perceived needs. For the anthropologist, the assumption is made that decisions, evaluations, power, and expertise will be common ingredients of the mix that need to be studied. What both vignettes have in common is that their principle figures—Kathryn Staiano in Oregon, Pakisa Tshimika in Congo—were individuals in a much larger arena of actors. They were able to witness changes occurring and crises arising, but no individual alone can transform something as labyrinthine as health care practices, institutions, and resources.

APPLYING ANTHROPOLOGY CLINICALLY

The reader may be relieved to learn that "clinical anthropology" only rarely refers to an anthropologist "practicing" on someone. Although the term *clinical anthropology* is still used (e.g., Rush 1996), the practitioner in question is always licensed in another area such as nursing, medicine, psychiatry, physical therapy, chiropractic, acupuncture, homeopathy, and many more fields. It is not clear how an anthropologist would "practice" clinically; I, for one, would not go to a fellow anthropologist for "treatment." However, the number of such licensed practitioners who have studied, read, and researched anthropology and bring their expanded understanding into the clinic is large.

Far more common is the term *clinically applied anthropology* (Chrisman and Johnson 1990) to describe the interface of anthropology, medical anthropology, and the clinical setting. This term is also used in the situation of a certified clinician who may have a degree in anthropology. It also extends to include the use of an anthropologist as interpreter and facilitator in a clinical setting.

One of the most common uses of an anthropologist in the clinic has been to serve as cultural translator between a client and the medical staff or practitioner. In a society as culturally pluralist as that of the United States or many other nations (see Chapters 3 and 9 for a review of represented traditions), sufferers seeking care are often not at home in the language of the doctor, nurse, or healer, or they have concepts and practices

vignette

The Oregon Health Plan[2]

The Oregon Health Plan (OHP) was a radical departure from "business as usual." At its core—and easily its most controversial feature—is a ranked list of medical, dental, and mental health conditions. Depending on how much money the Oregon legislature allocates to health care for Medicaid recipients each biennium, a condition may be "covered" or "not covered." It is the first (and to date only) national attempt to control health care costs by assertively and publicly rationing care. The list of condition/treatment pairs today contains 745 items, from "severe/moderate head injury," which heads the list, to "disorders of refraction and accommodation treated by radial keratotomy" which appears on line 745. The 1997 legislature agreed to allocate money to cover treatments to line 574, "non-cervical warts including venereal warts." This decidedly remarkable health care reform package, which included a strong emphasis on preventive care, prenatal care, and "comfort care" for those who were terminally ill, was intended to be a statewide reform, though in the initial phases it would apply only to the lowest income segment of the population—those eligible for Medicaid.

The concept of an open system of rationing care, an approach which was intended to eliminate the most expensive and least effective procedures and thereby free up money for a "basic health care package" for a larger number of people, drew almost immediate national and international attention, much of it unfavorable. While everyone seemed to agree it was time for major health care reform, few were willing to attempt such a risky approach. No one had yet seriously looked at the issues of cost-effectiveness of treatments and there was often a sense in those early newspaper and media accounts of a state headed in the wrong direction but applauded for the courage that it took to do so.

The Oregon Health Plan was conceived in the mid-1980s. Health care costs were consistently increasingly across the country at double-digit rates of inflation. The Oregon legislature, which is often constrained in its actions and ability to spend taxpayers' money by the initiative votes of Oregon citizens, was facing the prospect of diminishing general revenues and an increasing Medicaid caseload. The legislature wished to be responsive to its citizens who demanded good value for their tax dollars. Organ transplants were known to be extraordinarily expensive while often producing poor results. When the Oregon legislature had completed its funding decisions for the 87 Biennium, organ transplantation was no longer covered.

Medical ethicist Daniel Callahan began his book *What Kind of Life: The Limits of Medical Progress* with the following statement: "Early in December of 1987, Adam Jacoby 'Coby' Howard of Rockwood, Oregon, died of leukemia." He died, many argued, as a result of the state's new policy. It is a strange thing about Americans that they optimistically perceive all transplants to be lifesaving. When Coby Howard died, several legislators and many citizens across the state took up the issue. It had a certain political appeal and some politicians found it useful to their cause to support a revival of the transplant program. The program was resurrected, but shut down again after three months for lack of funds. John Kitzhaber, then president of the Oregon senate, argued eloquently throughout this period (and appeared on several national television programs) that technology had grown beyond our ability to afford it.

Priorities needed to be set. By saving money through reductions in treatments shown not to be cost effective, more pregnant women and children could receive basic health care services. This position became known as the Oregon Health Plan and while there were many players, it was and is a program principally associated with Kitzhaber, an emergency room physician and now governor of Oregon. The Health Services Commission (HSC), an 11-member commission, was appointed by the governor. The overview of the HSC describes the task awaiting it: Oregon acknowledges that all medical procedures are not equally valuable or effective. Therefore, in order to define an affordable, quality health care package, the state has to determine first which services are most beneficial. The legislature created the HSC to rank all health care services according to their importance to the entire population. The state legislature will then use this prioritized list to determine the Standard Benefit Package.

The Health Services Commission began its work in 1989. This was, in almost every respect, the most "democratically" conceived approach ever attempted to making health care decisions for a population. In the two years that followed, more than 25,000 volunteer hours were donated to this project. The final "formula" by which conditions and treatments were ranked was based on substantial public input, including 1,000 telephone Quality of Life surveys and solicitation of information at public meetings attended by more than 1,500 people. Testimony on illness and its treatment, including information on the most current medical technology, was obtained from 50 groups of health care practitioners. Testimony for each of these groups ran from one to eight hours. An actuarial firm was hired to estimate the costs of treatments. The commission turned to medical ethicists, social workers, providers, and consumers of service for additional input. The eventual ranking was based on 17 categories of severity (life threatening to self-limiting), health outcomes data, the cost of treatment, the quality of life with and without treatment, the value to the public of various health care statuses (independently mobile to immobile), the expected duration of the benefit, and ethical and other considerations. The cost-benefit ratio of health outcomes alone was tediously complex. It utilized the following factors:

the net benefit value ratio for condition/treatment pairs to be ranked;

the cost of treatment, including all medications and ancillary services as well as the cost of the primary procedure;

the years for which the treatment can be expected to benefit the patient with this condition;

the probability that a specific outcome will occur five years hence with or without treatment;

an indicator variable denoting the presence or absence of a specific health limitation or chief complaint for the specific outcome either with treatment or without treatment;

and the weight given by Oregonians to the specific health limitation or chief complaint ranging from no significant effect to death.

Did the Oregon Health Plan live up to its reputation as a systematic and somewhat mechanistic departure from traditional health care decision making? Has the prioritized list had the effect intended? Has the overall number of uninsured in the state diminished? Have health care costs been reduced? Have more children died for lack of a transplant? Are tiny premature infants who lie alone in some separate area of the newborn nursery denied aggressive treatment? The answer to all these questions is no. Indeed, a number of political, social, economic, legal, ethical, religious, and other factors have eroded the plan as it was originally designed.

For the state to begin the Oregon Health Plan, it required a "waiver" from the federal government from the usual constraints imposed on state Medicaid programs. The approval of the waiver was in some ways granted during the heat of a presidential campaign. The waiver request had been submitted to George Bush in 1991. The Bush administration, after months of delay, denied the waiver request. The State of Oregon then redesigned the list to meet several of the concerns identified by the Bush administration, most notably a concern that disabled persons would not receive adequate care under the OHP.

continued

continued from previous page

Many in Oregon believed the first Bush administration used that as an excuse to deny the waiver request and that the real reason for denial was that it proposed to create a model for a national health care insurance program. A second waiver request lay on someone's desk without further action for some time. Then, during a press conference, Bill Clinton was asked whether he would approve Oregon's radical request if he were elected president. Placed on the spot, he said he thought he would and there was little basis to deny the plan when in office since he was proposing national health care reform. But once in office, Clinton's administration proved equally cautious. National advocates for the disabled spoke up again. They argued that the results of the Quality of Life telephone survey had to be removed from the formula because the survey asked "healthy" people to make judgments about the quality of life of disabled persons. The Quality of Life survey was removed. The OHP also proposed that babies weighing under 500 grams (slightly over a pound) and less than 23 weeks gestation would not receive treatment. Lawyers pointed out that practitioners denying treatment might face prosecution under Baby Doe laws. The line on the list labeled "babies under 500 grams" was merged with a line for other newborns, which was well above the funding cutoff. Physicians specializing in transplantation argued eloquently that transplants were cost effective. Any transplants that had been low on the list moved up. The disabled advocacy groups came back arguing that the 17 categories of conditions that were a critical part of the list discriminated against the disabled. This too was removed. The subjective judgment of commission members was used to move conditions which did not seem to be placed appropriately (a "gut" test, one person noted). Then the formula which used health outcomes was altered and the costs of treatment were removed as a factor in ranking potentially life threatening or highly disabling conditions.

Originally, the state thought to review cases to determine which patients were terminally ill (i.e., with less than six months of life left) and deny payment for further treatment. This never occurred. Instead, the patient and his or her doctor jointly decide the point at which aggressive treatment is to be halted. If the patient wishes, he or she is eligible for hospice care, a service that was not covered under the pre-OHP medicaid program.

Today an additional 100,000 people have coverage for medical expenses under the OHP; 85 percent of OHP members are in managed care. Hospital emergency room visits have dropped by 5 percent and urgent care visits by 1 percent. But the original intent to control costs has not been achieved. Medicaid in Oregon today spends more than twice as much as it did only a few years ago. The state has instituted several measures in an attempt, once again, to control increasing costs, including charging some clients for "premiums," eliminating college students from coverage, lowering the value of assets which one may have and be eligible, and raising the line so that fewer conditions are covered. The line has now been raised to a position where the federal government is unlikely to give approval for any more changes. Conditions below the funding line are those that are self-limiting, cosmetic, or for which there is no effective treatment. All diagnostic services are covered, regardless of the individual's diagnosis, and most physicians treat the patient for minor illnesses, regardless of where they fall on the list. The economic "value" of all items below the funding line is less than 10 percent of the total cost of Medicaid services.

What the OHP has achieved is a public discussion about quality of life and the costs and value of treatments. This was a discussion in which thousands of Oregonians participated. It is perhaps, then, not surprising that Oregon voters approved the first physician assisted suicide law in the United States in 2000. ■

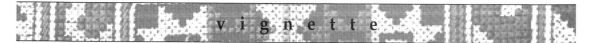

Preserving Public Health in the Ebola Zone[3]

Ebola struck in Kikwit Hospital in May 1995. Ebola is a viral hemorrhagic fever that kills about 90 percent of those it infects. There is no known cure. Nor is the ultimate source understood. At first patients, then medical staff, began dying in the hospital. Then those family and friends who washed and buried the dead also began dying. Soon, most of the remaining patients and some of the staff fled the hospital, some no doubt infected. The outbreak of ebola caused international health agencies like the World Health Organization, the International Red Cross, and the U.S. Centers for Disease Control to spring to action to contain and to understand the virus. International medical teams were sent to Kikwit to care for the sick and dying with ultracaution. Bodies were buried directly, the wards and rooms of the hospital were thoroughly cleaned, and epidemiological surveys were taken. Other than the hundred or so individuals who died in Kikwit, the feared epidemic did not reach the public, other cities, or spread abroad.

The importance of ebola in Kikwit, for our purposes, is the rest of the story that Dr. Pakisa Tshimika told the international press and this author. It is the story of the collapse of the fabric of health, and how Kikwit region responded. Kikwit is a city in Bandundu, one of the provinces of Congo (formerly Zaire). It is on the edge of the southern savanna of Africa, in the midst of vast oil palm plantations, where the Kwango river flows into the Kwilu, on which river barges take the raw oil downstream to refineries. A paved highway links the city to the national capital of Kinshasa in the west, and to the diamond hub Tshikapa in the east. Southward of Kikwit begin the open savannas, interspersed with riverside forests. Here, occasional villages of farmers may be seen, but population is sparse, around 12 per square (or about 35 per square mile) kilometer.

Kikwit, with a major hospital, was the center of several of the country's 300 health zones created in the 1980s when Zaire developed its own Primary Health Care (PHC) system following the World Health Organization plan launched following the 1976 Alma Ata Declaration of "Health for All." This region of Zaire, like much of the country, was beset with many of the basic health problems characteristic of high levels of contagious tropical diseases: an infant mortality rate of 130 per 1,000 births, endemic malaria, resurgence of sleeping sickness, increased sexually transmitted diseases including AIDS, tuberculosis, and widespread malnutrition. The Primary Health Care program was one area in which Zaire took positive initiatives during the 1970s and 1980s. In the spirit of the Health for All resolution, basic care in the form of a trained nurse with essential drugs was to be accessible to all. No one was to have to walk farther than 15 kilometers (9.3 miles) for this care.

Each health zone was organized into local primary health centers, regional midlevel centers, and a central regional hospital. In the local centers, nurses carried out basic care and public health initiatives such as inoculation. Ideally they were to see and refer the most serious cases to hospital centers. Medicines and other resources were distributed from central stocks to the local centers. Kikwit Hospital served as the center of such a set of zones; the supplies were brought in from church and international health agencies. Because of the unreliable nature of state medical supplies, the Primary Health Care system in Zaire was purposefully created in such a way that paralleled sources of medications from other governments (notably the United States Assistance for International Development, USAID). This "redundant" supply system was proposed in the late 1970s and early 1980s. Here

continued

continued from previous page

is how this happened in one region of Bandundu. In 1984 Tshimika, who is from the Chokwe region of southern Bandundu, invited physicians from private, state, and church hospitals in the region to his hospital, a church hospital. Along with a representative of the Ministry of Health, the group organized as six participating hospitals, each of which would coordinate local health centers from which they also would receive referral cases. Tshimika and many other medical personnel worked hard to find local and foreign "sponsors" for their health zones.

By the late 1980s, the Zairian government's role in the Primary Health Care system deteriorated. Inflation soared to 1,000 percent a year, and in one two-month period there were five ministers of health. The entire national budget became unreliable. At this point the government effectively and by default got out of the health care business entirely. The Ministry of Health became nonfunctional like other ministries of the Zairian government. Observers began to speak of the "collapse of the state." The 1991 riots in Kinshasa by Zairian soldiers and the destruction of many private enterprises brought the country into a state of deep moral crisis. Along with the collapse of infrastructural institutions such as the mail, roads, and ferries, the Primary Health Care zones also fell apart because governmental workers were no longer paid or, if paid, their salaries were as worthless as the hyperinflationary currency. After the riots in 1991 the foreign medical partners like USAID, the Canadian International Development Agency, Belgian assistance, and organizations like Oxfam and the United Nations Educational, Scientific, and Cultural Organization (UNESCO) withdrew because it became impossible to conduct their affairs in the midst of such chaos. Medicine stocks were stolen, vehicles were taken for private use or stolen, and personnel abandoned their posts. The national Primary Health Care office was finally closed in 1994.

The health care consequences of this, Tshimika stated, were increasing mortality and morbidity, and diseases thought to be under control such as measles and TB began to increase.

Sleeping sickness epidemics broke out anew in places along rivers. Typhoid and paratyphoid, previously unknown, appeared. And then came the outbreak of ebola in 1995. Tshimika was contacted by the international media because of the worldwide fear of this outbreak. But it was just the "tip of the iceberg," he said, revealing the extent of the disintegration of the health service infrastructure in Kikwit, and in Zaire as a whole.

Dr. Tshimika, who had once helped organize a neighboring zone in the area of Kajiji to the south of Kikwit and had played a central role in Bandundu public health planning, was also one of the individuals who could see the consequences of public health care collapse around 1990. He now became involved in trying to salvage public health in Kikwit through the creation of a local network of nongovernmental organizations (NGOs). Local supervision by motivated and interested individuals became central to new efforts at public health. In this sector, as in education and food production and distribution, private initiatives were all that remained. Where village nurses understood the issues, local clinics survived. The same was true of hospitals and clinics. But many of these now of necessity became fee-for-service operations, looking for support from outside church agencies, the United Nations, or other private sources. In Zaire and elsewhere in Africa, the NGOs became the structural wherewithal of health care delivery. Western governments had totally withdrawn from the Zairian scene; the "Zairian crisis" had become a way of life, Tshimika observed.

Out of the remnants of the old Primary Health Care structure, a consortium of local institutions created a program for the maintenance of public health. The loosely affiliated consortium called the Council for Development of Bandundu Health survived. It was able to play a major role in the ebola epidemic. Its participants included the organization Tshimika headed, the DESADEC/CEFMZ, a Mennonite Health and Development Agency; Oxfam Bandundu; Kikwit Catholic Diocese, a development department; Program Élargi de Vaccination (PEV), a government branch mainly subsidized by the

United Nations Children's Fund (UNICEF); Réseau Femmes et Développement Bandundu, a consortium of women's NGOs of Bandundu; Médecins Inspecteurs Urbaines, a group of Zairian physicians who had been involved in medical inspections; the Kikwit Catholic Diocesan Pharmaceutical Depot; and the Médecin Chef de Zone Kenge, one of the remaining health zone administrators. What is noteworthy about this group is that, although it contained remnants of government personnel, it was made up mostly of church and local civic groups with a keen desire to avert epidemics and to somehow maintain basic health services. A measure of the devotion of these groups to their cause was that all served as volunteers. Some of the agencies were affiliated with outside international institutions which gave some support. The corporate structure of the council was, however, totally decentralized, existing by the goodwill and common interests of its participants. As a set, these agencies working together were able to maintain some of the essential services that required the coordination of trained doctors and nurses, a dependable source of medicines, the support of the women, and the devotion of the churches.

In 1995 most politicians and higher-level administrators, as allies of the corrupt dictator Mobutu Sese Seko, had become enemies of the people in Zaire. In Kikwit they agitated to expel one of the ethnic groups whose members included some successful merchants with trucks. This was widely regarded as a diversionary tactic to maintain control. By mid-1997 the government of Mobutu was ousted by a rebel army that originated in the east of the country.

Although Dr. Pakisa Tshimika is not a medical anthropologist, he has led and participated in the campaign to create primary and public health structures in his region of central Africa during good times and very bad times. ∎

---

unique to their culture that are not understood by the practitioner from whom care is sought. An anthropologist who can translate clinical communications may not only help to avoid confusion and disaster, but may also contribute to the effectiveness of the treatment.

The application of anthropology in the clinic also extends to the very nature of the awareness of the cultural dimension in the sickness experience and in illness and healing. A better understanding of rites of passage in the lifecourse, and of the ritual character of sickness and healing, may offer practitioners a fuller appreciation of the cultural dimension of the experience. The most fundamental of these features is the recognition by the clinician that the transformation of signs of sickness and healing may range along the entire continuum of signs—signal, symptom, icon, index, symbol, name, and metaphor. The implications of this realization for the clinician are that he or she must recognize the reality of the whole of the person, not just the body. Even here, there must be an appreciation of the "lived body," not the body as inert organism. Then too the practitioner must realize that he or she is a "therapeutic specific," whose healing power may be substantial over and beyond the medicines which for their part also have a symbolic dimension. As clinical trials and comparative studies of placebos and nocebos, voodoo sickness and death, and healing by words, will, and prayer have shown, the power of the physician, nurse, or other healer as a "specific" is no longer medically deniable; these phenomena are scientifically confirmed processes. They may be explained by the continuity of the signs of life, or sickness and healing.

Another dimension of the presence of culture in the clinic is the importance of narrative—words, the imagined story of a life-shaping experience—both in the healing process and in the way medical knowledge is synthesized. This material was reviewed in "Narratives of Sickness and Healing" and "The 'Art of Healing' and the Construction of Clinical Reality" in Chapter 7. The ability of sufferers and healers to visualize and project alternative outcomes of a case gives them the sense of power over a situation and may spell the difference between despair and hope, which may, like a self-fulfilling prophecy, influence the outcome of the case. In like manner, narrative (i.e., story) offers a form within which to bring together many loose strands of disparate knowledge into a meaningful and unique body of learning about types of illnesses. The phrase "therapeutic emplotment" (Mattingly 1994, 1998) offers a catchy identifier for this process.

The clinician who studies anthropology may discover that "competence" is not equivalent to "care," in the words of Mary-Jo Delvecchio Good and Byron Good (see "Transmitting Medical Knowledge at Harvard Medical School" in Chapter 8). Rather, the two must of course be integrated, but that integration probably comes only from informed clinical experience and good clinical judgment. The importance of synthesizing experience with medical knowledge cannot be overemphasized. Anthropological understanding of how knowledge is embedded in signs and symbols, and iconic feelings and rhythms, may be useful in understanding the difference between effective and ineffectual therapeutic intervention.

Medical anthropologists have long tried to understand what makes for **efficacy** in clinical practice and healing. Writings on this issue have obviously sought to go beyond objective criteria of medical testing to the subjective sense of patients and sufferers that convinces them that they have not merely been treated, but feel and are convinced they are healed. The performance model of ritual signs and symbols may be helpful here to the clinician. Perhaps it is embarrassing and bordering on the unethical for the biomedical clinician to think of the clinic as a performance, in which the patient needs to be persuaded of medical efficacy. As already mentioned in Chapters 7 and 8, anthropologists' examinations of the ways clinical reality is constructed and decisions are made about treatment offer ways to examine subjective efficacy of the clinical experience. Kleinman's emphasis on the congruence of the **explanatory model** of the doctor (or nurse, healer) with that of the patient suggests one way that efficacy may be understood. Janzen's **therapy management process** and Marc Auge's **therapeutic itinerary** both emphasize the negotiated handling of the healing process for it to be regarded as effective.

The practical importance of narrative medical knowledge is evident in research on the extent to which medical doctors are able to speak with their patients about diagnoses, causes, and other issues pertaining to cure and care. A study by Wendy Levinson of clinical encounters in Colorado and Oregon suggests that those physicians who can talk easily with their patients, spend more time with them, and demonstrate compassion toward them are sued less often or not at all, even if their medical decisions formally differ little from those of their colleagues who are sued more often (1997).

Where does medical anthropology fit in this depiction of clinical judgment and medical knowledge? Those clinicians—physicians, psychiatrists, nurses—who are also anthropologists or who have become familiar with the idea of culture in shaping the clinical context and experience, will realize a greater facility in recognizing symbol, metaphor, narrative, classification of disease, labeling of signs and symptoms, and above all in recognizing that the patient's voice is important in healing. Anthropologists Noel Chrisman and Thomas Johnson, writing about "clinically applied anthropology" (1990:103–111), highlighted "ethnography" as the greatest tool that anthropology can contribute to the clinical context. This tool consists of imaginatively identifying and describing the fabric of meanings in relationships and behaviors, the hidden background of beliefs and assumptions that healer and patient, as well as family, bring to the clinical encounter.

LESSENING VIOLENCE IN SOCIETY WITHOUT MEDICALIZING IT

Violence is ever with us. As the statistical profiles of the Centers for Disease Control and the World Health Organization suggest (see Chapter 4), the category "accidents and violence" among the contagious and degenerative diseases almost hides a range of kinds of violence: work-related injuries, domestic abuse and violence, murders and injuries related to robbery and other crimes, as well as political violence of a more visible kind that results in soldiers and civilians injured and killed. When violence and its consequences take on a significant place in injury, death, and long-term social costs, then it deserves as much interest by medical anthropologists as other sources of morbidity and mortality. The question is what can medical anthropologists do about violence?

The anthropological interest in violence and its consequences has become a field of focus in anthropology in recent decades. Anthropologists have related to situations of violence in a number of ways. They have occasionally intervened directly in situations of potential violence to stop it; they may become human rights activists, mediation counselors, cultural brokers, or even part of peacekeeping teams in a region of conflict such as central Africa, the Balkans, and Haiti. Although some anthropologists may have done these things, this brief study of the application of anthropological insight in situations of violence is mainly about analyzing the setting and publicizing the context of such violence in writing. This is an area of concern for medical anthropology because violence kills people, it destroys the fabric of health, and leads to horrific outbreaks of disease.

But perhaps the most important contribution of anthropology to the study of violence has been, like so many other areas of life, to give the many kinds of violence a cultural and contextual understanding that at the same time highlights and raises to visibility the experiences of repression and terror in everyday lives of ordinary people, gives them meaning in terms of their particular social and cultural settings, and shows how people subvert, contest, and appropriate violence (Green 1998:3–7). Anthropological interpretation lifts out these very particular experiences and compares them to each other, providing in the process a universalizing language of scholarship to the study of violence. By acknowledging the experiences of ordinary people in often unjust circumstances, anthropologists can and do contribute to the rebuilding of a just world.

Work on the anthropology of violence has been done in a number of disparate quarters by numerous individuals. Longtime students of health, illness, and healing in China, Arthur and Joan Kleinman have connected the distinctive nature of depression and neurasthenia in that society to the pattern of violence during the Cultural Revolution (Kleinman and Kleinman 1991). As in many other settings, this violence was part of a long-term pattern of state-sponsored violence against its people in the name of control. More recently, Robert Desjarlais and Arthur Kleinman (1994:9–12) took a second look at the sources of violence in society and have identified many examples (e.g., civil wars in Afghanistan, Sri Lanka, Somalia, Northern Ireland, and Bosnia) where the breakdown of the state, rather than its repressive control, was the source of the violence. They suggested that the post-cold-war era may be characterized as a "New World Disorder" in which regional conflicts that blur the boundaries of nation-states will simmer on with many casualties, both physical and emotional. Some of the most interesting of the anthropological work with high levels of violence is focused on local or single national studies.

E. Valentine Daniel, an anthropologist of South Asian origin (the island republic of Sri Lanka), has tried to penetrate the origins and character of the particularly vicious civil war that has gone on there from the mid-1980s into the 1990s. In its simplest and perhaps distorting characterization, this civil war is between the Sinhalese-speaking Buddhists and the Tamil-speaking Hindus. The Tamil separatist militia, commonly known as the "Tigers," and the national, mostly Sinhalese, army, have exchanged extremely violent attacks on human targets that involve close physical assault, torture, and mutilation. The Sri Lankans do not have a monopoly on brutality in the modern world, to be sure. Nor have they always been a violent society. Indeed, until the war broke out, Sri Lankans considered themselves to be highly civilized and civil.

Daniel's writings have carried evocative titles such as "The Individual in Terror" (1994) and *Charred Lullabies* (1996), the title of an exhaustive book-length treatment of the subject. Among his many interests in these writings, several can be identified as illustrating the contribution of medical anthropology to the analysis and understanding of violence in modern societies. To begin with, Daniel sketched the broad cultural background of the conflict in Sri Lanka. He traced these societies deep into their histories, including ancient kingdoms and national lore and identity. He carefully examined several centuries of Portuguese, Dutch, and English colonialism in Sri Lanka, longer than many other regions, and the impact that colonial labor policies, migrations, educational opportunities, and differential entitlement may have had upon the island communities and the conflict between them. This careful historical background revealed an anthropological emphasis on cultural context.

Second, Daniel used case studies of events to understand the ways in which violence occurred. Based on many lengthy interviews at the sites of violence, and with the surviving victims wherever they may be, he reconstructed the particular words, symbols, and types of acts that typified the violence. In this case ethnography, he sought the close-up context in which the meaning of the violence originated for individuals. The meaning of particular acts of violence help us understand how perpetrators seek to control and destroy the victim not only through sheer physical injury, but through symbolic insult meant to remind them of the purpose of the violence. Thus, rape or mutilation in civil war violence is often more damaging emotionally to the victim than open warfare because it carries a message of terror that says: I insult your integrity as a person and a human being, and I hope you are so scared from this that you and your entire community become paralyzed with fear.

Daniel's work on the anthropology of violence is of interest for a third reason. He examined the way that the searing experience of violence leaves its mark upon the individual—both the perpetrator and the victim. Here the anthropologist borrowed some insights from psychology such as understandings about trauma, repression, and emotional effect. Because the experience of extreme physical violence is so deeply personal, it is well known that sufferers often cannot speak of their experience. But the damage and the consequences are often severe and lifelong, manifesting themselves in nightmares, symptoms of withdrawal, or physical behaviors that somatically mirror the deeply buried psychic wounds. Memory of the trauma can literally be lodged in a physical scar or an invisible psychic scar that is relived whenever an event occurs that triggers an association with the original experience. Daniel described in sympathetic detail how some of his interviewees required many hours before they could begin speaking about their traumatic experiences. Here the anthropologist becomes therapist and the process of story elicitation becomes extremely delicate. Ethnographic narrative becomes also the primary evidence of brutal abuse and of psychological trauma and trauma damage.

Daniel's writing on Sri Lanka applied the full strength of Charles Sanders Peirce's semiotics to recreate the power and nuances of the signs of cultural background leading up to violence in society, to the quality of the acts, the ways in which they remain internalized or embodied in the individuals who have suffered them, how they are remembered, and what occurs in the difficult process of healing that unfortunately comes to only a few of the victims. The full ramifications of suffering violence, and having any hope of recovering from it, recall the material presented in Chapter 6 on trauma and identity change. They are relevant here to the way that the fear and psychic scarring of violence may cause a kind of social paralysis and lead to a person's inability to continue normal life. The impact of the violence, the trauma, becomes a kind of transforming identity. The discussion on voodoo death and the nocebo and placebo effects in Chapter 7 are also relevant to the anthropology of violence. The fear induced by terror, or the threat of terror, often has as detrimental an effect on the individual's health as the curses described in voodoo death. Unless there is resolution of the conflict or other means of resolving the fear, long-term effects may be very destructive to the individual or they may lead to a search for revenge and the perpetuation of cycles of violence. The anthropological study of the culture of violence can often interpret the particular idioms of terror and their histories. Sometimes such understanding can also lead to effective resolution of the sources of violence.

Anthropological and other writing on violence can have a constructive impact on the restoration of healing if it speaks of the courageous ways that individuals refused to be intimidated by threat or act, or subtle ways that they subverted the culture of fear. Perpetrators of violence and terror depend on cowardice and secrecy, both the silence of victims and the lack of will in the international (including scholarly) community. Through their interpretation of the cultural context of violence, anthropologists can contribute significantly to "letting the world know" of the indignities of humans to each other.

The anthropology of violence has come to be very wary of exclusively medical interpretations of this area of human life, and has come to emphasize the larger moral framework of the topic. Nancy Scheper-Hughes dealt effectively with this issue in her book *Death without Weeping: The Violence of Everyday Life in Brazil* (1992), already noted several times in this book, which explores the broadest causes and consequences of violence to women and children in northeast Brazil. Based on 20 years of acquaintance with the region, she focused on particular men, women, and children by telling their stories in vivid ethnography, reinforced with quantitative data where necessary to make the analysis systematic. But she also connected these stories and statistics to the larger-scale forces of economic hardship and exploitation by the bosses of plantations and factories of northeast

Brazil. She extended and enriched her anthropological presentation with the depiction of the religious world of the people of northeast Brazil. Their frustrations and tragedies are situated within the beliefs and rituals of folk Catholicism that attends the very frequent deaths and funerals of everyday life. What makes this work compelling for our purposes is Scheper-Hughes's probing look at the way health workers and officials of the Brazilian government and industrial firms of the time explained away or even denied the levels of malnutrition by looking at the deaths of children as caused by disease. In other words, they "medicalized" this suffering, thereby giving it a superficially explained quality tending either to blame the victim or to make the problem a "chronic disease" whose "solution" is only more medical work—clinics, medicines, personnel—rather than to deal with exploitation, repression, disenfranchisement, and hopelessness. Medical anthropologists, in their approach to violence, dare not make a similar mistake and focus on the medicalized picture of trauma, for which therapy rather than the restitution of just society is the recommended solution. Thus, the substitution of a moral framework for a medical framework is essential for medical anthropology if it is to help the lot of the weak and oppressed peoples of the world.

WRITING MEDICAL ETHNOGRAPHY

Whatever else they do, anthropologists, including medical anthropologists, write. How they write has become a matter of intense interest not only within anthropology but in other disciplines such as sociology, communications, and, above all, literature. Mentioned in the opening section of Chapter 1, and in the "Medical Anthropology: A Brief History of Theory" section of Chapter 2, **ethnography** has emerged as one of the most characteristic and valuable tools of anthropology. This art was defined in the first of these settings as "close extended participation and observation . . . through which the vivid particulars of a single case study show the way to more general insight." Many other definitions of ethnography have been attempted by all kinds of authors and analysts. They tend to focus on the credibility of the writing, that is, on the way in which it seeks to convince the reader through its use of words, narrative styles, the ability to tell stories, and the author's authority within the context of the action being described (Geertz 1988).

However, lest this emphasis on writing in health, illness, and healing become too narrowly focused on anthropology, we must remember that anthropologists are not the only ones who write in medicine. It would be interesting to figure out the difference in practice and theory between the writing of medical ethnography and the writing of the medical case chart or report. There would be some close parallels in the vivid detail, the effort to cover both subjective and objective assessment of individuals, the attention to the passage of time, and perhaps the comparison of the immediate case to others. Most probably the anthropological ethnography would cast a broader net of observation and commentary than the medical case report in the search for family, societal, and historical connections to the case or event at hand. Not that medical writers would not look for case histories—genealogies, illness and disease backgrounds of family members—but the anthropologist would look for the ways in which particular words, symbols, and imagery would reflect the distinctiveness and the generality of the case, and represent social and cultural realities around the individual. The anthropologist, perhaps like a psychiatrist or psychologist, would look for contradictions in the way individuals speak and act, for inconsistencies, and for telltale suggestions that "there is more going on" than meets the eye.

Arthur Kleinman, in *Writing at the Margins* (1995:193–256), suggested that what defined and illustrated medical anthropology more than any other feature up to the year 2000 is the writing of ethnographies. Indeed, he spoke of a "new wave of ethnographies," of which he reviewed several that are representative and noteworthy of the topics and issues being addressed. It was not necessarily clear in earlier decades that medical anthropology would develop in this direction. Kleinman suggested that one of the reasons medical anthropology has developed into an ethnographical field is that the subjects considered most timely and interesting may be best studied and presented this way. One of these subjects, the culture of biomedicine, cannot really be studied through experiments and quantitative methods. But describing how medical people work, how values and perspectives infuse practice, how specific human situations like birthing, senility, menopause, and many other common life situations are lived and dealt with by medicine bring out a complex issue that can best be understood by writing about it.

This renewed emphasis on ethnography, story, and narrative has brought anthropology, including medical anthropology, into association with literature. Noteworthy monographs are recognized with prizes such as the Wellcome Medal and Award given by the Royal Anthropological Institute of Great Britain and Ireland to the monograph of the year that best reflects anthropology as applied to medical issues. The Society for Medical Anthropology, a section of the American Anthropological Association, actively rewards exemplary work through its annual awards for the best work in each of the following four categories: for the best undergraduate paper, the W. H. R. Rivers Award named after an early practitioner of medical anthropology; for the best graduate student paper, the Charles Hughes Award, named after a professor and leading figure in medical anthropology; for the best professional paper, the Steven Polgar Award, named after a founder of the discipline of medical anthropology; for large scale work representing superior research in gender and health, the Eileen Basker Memorial Prize.

CONCLUSION

This chapter has shown through five topical areas how anthropology may be used in specific applications to issues of health, illness, and healing. In the first application, anthropology's role was shown in the study of the spread of new and recurring old diseases—HIV/AIDS, tuberculosis, diabetes. Anthropologists have an increasing role to play in charting health education campaigns to combat such diseases. In the second application, the planning and creation of health care delivery, the significance of political, economic, and social dimensions were shown. Anthropological analysis of the complex ways these realms of life relate to health is useful in the grasp of past and current projects, and those that are planned in the future. Anthropology in the clinical setting, as a third application, shows to what extent the context of healing is symbolic and social. Here anthropology has much to offer as it identifies and helps shape the environment, language, aura, and signs of clinical practice. The study of violence and the analysis of social settings of violence have in recent years become a new attraction for medical anthropology. Here anthropologists have begun to apply their skills of observation and analysis to the causes of violence as well as the consequences of violence upon individuals and societies. Each of these areas touched on in this chapter—new diseases, health care delivery, the clinic, and violence—comprise an important dimension of the social fabric of health, of importance to the human community, and of interest to medical anthropologists.

All of these applications of medical anthropology, as well as others not mentioned here, have as their common methodological focus the "doing of ethnography," that is careful and detailed observation, and interpretive and analytical writing. This hallmark of anthropology has blossomed in recent years and is now recognized by clinicians, health administrators, and health researchers as well as the general public as the expertise of anthropologists. For this reason, it is fitting to close this chapter on "shaping of the fabric of health" with an enumeration of some journals that record the on-going activities of many medical anthropologists and types of practitioners. In the United States *Practicing Anthropology* and *Human Organization* are published by the Society for Applied Anthropology. The *Medical Anthropology Quarterly* is published by the Society for Medical Anthropology of the American Anthropological Association. *Medical Anthropology* is published as an independent journal. *Culture, Medicine and Psychiatry* is an independent journal edited at the Harvard University School of Social Medicine. *Social Science and Medicine* is an international journal that publishes studies and reports from medical anthropology as well as all of the social sciences applied to health issues. A growing list of newsletters, journals, and professional societies devoted to medical anthropology around the world attest to the popularity and relevance of this relatively new area of anthropology devoted to examining and ameliorating the social fabric of health.

REVIEW QUESTIONS

1. Identify the phrases or names that have been used for the practical application of anthropology in general and in the health field. Are there meaningful differences between the several terms and applications beyond their different times of origin?

2. Identify the circumstances that have led to the reemergence of an old disease. To the emergence of a "new disease." What have medical anthropologists done to study, understand, and come to terms with such new or renewed diseases?

3. What is the relationship of government to the delivery of health care services? Compare and contrast the two sketches of health care administration and reform, the first headed by a legislative body, the second in a setting of a collapsing state. Who were the decision makers and what were they trying to accomplish?

4. What does the medical anthropologist bring to clinical anthropology or clinically applied anthropology, since anthropology is not in and of itself therapeutic? Evaluate an example of anthropology in or about the clinic.

5. Based on examples in this textbook and elsewhere, discuss the dilemma anthropologists face when violence becomes medicalized—that is, explained as an illness or pathology whose solution is therapeutic.

6. Compare the medical chart taken of a patient in a hospital with a medical ethnography of the same setting. What is the difference in writing styles and in substance between the two genres of writing?

NOTES

1. This vignette was based on Christina Loehn's dissertation research (1994) conducted under the joint supervision of Professor Karl Schlesier and myself, on lengthy conversations with Loehn and Schlesier about the Cheyenne, and about this research in particular.

2. Written by Kathryn Staiano-Ross, who has worked as an anthropologist for the State of Oregon.

3. Based on a lecture (December 3, 1991) given by Congolese public health physician Dr. Pakisa Tshimika, an interview (May 15, 1995), and articles by Lawrence Altman in the *New York Times*, May 10–11, 1995, and follow-up conversation with Tshimika in October 2000.

BIBLIOGRAPHY

Abraham, John. 1994. Bias in science and medical knowledge: the Opren controversy. *Sociology* 28, no. 3 (August):717–37.

———. 1995. The production and reception of scientific papers in the academic-industrial complex: The clinical evaluation of a new medicine. *British Journal of Sociology* 46, no. 2 (June):167–91.

Achterberg, J., B. Dossey, and L. Kolkmeier. 1994. *Rituals of healing: Using imagery for health and wellness.* New York: Bantam.

Achterberg, Jeanne. 1985. *Imagery in healing: Shamanism and modern medicine.* Boston: Shambhala.

———. 1991. *Woman as healer.* Boston: Shambhala.

Ackerknecht, Erwin. 1971. *Medicine and ethnology.* Baltimore: Johns Hopkins University Press.

———. 1982. *A short history of medicine.* Baltimore: Johns Hopkins University Press.

Agarwal, Anil, and Sunita Narain. 1996. Pirates in the garden of India. *New Scientist* 152, no. 2053 (October 26):14–16.

Agich, George J., Yosaf F. Hulgus, and John Z. Sadler. 1994. On values in recent American psychiatric classification. *Journal of Medicine and Philosophy* 19, no. 3 (June):261–78.

Allen, Vernon, and Evert van den Vliert, eds. 1984. *Role transitions.* New York, Plenum.

Altman, Lawrence. 1995. 56 die in a month in Zaire outbreak of mystery disease. *New York Times,* May 10.

———. 1995. Deadly virus is identified in the outbreak in Zaire, *New York Times,* May 11.

American Journal of Psychiatry. 1994. Images in Psychiatry: Emil Kraepelin, 1856–1926. *American Journal of Psychiatry* 151, no. 3 (March):428.

American Psychiatric Association. 1952. *Diagnostic and statistical manual of mental disorders* (DSM-I). Washington, DC.

———. 1987. *Diagnostic and statistical manual of mental disorders* (DSM-IIIR). 3rd edition. Washington, DC.

Ancient healing: Unlocking the mysteries of health and healing through the ages. 1997. Lincolnwood, IL: Publications International.

Armelagos, George, T. Leatherman, M. Ryan, and L. Sibley. 1992. Biocultural synthesis in medical anthropology. *Medical Anthropology* 14:35–52.

Babineau, Timothy J., Bruce R. Bistrian, Patt Queen Samour, and Wendy Swails. 1996. A proposed revision of current ICD-9-CM malnutrition code definitions. *Journal of the American Dietetic Association* 96, no. 4 (April):370–74.

Backett, Kathryn C., and Charlie Davison. 1995. Lifecourse and lifestyle: The social and cultural location of health behaviours. *Social Science and Medicine* 40, no. 5 (March):629.

Baer, Hans A. 1982. On the political economy of health. *Medical Anthropology Newsletter* 14, no. 1:1–2, 13–17.

———. 1989. The American dominative medical system as a reflection of social relations in the larger society. *Social Science and Medicine* 23, no. 2:95–98.

Baer, Hans A., Merrill Singer, and Ida Susser. 1997. *Medical anthropology and the world system: A critical perspective.* Westport CT: Bergin & Garvey.

Balcazar, Hecter, Balen Cole, and Judith Hartner. 1992. Mexican-Americans' use of prenatal care and its relationship to maternal risk factors and pregnancy outcome. *American Journal of Preventive Medicine* 8, no. 1:1–7.

Baltes, Paul B., ed. 1978. *Life span development and behavior.* Vol. 1. New York: Academic Press.

Baltes, Paul B., and O. G. Brim, eds. 1979 and 1980. *Life span development and behavior.* Vols. 2 and 3. New York: Academic Press.

Barer, Barbara M. 1994. Men and women aging differently. Special issue: Social and cultural diversity of the Oldest-Old. *International Journal of Aging and Human Development* 38, no. 1 (January–February):29–41.

Barthes, Roland. 1967. *Système de la mode.* Paris: Editions du Seuil.

———. 1970. *Elements of Semiology.* Boston: Beacon.

———. [1972] 1985. Sémiologie et médecine. In *L'aventure sémiologique.* Paris: Editions du Seuil.

Bates, Don, ed. 1995. *Knowledge and the scholarly medical traditions.* Cambridge: Cambridge University Press.

Bayley, Carol. 1995. Our world views (may be) incommensurable: Now what? *Journal of Medicine and Philosophy* 20, no. 3 (June):271–85.

Bechot, Mauricio, and John Deely. 1995. Common sources for the semiotics of Charles Peirce and John Poinsot. *Review of Metaphysics* 48, no. 3 (March):539–67.

Becker, Ute, Ingeborg Jahn, Karl-Heinz Jockel, and Hermann Pohlabeln. 1995. Occupational life course and lung cancer risk in men: Findings from a socio-epidemiological analysis of job-changing histories in a case-control study. *Social Science and Medicine* 40, no. 7 (April):961–76.

Benoist, Jean, and Pascal Cathebras. 1993. The body: From an immateriality to another. *Social Science and Medicine* 36, no. 7 (April):857–66.

Benson, Herbert. 1975. *The relaxation response.* New York: Morrow.

———. 1979. *The mind/body effect: How behavioral medicine can show you the way to better health.* New York: Simon & Schuster.

———. 1996. *Timeless healing: The power and biology of belief.* New York: Scribner.

Bentley, Gillian R., Tony Goldbert, and Grazyna Jasienska. 1993. The fertility of agricultural and non-agricultural traditional societies. *Population Studies* 47, no. 2:269–82.

Berg, Marc, and Monica J. Casper. 1995. Constructivist perspectives on medical work: Medical practices and science and technology studies. *Science, Technology, and Human Values* 20, no. 4 (Autumn):395–408.

Berkman, Lisa F., Thomas A. Glass, A. Regula A. Herzog, Robert Kahn, and Teresa E. Seeman. 1995. Change in productive activity in late adulthood: MacArthur studies of successful aging. *Journals of Gerontology, Series B,* 50, no. 2 (March): S65–77.

Bibeau, Gilles, and Ellen Corin, eds. 1995. *Beyond textuality: Asceticism and violence in anthropological interpretation.* New York: Mouton de Gruyter.

Bird, Chloe E., and Catherine E. Ross, 1994. Sex stratification and health lifestyle: Consequences for men's and women's perceived health. *Journal of Health and Social Behavior,* 35, no. 2 (June):161–79.

Blad, John R., Dick J. Hessing, and Roel Pieterman. 1996. Practical reasons and reasonable practice: The case of euthanasia in the Netherlands. *Journal of Social Issues* 52, no. 2 (Summer):149–69.

Blakeley, Thomas, and Pamela Blakeley. 1994. Ancestors, Witchcraft, and Foregrounding the Poetic. In *Religion in Africa,* Thomas Blakeley, Walter van Beek, and Dennis Thomson, eds. Portsmouth, England: Heinemann; London: James Currey.

Boas, Franz. 1940. *Race, language and culture.* New York: Collier-MacMillan.

Bogoras, Waldemar. 1904–1909. *The Chukchee.* Part II. Leiden: E. J. Brill.

Boorse, Christopher. 1977. Health as a theoretical concept. *Philosophy of Science* 44:542–77.

Boserup, Esther. 1970. *Woman's role in economic development.* London: Allen & Unwin.

———. 1981. *Population and technological change: A study of long-term trends.* Chicago: University of Chicago Press.

Bourlag, Norman E. 1992. Lighting fires at the grassroots. *Food Technology* 46, no. 7:84–86.

Bourne, David, and Bruce Dick. 1979. Mortality in South Africa 1929–74. In *Economics of Health in South Africa.* Vol. 1. F. Wilson and G. Wescott, eds. Johannesburg: Ravan Press.

Breton, David L. 1994. Dissecting grafts: The anthropology of the medical uses of the human body. *Diogenes* 167:95–112.

Brinthaupt, Thomas M., Lorraine Bettini, Jon F. Nussbaum, and Brian Patterson. 1993. The meaning of friendship across the life-span: Two studies. *Communication Quarterly* 41, no. 2 (Spring):145–61.

Brody, Howard. 1977. *Placebos and the philosophy of medicine.* Chicago: University of Chicago Press.

Brown, Peter J., and Marcia C. Inhorn. 1990. Disease, ecology, and human behavior. In *Medical Anthropology: Contemporary Theory and Method.* Thomas M. Johnson and Carolyn E. Sargent, eds. New York: Praeger.

Buckley, Anthony. 1985. *Yoruba Medicine.* Oxford: Oxford University Press.

Burger, Bruce, S. Mark Pancer, Michael W. Pratt, Don Roth, and Silvana Santolupo. 1993. Thinking about parenting: Reasoning about developmental issues across the life span. *Developmental Psychology* 29, no. 3 (May):585–96.

Burke, Michael B. 1996. Sortal essentialism and the potentiality principle. *Review of Metaphysics* 49, no. 3:491–515.

Burns, John F. 1994. Bangladesh, still poor, cuts birth rate sharply. *New York Times,* September 13.

Byock, Ira R. 1995. The art of dying in America. *American Journal of Hospice and Palliative Care,* March–April:6–13.

Byrd, E. Keith, and P. Diane Byrd. 1993. A listing of biblical references to healing that may be useful as bibliotherapy to the empowerment of rehabilitation clients. *Journal of Rehabilitation* 59, no. 3 (July–September):46–51.

Cabanel, Guy-Pierre. 1977. *Médecine libérale ou nationalisée? Sept politiques à travers le monde.* Paris: Dunod.

Cai, Yang, and Tim Futing Liao. 1995. Socialization, life situations, and gender-role attitudes regarding the family among white American women. *Sociological Perspectives* 38, no. 2 (Summer):241–61.

Caldwell, John C. 1989a. Routes to low mortality in poor countries. In J. C. Caldwell and Gigi Santow, eds. *Selected readings in the cultural, social and behavioural determinants of health.* Canberra: Health Transition Centre, Australian National University.

———. 1989b. Mass education as a determinant of mortality decline. In J. C. Caldwell and Gigi Santow, eds. *Selected Readings in the Cultural, Social and Behavioural determinants of health.* Canberra: Health Transition Centre, Australian National University.

———. 1994. Review of, *Reaching health for all,* by Jon Rohde, Meera Chatterjee, and David Morley. *Health Transition Review* 4, no. 2:244–45.

———. 1994. The International Conference on Population and Development, Cairo: Is its plan of action important, desirable and feasible? *Health Transition Review,* 6, no. 1:71–72.

Callahan, Daniel. 1990. *What Kind of Life: The Limits of Medical Progress.* New York: Simon and Schuster.

Canguilhem, Georges. 1966. *Le normal et le pathologique.* Paris: Presses Universitaires de France.

Cannon, Walter B. 1942. "Voodoo" death. *American Anthropologist* 44, no. 2:169–81.

Capps, Lisa L. 1994. Change and continuity in the medical culture of the Hmong in Kansas City. *Medical Anthropology Quarterly* (New Series), 8(2):161–177.

Carey, John. 1994. Science-fiction medicine is fast becoming fact. *Business Week,* November 18:169.

Carroll, John T. 1995. Sickness and healing in the New Testament gospels. *Interpretation* 49, no. 2 (April):130–43.

Carstensen, Laura L., and Susan Turk-Charles. 1994. The salience of emotion across the adult life span. *Psychology and Aging* 9, no. 2 (June):259–65.

Cassel, Christine K., and Bruce C. Vladeck. 1996. ICD-9 code for palliative or terminal care. *New England Journal of Medicine* 335, no. 16 (October):1232–35.

Chang, Ming-Cheng, Ronald Freedman, and Te-Hsiung Sun. 1994. Taiwan's transition from high fertility to below-replacement levels. *Studies in Family Planning* 25 (November–December), 6, 317–32.

Chapireau, F. 1993. Méthodologie et concepts de la classification internationale des handicaps. *Neuropsychiatrie de l'Enfance* 41, no. 10:555–58.

———. 1994. La révision de la classification internationale des handicaps. *Annuaire de Médecine Psychologique.* 152, no. 10:689–92.

Chaput de Saintonge, D. M. 1994. Harnessing placebo effects in health care. Placebos in Medicine, part 2. *The Lancet* 344, no. 8928 (October 8):995–99.

Christensen, C. B. 1994. Peirce's transformation of Kant. *Review of Metaphysics* 48, no. 1 (September):91–121.

Chatters, Linda M., Jeffrey S. Levin, and Robert Joseph Taylor. 1995. Religious effects on health status and life satisfaction among black Americans. *Journals of Gerontology,* Series B, 50, no. 3 (May):S154–64.

Chew, Kenneth, S. Y. and Richard McCleary. 1994. A life course theory of suicide risk. *Suicide and Life-Threatening Behavior* 24, no. 3 (Fall):234–45.

Chrisman, Noel J., and Thomas M. Johnson. 1990. Clinically applied anthropology. In *Medical Anthropology: Contemporary Theory and Method.* Thomas M. Johnson and Carolyn F. Sargent, eds. New York: Praeger.

Chrisman, Noel J., and Thomas W. Maretzki, eds. 1982. *Clinically applied anthropology: Anthropologists in health science settings.* Boston: Kluwer.

Christian Science Monitor. 1996. The World. *Christian Science Monitor* July 23:2.

Cleland, John. 1993. Equity, security and fertility: A reaction to Thomas. *Population Studies* 47, no. 2:345–53.

Cleland, John, Chris Scott, and David Whitelegge. 1987. *World fertility survey; An assessment.* Oxford: Oxford University Press for the International Statistical Institute.

Clements, Forest. 1932. Primitive concepts of disease. *University of California Publications in American Archeology and Ethnology* 32, no. 2:185–252.

Cobb, Ann. 1977. Pluralistic legitimation of an alternative therapy system: The case of chiropractic. *Medical Anthropology* 1, no. 4:1–23.

———. 1981 Incorporation and change: The case of the midwife in the United States. *Medical Anthropology* 5, no. 1:73–88.

College of General Practitioners and Research. 1963. A classification of disease. *Journal of College of General Practitioners and Research Newsletter.* (London):204–16.

Collins, James, and David K. Shay. 1994. Prevalence of low birth weight among Hispanic infants with United States born and foreign-born mothers: The effect of urban poverty. *American Journal of Epidemiology* 139, no. 2:184–92.

Contact. 1993. Participatory evaluation [of health]. *Contact,* Special issue, 132 (August).

———. 1994. Population. *Contact,* Special issue, 135 (February).

Cordell, D. D., and V. Piche, eds. 1987. *African population and capitalism: Historical perspectives.* Boulder, CO: Westview.

Cordell, Dennis D., Joel W. Gregory, and Victor Piche. 1992. The demographic reproduction of health and disease: Colonial Central African Republic and contemporary Burkina Faso. In *The social basis of health and healing in Africa.* Steven Feierman and John M. Janzen, eds. Berkeley: University of California Press.

Corin, Ellen. 1989. Vers une réouverture sémiotique et culturelle du diagnostic psychiatrique: La santé mentale comme observable réseau. *Colloque INSERM.* P. Beuf, coordinator and ed. Vol. 192:455–70.

———. 1990. Facts and meaning in psychiatry: An anthropological approach to the schizophrenic world. *Culture, Medicine, and Psychiatry.* 14, no. 2. 153–188.

Correa, Hector, and Mohamed Ali El Torky. 1982. *The biological and social determinants of the demographic transition.* Washington, DC: University Press of America.

Cox, Donna M., and Marcia G. Ory. 1994. Forging ahead: Linking health and behavior to improve quality of life in older people. *Social Indicators Research* 33, nos. 1–3 (August):89–121.

Crandon-Malamud, Libbet. 1991. *From the fat of our souls: Social change, political process, and medical pluralism in Bolivia.* Berkeley: University of California Press.

Csordas, Thomas. 1990. Embodiment as a Paradigm for Anthropology. *Ethos* 18, no. 1:5–47.

———. 1994. *Embodiment and experience: The existential ground of culture and self.* Cambridge: Cambridge University Press.

Currer, Caroline, and Meg Stacey, eds. 1986. *Concepts of health, illness and disease: A comparative perspective.* New York: Berg.

Curtin, Philip D. 1992. Medical knowledge and urban planning in colonial tropical Africa. In *The social basis of health and healing in Africa.* Steven Feierman and John M. Janzen, eds. Berkeley: University of California Press.

Daniel, E. Valentine. 1984. *Fluid signs: Being a person the Tamil way.* Berkeley: University of California Press.

———. 1994. The individual in terror. In *Embodiment and experience. The existential ground of culture and self.* Thomas Csordas, ed. Cambridge: Cambridge University Press.

———. 1996. *Charred lullabies: Chapters in an anthropography of violence.* Princeton: Princeton University Press.

Das Gupta, Monica. 1995. Life course perspectives on women's autonomy and health outcomes. *American Anthropologist* 97, no. 3:481–92.

Dausset, Jean. 1994. Scientific knowledge and human dignity. *UNESCO Courier,* September:8–12.

Davis-Floyd, Robbie. 1992. *Birth as an American rite of passage.* Berkeley: University of California Press.

Dawson, Susan, Joachim Gunsalam, Neelam Khan, Lenore Manderson, Andres McNee, Ian Riley, and Veronica L. Tallo. 1995. Responding to cough: Boholano illness classification and resort to care in response to childhood ARI [acute respiratory infections]. *Social Science and Medicine* 40, no. 9 (May):1279–90.

De Medeiros, Narcisse. 1994. Culture sanitaire et décodage de messages télévisés de santé chez les Fon du Sud-Bénin. PhD dissertation. University of Montreal.

Desjarlais, Robert, and Arthur Kleinman. 1994. Violence and demoralization in the new world disorder. *Anthropology Today,* October:9–12.

Desowitz, Robert. 1997. *Tropical diseases: From 50,000 B.C. to A.D. 2500.* HarperCollins.

Dewhurst, Kenneth. 1966. *Dr. Thomas Sydenham (1624–1689): His life and original writings.* Berkeley: University of California Press.

Dodoo, F. Nii-Amoo. 1993. Education and changing reproductive behavior in Ghana. *Sociological Perspectives* 36, no. 3 (Fall):241–57.

Douglas, Mary. 1966. *Purity and danger.* New York: Praeger.

Douglas, Robert M., Gavin Jones, and Rennie M. D'Souza. 1996. The shaping of fertility and mortality declines: The contemporary demographic transition. *Health Transition Review,* vol. 6 supplement.

Dreyfus, Hubert L., and Paul Rabinow. 1983. *Michel Foucault, beyond structuralism and hermeneutics.* Chicago: University of Chicago Press.

Dubos, René. 1965. *Man adapting.* New Haven: Yale University Press.

———. 1968. *Man, medicine, and environment.* New York: Mentor Books.

Duis, Henk Jan Ten, Johannes Kingma, Henk J. Klasen, Elisabeth TenVergert, and Hinke Anja Werkman. 1994. A Turbo Pascal program to convert ICD-9CM coded injury diagnoses into injury severity scores: ICDTOAIS. *Perceptual and Motor Skills* 78, no. 3(June):915–37.

Dummond, Don E. 1975. The limitation of human population. *Science* 187.

Eberstadt, Nicholas. 1994a. Demographic shocks after communism: Eastern Germany 1989–1993. *Population and Development Review* 20, no. 1 (March):137–53.

———. 1994b. Marx and mortality: A mystery. *New York Times,* April 6. Nicholas Eberstadt, ed. 1981. *Fertility decline in the less developed countries.* New York: Praeger.

———. 1994c. Demographic shocks in Eastern Germany, 1989–1993. *Europe-Asia Studies* 46, no. 3 (May):519–34.

Ecob, Russell, Graeme Ford, Kate Hunt, Sally Macintyre, and Patrick West. 1994. Patterns of class inequality in health through the lifespan: Class gradients at 15, 35 and 55 years in the west of Scotland. *Social Science and Medicine* 39, no. 8 (October 15): 1037–51.

Edwards, Michelle. 1997. Personal communications.

Ehrlich, Paul, and Anne Ehrlich. 1971. *The population explosion.* New York: Simon & Schuster.

Elder, Glen H., Jr. 1994. Time, human agency, and social change: Perspectives on the life course. *Social Psychology Quarterly* 57, no. 1 (March):4–16.

Eliade, Miercea. 1964. *Shamanism: Archaic techniques of ecstasy.* Princeton: Princeton University Press.

Eliot, T. S. 1932. *Sweeney agonistes.* London: Faber and Faber.

Elling, Ray. 1986. *The struggle for workers' health: A study of six industrialized countries.* Farmingdale, NY: Baywood.

Epstein, Randi Hutter. 1996. The coming plague. *Geographical Magazine* 68, no. 1:24–7.

Erikson, Erik. 1963. *Childhood and society.* New York: W. W. Norton.

Estroff, Sue. 1993. Identity, disability, and schizophrenia: The problem of chronicity. In *Knowledge, Power, and Practice.* Shirley Lindenbaum and Margaret Lock, eds. Berkeley: University of California Press.

Fabrega, Horatio. 1973. *Illness and shamanistic curing in Zinacantan: An ethnomedical analysis.* Stanford, CA: Stanford University Press.

———. 1974. *Disease and social behavior: An interdisciplinary perspective.* Cambridge: MIT Press.

———. 1997. *Evolution of sickness and healing.* Berkeley: University of California Press.

Fadiman, Anne. 1997. *The spirit catches you and you fall down: A Hmong child, her American doctors, and the collision of two cultures.* New York: Noonday Press.

Farmer, Paul. 1992. *AIDS and accusation: Haiti and the geography of blame.* Berkeley: University of California Press.

———. 1994. AIDS-talk and the constitution of cultural models. *Social Science and Medicine* 38, no. 6 (March 15):801–10.

———. 1999 *Infections and inequalities: The modern plagues.* Berkeley: University of California Press.

Feeney, Griffith. 1994. Fertility decline in East Asia. *Science,* December 2:1518–24.

Feeney, Griffith, and Jianhua Yuan. 1994. Below replacement fertility in China? A close look at recent evidence. *Population Studies,* 48 November 3:381–95.

Feierman, Steven. 1985. Struggles for control: The social roots of health and healing in modern Africa. *African Studies Review* 28, nos. 2–3 (June–September):73–147.

Feierman, Steven, and John M. Janzen. 1992. The decline and rise of African population: The social context of health and disease. In *The social basis of health and healing in Africa.* Steven Feierman and John M. Janzen, eds. Berkeley: University of California Press.

Feierman, Steven, and John M. Janzen, eds. 1992. *The social basis of health and healing in Africa.* Berkeley: University of California Press.

Feldmann, Carole, and Dov Friedlander. 1993. The modern shift to below-replacement fertility: Has Israel's population joined the process? *Population Studies* 47, no. 2 (July):295–307.

Feuerstein, Marie-Louise. 1987 *Partners in evaluation: Evaluating development and community programmes with participants.* London: Macmillan.

———. 1993. Participatory evaluation: The Patna [India] Experience. *Contact,* no. 132 (August):1–15.

Figura, Starr. 1999. Diego Rivera's *The Communicating Vessels.* In *Mexican prints: From the collection of Reba and Dave Williams.* Edward J. Sullivan, ed.

Fortes, Meyer. 1984. Age, generation, and social structure. In *Age and Anthropological Theory.* David I. Kertzer and Jennie Keith, eds. Ithaca, NY: Cornell University Press.

Foster, George M., and Barbara Gallatin Anderson. 1978. *Medical Anthropology.* New York: John Wiley.

Foucault, Michael. 1972. *The archeology of knowledge.* New York: Pantheon Books. [1965] Translated by A. M. Sheridan Smith.

———. 1973. *Madness and civilization.* New York: Vintage/Random House. Translated by Richard Howard.

———. 1975. *The birth of the clinic: An archeology of medical perception.* New York: Vintage/Random House. Translated by A. M. Sheridan Smith.

————. 1979. *Discipline and punish: The birth of the prison.* New York: Vintage/Random House. Translated by Alan Sheridan.

————. 1980a. *Power/Knowledge.* New York: Pantheon. Translated by Colin Gordon.

————. 1980b. *The history of sexuality.* New York: Vintage/Random House. Translated by Robert Hurley

Frake, Charles. 1961. The diagnosis of disease among the Subanun of Mindanao. *American Anthropologist* 63, no. 1:113–32.

————. 1962. The ethnographic study of cognitive systems. In *Anthropology and human behavior.* T. Gladwin and W.C. Sturtevant, eds. Washington: Anthropological Society of Washington.

Frankel, Stephen. 1986. *The Huli response to illness.* Cambridge: Cambridge University Press.

Frankenburg, Ronald, ed. 1992. *Time, health, and medicine.* Newbury Park, CA: Sage Publications.

Frayer, David. 1989. Oral pathologies in the European Upper Paleolithic and Mesolithic. In *People and Culture in Change.* Israel Herskovits, ed. Oxford: BAR International Series no. 58.

Frazer, James G. 1911–15. *The golden bough,* London: MacMillan & Co. 12 vols. 3rd ed.

Freidson, Eliot. 1971. *Profession of medicine.* New York: Dodd, Mead.

Freudenheim, Milt. 1997. Dragging out HMO payments. *New York Times* April 17: C1–C2

Fried, Martha Nemes, and Morton H. Fried. 1980. *Transitions: Four rituals in eight cultures.* New York: W.W. Norton.

Fry, Christine L. 1984. *Dimensions: Aging, culture and health.* South Hadley, MA: Bergin & Garvey.

Fry, Janet. 1979. Native American cultural response to depopulation caused by epidemic disease. MA thesis, University of Kansas.

Furst, Peter. 1997a. American shamanism. In *Ancient healing.* Lincolnwood, IL: Publications International.

————. 1997b. Aztec, Maya and Inca healing. *Ancient healing.* Lincolnwood, IL: Publications International.

————. 1997c. Native American healing. *Ancient healing.* Lincolnwood, IL: Publications International.

————. 1997d. Asian shamanism. *Ancient Healing.* Lincolnwood, IL: Publications International.

Gajdusek, D. C. 1985. Hypothesis: Interference with axonal transport of neurofilament as a common pathogenetic mechanism in certain diseases of the central nervous system. *New England Journal of Medicine* 14, no. 312 (11):714–9.

Garcia-Moreno, Claudia, and Tomris Turmen. 1995. International perspectives on women's reproductive health. *Science* August 11:790–3.

Garrett, Laurie. 1994. *The coming plague: Newly emerging diseases in a world out of balance.* New York: Farrar, Straus and Giroux.

Garro, Linda C. 1994. Narrative representations of chronic illness experience: Cultural models of illness, mind, and body in stories concerning the temporomandibular joint. *Social Science and Medicine* 38, no. 6 (March 15):775–89.

Geertz, Clifford. 1973. *The interpretation of cultures.* New York: Basic Books.

————. 1988. *Works and lives: The anthropologist as author.* Stanford, CA: Stanford University Press.

Gelisen, Ilker, Byron J. Good, Mary-Jo Delvecchio Good, A. Guvener, Zafer Ilbars, and Isenbike Togan. 1994. In the subjunctive mode: Epilepsy narratives in Turkey. *Social Science and Medicine* 38, no. 6 (March 15):835–43.

Gibbs, Clarence J., and D. Carleton Gajdusek. 1978. Virus-induced subacute slow infections of the brain associated with a cerebellar-type ataxia. *Advances in Neurology* 21:359–72.

Gibbs, Clarence J., D. Carleton Gajdusek, and R. Latarject. 1978. Unusual resistance to ionizing radiation of the viruses of kuru, Creutzfeldt-Jakob disease, and scrapie. *Proceedings of the National Academy of Science* 75:6268–70.

Gillett, Grant. 1995. Virtue and truth in clinical science. *Journal of Medicine and Philosophy* 20, no. 3 (June):285–97.

Goldman, Abe. 1993. Agricultural innovation in three areas of Kenya: Neo-Boserupian theories and regional characterization. *Economic Geography* 69, no. 1:44–72.

Goleman, Daniel. 1993. Stress and isolation tied to a reduced life span. *New York Times,* December 7.

———. 1995. Making room on the couch for culture. *New York Times,* December 5.

Good, Byron J. 1977. The heart of what's the matter. *Culture, Medicine and Psychiatry* 1:25–58.

———. 1994. *Medicine, rationality, and experience: An anthropological perspective.* Cambridge: Cambridge University Press.

———. 1996. Culture and DSM-IV: Diagnosis, knowledge and power. *Culture, Medicine and Psychiatry* 20, no. 2: 127–32.

Good, Byron, and Mary-Jo Delvecchio Good. 1992. The comparative study of Greco-Islamic medicine: The integration of medical knowledge into local symbolic contexts. In *Paths to Asian medical knowledge.* Charles Leslie and Allan Young, eds. Berkeley: University of California Press.

———. 1993. Learning medicine: The constructing of medical knowledge at Harvard Medical School. In *Knowledge, Power and Practice.* Shirley Lindenbaum and Margaret Lock, eds. Berkeley: University of California Press.

Good, Byron J., Mary-Jo Delvecchio Good, Yasuki Kobayashi, Cheryl Mattingly, and Tseunetsugu Munakata. 1994. Oncology and narrative time. *Social Science and Medicine* 38, no. 6 (March 15):855–93.

Gore, Albert. 1992. *Earth in the balance: Ecology and the human spirit.* Boston: Houghton Mifflin.

Gowans, Christopher W. 1996. Intimacy, freedom, and unique value: A "Kantian" account of the irreplaceable and incomparable value of persons. *American Philosophical Quarterly* 33, no. 1:75–90.

Graham, Elaine L. 1995. Gender, personhood and theology. *Scottish Journal of Theology* 48, no. 3:341–59.

Green, Edward. 1994. *AIDS and STDs in Africa: Bridging the gap between traditional healing and modern medicine.* Boulder: Westview Press.

———. 1996. Purity, pollution and the invisible snake in southern Africa. *Medical Anthropology* 16:1–18.

———. 1999. *Indigenous theories of contagious disease.* Walnut Creek, CA: AltaMira.

Green, Linda. 1998. Lived lives and social suffering: Problems and concerns in medical anthropology. *Medical Anthropology Quarterly* 12, no. 1:3–7.

Greenbaum, Ellen. 1998. Resistance and embrace: Sudanese rural women and systems of power. In *Pragmatic women and body politics.* Margaret Lock and Patricia Kaufert, eds. Cambridge: Cambridge University Press.

Groen, Guy, J., and Vimla L. Patel. 1993. Comparing apples and oranges: Some dangers in confusing frameworks with theories. *Cognitive Science* 17, no. 1 (January–March):135–42.

Groves, David L., and Robin J. Wynne. 1995. Life span approach to understanding coping styles of the elderly. *Education* 115, no. 3 (Spring):448–57.

Guacci-Franco, Nathalie, Jerome L. Levitt, and Mary J. Levitt. 1993. Convoys of social support in childhood and early adolescence: Structure and function. *Developmental Psychology* 29, no. 5 (September):811–19.

Guillemard, Anne-Marie, and Martin Rein. 1993. Comparative patterns of retirement: Recent trends in developed societies. *Annual Review of Sociology* 19:469–504.

Gutfeld, Greg, and Marty Munson. 1993. Healing strokes: Friendship speeds recovery from brain attack. *Prevention* 45, no. 11 (November):10–12.

Haghighat, Rahman. 1994. Cultural sensitivity: ICD-10 versus DSM-III-R. *International Journal of Social Psychiatry* 40, no. 3 (Autumn):189–95.

Hahn, Robert. 1995. *Sickness and healing: An anthropological perspective.* New Haven: Yale University Press.

Hahn, Robert, and Arthur Kleinman. 1983. Belief as pathogen, belief as medicine: "Voodoo death" and the "placebo phenomenon" in anthropological perspective. *Medical Anthropological Quarterly* 14, no. 4:3, 16–20.

Hahn, Robert A., and Atwood D. Gaines, eds. 1985. *Physicians of Western medicine: Anthropological approaches to theory and practice.* Boston: D. Reidel.

Hammel, Eugene. 1984. Age in the Fortesian coordinates. In *Age and Anthropological Theory.* David I. Kertzer and Jennie Kieth, eds. Ithaca, NY: Cornell University Press.

Hamonet, Claude. 1985. *Handicap, le côté positif.* Colloquium on the handicapped and the law. Créteil, France: CTNRHI; Paris: Presses Universitaires de France.

———. 1990. *Les personnes handicapées.* Paris: Presses Universitaires de France.

———. 1992. Handicapologie et anthropologie. Doctoral thesis in social anthropology. University of Paris-5, Rene Descartes.

———. [1995] n.d. The normal and the pathological: A new approach based on the notion of "handicap." Unpublished manuscript.

Hamonet, Claude, A. M. Bégue-Simon, M. P. Brachet, and J. P. Thervet. 1985. Evaluer le dommage corporel: Nouvelles conceptions, nouveaux outils. *Revue française du Dommage corporel* 11:7–13.

Hansluwka, H. 1985. Measuring the health of populations, indicators and interpretations. *Social Science and Medicine* 20, no. 12:1207–24.

Hanson, F. Allan. 1970. The Rapan theory of conception. *American Anthropologist* 72:1444–47.

Haraway, Donna. 1993. The biopolitics of postmodern bodies: Determinations of self in immune system discourse. In *Knowledge, Power and Practice.* Shirley Lindenbaum and Margaret Lock, eds. Berkeley: University of California Press.

Harrison, Elizabeth G. 1995. Women's responses to child loss in Japan: The case of Mizuko Kuyo. *Journal of Feminist Studies in Religion* 11, no. 2 (Fall):67–93.

Hartmann, Betsy. 1987. *Reproductive rights and wrongs.* New York: Harper and Row.

Hartt, Frederick. 1969. *History of Italian renaissance art.* Englewood Cliffs, NJ: Prentice Hall.

Heckhausen, Jutta, and Joachim Krueger. 1993. Personality development across the adult life span: Subjective conceptions vs. cross-sectional contrasts. *Journal of Gerontology* 48, no. 3 (May):100–101.

Hedges, Chris. 1994. Key panel at Cairo talks agrees on population plan. *New York Times,* September 13: A4.

Helman, Cecil G. 1984. *Culture, health and illness: An introduction for health professionals.* London: John Wright.

———. 1985. Disease and pseudo-disease: A case history of pseudo-angina. In *Physicians of western medicine.* Robert A. Hahn and Atwood D. Gaines, eds. Boston: D. Reidel.

Helterline, Marilyn, and Marilyn Nouri. 1994. Aging and gender: Values and continuity. *Journal of Women and Aging* 6, no. 3 (Summer):19–38.

Hempel, Margaret. 1996. Reproductive health and rights: Origins of and challenges to the ICPD agenda. *Health Transition Review* 6, no. 1 (April):73–84.

Heppner, P. P. 1995. On gender role conflict in men—future directions and implications for counseling: Comment on Good et al. and Cournoyer and Mahalik. *Journal of Counseling Psychology* 42, no. 1 (January):20–24.

Herdt, Gilbert, and Shirley Lindenbaum, eds. 1992. *The time of AIDS: Social analysis, theory, and method.* Newbury Park, CA: Sage Publications.

Herskovits, Israel, ed. 1989. *People and culture in change.* Oxford: Broadcast Advertisers Reports International Series no. 58.

Hirsch, Barton J., and E. Ann Jolly. 1984. Role transitions and social networks: Social support for multiple roles. *Role transitions.* Vernon Allen and Evert van den Vliert, eds. New York: Plenum.

Horsfall, David. 1992. David Horsfall looks at the contrasting views of two population theorists: Thomas Malthus and Ester Boserup. *Geographical Magazine* 64, no. 12 (December): 45.

Huard, Pierre, Jean Bossy, and Guy Mazars. 1978. *Les medecines de l'Asie.* Paris: Editions du Seuil.

Hultkrantz, Åke. 1989. Health, religion and medicine in native North American Traditions. In *Healing and Restoring: Health and medicine in the world's religious traditions.* Lawrence E. Sullivan, ed. New York: Macmillan.

Hummer, Robert A., Isaac W. Eberstein, and Charles B. Nam. 1992. Infant mortality differentials among Hispanic Groups in Florida. *Social Forces* 70, no. 4:1055–75.

Hunt, Linda M. 1994. Practicing oncology in provincial Mexico: A narrative analysis. *Social Science and Medicine* 38, no. 6 (March 15):843–54.

Hunter, Jennifer. 1997. Personal communications.

Hunter, Kathryn Montgomery. 1996. Narrative, literature, and the clinical exercise of practical reason. *Journal of Medicine and Philosophy* 21, no. 3 (June):303–21.

Jackson, Jean E. 1994. The Rashomon approach to dealing with chronic pain. *Social Science and Medicine* 38, no. 6 (March 15):823–34.

Jackson, Michael, ed. 1996. *Things as they are: New directions in phenomenological anthropology.* Bloomington: Indiana University Press.

Jamieson, Anne. 1994. Aging, independence and the life course. *Journal of Social Policy* 23, no. 2 (April):282–85.

Janzen, John M. 1978a. "The comparative study of medical systems as changing social systems. *Social Science and Medicine* 12, no. 2B:121–30.

———. 1978b. *The quest for therapy in Lower Zaire.* Berkeley: University of California Press.

———. 1981. The need for a taxonomy of health in the study of African therapeutics. *Social Science and Medicine* 15B, no. 3 (July):185–94.

———. 1982a. *Lemba 1650–1930: A drum of affliction in Africa and the New World.* New York: Garland.

———. 1982b. Lubanzi: The history of a Kongo disease. In *African health and healing systems.* P. Stanley Yoder, ed. Los Angeles: Crossroads Press.

———. 1987. Therapy management: Concept, reality, process. *Medical Anthropology Quarterly* 1:1, 68–84.

———. 1992. *Ngoma: Discourses of healing in central and southern Africa.* Berkeley: University of California Press.

———. 1996–99. Vengeance, justice, forgiveness, and healing in the emotional-moral chess game of Rwandan and Burundian conflict. Unpublished manuscript.

———. 1999. Text and context in the anthropology of war trauma: The African Great Lakes region, 1993–4. *Journal of the Finnish Anthropological Society* 3, 37–57.

———. 2000. *Do I still have a life? Voices in the aftermath of war in Rwanda and Burundi.* Lawrence: University of Kansas, Department of Anthropology Monograph Series no. 20.

Janzen, John M., and Steven Feierman, eds. 1979. The social history of disease and medicine in Africa. *Social Science and Medicine* Special issue, 13B, 4.

Janzen, John M., and Gwyn Prins, eds. 1981. Causality and Classification in African Medicine and Health. *Social Science and Medicine* 15B, 3, July.

Janzen, Marike. 1996. Personal communication. Kuehlungsborn, Germany.

Jerrome, Dorothy. 1994. Friendship matters: Communication, dialectics and the life course. *Ageing and Society* 14, no. 1 (March):133.

Johansen, I. Elisabeth. 1996. Intron insertion facilitates amplification of cloned virus cDNA in Escherichia coli while biological activity is reestablished after transcription in vivo. *Proceedings of the National Academy of Sciences of the United States* 93, no. 22 (October 29):1246.

John Michael Kohler Arts Center. 1986. *Hmong art: Tradition and change.* Sheboygan WI: John Michael Kohler Arts Center of the Sheboygan Arts Foundation.

Johnson, Thomas M. 1994. Presidential message: On paradigm shifts in medical anthropology. *Medical Anthropology Quarterly* 35, no. 5:31–2.

Johnson, Thomas M., and Carolyn F. Sargent, eds. 1990. *Medical anthropology: Contemporary theory and method.* Westport, CT: Praeger.

Jones, Linda Corson, and Margarete Sandelowski. 1996. "Healing fictions": Stories of choosing in the aftermath of the detection of fetal anomalies. *Social Science and Medicine* 42, no. 3 (February):353–62.

Jordan, Birgette. 1983. *Birth in four cultures: A cross-cultural investigation of childbirth in Yucatan, Holland, Sweden and the United States.* Montreal: Eden Press.

Kahn, R., and T. Antonnucci. 1980. Convoys over the life course: Attachment, roles and social support. In *Life span development and behavior.* Vol. 3. Paul B. Baltes and O. G. Brim, eds. New York: Academic Press.

Katz, Phyllis A. and Keith R. Ksansnak. 1994. Developmental aspects of gender role flexibility and traditionality in middle childhood and adolescence. *Developmental Psychology* 30, no. 2 (March):272–83.

Katz, Richard. 1982. *Boiling energy: Community healing among the Kalahari !Kung.* Cambridge: Harvard University Press.

Katz, Richard, Megan Biesele, and Verna St. Denis. 1999. *Healing makes our hearts happy: Spirituality and cultural transformation among the Kalahari Ju/'hoansi.* Rochester, VT: Inner Traditions.

Kaufert, Patricia A. 1998. Women, resistance, and the breast cancer movement. In *Pragmatic women and body politics.* Margaret Lock and Patricia Kaufert, eds. Cambridge: Cambridge University Press.

Kaufman, Sharon. 2000. In the shadow of "Death with Dignity": Medical and cultural quandries of the vegetative state. *American Anthropologist* 102, no. 1:69–83.

Kazanis, Barbara W., and Ellen B. Kimmel. 1995. Explorations of the unrecognized spirituality of women's communion. *Women and Therapy* 16, nos. 2–3:215–28.

Keith, Jennie. 1980. The best is yet to be born: Toward an anthropology of age. *Annual Review of Anthropology* 9:339–64.

Kertzer, David I., and Jennie Keith, eds. 1984. *Age and anthropological theory.* Ithaca, NY: Cornell University Press.

Khan, H. T. Abdullah, and Robert Raeside. 1994. Urban and rural fertility in Bangladesh: A causal approach. *Social Biology* 41, nos. 3–4 (Fall–Winter):240–54.

King, C.D. 1945. The Meaning of Normal. *Yale Journal of Biology and Medicine.* 17:443–501.

Kleinman, Arthur. 1978. Concepts and a model for the comparison of medical systems as cultural systems. *Social Science and Medicine* 12, 2B:85–94.

———. 1980. *Patients and healers in the context of culture.* Berkeley: University of California Press.

———. 1988. *The illness narratives: Suffering, healing and the human condition.* New York: Basic Books.

———. 1995. *Writing at the margin: Discourse between anthropology and medicine.* Berkeley: University of California Press.

———. 1997. From one human nature to many human conditions: An anthropological inquiry into suffering as moral experience in a disordering age. *In Developing anthropological ideas: The Edward Westermarck Memorial lectures 1983–1997.* Jukka Siikala, Ulla Vuorela, and Tapio Nisula, eds. Helsinki: Transactions of the Finnish Anthropological Society, no. 41.

Kleinman, Arthur, Vena Das, and Margaret Lock. 1996. Introduction, Social Suffering. *Daedalus,* Winter: xi–xx.

Kleinman, Arthur, Leon Eisenberg, and Byron Good. 1978. Culture, illness, and care: Clinical lessons from anthropological and cross-cultural research. *Annals of Internal Medicine* 88:255–58.

Kleinman, Arthur, and Byron Good. 1985. *Culture and depression: Studies in the anthropology and cross-cultural psychiatry of affect and disorder.* Berkeley: University of California Press.

Kleinman, Arthur, and Joan Kleinman. 1991. Suffering and its professional transformation: Toward an ethnography of interpersonal experience. *Culture, Medicine and Psychiatry* 15, no. 3:275–301.

Koch, Henri. 1968. *Magie et chasse dans la fôret Camerounaise.* Paris: Editions Berger-Levrault.

Kozak, David. 1994. Reifying the body through the medicalization of violent death. *Human Organization* 53, no. 1 (spring):48–55.

Kuhn, Thomas. 1972. *The structure of scientific revolutions.* 2nd edition. Chicago: University of Chicago Press.

Kusikila kwa Kilombo. 1974. Kimongi, or a blighted society. In *An Anthology of Kongo Religion.* John M. Janzen and Wyatt MacGaffey, eds. Lawrence: University of Kansas Publication in Anthropology no. 5.

Lachenmann, Gudrun. 1982. *Primary health care and basic-needs orientation in developing countries.* Berlin: German Development Institute.

Laderman, Carol. 1983. *Wives and midwives: Childbirth and nutrition in rural Malaysia.* Berkeley: University of California Press.

———. 1991. *Taming the wind of desire: Psychology, medicine, and aesthetics in Malay shamanistic performance.* Berkeley: University of California Press.

———. 1992. A welcoming soil: Islamic humoralism on the Malay Peninsula. In *Paths to Asian medical knowledge.* Charles Leslie and Allan Young, eds. Berkeley: University of California Press.

———. 1996. The embodiment of symbols and the acculturation of the anthropologist. In *Embodiment and experience: The existential ground of culture and self.* Thomas Csordas, ed. Cambridge: Cambridge University Press.

LaFleur, William R. 1992. *Liquid life: Abortion and Buddhism in Japan.* Princeton, NJ: Princeton University Press.

Laman, Karl. 1962. *The Kongo III.* Stockholm: Studia Ethnographica Upsaliensia XII.

The Lancet. 1995. Leap of faith over the data tap. *The Lancet* 345, no. 8963 (June 10):1449–52.

Landy, David, ed. 1977. *Culture, disease and healing: Studies in medical anthropology.* New York: Macmillan.

Lane, Sandra D. 1994. From population control to reproductive health: An emerging policy agenda. *Social Science and Medicine* 39, no. 9 (November):1303–15.

Lannin, Donald R., Holly F. Mathews, and James P. Mitchell. 1994. Coming to terms with advanced breast cancer: Black women's narratives from eastern North Carolina. *Social Science and Medicine* 38, no. 6 (March 15): 789–801.

Larsen, Clark S., and David H. Thomas. 1982. The anthropology of St. Catherine's Islands. *American Museum of Natural History Anthropology Papers* 67.

Lassen, Henning. 1996. Personal communications. Kuehlungsborn, Germany.

Last, Murray. 1986. Introduction, the professionalisation of African medicine: Ambiguities and definitions. In *The Professionalisation of African Medicine.* Murray Last and Gordon Chavunduka, eds. Manchester, England: Manchester University Press.

———. 1990. Professionalization of indigenous healers. In *Medical anthropology: Contemporary theory and method.* Thomas M. Johnson and Carolyn F. Sargent, eds. Westport, CT: Praeger.

———. 1992. The importance of knowing about not knowing: Observations from Hausaland. In *The Social Basis of Health and Healing in Africa.* Steven Feierman and John Janzen, eds. Berkeley: Univeristy of California Press.

Laub, John H., and Robert J. Sampson. 1993. Turning points in the life course: Why change matters to the study of crime. *Criminology* 31, no. 3 (August):301–25.

Leavitt, Judith. 1986. *Brought to bed: Childbearing in America, 1750–1950.* New York: Oxford University Press.

Lee, Eunja, Igeta Midori, and Massato Osaka. 1995. A response [to Rhetorics, rituals and conflicts over women's reproductive power by Elizabeth G. Harrison]. *Journal of Feminist Studies in Religion* 11, no. 2 (Fall):95–101.

Legge, David. 1995. Research to support partnerships for public health. *Health Transition Review* 5, no. 2 (October):258–227.

L'Engle, Madeleine. 1974. *The summer of the great grandmother.* New York: Farrar, Strauss and Giroux.

Lessa, William A., and Evon Z. Vogt. 1979. *Reader in comparative religion.* New York: Harper & Row.

Leslie, Charles, ed. 1976a *Asian Medical Systems.* Berkeley: University of California Press.

———. 1976b The ambiguities of medical revivalism in modern India. In *Asian Medical Systems.* Charles Leslie, ed. Berkeley: University of California Press.

———. 1978. Theoretical foundations for the comparative study of medical systems. *Social Science and Medicine,* Special issue, 65–138.

———. 1992. Interpretation of illness: Syncretism in modern Ayurveda. In *Paths to Asian medical knowledge.* Charles Leslie and Allan Young, eds. Berkeley: University of California Press.

Leslie Charles, and Allan Young, eds. 1992. *Paths to Asian Medical Knowledge.* Berkeley: University of California Press.

Levine, Robert A. 1978. Adulthood and aging in cross-cultural perspective. *Items (SSRC)* 31–32, no. 1 (March):1–5.

Levinson, Wendy. 1994. Physician-patient communication: A key to malpractice prevention. *JAMA: Journal of the American Medical Association* 272, no. 20 (November 23): 1619–21.

Lévi-Strauss, Claude. 1963. The effectiveness of symbols. In *Structural Anthropology.* New York: Basic Books.

Lewin, Ellen. 1998. Wives, mothers, and lesbians: Rethinking resistance in the U.S. In *Pragmatic women and body politics.* Margaret Lock and Patricia Kaufert, eds. Cambridge: Cambridge University Press.

Lewis, Gilbert. 1975. *Knowledge of illness in a Sepik society.* London: Athlone Press.

Lex, Barbara. 1974. Voodoo death: New thoughts on an old explanation. *American Anthropologist* 76:818–23.

Liddell, Henry George, and Robert Scott. 1968. *A Greek-English Lexicon.* Oxford: Clarendon Press.

Lindenbaum, Shirley. 1979. *Kuru sorcery: Disease and danger in the New Guinea highlands.* Palo Alto, CA: Mayfield.

Lindenbaum, Shirley, and Margaret Lock, eds. 1993. *Knowledge, power and practice: The anthropology of medicine and everyday life.* Berkeley: University of California Press.

Lloyd, Peter. 1994. Growing up and growing old: Aging and dependency in the life course. *Man,* (September):740–42.

Lock, Margaret. 1991. Nerves and nostalgia: Greek-Canadian immigrants and medical care in Quebec. In *Anthropologies of medicine.* Beatrix Pfleiderer and Gilles Bibeau, eds. Brunswick, Germany: Friedrich Vieweg.

Lock, Margaret, and Patricia A. Kaufert, eds. 1998. *Pragmatic women and body politics.* Cambridge: Cambridge University Press.

Lock, Margaret, and Nancy Scheper-Hughes. 1990. A critical-interpretive approach in medical anthropology: Rituals and routines of disclipine and dissent. In *Medical anthropology: Contemporary theory and method.* Thomas M. Johnson and Carolyn E. Sargent, eds. New York: Praeger.

Loehn, Christina. 1994. Non-insulin dependent diabetes in the Southern Cheyenne Community. PhD dissertation, University of Kansas.

Loevinger, Lee. 1995. The paradox of knowledge. *Skeptical Inquirer* 19, no. 5 (September–October):18–22

Long, Thomas G. 1995. Waiting for the morning star. *Theology Today* 51, no. 4 (January):491–95.

Loudon, J. B., ed. 1976. *Social anthropology and medicine.* New York: Academic Press Association of Social Anthropology Monograph 13.

Lundberg, Shelly, and Robert C. Plotnick. 1995. Adolescent premarital childbearing: Do economic incentives matter? *Journal of Labor Economics* 13, no. 2:177–201.

Maas, Henry S. 1974. *From thirty to seventy.* San Francisco: Jossey-Bass.

———. 1984. *People and contexts: Social development from birth to old age.* Englewood Cliffs, NJ: Prentice Hall.

MacCormack, Carol. 1994. Ethnological studies of medical sciences. *Social Science and Medicine* 39, no. 9 (November):1229–36.

MacDougall, Jill R., and P. Stanley Yoder. 1998. *Contaminating theatre: Intersections of theatre, therapy, and public health.* Evanston, IL: Northwestern University Press

MacGaffey, Wyatt. 1991. *Art and healing of the BaKongo commented by themselves: Minkisi from the Laman Collection.* Stockholm: Folkens Museum - Etnografiska.

MacNaughton, R. J., and Sullivan, F. M. 1996. Evidence in consultations: Interpreted and individualised. *The Lancet,* October 5:941–44.

Mageo, Jeannette Marie. 1995. The reconfiguring self. *American Anthropologist* 97, no. 2:282–97.

Mahler, Halfdan. 1975. Health for all by the year 2000. *WHO Chronicle* 29:253–56.

———. 1977. Blueprint for health for all. *WHO Chronicle* 31:491–98.

———. 1988. Present status of WHO's initiative "Health for all by the year 2000." Annual Review of Public Health 9:71–97.

Mahowald, Mary B., and Lois Margaret Nora. 1996. Neural fetal tissue transplants: Old and new issues. *Zygon,* 31, 4, p615–34.

Maine, Henry. 1960. *Ancient law.* London: Dent.

Malinowski, Bronislaw. 1948. *Magic, science and religion.* Garden City, NY: Doubleday Anchor.

———. 1965. *Coral gardens and their magic.* 2 vols. Bloomington: Indiana University Press.

Malthus, Thomas. [1798] 1976. *Essay on the principle of population.* Philip Appleman, ed. New York: W. W. Norton.

Marquand, Robert. 1995. Healing role of spirituality gains ground. *Christian Science Monitor,* December 6.

Martin, Emily. 1987. *The woman in the body.* Boston: Beacon Press.

———. 1994. *Flexible bodies: The roles of immunity in American culture from the days of polio to the age of AIDS.* Boston: Beacon Press.

Marty, Martin E. 1994. The tradition of the church in health and healing. *International Review of Mission* 83, no. 329 (April):227–46.

Marwick, Charles. 1995. Should physicians prescribe prayer for health? Spiritual aspects of well-being considered. *JAMA: Journal of the American Medical Association* (May 24):1561–63.

Mattingly, Cheryl. 1994. The concept of therapeutic "emplotment." *Social Science and Medicine.* 38, no. 6 (March 15):811–23.

———. 1998. *Healing dramas and clinical plots: The narrative structure of experience.* Cambridge: Cambridge University Press.

Mauss, Marcel. 1960. *Sociologie et anthropologie.* Paris: Presses Universitaires de France.

Mazars, Guy. 1978. Les médecines indiennes. In *Les médecines de L'Asie.* Pierre Huard, Jean Bossy, and Guy Mazars, eds. Paris: Editions du Seuil.

McElroy, Ann, and Patricia K. Townsend. 1979. *Medical anthropology in ecological perspective.* North Scituate, MA: Duxbury Press.

McKeown, Thomas. 1976. *The modern rise of population.* New York: Academic Press.

McNeill, William H. 1976. *Plagues and peoples.* Garden City, NY: Anchor/Doubleday.

———. 1978. Disease in history. *Social Science and Medicine,* 12, no. 2B:79–81.

McQueen, David. 1978. The history of science and medicine as theoretical sources for the comparative study of contemporary medical systems. *Social Science and Medicine* 12:69–74.

Meillassoux, Claude. 1981. *Maidens, meal and money: Capitalism and the domestic Community.* Cambridge: Cambridge University Press.

Merleau-Ponty, Maurice. 1964. *Sense and Non-Sense.* Evanston, IL: Northwestern University Press.

Meyer, Bonnie, J.F. Connie Russo, and Andrew Talbot. 1995. Discourse comprehension and problem solving: Decisions about the treatment of breast cancer by women across the life span. *Psychology and Aging* 10, no. 1 (March):84–101.

Migdal, Susan, Ronald P. Abeles, and Lonnie R. Sherrod. 1981. *An inventory of longitudinal studies of middle and old age.* New York: Social Science Research Council

Mises, R., and N. Quemada. 1994. Classification des handicaps en pathologie mentale de l'enfant et de l'adolescent—Incapacités, désavantages et retentissement sur la qualité de vie familiale. *L'information psychiatrique,* no. 5 (May):439–52.

Moerman, Daniel. 1983. General medical effectiveness and human biology: Placebo effects in the treatment of ulcer disease. *Medical Anthropology Quarterly* 14 (August):3–13.

———. 1985. Physiology and symbols: The anthropological implications of the placebo effect. In *The anthropology of medicine: From culture to method.* L. Romanucci-Ross et al. eds. New York: Praeger.

———. 1998. Heart surgery: The anthropological implications of the placebo effect. In *The Art of Medical Anthropology: Readings.* Sjaak van der Geest and Adri Rienks, eds. Amsterdam: Het Spinhuis.

Monsalvo, Julio. 1993. Reviving primary health care through popular communication. *Contact* 130 (April):7–9.

Monsour, Ahlam Abdel-Hamid. 1994. The conceptualization of health among residents of Saskatoon. *Journal of Community Health* 19, no. 3:165–80.

Moore, Lorna, Peter Van Arsdale, JoAnn Glittenberg, and Robert Aldrich. 1980. *The biocultural basis of health: Expanding views of medical anthropology.* St. Louis: C.V. Mosby.

Mootz, Marijke. 1986. Health indicators. *Social Science and Medicine* 22 no. 2:255–63.

Moreland, J. P., and Stan Wallace. 1995. Aquinas versus Locke and Descartes on the human person and end-of-life ethics. *International Philosophical Quarterly* 35, no. 3:319–31.

Morella, Constance. 1994. Lost message from Cairo: Educate young women in U.S. *Christian Science Monitor,* September 23.

Morgan, Lynn M. 1996. Fetal relationality in feminist philosophy: An anthropological critique. *Hypatia* 11, no. 3:47–71.

———. 1997. *Community participation in health: The politics of primary care in Costa Rica.* Cambridge: Cambridge University Press.

Morris Charles W. 1971. *Writings on the general theory of signs.* The Hague: Morton.

Morsy, Sohier A. 1998. Not only women: Science as resistance in open door Egypt. In *Pragmatic women and body politics.* Margaret Lock and Patricia Kaufert, eds. Cambridge: Cambridge University Press.

Murdock, George P. 1967. *Ethnographic atlas.* Pittsburgh: University of Pittsburgh Press.

———. 1980. *Theories of illness.* Pittsburgh: University of Pittsburgh Press.

Navarro, Vicente. *1986. Crisis, health, and medicine: A social critique.* New York: Tavistock.

———. 1992. *Why the United States does not have a national health program.* Amityville, NY: Baywood.

———. 1993. *Dangerous to your health: Capitalism in health care.* New York: Monthly Review Press.

New York Times. 1997. The age boom: A special issue. *New York Times Magazine,* March 9.

Ngubane, Harriet. 1977. *Body and mind in Zulu medicine.* New York: Academic Press.

Nickson, Pat, and Nyangoma Karabole. 1992. Community-determined health development: The Experience of Boga. *Contact,* no. 128 (December):1–20.

Oaks, Laury. 1994. Fetal spirithood and fetal personhood: The cultural construction of abortion in Japan. *Women's Studies International Forum* 17, no. 5:511–24.

Obyesekere, Gananath. 1976. The impact of Ayurvedic ideas on the culture and the individual in Sri Lanka. In *Asian Medical Systems.* Charles Leslie, ed. Berkeley: University of California Press.

Orosz, Eva. 1994. The impact of social science research on health policy. *Social Science and Medicine* 39, no. 9 (November), 1287–94.

Ortiz de Montellano, Bernard R. 1989. Mesoamerican religious tradition and medicine. In *Healing and restoring: Health and medicine in the world's religious traditions.* Lawrence E. Sullivan, ed. New York: Macmillan.

Ostor, Akos. 1984. Chronology, category, and ritual. In *Age and Anthropological Theory.* David I. Kertzer and Jennie Keith eds. Ithaca, NY: Cornell University Press.

Ots, Thomas. 1991. Phemonology of the body: The subject-object problem in psychosomatic medicine. In *Anthropologies of Medicine.* Beatrix Pfleiderer and Gilles Bibeau, eds. Brunswick: Friedrich Nieweg.

Packard, Randall. 1989. *White plague, black labor: Tuberculosis and the political economy of health and disease in South Africa.* Berkeley: University of California Press.

Palmer, Nancy Nyberg, 1993. The impact of maternal education on infant and child mortality and morbidity in the Cameroon grasslands. Ph.D dissertation University of Kansas.

Parmenter, Trevor R. 1994. Quality of life as a concept and measurable entity. *Social Indicators Research* 33, nos. 1–3 (August):9–46.

Parsons, Talcott. 1951. *The Social System.* New York: Free Press.

Patterson, K. David. 1979. Health in urban Ghana: The case of Accra 1900–1940. *Social Science and Medicine* 13B, no. 4, 251–268.

Paul, Benjamin, ed. 1955. *Health, culture and community: Case studies of public reactions to health programs.* New York: Russell Sage Foundation.

Payer, Lynn. 1988. *Medicine and culture: Varieties of treatment in the United States, England, West Germany and France.* New York: Henry Holt.

Pearce, Fred. 1994. Deserting dogma. *Geographical Magazine* 66, no. 1:24–29.

Peirce, Charles Sanders. 1938. *Collected Papers.* Vols. 1–6. C. Hartshorne and P. Weiss, eds. Cambridge: Harvard University Press.

———. [1940] 1955. *Philosophical Writings of Peirce.* Justus Buchler, ed. New York: Dover.

———. 1958. *Collected Papers.* Vols. 7–8. A. Bucks, ed. Cambridge: Cambridge University Press.

Pfleiderer, Beatrix, and Gilles Bibeau, eds. 1991. *Anthropologies of medicine: A colloquium on West European and North American Perspectives.* Brunswick: Friedrich Vieweg.

Pigg, Stacy Leigh. 1995. Acronyms and effacement: Traditional medical practitioners (TMP) in international health development. *Social Science and Medicine* 41, no. 1 (July):47–69.

Plath, David W., ed. 1983. *Work and lifecourse in Japan.* Albany: State University of New York Press–Albany.

———. 1980. *Long engagements: Maturity in modern Japan.* Stanford, CA: Stanford University Press.

Polgar, Steven. 1968. Health. *International encyclopedia of the social sciences* 6:330–36. New York: MacMillan.

———. n.d. Health action in cross-cultural perspective. In *Handbook of Medical Sociology.* H.E. Freeman, Sol Levine, and L. B. Reeder, eds. Englewood Cliffs, N.J.: Prentice Hall, Inc.

———. 1975. Population, evolution and theoretical paradigms. In *Population, Ecology and Social Evolution.* Steven Polgar, ed. The Hague: Mouton.

Polgar, Steven, ed. 1975. *Population, ecology and social evolution*. The Hague: Mouton.

Popper, Karl. 1964. *The Poverty of Historicism*. New York: Harper & Row.

Porkert, Manfred. 1974. *The theoretical foundations of Chinese medicine: Systems of correspondence*. Cambridge: MIT Press.

Pulkkinen, Lea, and Anna Ronka. 1994. Personal control over development, identity formation, and future orientation as components of life orientation: A developmental approach. *Developmental Psychology* 30, no. 2 (March):260–72.

Quadagno, Jill, and John M. Janzen. 1987. Old age security and the family life course: A case study of nineteenth-century Mennonite immigrants to Kansas. *Journal of Aging Studies* 1, no. 1:33–49.

Raso, Jack. 1995. Mystical medical alternativism. *Skeptical Inquirer*. 19, 5 (Sept–Oct), p. 33–38.

Rhodes, Lorna Amarasingham. 1990. Studying biomedicine as a cultural system. In *Medical anthropology*. Thomas M. Johnson and Carolyn A. Sargent, eds. Westport, CT: Praeger.

Richman, Sheldon. 1994. Cairo's faulty assumption: Population growth isn't antithetical to progress; it's a result of it. *Christian Science Monitor* September 23:19.

Riley, Matilda White. 1968. *Aging and Society*. New York: Russell Sage Foundation.

———. 1979. *Aging from birth to death: Interdisciplinary perspectives*. Boulder, CO: Westview Press.

Rivers, W. H. R. 1924. *Medicine, magic, and religion*. London: Kegan Paul, Trench, Trubner.

Robertson, Alexander F. 1991. *Beyond the family: The social organization of human reproduction*. Berkeley: University of California Press.

Rodwin, Victor C. 1984. *The health planning predicament: France, Quebec, England, and the United States*. Berkeley: University of California Press.

Romanucci-Ross, Lola. 1969. The hierarchy of resort in curative practices: The Admiralty Islands, Melanesia. *Journal of Health and Social Behavior* 10:201–209.

Rosen, G. 1958. *A history of public health*. New York: M.D. Publications.

Roth, Julius. 1963. *Timetables: Studying the passage of time in hospital treatment and other careers*. Indianapolis, IN: Bobbs-Merrill.

Rush, John A. 1996. *Clinical anthropology: An application of anthropological concepts within clinical settings*. Westport, CT: Praeger.

Rwangabo, Pierre-Claver. 1993. *La médecine traditionnelle au Rwanda*. Paris: Karthala.

Sarbin, Theodore R. 1984. Role transition as social drama. In *Role Transitions*. Vernon Allen and Evan Vana de Vliert, eds. New York: Plenum Press.

Saussure, Fernand de. [1959] 1915. *Course in General Linguistics*. New York: McGraw-Hill.

Sautter, Gilles. 1966. *De l'Atlantique au fleuve Congo: Une géographie du sous-peuplement*. The Hague: Mouton.

Scheper-Hughes, Nancy. 1992. *Death without weeping: The violence of everyday life in Brazil*. Berkeley: University of California Press.

Scheper-Hughes, Nancy, and Margaret M. Lock. 1987. The mindful body: A prolegomenon to future work in medical anthropology. *Medical Anthropology Quarterly* 1:6–41.

Schneider, David M. 1968. *American kinship: A cultural account*. Englewood Cliffs, NJ: Prentice Hall.

———. 1984. *A critique of the study of kinship*. Ann Arbor: University of Michigan Press.

Schoepf, Brooke Grundfest. 1995. Culture, sex research and AIDS prevention in Africa. In *Culture and sexual risk: Anthropological perspectives on the epidemic*. H. ten Brummelhuis and G. Herdt, eds. Philadelphia: Gordon and Breach.

———. 1998. Inscribing the body politic: Women and AIDS in Africa. In *Pragmatic women and body politics*. Margaret Lock and Patricia A. Kaufert, eds. Cambridge: Cambridge University Press.

Sebeok, Thomas. 1994. *Signs: An introduction to semiotics*. Toronto: University of Toronto Press.

Sedler, Mark J. 1994. Foundations of the new nosology. *Journal of Medicine and Philosophy* 19, no. 3 (June):219–39.

Seidelman, William E. 1996. The path to Nuremberg in the pages of JAMA, 1933–1939. *JAMA: The Journal of the American Medical Association* 276, no. 20:1693–97.

Selye, Hans. 1950. *The physiology and pathology of exposure to stress: A treatise based on the concepts of the general-adaptation-syndrome and the diseases of adaptation.* Montreal: Acta.

———. 1956. *The stresses of life.* New York: McGraw-Hill.

———. 1976. Stress in health and disease. Boston: Butterworths.

———. 1977. The stress of my life: A scientist's memoires. Toronto: McClelland and Stewart.

Sheriff, John. 1989. *The fate of meaning: Charles Peirce, structuralism, and literature.* Princeton: Princeton University Press.

———. 1994. *Charles Peirce's guess at the riddle: Grounds for human significance.* Bloomington: University of Indiana Press.

Simon, Julian. 1977. *The economics of population growth.* Princeton: Princeton University Press.

Sindzingre, Nicole. 1985. Presentation: Tradition et biomédecine. *Sciences sociales et santé* 3, nos. 3–4:9–26.

Singh, Ram D. 1994. Fertility-mortality variations across LDCs: Women's education, labor force participation, and contraceptive use. *KYKLOS* 47, no. 2:209–30.

Smith, Michael G. 1974. *Corporations and Society.* London: Duckworth.

Solzhenitsyn, Aleksandr. [1973–75] 1992. *Gulag Archipelago.* 3 vols. translated by Thomas Whitney. Boulder, CO: Westview Press.

Sonko, Sheriff. 1994. Fertility and culture in sub-Saharan Africa: A review. *International Social Science Journal* 46, no. 3:397–412.

Sontag, Susan. 1977. *Illness as metaphor.* New York: Farrar, Straus and Giroux.

———. 1988. *AIDS and its metaphors.* New York: Farrar, Straus and Giroux.

Staiano, Kathryn Vance. 1979. A semiotic definition of illness. *Semiotica* 28, 1–2.

———. 1982. Medical semiotics: Redefining an ancient craft. *Semiotica* 38, no. 3–4:319–46.

———. 1986. *Interpreting signs of illness: A case study in medical semiotics.* New York: Mouton de Gruyter.

———. 1989. Semiotics and medical semiotics. *Semiotica* 77, no. 4:491–95.

———. 1992a. Biosemiotics, ethnographically speaking. In *Biosemiotics: The semiotic web.*

Thomas A. Sebeok and Jean Umiker-Sebeok, eds. New York: Mouton de Gruyter.

———. 1992b. The semiotic perspective. In *The social construction of illness: Illness and medical knowledge in past and present.* Jens Lachmund and Gunnar Stollberg, eds. Stuttgart: Franz Steiner.

———. 1997. Personal correspondence. March 31 and August 15.

Staiano-Ross, Kathryn, and Sunil Khanna. 1999. *A Body of Signs. Recherches Sémiotiques/Semiotic Inquiry* 19, no. 1:3–23.

Starke, Linda. 1994. Fertility rates: The decline is stalling. *World Watch* 7, no. 2:37–39.

Stengers, Isabelle. 1995. Do we know to read messages in the sand? *Diogenes,* no. 169 (Spring):179–97.

Steuer, R. O., and J. B. de C. M. Saunders. 1959. *Ancient Egyptian and Cnidian medicine.* Berkeley: University of California Press.

Stokes, C. Shannon. 1995. Explaining the demographic transition: Institutional factors in fertility decline. *Rural Sociology* 60, no. 1:1–22.

Sullivan, Lawrence E. 1989. Religious foundations of health and medical power in South America. In *Healing and restoring: Health and medicine in the world's religious traditions.* Lawrence E. Sullivan, ed. New York: Macmillan.

Taché, Jean, Hans Selye, and Stacey B. Dey, eds. 1979. *Cancer, Stress and Death.* New York: Plenum.

Tadesco, Frank M. 1996. Rites for the unborn dead: Abortion and Buddhism in contemporary Korea. *Korea Journal* 36, no. 2 (Summer):61–74.

Taylor, Anne Christine. 1996. The soul's body and its states: An Amazonian perspective on the nature of being human. *Journal of the Royal Anthropological Institute* 2, no. 2:202–217.

Taylor, Charles. 1985. The person. In *The category of the person.* Michael Carrithers, Steven Collins, and Steven Lukes, eds. Cambridge: Cambridge University Press.

Taylor, Christopher. 1992. *Milk, honey, and money: Changing concepts in Rwandan healing.* Washington DC: Smithsonian Institution Press.

Temkin, Owsei. 1973. Health and disease. In *Dictionary of the History of Ideas* 2:113–18.

Thomas, Neil. 1991. Land, fertility, and the population establishment. *Population Studies* 45, no. 3:379–397

Tompkins, Nancy. 1996. *Roe v. Wade and the fight over life and liberty.* New York: Franklin Watts.

Tshimika, Pakisa. 1991. Lecture. University of Kansas. December 3.

———. 1995. Interview. May 15.

———. 2000. Lecture. University of Kansas, November 15.

Tuchman, Barbara W. 1978. *A distant mirror: The calamitous 14th century.* New York: Ballantine.

Turnbull, Colin M. 1983. *The human cycle.* New York: Simon & Schuster.

Turner, Victor W. 1967. *The forest of symbols: Aspects of Ndembu ritual.* Ithaca, NY: Cornell University Press.

———. 1968. *The drums of affliction. A study of religious processes among the Ndembu of Zambia.* Oxford: Clarendon.

———. 1969. *The ritual process: Structure and anti-structure.* Chicago: Aldine.

Turney, Jon. 1996. Public understanding of science. *The Lancet* 347, no. 9008 (April 20):1087–91.

Tylor, Edward. 1958 [1871]. *Primitive culture.* New York: Harper and Row.

U.S. Department of Health and Human Services (USDHHS). 1990. *Healthy people 2000: National health promotion and disease prevention objectives.* Publication no. PHS 91-50212. Washington, DC: USDHHS.

United Nations High Commission for Refugees. 1994. Morbidity and mortality report for week ending 30 October, Mugunga Camp, Zaire. Unpublished Manuscript.

Unschuld, Paul. 1975a. Medizin und Ethik: Sozialkonflikte im China der Kaiserzeit. Wiesbaden: Franz Steiner Verlag.

Unschuld, Paul. 1975b. Medico-cultural conflicts in Asian settings: An explanatory theory. *Social Science and Medicine* 9:303–312.

———. 1985. *Medicine in China: A history of ideas.* Berkeley: University of California Press.

———. 1986. *Nan-ching: The classic of difficult issues.* Translated and annotated by Paul Unschuld. Berkeley: University of California Press.

———. 1992. Epistemological issues and changing legitimation: Traditional Chinese medicine in the twentieth century. In *Paths to Asian Medical Knowledge.* Charles Leslie and Allan Young, eds. Berkeley: University of California Press.

Van der Geest, Sjaak. 1994. Christ as a pharmacist: Medical symbols in German devotion. *Social Science and Medicine* 39, no. 5 (September):727–33.

Van der Geest, Sjaak, and Susan Reynolds Whyte. 1989. The charm of medicines: Metaphors and metonyms. *Medical Anthropology Quarterly* 3, no. 4:345–67.

Van der Geest, Sjaak, Susan Reynolds Whyte, and Anita Hardon. 1996. The anthropology of pharmaceuticals: A biographical approach. In *Annual review of anthropology* 25:153–78.

Van Gennep, Arnold. [1960] 1908. *The rites of passage.* Chicago: University of Chicago Press.

Van Uexkuell, Thomas and W. Wesiack. 1988. *Theorie der humanmedizin: Grundlagen aerztlichen denkens u. handelns.* Munich: Urban & Schwarzenberg.

Vaughan, Megan. 1991. *Curing their ills: Colonial power and African illness.* Cambridge: Polity Press; Oxford: Basil Blackwell.

Vergara, Alfredo, and David Swerdlow. 1994. Population survey, nutrition, mortality, Camp Mugunga, Zaire August 13–August 14, 1994. Centers for Disease Control and Prevention, for Medical Coordination, United Nations High Commission for Refugees, Goma, Zaire. Mimeo.

Warren, Dennis. 1979. The role of emic analyses in medical anthropology: The case of the Bono in Ghana. In *African Therapeutic Systems.* Z. A. Ademuwagun, J. A. A. Ayoade, I. E. Harrison, and D. Warren, eds. Waltham, MA: Crossroads Press.

Weber, Max. 1982. The Techiman. Bono ethnomedical system. In *African Health and*

Healing Systems: Proceedings of a Symposium. P. Stanley Yader ed. Los Angeles: Crossroads Press.

————. 1964 *The theory of social and economic organization.* Glencoe, IL: Free Press; London: Collier MacMillan.

Weiss, Meira. 1995. Of man and beast: From "Person" to "Non-person." *Semiotica* 106, nos. 1–2:55–76.

Wellin, Edward. 1955. Water boiling in a Peruvian town. In Benjamin Paul, ed. *Health, Culture, and Community.* New York: Russel Sage Foundation.

Wellin, Edward. 1977. Theoretical orientations in medical anthropology. In *Culture, disease, and healing: Studies in medical anthropology.* David Landy, ed. New York: Macmillan.

Westerdorf, W. 1978. Altes Aegypten. In *Krankheit, heilkunst, heilung.* H., Schipperges, E. Seidler, P.U. Unschuld, eds. Freiburg, Germany: Karl Alber.

What is medical anthropology? 1981. *Medical Anthropology Newsletter:*7–8.

Wilson, Francis, and Gill Wescott, eds. 1979. *Economics of health in South Africa.* Vol. 1, *Perspectives on the health system;* Vol. 2, *Hunger, work and health.* Johannesburg: Ravan Press for the Southern Africa Labour and Development Research Unit.

Wimsatt, James I. 1996. Rhyme, the icons of sound, and the Middle English "pearl." *Style* 30, no. 2 (Summer):189–214.

WIN News. 1995. The unmet needs of reproductive health. *Win News* 21, no. 2 (Spring):36.

Wolpe, Paul Root. 1994. The dynamics of heresy in a profession. *Social Science and Medicine* 39, no. 9 (November):1133–49.

World Health Organization (WHO). 1957. *International classification of diseases.* 7th ed. Geneva: WHO.

————. 1960. *Statistical annual.* Geneva: WHO.

————. 1965. *International classification of diseases.* 8th ed. Geneva: WHO.

————. 1970. *Statistical annual.* Geneva: WHO.

————. 1978. *Primary health care* [The Alma Ata Declaration]. Geneva: WHO.

————. 1980a. *International classification of impairments, disabilities and handicaps.* Geneva: WHO.

————. 1980b. *Statistical annual.* Geneva: WHO.

————. 1990. *Statistical Annual.* Geneva: WHO.

————. 1999. *World Health Report.* Geneva: WHO.

Wright, Randall. [1982]1991. Rethinking the Middle/Upper Paleolithic transition. In *Inquiry and debate in the human sciences.* Sydel Silverman, ed. Chicago: University of Chicago Press.

Wrigley, E. A. 1969. *Population in history.* New York: McGraw-Hill.

WuDunn, Sheryl. 1996. In Japan, a ritual of mourning for abortions. *New York Times,* January 25.

Yoder, P. Stanley. 1995. Examining ethnomedical diagnoses and treatment choices for diarrheal disorders in Lubumbashi Swahili. *Medical Anthropology* 16:211–47.

————. 1997. Negotiating relevance: Belief, knowledge and practice in international health projects. Special Issue. *Medical Anthropology Quarterly.*

Young, Allan. 1993. A description of how ideology shapes knowledge of a mental disorder (Posttraumatic Stress Disorder). In *Knowledge, power and practice: The anthropology of medicine and everyday life.* Berkeley: University of California Press.

————. 1995. *The harmony of illusions: Inventing post-traumatic stress disorder.* Princeton: Princeton University Press.

Young, James. 1981. *Medical choice in a Mexican village.* New Brunswick, NJ: Rutgers University Press.

Zhang, Junsen. 1994. Socioeconomic determinants of fertility in Hebei province, China: An application of the sequential logit model. *Economic Development and Cultural Change* 43, no. 1:67–71.

Zimmerman, Francis. 1982. *The jungle and the aroma of meats: An ecological theme in Hindu medicine.* Berkeley: University of California Press.

————. 1989. *Le discours des remèdes au pays des épices.* Paris: Payot.

————. 1995. *Généalogie des médicines douces.* Paris: Presses Universitaire de France.

GLOSSARY

This glossary offers a quick reference of commonly used medical anthropology terms and phrases; they have been marked in bold in the text, at first use, and again later in passages where they are important. Some of these terms and phrases are specialized definitions of common English words, others have been coined by anthropologists for special issues and have become technical terms. They are best used with reference to the author who coined them. Consult the index for fuller reference to the use of these terms throughout the book.

A

Adaptation   The adjustment of organisms to an environment, and the mutual relationship to other organisms through energy exchanges.

Anthropology, action   The use of anthropology within communities and societies upon the request of the community, rather than government or other agency originated projects.

Anthropology, applied   The application of anthropology to issues and problems in society; may be focused on economic or social "development" as well as health care and "clinical" work.

Anthropology, practicing   A more recent term for anthropologists doing anthropology outside of the academic setting.

Anthropology, public service   Most recent term for anthropologist who work outside of academic institutions, often for health care related agencies on health issues.

Authority   The consensual exercise of power in a legitimate manner; may be of differing types, e.g., **traditional~**: through the sanctity of immemorial traditions; **rational-legal~**: the impersonal, rational, legal application of commands and coordination in a bureaucracy; **charismatic~**: derived from the attributed forceful aura of an individual practitioner or founder (see Max Weber 1964).

B

Balance   a widespread paradigm or idea of health.

Biocultural (perspective)   A theoretical perspective in anthropology that seeks to bridge biological and cultural realms, through analyses of adaptation, evolutionary ecology, and the relation of ideas to material and environmental forces and constraints.

Biology, biological approach   In medical anthropology, the perspective that focuses on the physical patterns of health and illness, may be combined with social and cultural perspectives.

Biomedicine   The term currently used in anthropology to describe mainstream modern Western medicine, with its basis in science and emphasis on the physical body.

Birthrate (natality)   The number of newly born each year in a population, per 1000 individuals.

Body   A term of many uses in anthropology, including the literal physical and organic body of medicine and science, as well as the current use of body as a metaphor that mirrors individual experience, and social and political forces; this "body" in medical anthropology emphasizes the emotions and non-rationalized aspects of health and illness; see **Embodiment.**

C

Clinical reality   Negotiated agreement between patient, healer, and significant others around the meaning of their encounter.

Communitas   A community or group of individuals whose relationship is characterized by "anti-structure," or continuing liminal status associated with their social marginality due to transition or crisis of chronic illness (Victor Turner 1969).

Comparison, comparative   The search for common characteristics and broad understanding in human society and behavior through the study of two or more examples of a given phenomenon.

Corporation, corporate   Key concept in corporation theory that may be used by medical anthropologists to study human organization, including medical structures in relation to society and the state; a **corporate category** is a group of individuals identified by a common criterion, whereas a **corporate group** designates such individuals organized to conduct their affairs, including a spokesperson to the outside.

Critical (political economic, cultural literary) perspective   An approach to medical anthropology that combines class-based analysis and cultural interpretation in the study of medical and health phenomena.

Cultural constructivism   Language holds the key to culture, and culture and documents of experience may be "read" as text and interpreted.

Culture of biomedicine   The identification of culturally distinctive features of mainstream scientific medicine; see **Medical culture.**

Culture, cultural approach   In medical anthropology, the perspective that focuses on knowledge and symbols as independent in relation to health, illness, and healing; may be combined with biological and social perspectives.

Culture   Creatively fashioned techniques, lifeways, social patterns, and deeply held convictions and assumptions in a community; these are stored in and articulated by language, they are learned, they may change to adjust to the limits of material conditions; a most remarkable human resource for adaptation through ideas, techniques, and organization.

Culture-bound syndrome   The view that affliction syndromes and treatments may be specific to particular cultures, and thus not comparable as universal conditions.

D

Death (mortality) rate   The number of individuals per thousand who die in a given year in a society or population.

Demographic transition   A constellation of features in the modern population explosion followed by an eventual leveling off of population growth.

Demography   The study of population.

Diagnosis   The determination of a disease or condition by its signs and symptoms.

Diagnostic and Statistical Manual (DSM)   Classification of psychiatric and psychological conditions sponsored by the American Association of Psychology.

Disease   a condition that is objectively identified with a medical label or diagnostic name, based on externally established signs; may be identified with or without there being a subjective perception of illness by the individual; objective condition or pathology as determined by a medical professional; becomes relativized in the ecological perspective.

E

Efficacy   Term used by anthropologists in their search for criteria that could be applied to characterize successful healing cross-culturally.

Embodiment   The idea in anthropology that experiences, social forces, and cultural ideas are imprinted upon identity and self—the body; may be seen especially forcefully in the internalization of the emotional register of violence and trauma, but also gender roles, occupation, and class.

Epidemiology   The study of disease patterns and frequencies, a basic tool of public health.

Epistemology   A branch of philosophy that investigates the origin, structure, perception, and validity of knowledge.

Ethnography   The close range and extended participation and observation of a society by an anthropologist in order to gain general insights by a thorough acquaintance of the particular.

Ethnomedicine   Term used to describe the cultural dimension of a medical tradition; has also been used recently to characterize mainstream scientific biomedicine.

Etiology   Term used in medicine and sometimes medical anthropology for the cause or origin of disease or illness.

Eustasis   A way of seeing the human condition in terms of the dynamic balance between forces of disease and health.

Explanatory model   A view of the context of healing espoused by Arthur Kleinman (1980) that looks at illness cause, meaning of symptoms, nature of the pathology, course of sickness and treatment as understood both by the healer and the patient. The two perspectives need to be congruent for healing to be efficacious.

F

Fabric of health   Ideas and practices in healing traditions and health campaigns, the social patterns and institutions by which they are carried; a metaphor used to speak about health, illness, and healing as represented in social and cultural images, institutions, and ideas about health; the practices, social arrangements, words and related concepts, codes for health.

Fertility rate   The number of children born on average to women of reproductive years in a society; also recorded as live births of those infants who reach age one.

Functionalism   The theoretical viewpoint in anthropology whereby behavior meets biological, material, community, emotional, and spiritual needs.

G

Genetic change   One of the modes of adaptation, the most long-term, whereby adjustments to external stress are made through reproductive advantage and disadvantage among organisms in an environment.

Gerontology   The study of the elderly; of the process of change over the life span.

Gnosis   Ancient Greek term for knowledge, basis of many medical terms— e.g., diagnosis, prognosis, nosology.

H

Healing   Both the sufferer-defined resolution of the sickness, as well as the medically defined transformation of the disease or disorder—associated with wholeness.

Health   A scheme of thought and life used to refer to an abstract ideal of wellbeing; but often expressed in more particular idioms such as "the absence of disease," "adaptation to the envionment," sustainability, or other dynamic process relating individuals and society to wellbeing.

Hierarchy of resort   The conventional pattern of the sequence of different consultations with medical practitioners or therapies in an unfolding case (see Romanucci-Ross 1969).

Holism, holistic   An aspect of anthropological inquiry that uses a broad multi-disciplinary approach in the study of a single human community or tradition.

Human development   The study of human growth and development across the life of individuals; scholarly interest in the formative influences and learning of individuals over their entire life.

Humors   Bodily fluids or properties—blood, bile, phlegm, wind, air—that are considered fundamental aspects of life forces in many classical medical traditions.

I

Icon   A sign that contains its meaning in its very form and nature, has a formal similarity between its signifier and that which it denotes.

Illness   The sufferer's perception of the individual experience of suffering; may occur with or without disease being identified; culturally embedded, subjective definition given to suffering by the patient, and to behavior in which it is expressed.

Imbalance   Widespread etiological idea of source of illness in Old World traditions, in which elements (earth, water, air) and humors (blood, bile) or thermal states (hot, cold) are not in their appropriate relationship; see **Balance.**

Index   A sign whose signifier is contiguous with that which it signifies, or is a sample of it, is identical to or actually accounts for the object—i.e., the ideal of a scientific fact.

Infant mortality rate (IMR)   Deaths per 1,000 children in a population born per year.

International Classification of Disease (ICD)   The most widespread example of medical classification, developed by the World Health Organization.

International Classification of Impairments, Disability and Handicaps   A widely used classification of conditions of disability sponsored by the World Health Organization.

Interpretant   One of the terms of C. S. Peirce's triadic sign; describes the intentional reaction, interpretation, or name for the representamen and its object.

Intrusion   Widespread idea of the cause of illness, by agent or substance that has entered the human space or body—e.g., spirits, germs, dirt.

K

Kuru   A fatal viral infection identified among the Fore of highland New Guinea that resulted from drinking the bodily fluids of deceased kin to commemorate them.

L

Life course (perspective)   The study of human life with an emphasis on the stages of growth, on transitions, and crises; emphasis on the life of an individual, as defined by society's patterns of the rhythms of life for male and female, the constraints and the opportunities.

Life cycle   The typical course of an individual in a society, as well as the cycle of a family or household, individuals related by social bonds.

Life expectancy   The average life expectancy at birth of infants born in a given year in a population.

Life span   A perspective on the study of humans that features the entire span of the life of an individual.

Liminality   The transition phase of a rite of passage during which an individual or group is "outside" conventional social roles and statuses; ambiguous status that is neither/nor, expression of paradoxical, contradictory, painful, and chronic conditions; see **Rites of Passage.**

M

Marxism　Social ideology and social science theory based on the work of Karl Marx whereby class conflict inherent in a capitalist socio-economic system will give rise to a revolution ushering in collective state-controlled sponsorship or social program.

Medical culture (national, international)　The broadest common denominator in a society of that which is identifiably medical, with no regard for institutions, roles, or structures. (See Last 1986, 1990, 1992).

Medical pluralism　The coexistence of multiple medical traditions, or bodies of practice and thought, within the same society.

Medical systems　A comparative perspective in medical anthropology that attributed to medical practices and traditions a recognizable coherence like a social system.

Medicine, the medical　In anthropology, refers to generic practices from whatever tradition intended to address or alleviate what people and practitioners consider to be an affliction in need of attention; considered by anthropologists to be a part of human culture in adaptation.

Metaphor　A sign or expression that gives a thing a name or property that belongs to something else, the use of an image taken to describe or define another realm or experience.

Modern (modernity, modernization)　The view of social science theory and social ideology whereby society should or does progress toward rational, individualized, free market orientation, and away from traditional, collective, and irrational perspectives.

Morbidity　The rate of infection or incidence of a disease in a population, calculated per 1,000 individuals per year.

N

Name　A sign for Thomas Sebeok (1994) that refers to a single example of a class, features uniqueness and singularity.

Narratives of suffering, illness narratives　The focus of an approach of medical anthropology that highlights individual experiences and the subjective dimension.

Nocebo　Like the placebo, but negative; an agent or symbolic force that can affect the health and wellbeing of individuals; see **Placebo.**

Nosology　The discipline of classifying medical knowledge around the symptoms and signs of a given condition of distress.

Nutrition　A central aspect of the ecological perspective in anthropology, featuring the intake and outflow of energy, the nature and requirements for a given organism or species to survive, adjust to pressures upon it; generally applied to the human community in medical anthropology.

O

Object   Term of triadic sign of C.S. Peirce to describe the stimulus of sensation or the ground of signification; in medical anthropological application, the disease or source on which labelling and interpretation is made.

Organisms, community of   An idea central to the ecological or biocultural perspective, whereby all living beings are seen as part of a single energy or nutrition circuit, adapted and dynamically related.

P

Pain   Sensation of suffering that has been studied by medical anthropology for the way it reflects cultural shaping and expression.

Paradigm   Assumptions and working practices in the creation of knowledge; for Kuhn, universally recognized scientific achievements that for a time provide model problems and solutions to a community of practitioners.

Person, personhood   The social characterization of the individual human being in a society, society's understandings and laws of how an individual will be represented and treated, given autonomy, how life will be defined.

Placebo (effect)   Originally used to describe treatment intended "to please," has become the name for ostensibly neutral substances in clinical trials, but increasingly noted to carry symbolic force in its own right; the impact of such substances and acts on individuals receiving them.

Political economy   An analysis of economic and power relations and institutions based on class; used by medical anthropology to understand the relationship of class, privilege, and oppression to health.

Population (profiles)   The study of organisms—human populations—over time with attention to the relative ratios of birth rates to death rates, and the changes in these ratios over time.

Power   The ability of some individuals or groups to manipulate and control other individuals and groups; sometimes applied to those who have or hold the power of healing and the resources of medicine.

Primary Health Care   A campaign initiated by the World Health Organization in the 1970s to establish basic care in communities throughout the world; "Health for all by the year 2000" was its slogan.

Profession   Full-time pursuit by persons of specialized skill, usually for pay by customers, or by an agency that buys their skills, of use in understanding organization of medicine and medical practitioners.

Prognosis   The foretelling of the outcome of the course fo a disease on the basis of the diagnostician's understanding of the case and in light of other prior cases.

R

Representamen   Term of triadic sign in C.S. Peirce's scheme to describe the sensory expression such as a pain, feeling, or perception of the object, for example a disease or injury.

Reproductive health   A phrase that captured debate and action in family and population planning in the postcolonial world, it focused on the improvement of health for women and children; women's rights, population control, family planning, and primary health care.

Research   A focused inquiry that through the use of a consistent methodology yields findings that are made public through teaching or publication or are applied to solve a problem.

Rites of passage   Transitions between life's stages and through crises; phrase coined by Arnold Van Gennep (1960 [1908]); highlights passing through a "threshold" and being betwixt and between, in limbo.

Ritualization   Recourse to special symbols and metaphors that heighten expression and offer understanding of the moments of passage or crisis of individuals and groups.

S

Sectors of health care   A perspective in medical anthropology that divided medical practices and traditions into folk, popular, and professional groupings.

Semiosis   The ongoing process of signification, seen by medical anthropologists as useful in understanding the fluid or transformative character of signs in sickness and healing.

Semiotics   The perspective of signs that express both the subjective realm of individuals and the objective, public world of symbols, codes, and laws, as well as a range of signs from those that are predetermined to those that are intellectually defined.

Shamanism   Considered the most ancient form of healing, characterized by a calling in the form of trance, a journey of the soul, association with spirit familiars, and curing through retrieving errant souls.

Sickness   The subjective experience of suffering; or an experience that disrupts ordinary life, may be identified with a group experience.

Sign   A sensory object or presence that can be felt, heard, smelled, seen, or tasted, which conveys some additional association with a message or meaning.

Signal   Sign that triggers some reaction on the part of its receiver, may be either mechanical and unconscious, or culturally and consciously coded; in Sebeok's scheme, it is the "most compulsive" of the types of signs.

Social reproduction of health   The view in medical anthropology that health is sustained by socially created conditions; that social units—family (the dependent and the active), community, networks of support, sometimes the state—contribute to the distribution of resources to children, the elderly, the sick, and the marginal to assure the effective continuum of generations, thus health.

Society, social approach   In medical anthropology, the perspective that focuses on behaviors, relations, and authority patterns in matters of health and medicine; may be combined with biological perspective.

Somatic, somatization   A condition such as depression or other "mental" illness that is expressed through physical symptoms.

Soul loss   The most frequent illness diagnosis in shamanic healing; leading etiology of affliction in Asian and American traditions of shamanism, requires "soul retrieval" as cure.

Structural-functionalism   The combined perspective that human actions and institutions are interrelated in an orderly, organic manner, and that human actions serve to meet functional needs.

Structuralism   The theory that holds that society's institutions are inter-related in a complementary manner to create a balanced whole .

Suffering   The subjective, usually more chronic, condition of affliction or painful existence; broader than sickness, the existential experience of life of hardship and difficulty, may be permanent human condition, often accounted for in religion and wisdom literature.

Symbol   A sign of identity verified by a point of reference outside itself, that is its reference to that sign is of an arbitrary nature; may affect human communication profoundly as it expresses strong emotions, motives and attachments that influence sickness and healing; a sign without either similarity or contiguity, no intrinsic relationship between the itself and its object, an accident of history, such as language.

Symbolic (effect of healing)   Strong force little understood observed in shamanism and most other types of healing.

Symptom   A happening or attribute that indicates the personally felt, subjective evidence of physical disturbance; in Sebeok's view, a compulsive, automatic, non-arbitrary sign which has a natural link to that which it signifies.

T

Taxonomy   From the Greek word for "arrangement" (e.g., syntax in language), is applied to the ordering of terms for signs and symptoms of disease and distress.

Therapeutic itinerary (*itinéraire thérapeutique*)   phrase coined by Marc Augé (Sindzingre 1985) to describe the totality of therapeutic steps and processes, including detours and curves, in a quest for therapy.

Therapy management (group, process)   Phrase coined by J.M. Janzen (1978) with reference to Kongo society of Western Equatorial Africa to describe the process of negotiation for control of therapeutic resources, and the group of people who share in the decisions of care giving).

W

Wholeness   That state which healing restores, defined in a multitude of culturally specific ways.

INDEX

A

Aborigine cultures, 88
Abortion issues, *137*, 138, 142, 168; *see also* Reproductive and sexual health issues
Accidents, and health issues, 87, 88, 96
Acquired immune deficiency syndrome (AIDS); *see* AIDS
Action anthropology, 245
Acupuncture, 59, *59*, 60
Adaptation issues, 32, 33, 79, 166–167, 183
Aesculapius, *51*, 53, *54*, 56, 189, 225
African cultures; *see also specific country; specific culture*
  birthrate issues, 102–103
  Boga project, 65–67, 73
  color codes, 62–63, 157
  and conception, ideas about, 140–141
  death rate issues and, 103
  demographic transitions and, 103
  fertility rate issues and, 103
  and flow/blockage, concept of, 63
  food production, 100
  healing issues and, 37, 146–147, 174
  health care delivery and, 250, 255–257
  health issues and, 37
  IMR issues and, 103
  industrialization, 103
  medical knowledge, 190, 194
  medical pluralism, 235–236
  medical traditions and, 189, 213
  medicines and, 13–15, 157, 225
  morbidity rate issues and, 103
  political economy issues and, 31
  self-help communities, 146–147
  shamanism and, 213
  and sickness, experience of, 152
  sociocultural issues and, 37–38
  thermal ideas of disease and, 52, 63–64
  violence issues and, 96, 107
Aging from Birth to Death (Riley), 117
Aging issues, 117, 123, 126–127, 134
AIDS
  epidemics and, 88, 94
  immune system and, 193
  medical anthropology, and study of, 246–247
  primary health care and, 73
  research in, 8
  socio-economic issues and, 24
  violence issues and, 105
AIDS and Accusation (Farmer), 247
AIDS and Its Metaphors (Sontag), 180
Alaska, Tlingit culture, 123
Alcoholics Anonymous (AA), 146
Alexander the Great, 91
Allopathic medicine, 214; *see also* Biomedicine
Alma Ata Declaration, 72
Alternative therapies, 24; *see also* Biomedicine
Amazonian rain forest cultures, soul loss and, 61
American Anthropological Association, 18, 264, 265
American Council of Learned Societies, 37
American cultures; *see also* Central American cultures; North American cultures; South American cultures; United States (U.S.) cultures; *specific country; specific culture*
  and conception, ideas about, 140–141
  health care practices and, 22
  health issues and, 62
  and medicinal plants, use of, 61
  population issues and, *86*
  ritual therapies and, 61–62
American Dietetic Association, 201
American Indian cultures; *see also* Indian cultures
  anorexia nervosa and, 205
  "ghost sickness" disease and, 204
  health care programs and, 249
  health issues and, 52
  medical knowledge and, 194
  and medicinal plants, use of, 61
  modernity and, 31
  Navajo-Ramah culture, 61
  Pueblo cultures, 62, 249
  ritual therapies and, 61–62
  shamanism and, 193
  soul loss and, 61
American Kinship, A Cultural Account (Schneider), 28
American Medical Association (AMA), 82n4, 227
American Psychological Association, 203, 206
Anderson, Barbara, 31
Andes Mountains, cultures of, 90
Anger, treatment for, 161–162, 183
Anthropology and Medicine, 18